JOINT ATTENTION: COMMUNICATION AND OTHER MINDS

Some time around their first birthday most infants begin to engage in a series of behaviours designed to bring it about—say, by means of pointing or gaze-following—that their own and another person's attention are focused on the same object. Described as manifestations of an emerging capacity for *joint attention*, such triangulations between infant, adult, and the world are often treated as a developmental landmark and have become the subject of intensive research among developmentalists and primatologists over the past decade. More recently, work on joint attention has also begun to attract the attention of philosophers. Fuelling researchers' interest in all these disciplines, we find the intuition that joint attention plays a foundational role in the emergence of communicative abilities, in children's developing understanding of the mind and, possibly, in the very capacity for objective thought.

This book brings together, for the first time, philosophical and psychological perspectives on the nature and significance of the phenomenon of joint attention, addressing issues such as: How should we explain the kind of mutual openness that joint attention seems to involve, i.e. the sense in which both child and adult are aware that they are attending to the same thing? What sort of grip on one's own and other people's mental states does such awareness involve, and how does it relate to later-emerging 'theory of mind' abilities? In what sense, if any, is the capacity to engage in joint attention with others unique to humans? How should we explain autistic children's seeming incapacity to engage in joint attention? What role, if any, does affect play in the achievement of joint attention? And what, if any, is the connection between participation in joint attention and grasp of the idea of an objective world? The book also contains an introductory chapter aimed at providing a framework for integrating different philosophical and psychological approaches to these questions.

CONSCIOUSNESS AND SELF-CONSCIOUSNESS

This series presents the fruits of a joint philosophy and psychology research project whose aim is to advance understanding of the natures of consciousness and self-consciousness by integrating philosophical work with experimental and theoretical work in developmental psychology, cognitive psychology, and neuropsychology.

ALSO PUBLISHED IN THE SERIES:
Time and Memory, edited by Christoph Hoerl and Teresa McCormack

Agency and Self-Awareness, edited by Johannes Roessler and Naomi Eilan

Joint Attention: Communication and Other Minds

Issues in Philosophy and Psychology

edited by

Naomi Eilan, Christoph Hoerl, Teresa
McCormack, and Johannes Roessler

CLARENDON PRESS · OXFORD
2005

OXFORD
UNIVERSITY PRESS

Great Clarendon Street, Oxford OX2 6DP

Oxford University Press is a department of the University of Oxford.
It furthers the University's objective of excellence in research, scholarship,
and education by publishing worldwide in

Oxford New York

Auckland Cape Town Dar es Salaam Hong Kong Karachi Kuala Lumpur
Madrid Melbourne Mexico City Nairobi New Delhi Shanghai Taipei
Toronto

With offices in

Argentina Austria Brazil Chile Czech Republic France Greece
Guatemala Hungary Italy Japan Poland Portugal Singapore
South Korea Switzerland Thailand Turkey Ukraine Vietnam

Oxford is a registered trade mark of Oxford University Press
in the UK and in certain other countries

Published in the United States
by Oxford University Press Inc., New York

A catalogue record for this title is available from the British Library

Library of Congress Cataloging in Publication Data

Joint attention : communication and other minds : issues in philosophy and psychology / edited
by Naomi Eilan ... [et al.].
     p. cm.
Includes bibliographical references and Index.
1.   Joint attention. I.   Eilan, Naomi.
BF323. J63J65 2005   153.7'33—dc22   2004024898
ISBN 0–19–924564–9
ISBN 0–19–924563–0 (pbk.)

1 3 5 7 9 10 8 6 4 2

Typeset by Newgen Imaging Systems (P) Ltd., Chennai, India
Printed in Great Britain
on acid-free paper by
Biddles Ltd,
King's Lynn, Norfolk

Preface

This book is the third in the interdisciplinary OUP series dedicated to the work of the AHRB Project on Consciousness and Self-Consciousness, the previous ones being *Time and Memory* and *Agency and Self-Awareness*. These, in turn, were preceded by two volumes, *Spatial Representation* (OUP) and *The Body and the Self* (MIT), both produced by the King's College Cambridge Spatial Representation Project.

Bernard Williams is reported to have commented about the first volume, *Spatial Representation*, that it is remarkable how far one can get on a purely solipsistic basis. The problem Williams was pressing was this. Anyone would agree that the capacity to represent the world spatially is absolutely critical for getting objective thought off the ground. The question is whether an account of objective thought that does not make explicit the role of social cognition could possibly be complete. Many developmentalists and philosophers share Williams's intuition that it can't be. The difficulty, though, is to show how and why this is true. This volume, twelve years on, is an attempt to engage head-on with his challenge.

One reason why the phenomenon of joint attention is so fascinating is that it occurs relatively early on in development (from the age of 12 months on) and seems, intuitively, absolutely fundamental to the very possibility of thought. When we try to explain what exactly it is, and why it seems so fundamental, we run immediately into questions about the relation between social interaction and spatial cognition in providing for the idea of an objective world. These questions, in turn, raise fundamental issues about how we explain our access to others' and our own mental states, and about the relation between communication and our knowledge of other minds. The phenomenon of joint attention also demonstrates in a remarkably vivid way why neither philosophers nor psychologists can go it alone in areas of such fundamental importance for understanding the nature of thought. For many of the issues we encounter here turn on getting right the relation between empirical data and a priori, largely epistemological concerns. So in trying to explain the phenomenon, we cannot but begin to address the challenge posed by Williams.

This volume is also a tribute to George Butterworth, whose pioneering work on joint attention has been of such importance to many developmental psychologists. He was going to contribute to this book, and he contributed to many of the interdisciplinary discussions that preceded it. But his influence on the kind of work done within the framework of both projects extends far beyond his particular contributions to empirical work on joint attention. He shared, and did much to foster, a vision of interdisciplinary work which has informed both projects and which he associated with Piaget—the idea that empirical work on developmental mechanisms must be informed by and inform central epistemological concerns in philosophy.

This collection of papers has its origins in two workshops held by the AHRB Project on Consciousness and Self-Consciousness. Many of the papers in this volume were first presented at the second workshop. Others were commissioned. Our very greatest debt is to the contributors, for their papers and the immensely stimulating discussions surrounding them, during and after the workshops. We owe a particular debt of gratitude, and apologies, to those contributors who have waited patiently for so long for the rest of the book to catch up with them.

We would like to thank the AHRB for the grant that made the project and the workshops possible and the University of Warwick for its generous supplementation of the grant. The Philosophy Department at Warwick provided an ideal environment for pursuing the project. We want in particular to acknowledge with much gratitude the unflagging vision and support provided by the head of department, Michael Luntley. Peter Momtchiloff has been, as always, invaluably supportive and encouraging, and we thank him for this. We are also very grateful to Jean van Altena and Jacqueline Baker for seeing the book through to press.

Contents

Notes on Contributors   ix

1. Joint Attention, Communication, and Mind   1
   NAOMI EILAN

2. Joint Attention and Understanding the Mind   34
   JANE HEAL

3. What Chimpanzees Know about Seeing, Revisited:
   An Explanation of the Third Kind   45
   JOSEP CALL AND MICHAEL TOMASELLO

4. Joint Attention and the Notion of Subject: Insights from
   Apes, Normal Children, and Children with Autism   65
   JUAN-CARLOS GÓMEZ

5. Before the 'Third Element': Understanding Attention to Self   85
   VASUDEVI REDDY

6. Infants' Understanding of the Actions Involved in
   Joint Attention   110
   AMANDA L. WOODWARD

7. Infant Pointing: Harlequin, Servant of Two Masters   129
   FABIA FRANCO

8. Understanding the Role of Communicative Intentions
   in Word Learning   165
   MARK A. SABBAGH AND DARE BALDWIN

9. What Puts the Jointness into Joint Attention?   185
   R. PETER HOBSON

10. Why do Children with Autism have a Joint Attention
    Impairment?   205
    SUE LEEKAM

11. Joint Attention and the Problem of Other Minds   230
    JOHANNES ROESSLER

12. Joint Reminiscing as Joint Attention to the Past   260
    CHRISTOPH HOERL AND TERESA McCORMACK

13. Joint Attention and Common Knowledge 287
    JOHN CAMPBELL

14. Joint Attention: Its Nature, Reflexivity, and Relation to
    Common Knowledge 298
    CHRISTOPHER PEACOCKE

Author Index 325
Subject Index 331

Notes on Contributors

Dare Baldwin is Professor of Psychology at the University of Oregon and a former fellow at the Center for Advanced Study in the Behavioral Sciences. Her current research pursues two trajectories: examining the foundational role that early emerging social understanding plays in language development, and investigating action-processing mechanisms that support the emergence of social understanding. She is a recipient of the American Psychological Association's Distinguished Scientific Award for Early Career Contribution, the Boyd McCandless Award, and the John Merck Scholars Award. Her research is currently funded by the National Science Foundation.

Josep Call received his Ph.D. in Psychology in 1997 from Emory University, Atlanta (USA) and worked at the Yerkes Primate Center (USA) from 1991 to 1997. From 1997 to 1999 he was a lecturer at the University of Liverpool (UK). Since 1999 he has been a research scientist at the Max Planck Institute for Evolutionary Anthropology and co-director of the Wolfgang Köhler Primate Research Center in Leipzig (Germany). His research interests focus on comparative cognition in the social and physical domains. His publications include numerous research articles and book chapters on primate social behaviour and comparative cognition and a book, *Primate Cognition* (with M. Tomasello, Oxford University Press, 1997). Currently, he is preparing a comprehensive book on *The Gestural Communication of Apes and Monkeys* (with M. Tomasello, Lawrence Erlbaum Associates).

John Campbell is Willis S. and Marion Slusser Professor of Philosophy at the University of California, Berkeley. He was Wilde Professor of Mental Philosophy at Oxford University. He is the author of *Reference and Consciousness* (OUP, 2002) and *Past, Space and Self* (MIT Press, 1994). He is currently working on causation in psychology.

Naomi Eilan is Professor of Philosophy at the University of Warwick. She was Co-director of the King's College Spatial Representation Project and Director of the Warwick AHRB Consciousness and Self-Consciousness Project. She is co-editor of several joint philosophy and psychology books, including *Spatial Representation* and *Agency and Self-Awareness*. Her research interests and publications turn on problems that lie at the interface of metaphysics, theory of content, epistemology, and psychology, especially as these relate to issues in explaining aspects of consciousness and self-consciousness.

Fabia Franco is a developmental psychologist and works at Middlesex University. Her main research interests are in the field of infant development of communication and social cognition.

Juan-Carlos Gómez is a lecturer at the School of Psychology, University of St Andrews, and a member of the Centre for the Study of Social Learning and Cognitive Evolution. He works on cognitive development and evolution in primates, children, and autism. He is the author of *Apes, Monkeys, Children and the Growth of Mind* (Harvard University Press, 2004).

Jane Heal is Professor of Philosophy at Cambridge University and a Fellow of St John's College. She has written on philosophy of mind and language, and was one of the initiators of the so-called simulation approach to psychological concepts. Publications include *Fact and Meaning* (Blackwell, 1989) and *Mind, Reason and Imagination* (CUP, 2003), a collection of essays on philosophy of mind.

Peter Hobson is Tavistock Professor of Developmental Psychopathology in the University of London, based at the Tavistock Clinic and the Behavioural and Brain Sciences Unit, Institute of Child Health, University College, London. He has a Ph.D. in experimental psychology from Cambridge University, and is a psychiatrist and psychoanalyst. His research in lifespan developmental psychopathology centres around the significance of interpersonal relations for cognitive and social development. He has written two books, the most recent entitled *The Cradle of Thought* (Pan Macmillan, 2002).

Christoph Hoerl is a lecturer in the Department of Philosophy, University of Warwick, and was previously AHRB Institutional Research Fellow in the Project on Consciousness and Self-Consciousness at Warwick. He is also Co-director of the AHRB Project 'Causal Understanding: Empirical and Theoretical Foundations for a New Approach'. His research interests include episodic memory, temporal and causal reasoning, and the nature and development of psychological understanding. He is co-editor of the book *Time and Memory: Issues in Philosophy and Psychology* (OUP, 2001).

Sue Leekam is a Reader in Developmental Psychology at the University of Durham. After completing a Ph.D. at the University of Sussex in 1988 and postdoctoral work in Melbourne, Australia, she took a lectureship at the University of Kent followed by a readership at the University of Durham in 2000. Her publications in the field of autism and developmental disorders reflect a particular interest in the developmental changes that occur in children's social interaction and symbolic development.

Teresa McCormack is a lecturer at the School of Psychology, Queen's University, Belfast, and a Co-director of the AHRB Project 'Causal Understanding: Empirical and Theoretical Foundations for a New Approach'. She has researched and published on memory development and the development of temporal and causal abilities in children. She is co-editor of the book *Time and Memory: Issues in Philosophy and Psychology* (OUP, 2001).

Christopher Peacocke is Professor of Philosophy at Columbia University, and a Fellow of the British Academy. He was previously Professor at New York University, a Leverhulme Research Professor, and Waynflete Professor of Metaphysical Philosophy at Oxford University. His books include *A Study of Concepts*, *Being Known*, and *The Realm of Reason*. His current research interests within the philosophy of mind include thinkers' understanding of their own and others' mental states, the nature of self-knowledge, the individuation of intentional content, and the nature of awareness in perception, thought, and emotion.

Vasudevi Reddy is Reader in Psychology at the University of Portsmouth. Her research has included studies of non-compliance across cultures, infant shyness and teasing, interpersonal play in autism and Down's syndrome, and interaction in mirrors. Her primary interest is in processes of interpersonal engagement and knowledge of other minds. She is currently writing a book for Harvard University Press called *Teasing, Shyness and Showing Off: Understanding Minds in Infancy*.

Johannes Roessler is a lecturer in Philosophy at the University of Warwick and was previously an AHRB Institutional Research Fellow in the Project on Consciousness and Self-Consciousness at Warwick. He is Co-director of a new AHRB Project on Causal Understanding. His research interests include self-awareness, perceptual knowledge, the nature of psychological understanding, Kant, and Wittgenstein. He is co-editor of *Agency and Self-Awareness: Issues in Philosophy and Psychology* (OUP, 2003)

Mark Sabbagh is an Assistant Professor of Psychology at Queen's University at Kingston. His current experimental research interests focus on children's understanding of mental states and how this understanding affects children's word learning in everyday settings. In addition he is active in research investigating the neurological underpinnings of mental state decoding and reasoning in both adults and young children.

Michael Tomasello received his Ph.D. in Psychology in 1980 from the University of Georgia (USA) and taught at Emory University and worked at Yerkes Primate Center (USA) from 1980 to 1998. Since 1998 he has been Co-director of the Max Planck Institute for Evolutionary Anthropology, Leipzig, Germany. Research interests focus on processes of social cognition, social learning, and communication in human children and great apes. Books include *Primate Cognition* (with J. Call, OUP, 1997), *The New Psychology of Language: Cognitive and Functional Approaches to Language Structure* (edited, Erlbaum, 1998), *The Cultural Origins of Human Cognition* (Harvard University Press, 1999), *Constructing a Language: A Usage-Based Theory of Language Acquisition* (Harvard University Press, 2003).

Amanda Woodward is Associate Professor in the Department of Psychology and the Committee on Human Development at the University of Chicago. She is chair of the Psychology Department's graduate program in Developmental Psychology, Co-director of the Center for infant studies, and a core member of the Center for Early Childhood Research. Her research focuses on social understanding during the first year of life, including infants' reasoning about people's actions and on the linkages between early social knowledge and language development. Professor Woodward's research has been recognized by several awards, including the John Merck Fund Young Scholars Award (1994), the Division 7 American Psychological Association Boyd McCandless Award for an Early Career Contribution to Developmental Psychology (2000), the Neubauer Faculty Development Fellowship in the College, University of Chicago (2001), and a James McKeen Cattell Sabbatical Fellowship (2003–4).

1

Joint Attention, Communication, and Mind

Naomi Eilan

1. INTRODUCTION

Sometime around their first birthday most infants begin to engage in relatively sustained bouts of attending together with their caretakers to objects in their environment. By the age of 18 months, on most accounts, they are engaging in full-blown episodes of joint attention. As developmental psychologists (usually) use the term, for such joint attention to be in play, it is not sufficient that the infant and the adult are in fact attending to the same object, nor that the one's attention cause the other's. The latter can and does happen much earlier, whenever the adult follows the baby's gaze and homes in on the same object as the baby is attending to; or, from the age of 6 months, when babies begin to follow the gaze of an adult. We have the relevant sense of joint attention in play only when the fact that both child and adult are attending to the same object is, to use Sperber and Wilson's (1986) phrase, 'mutually manifest'. Psychologists sometimes speak of such joint-ness as a case of attention being 'shared' by infant and adult, or of a 'meeting of minds' between infant and adult, all phrases intended to capture the idea that when joint attention occurs everything about the fact that both subjects are attending to the same object is out in the open, manifest to both participants.

The phenomenon of joint attention, under that description, was initially studied by developmental psychologists interested in the development of pre-verbal and early verbal communication during the second year of life—interested, that is, in the emergence of pointing and the transition from pointing to the accompaniment of such pointing with various pre-verbal 'comments' and finally, by the time children are 2 years old, to the production of basic sentences in the context of short conversations. And the importance of joint attention for the development of such early verbal communications is hard to overestimate. As Bruner (1977, p. 287) puts it, joint attention 'sets the deictic limits that govern joint reference, determines the need for referential taxonomy, establishes the need for signaling intent, and eventually provides a context for the development of explicit predication'. But commenting on this work retrospectively some thirty years later, Bruner (1995, p. 1) notes that there was a sense in which the phenomenon of joint attention itself was simply taken for granted. In particular, he says, '[e]pistemological questions [such as how infants and toddlers 'come to know about other minds or how they come to realize that other minds know theirs'] never entered the discussion'. Nor, he says, did the questions of the nature of the mental concepts that the babies and toddlers use when engaging in bouts of joint attention.

Turning now to philosophy, at least some of the epistemological issues raised by the phenomenon of joint attention, or analogues of them, have, of course, been intensely discussed, with respect to adults, under the heading of mutual or common knowledge. The concept question, that is the question of the kind of mental understanding implicated in joint attention, however, has not. Let me first say a few words about the former, and use them to lead on to the latter, which has, in recent years, become of interest to developmental psychologists.

The notion of mutual or common knowledge has been thought of as the key to explaining verbal communication, and, more generally, rational co-operative activity. Many analyses of it appeal to the possibility of infinitely iterated beliefs in order to explain what such openness consists in—and then try to find ways of either justifying stopping it at some arbitrary level of complexity or of providing subjects with bases from which they can compute an infinite regress. Thus to take a much discussed example of Schiffer's (1988), suppose you and I are sitting at a table with a candle between us. In such a situation, in normal conditions we will have mutual knowledge of the fact that we can both see the candle. A typical philosophical analysis of what must be true of me, say, if this is a case of mutual knowledge, will ascribe to me at the very least the belief that you see the candle, the belief that you believe that I see the candle, the belief that you believe that I believe that you see the candle. The debate then turns on how one deals with the further, infinite iterations that many feel should follow to explain complete openness, given the finiteness of human minds.

Now, if something along these lines is the right thing to say about the kind of mutual awareness implicated in joint attention, it is hardly surprising that developmental psychologists had shown no interest in it. Not merely because it seems absurd to explain what is going on in the infant's mind by appeal to the capacity for such infinitely iterated knowledge structures, but because one of the most robust findings in developmental psychology is that children before the age of 4 just don't have the concepts of belief and knowledge needed for formulating even the first step. And one response, when presented with such an account, might be: that just shows that it is wrong to describe toddlers as engaging in bouts of joint attention. They may well be capable of bringing it about, causally, e.g. by pointing, that others attend to what they attend to, and they may respond to adults' attempts to draw their attention to objects, but that is all there can be to it—in particular, the idea of some kind of mutual awareness here must go by the board.

The alternative response is: the fact that babies engage in joint attention just shows, particularly vividly, what is wrong with the iterated belief ascriptions approach to explaining mutuality of awareness here, which is anyway unsatisfactory for the adult case as well. There is something utterly simple and basic about the transparency of our minds to each other in the case of joint attention which this whole kind of account misses. The very idea that we have to iterate beliefs *ad infinitum* in order to capture the phenomenon of mutual awareness only gets going because of an assumption of basic opacity as a starting-point.

There is something very attractive and suggestive about this immediate reaction, but it turns out to be extremely difficult to articulate and make good. For one thing, if the phenomenon of joint attention is to take us forward on the epistemological front, this will only happen if we can explain how we should account for the way in which each person represents what is going on in others' minds when it is achieved. Whatever in general we want to say about the kind of mental understanding we find in joint attention, it will presumably involve ascribing to the baby some kind of grip on the notion of attention. But what is attention? Despite the centrality of the those of attention in our mental life, there has been very little philosophical work on what exactly our intuitive, everyday concept of attention actually means—about how it is connected with, on the one hand, grasp of physical concepts such as those of space and causation, and, on the other hand, grasp of mental concepts such as those of perception, action, and various affective concepts. There is a clear contrast here with other concepts, possession of which has been the subject of intense research among developmental psychologists, such as the concepts of belief, desire, and intentional action. So, solving for the children's case with respect to the concept of attention is a matter of simultaneously discovering the role played in our adult common-sense psychology by the concept of attention.

However, whatever we say about the child's (and adult's) concept of attention in general, this will only help with explaining the kind of transparency of minds we assume exists in cases of joint attention if we can also say something about the kind of social interaction we have in play in such cases, which seems, intuitively, to guarantee such transparency. After all, such transparency is not something we assume always exists—for example, when we observe someone's behaviour and use that to form hypotheses about what they must be thinking. So there is something special about the joint attention situation, which it shares with other cases of social interaction, e.g. rational co-operation, verbal communication, and so forth, in which we want to say that minds are transparent to each other. And this brings us to the third big issue raised by the phenomenon of joint attention.

Many philosophers and developmental psychologists share the intuition that treating the child's developing mental capacities as emerging in the context of social interaction yields a picture of understanding that is fundamentally different from one on which mental understanding is a matter of theorizing about observed behaviour. Here too, though there is something attractive and intuitively suggestive about the idea of a different picture, it is not at all easy to formulate what this difference is exactly. What exactly is it that turns out to be different in the account we give of our everyday psychological terms, and of their referents, if we hold that mental life emerges in the context of social interaction. Indeed, what exactly do we mean by social interaction? And how does our understanding of development contribute to spelling out the answer?

So, there is the question of the kind of mutual awareness we find in joint attention, in virtue of which we think of minds as being transparent to each other (call this the 'Epistemological Question'). And there is the question of the kind of understanding of attention which a child at the age of 1–2 might plausibly be thought of as possessing and bringing to bear on these situations (call this the 'Concept Question'). And there is the question of how we should conceive of the kind of social interaction involved in joint attention, in virtue of which the concept of attention can be deployed in a way that yields mutual awareness (call this the 'Social Question'). And finally, there is the issue of how exactly these three questions are related to each other.

There are, in fact, many ways one might relate them. In what follows I propose one framework for doing so, which in turn yields one way of distinguishing between two different accounts of joint attention. These two types of theory give different answers to our three questions, and relate them in different ways. As I will be setting up issues, the difference turns on how each theory addresses two fundamental issues raised by the phenomenon of joint attention. (a) What, if any, is the connection between the capacity to engage in joint attention triangles and the capacity to grasp the idea of objective truth? (b) How do we explain the kind of openness or sharing of minds that occurs in joint attention? In developing these ideas I will be drawing heavily on the papers collected here. This is not at all to say, though, that their authors would necessarily agree with this way of setting up the issues. And it is even less to say that the questions I will be raising begin to scratch the surface of the rich assortment of fascinating issues raised by each paper in its own right.

2. LOCATING THE PHENOMENON OF JOINT ATTENTION

2.1 A Preliminary Definition

To get going, it will help to have before us the following relatively uncontroversial breakdown of the looking patterns that lead up to the emergence of the phenomenon labelled 'joint attention', and of the attentional behaviours that develop in the course of its maturation. Up until the age of 4 or 5 months, infants look mainly at their caregivers. Attentional focus switches to physical objects at about 5 months. Between the ages of 6 and 9 months we find the beginning of gaze alternation between objects and adults, where this includes first bouts of gaze-following, restricted by the visibility of the object to the infant. Pointing and more sophisticated forms of gaze- and point-following, coupled with the phenomenon of social referencing (in which infants appear to look to the adults to get emotional

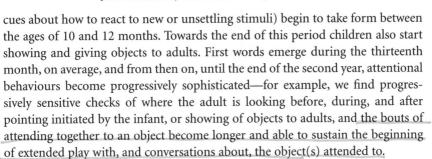

cues about how to react to new or unsettling stimuli) begin to take form between the ages of 10 and 12 months. Towards the end of this period children also start showing and giving objects to adults. First words emerge during the thirteenth month, on average, and from then on, until the end of the second year, attentional behaviours become progressively sophisticated—for example, we find progressively sensitive checks of where the adult is looking before, during, and after pointing initiated by the infant, or showing of objects to adults, and the bouts of attending together to an object become longer and able to sustain the beginning of extended play with, and conversations about, the object(s) attended to.

On most accounts, joint attention, in the sense we are interested in, begins to manifest itself at about 12 months, when we find the beginning of periods of sustained attending together to objects in the environment As I will understand the term 'joint attention', to say of an event that it is an event of two subjects (or more) jointly attending to the same object is to be committed, at least, to the truth of the following four claims about the event.

a. There is an object that each subject is attending to, where this implies (i) a causal connection between the object and each subject, and (ii) awareness of the object by each subject.
b. There is a causal connection of some kind between the two subjects' acts of attending to the object.
c. The two subjects' experiences exploit their understanding of the concept of attention.
d. Each subject is aware, in some sense, of the object *as* an object that is present to both subjects. There is, in this respect, a 'meeting of minds' between both subjects, such that the fact that both are attending to the same object is open or mutually manifest.

Let us say that when these conditions are met, we have in play a 'joint attention triangle'. Very loosely, so-called rich theories say that it is right to ascribe to 1–2-year-olds participation in joint attentional triangles thus conceived. 'Lean' theories put pressure on condition (c), and thereby on (d). A radically lean claim would be that there is no understanding of any kind of the concept of attention at this age and that, therefore, between the ages of 1 and 2 conditions (a) and (b) only apply. A modestly rich account will say that there is some understanding of attention, but that it is not sufficient to generate mutuality, so only conditions (a)–(c) apply. (In the case of primate research, where all are agreed that mutuality is not achieved, all rich interpretations are modestly so: they say that some kind of understanding of attention is in play, whereas lean ones deny any.)

There are, however, two critical ambiguities in this loose description of the rich/lean debate. Clarifying these will yield several additional stipulations about the way I will be using the notion of 'joint attention', and allow a more focused introduction of the kinds of questions I will be pursuing.

The first ambiguity is this. The term 'rich' is sometimes used to refer to what the causal co-ordinations of attention *provide for* between the ages of 1 and 2. A rich theory will say that these co-ordinations provide for mutual awareness; a lean theory will deny it. On another reading, a 'rich' theory is a theory which says that *sophisticated conceptual abilities* are *deployed* by children engaged in causal co-ordinations of attention; a lean theory will deny it. The difference between these two readings comes out when we reflect on the possibility of claiming that the causal co-ordinations of attention we find among 1–2-year-olds are rich in the first sense—that is, yield mutual awareness—but that this requires ascribing to them only lean, unsophisticated conceptual abilities, which would be a lean claim in the second sense.

The second ambiguity is this. Condition (c) refers to the mental understanding implicated in causal co-ordinations of attention among 1–2-year-olds. There are two distinct issues that fall under this heading. The first is the question of which particular mental concepts are implicated in joint attention conceived of as rich in the first sense. In particular, this is the question of what notion of attention we should be ascribing to children if we say that between the ages of 1 and 2 they participate in joint attention triangles. (This is what I earlier on called the 'Concept Question'). The second is: what model of mental understanding should we use to explain the child's use of these concepts? The central issue here is whether, and in what sense, the social interaction involved in joint attention suggests an alternative to the claim that children's mental understanding is a matter of grasping a theory. (This is one aspect of what I earlier called the 'Social Question'.)

Now, as I will be using the notion of 'rich' throughout this chapter, unless I specify otherwise, it will refer to theories that hold that the kinds of causal co-ordinations of attention we find among 1–2-year-olds provide for mutual awareness. In the first half of this chapter I will be concerned with building up to a progressively refined definition of such a theory. In the second half of the chapter I will be considering two current approaches to joint attention, both of which describe themselves as 'rich'. As we will see, there is a question whether both can, or would want to, meet the requirements I will be using to define richness. At that point I will return to questions about the sophistication of abilities required of children participating in joint attention triangles. For the moment, though, my concern will be to develop one substantive version of a rich theory in a way that will allow me to raise some of the fundemantal problems to which joint attention gives rise.

So the kinds of rich theory we are concerned with are ones that hold that the kinds of co-ordinations of attention engaged in by 1–2-year-olds provide for a form of mutual awareness. This yields our first question: how must we conceive of the child's understanding of attention if we are to credit her with the capacity for mutual awareness that she and the adult are attending to the same object? On the face of it, this question does not get us very far. We are faced with the task of solving simultaneously for two hard and controversial issues. What is attention? And how do we explain mutual awareness? Luckily, two additional major claims made in the early literature about what joint attention provides for yield further constraints on how we might go about answering these questions.

The first, which we find in the quote above from Bruner, is the idea that the joint attention triangle makes possible the development of linguistic communication. In particular, there is the idea that the existence of a common object of attention provides for something like a joint field of reference, which enables linguistic communication about it to get going and develop. So, supposing that we think of joint attention in this way, an additional, constraining question we can ask is: What kinds of constraints does this impose on the conceptual abilities implicated in it? And, further, what bearing does this have on how we explain mutual awareness?

The second major claim about what joint attention provides for is the idea we find in Werner and Kaplan (1963): namely, that joint attention provides for a contemplative or theoretical attitude to the world, where this is contrasted with a purely practical attitude. This is the idea that by thinking of the object as a common object of attention, something new comes into play that was not available in earlier dyadic interactions with objects. There is, on this account, the beginning of interest in how things are, in truth for its own sake, again contrasted with a purely practical engagement with the world. So, supposing we think of joint attention in this way, another question we might ask is: What kinds of constraints does this impose on the conceptual abilities implicated in it? And how does this link up with the idea of joint attention providing for communication and mutual awareness?

2.2 Davidson on Triangulation, Objectivity, and Communication

One way of connecting these questions is to be found in the philosopher Donald Davidson's account of the kinds of triangulations he thinks have to be in place for objective thought to be possible (Davidson, 2001). His particular account is one that lean developmental approaches to the capacities of 1–2-year-olds might well avail themselves of. A brief summary of his claims, then, will serve as a useful way of formulating the challenges that rich accounts must meet, and distinguishing between two major ways of addressing these challenges.

In 'The emergence of thought', Davidson argues that thought requires a kind of triangular interaction between (at least) two subject and objects in the world. There are two levels on which this triangulation takes place, each providing a necessary condition for thought.

The first necessary condition is a condition that can be observed to obtain 'in nonhuman animals and in small children' (2001, p. 128). This 'basic situation is one that involves two or more creatures simultaneously in interaction with each other and with the world they share; it is what I will call *triangulation*. It is the result of a threefold interaction, an interaction which is twofold from the point of view of each of the other two agents: each is interacting simultaneously with the world and with the other agent. To put this in a slightly different way, each creature learns to correlate the reactions of the other with changes or objects in the world to which it also reacts' (p. 128). Davidson goes on to give examples of what he means, which include the behaviour of schools of fish, the responses of monkeys to a variety of calls issued by other monkeys which they use as guides to behaviour, and unspecified correlations of 'young children's' responses to the environment with those of adults.

This kind of triangular situation can be accounted for by appeal to more or less sophisticated forms of conditioning, and need not involve the capacity for any kind of representation. But there are several aspects of thought, according to Davidson, which could not be accounted for in the absence of the triangle. The most important for our purposes is what Davidson calls the 'objectivity of thought'.

Thought is objective in the sense that it is made true by a world that is independent of what the thinker takes it to be. For this to be in place, the thinker must appreciate it, which in turn involves a capacity to appreciate that thoughts can be true or false depending on how things are in that world. According to Davidson, what gives us the idea that we might be mistaken, right or wrong, is the kind of interaction described in the basic triangulation. In this situation two or more creatures correlate their reactions to the world. Once these correlations are set up, each creature is in a position to expect the associated phenomenon when it perceives the associated reaction of the other. What introduces the possibility of error is the occasional failure of the expectation; the reactions do not correlate. If this is right, then this gives us one sense in which we might say that thought is essentially social.

Although this kind of precognitive triangulation is essential for thought, it is not sufficient, according to Davidson. The other condition that creatures must meet if they are to be credited with the capacity for objective thought is that they be language-users. As he sees it, utterances are the only sufficiently structured form of behaviour that can serve as evidence, from the triangulator's perspective, for there being a common world and for its exact nature. It is only the production and interpretation of speech behaviour in the context of communication that actually requires the subject to deploy the concept of objective truth.

A notable feature of Davidson's account of this second level of triangulation is that the subject's exploitation of the concept of objective truth is embedded in her formulation and interpretation of communicative intentions, where the latter are conceived of along roughly Gricean lines. Such an account attributes to each speaker an intention to get her audience to form beliefs about her, the speaker's, beliefs. That is the speaker's primary intention. Her secondary intention is to produce an utterance that has features that will provide the audience with evidence about the contents of her belief. Her third intention is that her primary intention be recognized by the audience, and serve as the audience's reason for acquiring a belief about the speaker's belief.

Now, there is a very great deal going on here, and it will serve as a useful point of reference to which I will return throughout this chapter. For the immediate purposes of highlighting central theoretical debates among developmentalists, though, I want to note four features of the way in which Davidson connects triangulation, objectivity, mutual awareness, and communication.

1. The first point is, simply, that on Davidson's account *some kind of triangulation* is essential for the subject to have a conception of an objective world, a world that makes her thoughts true or false. √

2. The second point concerns the *particular kinds of triangulation* that Davidson thinks have to be in place, and the relation between them. Triangulation comes in on two levels for Davidson. First there is precognitive triangulation, based on more or less sophisticated forms of conditioning. Then there is a reflective triangulation that gets going in virtue of the exploitation of reflexive communicative intentions. One striking feature is that we only have the *subject* making something of the world once we have in play a sophisticated reflective theory of mind. It is either that, or wholly non-cognitive triangulation. A second striking feature in this two-tier account is the absence of any obvious developmental or explanatory connection between the two levels. By an absence of a developmental connection I mean the absence of anything that explains how subjects get, developmentally (or indeed phylogenetically), from precognitive triangulation to the kind of reflective deployment of communicative intentions that Davidson thinks are essential for linguistic communication. There is a correlative explanatory gap: it is not clear how and whether anything that happens on the precognitive level serves to explain the achievements on the reflective level. On the precognitive level there is a causal, presumably perceptual relation between each subject and objects in the world, and between the two perceptions. Neither seems to play any role in explaining the mechanism of triangulation on the reflective level.

3. The third distinctive feature I want to have before us is this. The subject's take on the idea of an objective world and her take on the other's mind both rely, essentially, on exploiting the capacity to distinguish between true and false beliefs in interpreting the behaviour of the other. Indeed, the concept of belief comes in twice over. First, the audience acquires beliefs about the way the world is, by acquiring beliefs about the speaker's beliefs (and the speaker's primary intention is that the audience do so). Second, the audience, A, can, on this picture, understand which belief it is that the speaker, S, wants her to acquire, but fail to acquire it because, for example, she suspects S of duplicity—i.e. of providing linguistic evidence for beliefs S does not in fact hold. The capacity to assume sincerity, i.e. absence of deception, is essential for successful communication to occur.

4. The fourth striking feature of Davidson's account turns on the extreme elegance and simplicity with which communication, objectivity, and mutual awareness are connected on the cognitive level. More specifically, it is by manifesting and interpreting the kind of complex embedded communicative intentions described earlier that (a) communication is meant to be achieved; (b) the idea of truth is supposed to get a purchase; (c) mutual awareness is said to be secured. It is a consequence of this that the kind of social interaction in play from the subject's perspective is, essentially, the product of such complex intentions, manifested and understood.

2.3 Joint Attention as a Midway House

Each of these features in Davidson's way of connecting objectivity, communication, and mutual awareness is important in locating central issues in the developmental debates about the nature of joint attention, in a way that links up with central philosophical concerns. I will use the first three to formulate a progressively refined definition of a rich theory, and the fourth to introduce a distinction between two kinds of rich theory. It is this distinction that will occupy us for the remainder of the chapter.

1. In philosophy, the most radical rejection of the idea that triangulation is critical for either a sense of an objective world or for grasp of mental concepts says that having an idea of an objective world out there is wholly independent of any grasp of mental concepts at all. A less radical rejection would agree that a grip on the idea of an objective world is interdependent with the capacity to ascribe mental states, but insist that the child need only be able to ascribe mental states such as perception to itself, in order to be credited with the idea of an objective world. (See below for more on this.)

In developmental psychology, the clearest opposition to the insistence on the importance of triangulation is to be found in theories that hold that a sense of an objective world and the capacity to 'mind read' develop along parallel lines. There are many versions of this position, two of which are the following.

On the first, in each sphere, the child progresses from perception of physical (and, perhaps, psychological) properties, to theorizing about them, drawing on generally developing capacities for causal understanding, counterfactual reasoning, and so forth in each sphere. This is probably the dominant picture, with theory of the world and theory of the mind progressing in parallel, and, with respect to the latter, reaching the basic format to be found in adult 'theory of mind' at about the age of 4. On the second parallel-development view, physical understanding progresses as described above, without any need for psychological understanding. But psychological understanding has its roots in what are sometimes called the 'proto-conversations' in which the infant engages in early dyadic interactions.

The idea is that these interactions yield a different kind of understanding of mental properties than that provided by the theory model. This is sometimes described as a first- and second-person understanding, as opposed to the third-person understanding posited by the theory approach, and sometimes described as an essentially first-person-plural understanding, where this again is contrasted with third-person understanding. These are issues to which we will return. For the moment, what matters is that, on some views, either everything needed for such understanding is already there in these early interactions, or will develop through these interactions as years go by, but, crucially, the introduction of the third element, the physical object or world, adds nothing to the understanding to be had from dyadic interaction. (See Chapter 5 for an argument for this view.)

The possibility of holding these kinds of parallel-development views shows up an ambiguity in the way we have so far defined rich theories in terms of what they provide for. On one understanding a theory is rich if, as a matter of fact, children have the wherewithal at this age for engaging in rich attentional triangles, but what provides them with these capacities is to be explained independently of their actual engagement in the co-ordination of attention. This might be one kind of 'rich' parallel-view theory. On this reading, 'provides for' means merely 'implies'. On another reading, 'provides for' means something stronger: namely, that the kinds of triangulation engaged in during joint attention episodes actually play some role in yielding these capacities. This is Davidson's idea. This is a natural reading of theories that claim that joint attention should be considered a landmark in children's development. As we will see, though, it is questionable whether this is the correct reading of one of the theories that makes this claim. For our immediate purpose of building up an account of richness, I add this to the definition. A rich theory is one that shares with Davidson the idea that the triangulations engaged in by 1–2-year-olds have some such explanatory role.

2. It is no accident that there is no connection between Davidson's two levels of triangulation. In fact it is over-determined by two positions he holds. The first is that our concepts of belief, intention, desire, and the like—i.e. our propositional attitude concepts—get their meaning only in virtue of being deployed in certain patterns of explanation which draw essentially on the other concepts in the package. According to Davidson, this introduces a deep conceptual difficulty about saying anything about any midway developmental positions a child might occupy relative to our mature theory of mind. The second position he holds is that all representational content is conceptual content governed by rationality constraints. What this rules out is any idea of perceptions having a representational content that is non-conceptual, in not being governed by these constraints. And this in turn rules out the idea that children have representational abilities prior to the age of 12 months, which, in some way, provide a basis for conceptual abilities they might develop during their first year.

Consider now a 12-month-old baby about to embark on progressively sophist-icated co-ordinations of attention with adults. All developmental psychologists would agree that she comes armed with a rich battery of perceptual representa-tional capacities; and many would argue that these are not yet conceptual. With respect to the physical world, almost all psychologists (and primatologists) assume that the child (and chimpanzee) has some kind of primitive intuitive physics embedded in her perception of the physical world in virtue of which it is right to speak of it as representing it. So there is an explicit rejection here of the idea that empirical content with respect to the physical world needs to be the product of triangulation. As to the psychological world, we find a much wider spectrum of claims. First, there is an increasing amount of work showing that prior to the age of 12 months, infants are able not merely to distinguish animate from inanimate movements, but that they also develop during this period a progressively fine-tuned perceptual individuation of movements relative to the objects at which they are directed. As Chapter 6 shows, this kind of individuation begins to be applied to gazes and pointings too, prior to the onset of the use of either for the purposes of communication. Secondly, all psychologists would agree that during the months of intensive dyadic interaction with adults, infants develop supremely fine-tuned ways of exchanging emotions with adults, and a rich assortment of behaviours that enable this exchange. Opinions range here from those who hold that all the child detects in these exchanges are physical properties, to those who hold that they are perceptually detecting psychological properties, in particular emotions, to those who hold that we have here full-blown conceptual representations of other persons as subjects of emotions and other psychological properties (for discussion of these options see Chapter 11, for defence of the strong claim see Chapter 5).

Whatever position one takes on exactly how strong psychological awareness is by the age of 12 months, all would agree at least on the following. The child, *contra* Davidson's precognitive triangulator, comes to episodes of triangulation richly endowed with representational abilities with respect to the physical world, a rich assortment of social, interactive abilities, and, perhaps, some abilities to detect some psychological properties. So, on this score alone, the triangle in which they engage is richer than Davidson's precognitive one. And one question we might ask is: what are the particular *non-conceptual* representational skills the child brings to bear on these co-ordinations? And how do they explain, and in what sense, what happens in these co-ordinations?

Secondly, every developmental psychologist is committed to the idea that there must be some form of *conceptual* development, some story to tell about how the child's mental (and other) concepts develop so that she ends up possessing a full-blown understanding of propositional attitude psychology. This is, for many, the hardest question in which developmentalists are engaged. This is not to say that Davidson has not identified a deep conceptual difficulty with telling a developmental story about concepts which, in their mature stage, are all interdependent. On the contrary, he has pin-pointed a challenge relative to which some of the deep disagreements among developmentalists can be understood. At the very least, it brings out the significance of showing that in addition to asking which particular concepts we should be ascribing to children (the 'Concept Question'), we need, at the same time, to ask about what model of mental understanding in general we should be appealing to here (which is where the 'Social Question' comes in).

So another question we need to ask about joint attention triangles between the ages of 1 and 2 is: how should we explain the kinds of mental concepts, and the form of mental understanding that might be in play at this stage, before the development of a full-blown propositional attitude psychology?

Finally, there is the question of the connection between the non-conceptual skills the child brings with her and the conceptual abilities she develops during the first year. As we shall see, the two kinds of theories we will be distinguishing deliver somewhat different answers to these questions. But they would all accept a particular constraint that is best brought out when we turn to the third feature of Davidson's account.

3. Davidson's cognitive triangulation relies, essentially, on exploiting the concept of belief. A constraint that all would accept with respect to these cognitive skills is that the third feature in Davidson's account of cognitive triangulation does not apply to children at this age. It is common ground among all developmentalists that children at this age cannot distinguish between true and false beliefs in interpreting the behaviour of others. This is generally taken to be established by the failure of children before the age of 4 to pass the famous 'false belief task'. This task tests for a child's capacity to distinguish between true and false beliefs in predicting what a protagonist in a story will do or believe. Prior to the age of 4, children use only what they take to be the true state of affairs to engage in such predictions; they assume, that is, that the other believes what they themselves take to be the case. At about the age of 4, they can exploit an understanding of someone else having beliefs that misrepresent the world in order to predict their future behaviour and beliefs.

Suppose we accept this as a reliable indicator that at the age of 1–2 children cannot employ a concept of belief of a kind needed for ascribing to them full-blooded Gricean intentions. One motivation for rejecting a rich theory of joint attention, as we have so far defined it, might run as follows. Suppose you share Davidson's intuitions that the capacity for distinguishing true from false beliefs in interpreting the behaviours of others is essential for being credited with any idea of an objective world. Suppose, moreover, you hold that Davidson describes the only way in which mutual awareness can come into triangulation. This would be one way of motivating a lean interpretation of the kinds of triangulation we find in 1–2-year-olds. It would be a way of motivating the claim that from this perspective there is nothing of interest happening in the kinds of causal co-ordination of attention to objects that we find in 1–2-year-olds. From this perspective, that is, these co-ordinations could as well be treated as precognitive. On this kind of account, as far as the connections between triangulation, objectivity, and mutual awareness are concerned, there is no developmental midway house between Davidson's precognitive triangulations and the reflective deployment of a theory of mind in Gricean-like communication.

While this is one possible way of using Davidson's arguments, there is something perverse about it. A datum as robust as that of children's failure before the age of 4 to pass the false belief test is their success between the ages of 1 and 2 in communication. An equally plausible response to Davidson would be to turn his argument on its head. Given that there is success in communication at this age, then, on Davidson's own account, this should suffice for being credited both with a kind of mutual awareness and a kind of grip on the idea of an objective world. The task, on this way of looking at it, is to find what this could amount to in the absence of the subject's capacity to deploy the distinction between true and false belief to explain others' behaviour.

What I will mean by a rich theory, henceforth, is a theory that holds that the triangulations we find between adults and 1–2-year-olds constitute precisely such a midway house between precognitive triangulations and triangulations explained by appeal to full-blown Gricean communicative intentions. Such a theory insists, that is, that it is right to hold that children between the ages of 1 and 2 participate in joint attention triangles as we have defined them. The sense in which such triangles constitute a midway house is twofold. First, what these triangles deliver is a weakened version, in some way, of the full-blown objectivity and mutual awareness we find in adults. Second, the conceptual and preconceptual skills that go into achieving such objectivity and mutual awareness are, in some way, more primitive than the kinds of conceptual skills drawn on by Davidson's reflective triangulators.

One way of describing the agenda set by this definition is that it takes as its endpoint the stage reached at about 2 years old, when conversations about absent objects truly get going, and when no one is in any doubt that children are making assertions with definite truth-values. The question then is: how should we describe the progress during the second year towards that end-point? This is where the theories we are considering differ. A useful way of introducing the difference between them is by bringing in the last ingredient in Davidson's story.

4. According to Davidson, the possession and interpretation of complex embedded intentions is the vehicle of the kind of triangular social interaction that yields truth, mutuality, and communication. One way of dividing up current approaches to joint attention into two groups, both of which count themselves as 'rich', turns on whether or not they appeal to such embedded intentions, scaled

down for the child case, in explaining the way in which the phenomenon of joint attention yields an understanding of objectivity and mutual awareness. The most influential exponent of a theory that does this is Tomasello (1995, 1999). In the opposite camp I place theories influenced by several key ideas of Werner and Kaplan (1963). In doing so I will be drawing together work represented in this volume in a way that is not necessarily the way its authors would present it. The point of the distinction between the two kinds of theories, though, is not to commit the writers I draw on to accepting this characterization of the significance of their work, but to set up a way of beginning to examine some of the fundamental problems they raise. I begin the next part of this chapter with a brief description of some of the empirical data upon which both theories are agreed. I then go on to give a brief sketch of each theory. Finally, in the last two sections, I consider how their differing answers to the epistemological, concept, and social questions affect the accounts they give of the two basic ingredients in our definition of a rich theory. These are the idea that joint attention in 1–2-year-olds yields a grip on the idea of an objective world and the idea that joint attention at this age yields mutual awareness.

3. TWO THEORIES

3.1 Pointing and Gaze-Following

There are two forms of behaviour other than speech itself which have been taken as indications of the child's developing understanding of attention during the second year. The first is pointing; the second is the progressively sophisticated forms of gaze-following and checking that accompany pointing during the second year. The two types of theory we will be considering each yield different accounts of the significance of each, so a few introductory words about each will be helpful.

The actual gesture of pointing emerges spontaneously as early as 3 months. (See Chapter 7 for a discussion of the gesture and its pattern of emergence, and Chapter 6 for the later emergence of its perceptual detection.) However, most psychologists agree that it is only at the age of about 12 months that it begins to be used with what appears to be some kind of deliberative intent. In a pioneering paper Bates, Camaioni, and Volterra (1976) distinguished between two kinds of pointing that emerge at roughly this age: proto-imperative and proto-declarative. The first was interpreted as a request for an object (the baby appears satisfied when he gets the object). The interpretation of the second is more controversial; but, described maximally neutrally, it is a form of pointing the aim of which appears to be simply to get the adult to engage with the baby's attention to the object (the baby seems satisfied when this has occurred).

Declarative pointings are not produced by chimpanzees, nor, usually, by autistic children. In both cases, moreover, researchers have strong intuitions that joint attention, in the sense of mutual awareness, is lacking. Bates *et al.*'s idea was that declarative pointings provide a bridge to verbal communication. If we think that wherever there is genuine communication in play, there is mutual awareness of a joint field of reference, then the idea that we have a route into explaining the emergence of communication by appeal to psychological abilities underpinning declarative pointing seems very attractive.

However, given the minimal description of the behavioural difference between declarative and imperative pointing, the scope for different explanations is very wide indeed. Two such radically different accounts are provided by the two theories we will be considering. This difference is, in turn, connected with the difference in the way they account for the significance of the way in which gaze-following and so forth develop during the second year. A study of particular interest here is one conducted by Butterworth and Franco (1993), who found that the pattern of gaze-checking changed over this year from looking at the adult after the pointing, to during the pointing, and after it, and finally, at the age of 18 months, we find the beginning of what they call anticipatory looks, gazes at the adult before the child embarks on pointing. This is suggestive of an increased sensitivity to the fact that the adult may not be attending to what engrosses the child. This is strengthened when combined with findings that it is at the age of about 18 months that children begin to display sensitivity to whether or not the adult can see the object that they themselves can see. For example, if the object is placed behind the adult we find, initially, far more pointing and vocalization than if both adult and child can see it. Moreover, pointing decreases markedly if the interesting event is a sound emanating from an object invisible to both adult and child, and becomes pretty random if a paper bag is placed over the adult's head.

A natural way of putting these findings is that the child is manifesting a developing understanding that the adult may not be attending to what she, the child, is attending to, and that something has to be done to get her to attend. The bearing this has on how we cash objectivity and mutual awareness turns on how we cash the concept of attention used in such reasoning. And it is here that we come to the main division between our two kinds of theory, the first of which I now briefly outline.

3.2 A Sketch of Two Theories

1. According to Tomasello (1995, pp. 104 f.), between the ages of 9 and 18 months the child undergoes a cognitive revolution akin in significance and structure to the revolution it undergoes between the ages of 3 and 4. During the latter, the child progresses from understanding 'other persons in terms of their thoughts and beliefs' to understanding 'that others have thoughts and beliefs that may differ from their own', and eventually to understanding 'that others have thoughts and beliefs that may not match the current state of affairs (false beliefs)'. During their

second year of life children have an analogous, agency-based understanding of persons that develops along similar lines. That is, they progress from understanding 'other persons in terms of their intentions' to understanding 'that others may have intentions that may differ from their own', and eventually to understanding 'that others have intentions that may not match with the current state of affairs (accidents and unfulfilled intentions)'.

The first step of the agency-based revolution occurs at about 9 months, when children achieve their own newly formed capacity for means–ends reasoning, and hence for a distinction between goals and the means to achieve them. They apply this understanding to their own actions and, by simulation, to the perceived activities of others. They also apply this to their own and others' looking behaviour, conceived of as a kind of object-directed action. This is how they think of attention.

At around 12 months they begin to manifest a grip on the possibility of manipulating others' attentive behaviour by pointing and then by uttering their first words—both vehicles for such manipulation, first to objects, and then, when predication sets in, to properties or aspects of objects. These manipulations performed and responded to, constitute an implementation and comprehension of a primitive form of communicative intention. What makes it primitive is that it employs agency-related notions only; that is, it does not use the concept of belief. But they have the same kind of embedded structure as do Gricean communicative intentions. So the pointing child will have intentions relative to the other's intentional states (attendings), and will realize when she responds to an adult's pointings that the adult has intentions relative to her intentional lookings. More specifically, the communicative intentions expressed (and understood), say in pointing, are that you share attention with me to this object. Sharing attention, in turn, is conceived by the child as a kind of doing together. So inviting someone to attend to an object, say by pointing, or responding to an invitation to do so, is a matter of entering into an agreement of kinds to do something together, namely look at the object.

During the second year children begin to manifest a grip on the idea that others may be attending to something other than what they are attending to. The manifestations of this grip are, first, the increasing sensitivity to where the adult is looking and, second, the production of predication which sets in, on Tomasello's account, at about 18 months (where predication is conceived of as a kind of attention-directing to aspects of objects the adult may not be attending to). At about 18 months, too, they begin to manifest a grip on the idea that intentions may fail to meet their success conditions, primarily when they begin to correct failed messages.

2. According to Werner and Kaplan (1963), the triangulations we find in joint attention are the first manifestations of the child's adoption of a contemplative stance, where this is contrasted with a purely practical stance. As they put it: 'Thus the act of reference emerges not as an individual act, but as a social one: by

exchanging things with the Other, by touching things and looking at them with the Other. Eventually a special gestural device is formed, *pointing* at an object, by which the infant invites the Other to contemplate an object as he does himself' (p. 43).

The central metaphor they use to describe the role of triangulation is the familiar Gestalt metaphor of polarization or distancing. Prior to triangulation, objects exist as 'things of action'. The transformation that begins to take place when joint attention sets in transforms objects from 'ego-bound things of action to ego-distant things of contemplation'. A correlative distancing of the infant from the adult takes place, though Werner and Kaplan are less explicit about what exactly this involves.

The main picture behind this metaphor is, I think, something like the following. Prior to triangulation, the child is engaged in two kinds of dyadic relations: perception of objects and mutual affect regulation with persons. When the child shows the object to another, successful showing requires taking into account the other's perspective, taking into account what she sees, and so forth. This entails a distancing of the child from the object for the child to succeed, in that the object cannot be treated by her purely as an affordance for her own actions. But showing it to someone else requires more than mere mutual affect regulation. When all we have in play is the latter, the adult need be treated as nothing more than an affective affordance. But introducing a third element requires treating her as someone who can have a take on the world, can have a perspective on it—where the differentiation comes in, in the more the child needs to take into account the difference of perspective. Taking the latter into account simultaneously strengthens the grip on the idea of a mind-independent world. Awareness of others as having a different perspective and awareness of the world as being as it is independently of one's own perspective come together.

So much for the picture. Werner and Kaplan themselves said very little that gave developmental flesh to it. Their main interest was in the development of language as a 'tool of knowing', contrasted with the Vygotskyan idea that language is primarily a 'tool for doing'. This distinction has informed many attempts to characterize the difference between proto-imperative and proto-declarative pointing (see Chapter 7), where the idea was that a correct account of the distinction would lend support to the picture. Debates about the distinction do give us something on which to hang more precise developmental claims. The one I want to have before us is Bates *et al.*'s (1976) original one, which is fitted by them into a distinction between two stages in means–ends reasoning: (a) the use of adults as a means to obtaining an object ('person to object'); and (b) the use of objects to obtain affective engagement with adults ('object to person'). Proto-imperatives were seen as an exemplification of the first; proto-declaratives as a form of the second. The theories I will be collecting under the Werner and Kaplan heading can all be seen as attempting to put flesh on the ideas we have been sketching by explaining joint attention in the terms Bates *et al.* use for the motivational structure and aims of declarative pointing. They can all be seen as attempts to articulate the idea that affective engagement is in some sense the engine of the child's beginning to adopt the contemplative stance. (For the expansion of this basic structure in accounting for the role of joint reminiscing in providing children with the idea of an objective past, see Chapter 12.)

This will have to do as a brief introductory sketch of the two theories. What I now want to do is compare Tomasello's account of the concept of attention with one that would be developed naturally in connection with the Werner and Kaplan picture, and consider the different answers implicit in these accounts to two questions, each one of which will be the topic of the two sections that follow. First, how, and in what sense, does the child's concept of attention contribute to joint attention being a manifestation of her grip on the idea of an objective world? Second, how does each theory's account of the nature of social interaction explain the sense, if any, in which, the kinds of joint attention triangles in which children participate yield mutual awareness.

3.3 Joint Attention and Objectivity

According to Tomasello, the child's understanding of attention between the ages of 1 and 2 can be accommodated wholly by her general understanding of others as agents, entities capable of intentional action. Specifically, for her, attention is a kind of 'intentional perceiving'. But what does 'perceiving' mean for the child? There seem to be two options. On one, perceiving is conceived of as a kind of physical action, an intentional turning of the head and directing of the gaze. This really would be a purely agentive notion of attending, considered as a kind of *physical* action. This does not appear to be Tomasello's own view—he insists that children of that age have a grip on attention as a *mental* activity. The question then is: what kind of mental activity? A natural response would be that they have some concept of perceiving, understood as a way of taking in information about the world. Attending is an active taking in of information. This would seem to be roughly what the adult everyday conception of attention involves. But we are then owed an account of what the child's understanding of the idea of taking in information about the world consists in.

More importantly, however, when our concern is specifically with the idea that joint attention yields objectivity, there is the question of what it is, or could be, about the child's concept of attention that could accommodate that, such that when she thinks she and the adult are sharing attention to an object, she is manifesting a grip on the idea of an objective world. If we take our everyday concept of attention as a guide to what we might expect of children, then the intuitive answer would turn precisely on grasp of the idea that attending is a way of acquiring information or knowledge about the world, a way of taking in the passing show.

The absence of any explicit consideration of this ingredient in our concept of perception reflects what is often a missing ingredient in current developmental discussions of children's early mental understanding, prior to their grasp and use of the concept of belief. If we look at Davidson's theory, the subject's concept of belief has two roles. It is used to interpret the behaviour of others (in a way that can be used to explain and predict their behaviour); and it is the vehicle for the subject's grasp of the idea of objective truth. Suppose, now, we consider children before they acquire the concept of belief. On the face of it, we need to consider the progenitors of our concept of belief in both its roles. In effect, Tomasello gives their grip on the notion of attention a role analogous to the explanatory use of belief, in keeping with a general developmental interest in recent years in finding progenitors for the child's later theory of mind. But his explicit theory does not ask the question of how, in virtue of their grasp of the concept of attention, children might be credited with some kind of primitive grip on the idea of objective truth, more primitive than, and perhaps more basic than, the kind of grip on the idea of an objective world given by Davidson's appeal to our grasp of the concept of belief.

When we do raise this question explicitly, there are several routes we might take in developing what Tomasello in fact says. One would be to say that at this age there isn't anything like a grip on the idea of objective truth. The latter comes only later, with the child's use of the concept of belief. (This was the kind of reasoning behind one version of a lean theory, mentioned earlier. If Tomasello's theory were to take this line, it would not fit our specification of a rich theory in this respect.) Another option is to say that children of this age do have some grip on the idea of objective truth; but for an explanation of that we must turn, at least in part, to their understanding of attention as a directed way of taking in information about the world. To do this is to give up on the idea that it can all be accommodated within an agentive conception of mind—and a version of this is what the second theory we will be considering says. Finally, there is the option of treating the child's conception of attention at this age as purely agentive; attending is a kind of physical action that involves directing head and eyes towards an object. The claim might then be that at this age children have a purely intentional analogue of the later conception of objective truth, an analogue of the distinction between truth and falsity when, from 18 months on, they manifest a grip on the conditions of success for an action, they have the idea of misfired or unsuccessful actions, in their own and others' case. One might then say that for them 'true' just means 'conducive to successful action'. Of all the options, this probably best captures the spirit of Tomasello's account of the pre-belief mind.

As I noted, the fact that we do not have obvious answers here is due to a large extent to the fact that interest in the child's concept of attention is driven mainly not by the urge to find a replacement at this age for the concept of belief *qua* vehicle of the child's grasp of the idea of objective truth, but by the need to find a more primitive version of the explanatory role that belief plays. The opposite is the case for those inspired by Werner and Kaplan, for whom, as we noted, the question of what gives the child something like an objective take on the world is the driving question, because this is one of the two main things that triangulation is said to deliver. In fact, much work on the development of joint attention suggests precisely that. Franco herself interprets the results of her experiments as showing that the baby is beginning to manifest an understanding of the connection between looking and seeing. Although she does not expand on what the child's notion of seeing is at this stage, the way she describes what the understanding of the connection comes to, in effect brings in the ingredient in our concept of attention that we said seemed to be absent in Tomasello's account of the child's concept of attention. This is the link between attending to something and finding out about it. The child's concept of attention, on this view, is a vehicle for an elementary grip on the concept of knowledge. The question then is: what is it exactly about the child's behaviour in these cases that suggests that she is exploiting some such grip on the notion of attention?

When we ask the question in this way, the most striking feature of the child's behaviour is the way she exploits spatial understanding in checking whether the adult can see the object she is pointing to. In doing so, she is manifesting a grip on the idea that the spatial world is there independently of whether the adult perceives it. She is manifesting, that is, a grip on the idea of a world that is there independent of perception, which is one of the traditional ways, in philosophy, of formulating what our grip on the objective world consists in. This in turn helps give substance to the idea that she thinks of attending to the world as a way of acquiring knowledge about something that is there anyway, independently of her own and the adult's responses to it.

Naturally, we want more than this first glimmer to have a full understanding of both knowledge and the idea of an objective world. With respect to the latter, for example, one thing we may look for is the use of spatial concepts in explaining *why* objects can or cannot be perceived—that is, some grip on a systematic understanding of the conditions under which objects can be perceived, which the child can exploit in making it the case that the adult can see what she is pointing to. This is the kind of grip on the idea of an objective world that is tested for by Yaniv and Shatz (1988), for example, who found progressively sophisticated understanding of the conditions of perceivability associated with different modalities between the ages of 2 and 4. But the basic exploitation of spatial understanding in the act of directing another's attention to an object seen by the child but unseen by the adult can be viewed as a manifestation of the core from which such understanding develops.

In philosophy a distinction is sometimes drawn between communication-theoretical and thought-theoretical approaches to explaining what gives the subject an idea of an objective world. The classical communication-theoretical view is

Davidson's—we arrive at the idea of a world by triangulating our own and others' responses to that world; the world is the common cause of both sets of reactions to it. On the thought-theoretical view, which stems from developments of Kantian insights, what gives the subject the idea of an objective world is his use of spatial concepts within the framework of a primitive theory of perception, which includes, among other things, a basic grasp of the conditions of perceivability. On a version developed by John Campbell (1986), the idea here is that a full explanation of what this involves will itself yield the idea of different perspectives on the same world. (For example, in explaining to myself why I can or cannot see something, the idea of different perspectives on the same place has to be brought in.)

As I noted earlier, this thought-theoretical claim in philosophy has its counterpart in developmental psychology, where the claim is that the capacity for triangulation plays no fundamental role in providing the child with the wherewithal to grasp the idea of an objective world. The kind of work cited by Franco suggests an interesting middle position between parallel-development, or thought-theoretical, views, on the one hand, and communication-theoretical and interactive theories on the other. Certainly, the baby seems to be drawing on spatial understanding and a rudimentary grip on conditions of perceivability prior to and during her use of declarative pointings and vocalizations about what she can see. But she is applying this understanding in the first instance not to her own perceptions, as the thought-theoretical position has it, but to those of the adult; and the reason she is doing so is to establish that they are both attending to the same thing, where the aim, in turn, is to go on to 'comment' on it. That is, the kind of objectivity to be gleaned from an understanding of perception is being put to use in establishing a common world with another subject, in order to communicate about it. Communication comes in not as the basis for objectivity, *contra* Davidson, but as its motivator. And spatial understanding, as implicated in a grip of perception comes in, in this context, not in order to explain the course of one's perceptions, as the thought-theoretician has it, but in order to enable communication. (For this way of relating communication and objectivity in the case of joint reminiscing see Chapter 12.)

There is a great deal more work to be done, for this kind of theory, in spelling out the connection between joint attention and grasp of the idea of an objective world. One aspect of this will concern us soon. But before we come to it, we must turn to our next question: what do we mean when we speak of the child's 'urge to communicate', and how does what we mean affect the kind of account we give of the sense of openness or transparency, or sharing of minds, that a rich theory says applies to children engaging in triangulations of attention?

3.4 Joint Attention and Mutuality

Imagine a 14-month-old baby pointing to an object and looking back and forth between object and adult, where this is accompanied by gurgles of delight, which it is natural to treat as something like non-verbal commentary on the object (see Chapter 7). There is no doubt that the pointing is an intentional activity. Suppose we ask what the content of the intention is. A natural response would be that the child points with the intention of drawing the adult's attention to the object, or getting the adult to look at the object. According to Tomasello, though, we should think of the intention as being more complex: as having, that is, the same structure as a Gricean communicative intention, but without reference to beliefs. The intention which infants need to recognize when responding to a pointing is 'You intend for [me to share attention to (X)]' (Tomasello, 1999, p. 102). Naturally, the question arises: what do children mean by 'share'? Tomasello's answer is that it will involve at the very least the child thinking of her own response to an adult's pointing as a case of looking because this is what the adult wants her to do, and the correlative understanding of what she intends the adult to do when she, the child, points: namely, to look because the child wants her to. Presumably this is how she will think of the adult's and her own lookings when she takes the intentions to have been satisfied. This is the first stepping-stone in the Gricean analysis: communication occurs only when the audience responds to the speaker's intention for the reason that the speaker wants her to.

This position is over-determined by several ingredients in Tomasello's theory: some unique to his particular account of the child's agency-based conception of the mind, some shared with Davidson's appeal to Gricean communication intentions to explain how openness is achieved. The one I want to have before us is, I think, independent of his particular appeal to agency, though it is expressed in those terms. It turns on what one takes the basic perceptual input to be for each subject engaged in joint attention. Very roughly, as one would expect, the more complex the input, the less the sophistication required of the mechanism. What Tomasello shares with an essentially Gricean approach is the idea that triangulation of the kind that yields mutual awareness rests on a combination of relatively simple input and relatively sophisticated mechanisms of triangulation. The opposite tack, which I think is the essential idea behind the intersubjectivity approach, reverses the order: the input is thought of as more complex, the mechanism for achieving mutual awareness more simple. I begin with a few general comments about mechanism, and then move on to the difference between our two theories.

Our original definition of joint attention was as follows.

a. There is an object that each subject is attending to, where this implies (i) a causal connection between the object and each subject, and (ii) awareness of the object by each subject.
b. There is a causal connection of some kind between the two subjects' acts of attending to the object.
c. The two subjects' experiences exploit their understanding of the concept of attention.

    d. Each subject is aware, in some sense, of the object *as* an object that is present to both subjects. There is, in this respect, a 'meeting of minds' between both subjects, such that the fact that both are attending to the same object is open or mutually manifest.

The mechanism question is, in effect, a question about the relation between (b) and (c). In crude outline, there are three types of position one might hold here. At one extreme is the claim that when joint attention meets condition (d), i.e. generates mutual awareness, this requires that the causal co-ordinations described in (b) be essentially intentional rational activities. Causal co-ordinations that yield mutual awareness are a form of rational co-operation. This would appear to be Tomasello's position. At the other extreme are positions, mooted for example by Campbell in Chapter 13, that the causal co-ordinations that yield rich joint attention are, or could be, wholly subpersonal, and work through, for example, causal influences on primitive orienting mechanisms. Finally, there is a midway position, implicit in theories that appeal to emotion and affect to explain mutuality. On this view, the mechanisms that sustain mutuality-yielding joint attention triangles are personal-level, conscious ones, but these are non-rational and can operate even in the absence of reflective concept grasp—as they do in case of mutual affect regulation in young infants.

Leekam's work on autism is strongly suggestive of the claim that mutuality-sustaining co-ordinations of attention in normal babies are personal-level ones (autistic children's orienting responses to pointings and so forth are wholly intact, but joint attention rarely occurs). I will return later to implications of this view. For our immediate purposes, though, I want to focus on the debate between the two personal-level explanations: on the one hand, the kind of theory proposed by Tomasello, on which intentional co-ordination is the source of mutuality; on the other, Hobson's account, on which it is a developed form of mutual affect regulation that sustains it (and the absence of such mechanisms between autistic children and adults that explain the absence of joint attention between them). Our question, then, is: what does this difference come to, and what are the issues raised by it?

In terms of actual claims about the mechanism of mutuality, the substantive disagreement can be phrased as follows. On the affective theory, the content of the intention with which the child points to an object just is that the adult attend to the object; mutuality is explained by a separate mechanism, the mutual affect regulation that sustains the attending of adult and child to the same object, once the adult has responded to the pointing. (We will return shortly to how this is supposed to work.) On Tomasello's theory the content of the intention is meant to guarantee that if the intention is fulfilled, mutual awareness will result. One reason for this is that the child's agentive conception of the mind is supposed to do all the work; appeal to emotion doesn't come in here at all for him. But there is arguably a deeper reason, which turns on the feature Tomasello shares with

Davidson's appeal to Gricean intentions for similar purposes, where this brings in fundamental issues about how we explain the contents of subjects' experiences when the state they are in has the kind of openness we think joint attention situations manifest. This is the issue to which I now turn.

Any analysis of joint attention, in the sense with which we are concerned, i.e. one that involves openness and mutual awareness, begins with the observation that, for there to be joint attention in play, it is not sufficient that both subjects in fact attend to the same object. In joint attention everything about the fact that both are attending to the same object is out in the open, manifest to both subjects. On the first kind of account, the first step in spelling out what is required for joint attention is to say that the very least each participant in the triangle must perceive is the other's attention to the object. This is the basic perceptual input to any achievement of mutual awareness in joint attention. The next step in analysing joint attention is to note that the mere perception by each subject of the other's attention to the object will not suffice for openness. I can see that you are looking at an object, and you can see that I am, without either of us being aware of the other's perception of one's own perception, say because, as in Peacocke's example (Chapter 14), each of us falsely believes that a thick planed glass through which we see each other is a one-way mirror. If this is what we believe, our minds are not transparent to each other in the way they are in real joint attention situations. One natural thought then is that in joint attention, not only are we each aware of the other's perception of the object, but we are each aware of the other's awareness of our own perception of the object. What was lacking in the dividing glass case was the recognition by each of us that our own perception of the object is open to view to the other.

Now, notoriously, once we set things up in this way, it seems that this can only be the first step in the analysis of what real openness consists in. We think that at the very least this recognition by each of us that the other is aware of our perception must itself be included in the total account of what we are each aware of—that this is part of what complete transparency requires. The question then becomes: can we find ways of explaining such openness without characterizing what it comes to by appeal to an infinite regress of iterations? (See Chapters 13 and 14.)

The step I want to keep in focus, though, is the first iteration. This is the step that takes us from the perception of the other's perception of the object to a second level of thought in which we describe each subject as being aware that the other is aware of her perception of the object. The feature here that I want to highlight is that, on this kind of account, the interpersonal ingredient in joint attention only gets going via such an iteration. It is only via such iteration that, for each subject, the idea of one mind being available to the other gets expressed. One way of characterizing the second theory is to say that it tries to side-step the need for this first move up a level in thought by characterizing the initial input in a way that already contains within it this interpersonal ingredient. This is one aspect,

I think, of the general idea behind the intersubjectivity approach, on which the joint attention to the object is, so to speak, inserted into a framework of dyadic affective relations. To make this a bit less metaphorical, I want to break down the description into three steps. First I describe what I will call 'non-reflective reciprocal openness' in earlier mutual affect regulation. Then I will describe what a reflective version of it looks like. Finally I will make a few comments about how it might be applied to cases of joint attention to a third object.

In early stages of mutual affect regulation we find processes such as the child smiling, the adult responding with a related expression of an emotion, to which the child again responds with another expression of a related emotion, and so on, until one of them gets bored or distracted. (See Chapter 5.) There are two features of these kinds of exchanges that I want to highlight. The first is that the state of mind, the emotion, is expressed directly by the face, without any essential mediation of intent. The second is that the detection of this state by the other is naturally accompanied by the production of an expression of emotion (which can again be responded to immediately by the child, and so forth). As Hobson puts it (Chapter 9), in these kinds of exchanges, to detect and to respond with a new or related emotion come to the same thing. The sense in which minds are reciprocally open to each other here can be put metaphorically, though familiarly, as follows. Each sees her own smile reflected in the smile of the other, and so on, until the process comes to a halt.

Suppose now, as the second year progresses, we begin to equip the child with the conceptual wherewithal to understand what is going on in such cases and allow these concepts to imbue her experiences. She will now see smiles of delight, say, *as* responses to her own smiles of delight, where this perception of the other's emotion is still accompanied by the immediate response on her own part, which triggers more smiling from the adult, and so forth, until, for whatever reason, the process comes to a halt. Note there is a mimicking over time of the iterations we find in definitions of common knowledge—but what we have here is just a causal chain. At any one time, all that is required for full reflective reciprocal openness is that each participant is aware of the perceived expression of delight, say, as a response to her own.

The hard question now is: how can this help with joint attention, where, after all, what we are supposed to be mutually aware of is not our feelings for each other but our attention to a third object. This is where we come to one of the central metaphors that inform at least some versions of the intersubjectivity approach. The idea is that we can retain the same reciprocal structure when explaining the openness of joint attention by giving some account of the way the reciprocated feelings now begin 'to include' objects in the world. That is the metaphor. The hard question is: can we explain what 'include' means here in such a way that we can make cognitive sense of the world becoming available to both subjects in virtue of a mechanism of mutual affect regulation? The problem here is in some sense the converse of the problem generated by the first theory. On that account the basic input to each subject's perceptions of others' psychological states was a psychological state that consisted in the other's relation to an object—there was no aspect of it that related the other's perceptual state to oneself, and nothing that showed in it that the other was aware of the state one is in. Here the problem is that while there is plenty of the latter, what we don't yet have a sense of is how this mechanism brings an object into view in such a way that it is obvious to the subject that there is an object that both are attending to.

This lacuna is due to a large extent to unfinished business for this kind of theory in explaining the sense in which joint attention triangles provide for the idea of an objective world. And before continuing with a comparison on the mutuality front, I want to say a few brief words about that. Earlier, I suggested that a defender of the Werner and Kaplan idea, that triangulation in joint attention yields a first glimmer of the idea of an objective world, might appeal to the way in which the child shows progressive sensitivity to the spatial conditions of perceivability before, during, and after pointing. It is this sensitivity, one might think, that is the manifestation of the child's grasp of the idea that there is a common object to which both are attending. The problem in what we have so far said on this score is this. Mere sensitivity to spatial considerations when engaged in some form of interaction with another does not suffice to show that these sensitivities are inputs to the idea of a world out there independently of one, inputs to the idea of an objective world. As Call and Tomasello show in Chapter 3, apes display remarkable sensitivities when their interest is obtaining food, without this giving rise to any temptation to think that they are engaging in the kind of mutual attention we think the child can engage in. Add to that Gomez's observation (Chapter 4) that at least hand-reared apes engage in long sessions of affective contact attention, then, on the face of it, we have the same capacities in place and no joint attention. This is one place where, and one reason why, the kind of approach proposed by Tomasello, on which it is the absence of the capacity to form co-operative intentions that explains the absence of joint attention, becomes so attractive.

Gomez's own suggestion is more congenial to the Werner and Kaplan account. Apes can use spatial understanding—for example, in getting humans to do things for them, they can engage in bouts of affective contact attention—but they cannot 'put the two together' to get declarative pointing. What does this putting together amount to? One suggestive answer, proposed by Roessler, turns on Franco's suggestion that infants' first expressions of delight, fear, and so forth that accompany declarative pointing should be seen as the beginning of commentary on the world. The 'putting together' on this picture, which is lacking in the apes, is the directing of the emotion towards an object in a way that constitutes an evaluation of it. What makes it true to say that the child is using spatial concepts in a way that manifests a grip on the idea of a world out there to which she and the adult are responding is her use of such expressions of emotion as primitive predications.

For it to be true that this is what the child is doing, as Roessler points out, there must be some sense in which this use of affective responses is imbued with some sense of getting it right in some respect. Things are scary or not, funny or not. The suggestion is that this primitive sense of right and wrong begins to be manifested as social referencing sets in, where the appropriateness or not of the responses is precisely what the child is seeking reassurance about. One way of putting this is that affect regulation becomes, at this stage, regulation of the *appropriateness* of the response to the world. (For a related, far more sophisticated version of the normative and objectivity-yielding role of such affect regulation see Chapter 12 on its role in joint reminiscing.)

With this all too hasty sketch of an idea in place, let us return to mutuality and to the question of how appeal to mutual affect regulation can begin to explain a sense in which, for the child, everything about the fact that she and the adult are attending to the same object is out in the open. Drawing on the idea that affect expression begins to function as a primitive form of predication of properties to objects perceived and pointed at, the basic idea might be put as follows. What it means to say that affective expressions begin to 'include' the world just is that they begin to function in this quasi-predicative way. But the basic mechanism of recip-rocal affect regulation is not lost in their taking on this role. So, as joint attention to a third object sets in, when the child sees her own smile reflected in the adult's, what she is seeing and responding to in this way is a reciprocated response to an object, a reciprocated primitive commentary on it. This is what the openness of joint attention consists in during this early period. Reciprocated smiles are recip-rocated comments on the world. So long as they keep smiling at each other, so to speak, mutual awareness is sustained.

Earlier, I introduced the difference between the two theories by saying that they might be compared by appeal to relative pay-off between complexity of mechan-ism for delivering mutuality and complexity of basic perceptual input. In terms of the rich/lean debate, this shows up a further ambiguity in the way the terms are used. Not only do we need the distinction we already drew between the rich/lean distinction as it applies to claims about what joint attention delivers, on the one hand, and as it applies to claims about what joint attention requires, on the other. What we have been discussing now is a further ambiguity in the description of what the account requires of the child. On the one hand, we may require the capacity for complex embeddings and relatively simple input; on the other, we may require complex perceptual input and non-complex mechanisms. The affect theory requires essentially reciprocal, and in this sense complex, perceptual inputs to create mutual awareness, and a simple mechanism to sustain it. Tomasello's theory has a relatively simple basic input, the child's perception of the adult's perception of an object, and relatively complex mechanisms for creating and sus-taining mutual awareness. Note that the difference between the two accounts is *not* that one requires self-consciousness and the capacity to apply the concept of attention to one's own and others' states and the other doesn't. It is, rather, that reflections and self-awareness on the affect theory do not have the regress-generating role of trying to capture everything that is going on in the relation between the two subjects from the outside.

There is a connection here, though certainly not a one-to-one mapping, between this way of distinguishing psychological theories and one difference between two of the philosophical accounts in this volume concerned specifically with the epistemological problem of mutuality. Campbell defends what he calls a relational view of joint attention, on which mention of the other, as co-attender, is essential to the specification of the content of the experience we have in joint attention. Appeal to the reciprocity of affective regulation might be one way of spelling out the conditions that have to hold, at least in the case of child–adult interactions, for it to be true that the other does figure as a co-attender in the contents of one's experience. It would be one way of spelling out what it means to say, as Campbell does, that the occurrence of the other as co-attender in the contents of one's experience is a primitive phenomenon of consciousness. To take this approach, though, is to insist that the kind of co-ordination of attention we find is personal-level and conscious, *contra* Campbell's own suggestion, but in line with his in not requiring second-order embeddings of first-order states in explaining the nature of mutual awareness here.

In contrast, the solution to mutuality proposed by Peacocke does explicitly assume that the basic perceptual input in the case of joint attention is not inter-personal, but is, rather, the perception of the other's perception of the object and, correlatively, that some kind of second-level reflection is required for getting the relation between the two perceptions going. The account proposed by Peacocke himself to explain how openness is secured requires, in addition to many other capacities, the capacity to entertain thoughts that refer to themselves. If this is the kind of solution that Tomasello would advocate for the adult case, then he would have to say that children between the ages of 1 and 2 do not achieve fully open joint attention. This is, in fact, the position advocated by Peacocke, who suggests that we need a developmental story of how a child eventually reaches full open-ness as he defines it. If this is the line that Tomasello would want to take, his theory would not be rich in this sense.

A different option, obviously, is to appeal to the intersubjectivity approach to explain the kind of openness we find in joint attention episodes in children. The bearing this has on epistemological issues, though, depends on whether, and how, one extends this to adult cases of joint attention, and whether, and how, such an extension is used to help with other cases in which openness is an issue: mutual knowledge and the like. For example, sticking to joint attention, one claim might be that the affect theory may be right for children, but for the adult case this kind of account won't do, and that what infant joint attention delivers is impoverished in essence, rather than in detail, relative to what adults have. An alternative response is that there are ingredients in the intersubjectivity account that do have direct bearings on the basic account we give of the openness of adult minds to each other, in actual joint attention cases and in others. Whatever response one chooses here will rest on, and raise, a host of interconnected issues which I have not even begun to consider, but which are addressed in detail in other chapters in this volume.

4. CONCLUDING COMMENTS

All of this bears directly on the extent to which one thinks that joint attention, and getting it right, do, as Heal suggests in Chapter 2, provide the materials for a different account of the nature of mental understanding from the kind we get when we focus on children's capacity to employ the concept of belief in the context of explaining and predicting others' behaviour. I end with a few words on this question.

Davidson says that the role he assigns triangulation in providing subjects with the distinction between truth and falsity shows one sense in which thought is an essentially social phenomenon. He is referring here to the precognitive triangulations in which basic correlations of expectations give the beginning of a sense of right and wrong. As I noted, one difficulty in his account is that it is not clear what, if anything, of this survives when we turn to the cognitive level. The two theories we have been considering might provide an alternative midway version of this story, though it is not clear if one of them would want to.

I suggested earlier that the most plausible account of the way in which, on Tomasello's theory, a child between the ages of 1 and 2 might be credited with an analogue of the distinction between truth and falsity would appeal to the child's capacity to distinguish between failed and successful actions. However, if this is to fit with Davidson's suggestion about the distinctive role of triangulation, Tomasello would have to say that the child first exploits this distinction in the context of joint attention—for example, in correcting failed messages and so forth. It is not clear to me that this is something he would want to say, for there is a strong suggestion that the child first applies this distinction to her own actions, and only then, by a basic simulative process, to those of others. In this sense joint attention co-ordinations are just one opportunity among others to exploit the capacity for distinguishing successful and failed actions. On this count, then, his theory would not make thought essentially social in the sense that Davidson suggests.

Werner and Kaplan's approach fits more naturally with this particular way of describing the essentially social nature of thought. A plausible interpretation of it would be to say that the child first exploits her grip on the conditions of perceivability, and in this sense objectivity, in the context of joint attention, where the aim is communicative. If we adopt the suggestion that the child's first comments about the world are expressions of emotions, and that what she is discovering is the appropriateness or otherwise or these responses, this would be one way of doing justice to the thought that triangulation is having a constitutive role in providing the child with the beginning of a grasp of the distinction between truth and falsity.

However, our discussion of the two theories shows that there is also a sense in which, for Davidson, thought is *not* essentially social, which comes out when we focus specifically on the question of how we explain thought about minds, how we explain our grasp of mental concepts. When he first introduces the notion of triangulation on the precognitive level, he describes it as follows: 'It is the result of a *threefold* interaction, an interaction which is *twofold* from the point of view of each of the two agents: each is interacting simultaneously with the world and with the other agent. To put this in a slightly different way, each creature learns to correlate the reactions of the other with changes or objects in the world to which it also reacts' (Davidson, 2001, p. 128; my emphasis). One aspect of this survives in the reflective version. What each subject is given evidence for is the other's relation to the world, here in the shape of verbal expressions of the other's beliefs about the world. This is the similarity with Tomasello's account of joint attention—the basic input to triangulation is the other's relation to the world. Any relation between the two subjects comes in only subsequently, and reflectively, as a means of achieving triangulation.

Now one question that one might raise for this approach is: to what extent is joint attention, or any triangulation, doing more than provide conveniently close at hand materials for the kind of understanding one might get when theorizing about some else's beliefs in the course of explaining and predicting her behaviour? (This is the way Heal presents the challenge of describing the sense in which the phenomenon of joint attention does really provide an alternative description of the end-point as far as mental understanding is concerned.) For, in effect, the basic input to the triangulations, for both Tomasello and Davidson, is exactly the same kind of input one would have when theorizing and explaining someone's behaviour in the third person. One way of putting this is that on this approach third-person interpretation is the basis for any sense of first- and second-person relations, the materials for which are derived from those used in third-person interpretations. It is true that language is essential on Davidson's account. But this is because it provides sufficiently structured evidence of the other's beliefs about the world. The fact that language is being directed at the interpreter herself appears to play no foundational role.

In this respect the intersubjectivity approach does, if it can be made good, provide the materials for thinking that the sense in which joint attention is an essentially social phenomenon does give rise to a radically different account of the nature of mental concepts—one that distinguishes them radically, say, from the concepts we use in theorizing about the physical world. The idea here is sometimes put in terms of its giving the first–second-person relation priority over the third person. But some care is needed in expressing the disagreement in this way.

It is part of the story that Werner and Kaplan tell, and certainly part of the story as I have developed it here, that we only get the first and second person when it is true to say of the child that she can also employ the concept of perception in an essentially third-person way, for example in checking where the adult is looking. This is one difference between their version and other defences of the intersubjectivity approach—for example, Reddy's (Chapter 5) on which the early dyadic interactions of their own provide for a first- and second-person understanding, independently of any need for triangulation to a third object. The difference between the Werner and Kaplan approach and the kind I have been attributing to Tomasello and Davidson is, rather, that on the former but not the latter the explanatory role gets its first articulation in the service of promoting first–second-person interaction, the roots of which are explained independently, in early reciprocal affect regulation. One way of capturing in slogan form what this difference comes to is in terms of their respective answers to the following question: can we, and should we, give an account of the first–second-person distinction that makes it not derivative of the account we give of the the way mental concepts are used in third-person explanations? The intuitions driving the Werner and Kaplan approach are that we can and we should; those informing the Tomasello approach are, at least, that we needn't. As to whether we can or should—the papers collected here do much towards beginning to unravel the issues that need to go into articulating what exactly this question comes to.

REFERENCES

BATES, E., CAMAIONI, L., and VOLTERRA, V. (1976), 'Sensorimotor performatives', in E. Bates (ed.), *Language and Context: The Acquisition of Pragmatics*. New York: Academic Press, 49–71.

BRUNER, J. (1977), 'Early social interaction and language acquisition', in H. R. Schaffer (ed.), *Studies in Mother–Infant Interaction*. New York: Academic Press, 271–89.

—— (1995), 'From joint attention to the meeting of minds', in C. Moore and P. Dunham (eds.), *Joint Attention: Its Origins and Role in Development*. Hillsdale, NJ: Erlbaum, 1–14.

BUTTERWORTH, G., and FRANCO, F. (1993), 'Motor development: communication and cognition', in L. Kalverboer, B. Hopkins, and R. H. Gueze (eds.), *A Longitudinal Approach to the Study of Motor Development in Early and Later Childhood*. Cambridge: Cambridge University Press, 153–65.

CAMPBELL, J. (1986), 'Conceptual structure', in C. Travis (ed.), *Meaning and Interpretation*. Oxford: Blackwell Publishers, 159–74.

DAVIDSON, D. (2001), 'The emergence of thought', in *Subjective, Intersubjective, Objective*. Oxford: Oxford University Press, 123–34.

SCHIFFER, S. (1988), *Meaning*. Oxford: Oxford University Press.

SPERBER, D., and WILSON, D. (1986), *Relevance: Communication and Cognition*. Cambridge, Mass.: Harvard University Press.

Tomasello, M. (1995), 'Joint attention as social cognition', in C. Moore and P. Dunham (eds.), *Joint Attention: Its Origins and Role in Development*. Hillsdale, NJ: Erlbaum, 103–30.

—— (1999), *The Cultural Origins of Human Cognition*. Cambridge, Mass.: Harvard University Press.

Werner, H., and Kaplan, B. (1963), *Symbol Formation*. Hillsdale, NJ: Erlbaum.

Yaniv, I., and Shatz, M. (1988), 'Children's understanding of perceptibility', in J. W. Astington, P. L. Harris, and D. R. Olson (eds.), *Developing Theories of Mind*. Cambridge: Cambridge University Press, 93–108.

2

Joint Attention and Understanding the Mind

Jane Heal

1. INTRODUCTION

What might episodes of joint attention in infants and young children contribute to the development of their competence with psychological concepts? What have such episodes to do with the child's coming to an increasingly rich understanding of the fact that the world contains many people, of whom he or she is one? This paper offers some brief, speculative reflections on this issue in the light of the intimately related question of the nature of the adult grasp of psychological concepts.

A question which motivates the approach of the paper is this: is it possible that philosophers of the mainstream analytic tradition (and psychologists influenced by them) are working with a distorted view of the nature of our fully-fledged adult competence with psychological concepts? To put matters very briefly and tendentiously, a suspicion I would like to air is that prediction and quasi-scientific understanding have been overemphasized as elements in a grasp of the psychological, while co-operation and communication have been underemphasized. If this suspicion is right, then it follows that the already immensely difficult task of developmental psychologists—for example, in understanding the role of joint attention—has had more, unnecessary difficulties added to it.

Psychologists studying the development of infants and children are faced with peculiarly fascinating, but also peculiarly intractable, problems. A central question is what concepts, and what psychological states and competences, the infant or young child possesses at the various stages of his or her growth to maturity. A starting-point in offering an answer must be observations of the behaviour of infants and children in different situations at different ages. We may, for example, note that typically an infant of 6 months responds in such-and-such a way to this or that stimulus, while an infant of a year behaves differently. We may also note that an infant who at one age undergoes a kind of stimulation S_1 will later respond differently to stimulation S_2 from a child who has not earlier undergone stimulation S_1. And so forth and so on. (The other papers in this volume give us much fascinating evidence on these matters.) Having marshalled the observations to give a picture of the possible sequences in which abilities and responses may develop, and in what kinds of environment, there is then the problem of working out the nature of the underlying psychological reality which manifests itself in the propensity to this whole pattern of behaviour.

Already at the stage of assembling and setting out the evidence there will be controversial issues: namely, how richly to describe the stimuli which impinge on the child and the responses which the child produces. In offering hypotheses about the underlying psychological reality, further methodological and conceptual questions proliferate. Should we invent new concepts especially to describe the psychological configurations of the very young child, or is the vocabulary suitable for describing adults also appropriate here? Should we favour accounts which credit the infant with a rich innate cognitive endowment, or should we be predisposed to allow only more meagre starting resources? Should we regard impinging external situations as helping to trigger maturation of innate capacities, or, alternatively, should we regard them as providing material for learning? It is only in the light of assumptions on all these matters that the actual observations will suggest a particular theory. And psychologists who favour one set of assumptions are well aware that rival sets are thought by others, on either a priori or a posteriori grounds, to be more fruitful or appropriate. The whole enterprise of psychological theorizing about young children seems, to a sympathetic outside observer like myself, to resemble an attempt to solve a set of simultaneous equations where there are many more unknowns than equations.

But one thing which would make the task even more difficult, by setting reflection off in the wrong direction, is any serious misconception about the end-point towards which the child's process of maturation is taken to lead. The interest of the earlier stages lies, in part at least, in the fact that they are precursors to the fully-fledged adult competence. The fascinating questions are how much of that competence, or what precursors of that competence, are present at early stages of development, and what kind of impetus drives the development forward. But if we misdescribe the nature of the fully-fledged competence, then our theorizing about the earlier stages will be undertaken in the light of a misunderstanding. And given the amount of flexibililty and choice already available, theorists gripped by such a misunderstanding may well find themselves able to plough on for a long time down what may ultimately prove to be a blind alley.

This is why laying on the table a variety of views of the nature of the adult grasp of psychological concepts is worthwhile, and why it is important not to accept unquestioningly any current orthodoxy. Psychologists and philosophers have in recent decades exchanged ideas and developed shared perspectives in a very fruitful way. Psychologists have contributed their data and theorizations to the debate, while philosophers have offered their conceptual structures and clarifications. But in doing their share of the work, philosophers need to reflect on whether they might not be offering a partly misleading model. And it might help psychologists to be aware that there is more than one philosophical view to play with.

In the next sections I shall sketch two lines of thought about joint attention, and in the final section I shall speculate about how combining the most plausible elements of each might require us to modify our conception of the nature of fully-fledged grasp of psychological concepts. Dunham and Moore provide a pointer to the themes I want to explore when they write: '[A]t a more theoretical level of analysis, the functional properties of joint attentional experiences, originally emphasised in the context of early language and communicative development, are now implicated in a much broader array of developmental phenomena including, in particular, the infant's incipient understanding of the mental life of others' (Moore and Dunham, 1995, p. 17). This change of focus, from communication to psychology more broadly conceived, is indeed a striking feature of the literature on joint attention, a feature apparent even to a naïve but interested amateur like myself. But what is the significance of the shift, and is it right to think that there really are two different topics here?

2. JOINT ATTENTION AND 'THEORY OF MIND'

The explicit suggestion of recent writing on joint attention is that it is an important precursor to a fully-fledged grasp of psychological notions, i.e. is 'implicated in . . . the infant's incipient understanding of the mental life of others', as Dunham and Moore say. There is considerable intuitive plausibility to this idea. Moreover, there is some empirical evidence to support it from observations that deficits in understanding of the psychological follow on from deficits in normal shared attention behaviour.

Those who favour this view, however, elaborate it against a background assumption that psychological notions should be understood in a particular way. Shared attention, they suggest, plays an important role in the acquisition of so-called theory of mind. (Baron-Cohen (1995) provides one example of this approach and this way of talking, but it is shared by many others.) Let us consider this further assumption and its implications.

In speaking of grasp of 'theory of mind' as what is required for mastery of psychological concepts, writers show that they accept the understanding of psychological concepts which has become orthodox among analytically minded philosophers and which is also widely accepted among cognitive scientists and some psychologists. This mainstream analytic understanding sees mastery of psychological concepts as possession of conceptual tools for predicting and explaining the behaviour of others. Psychological concepts are thus seen as similar to the concepts of natural science. They are taken to supply a way of thinking about the inner causal structure of human beings and about the causal roles and relations of the various hypothesized items (beliefs, desires, perceptions, feelings, etc.) which constitute that inner structure. (For an introduction to this way of viewing matters, see Smith and Jones (1986). A set of classic writings on these themes is collected by Block (1980), and a useful recent survey of the area, with references to much of the literature, is supplied by Davies (1995).)

Certainly it would be agreed on all sides that psychological concepts differ significantly from those of naïve physics, chemistry, or meteorology. In particular, they differ from them in significant features of their logical shape. Central psychological concepts are of representational states, with all the complexities and possibilities (false belief, unfulfilled desire, etc.) which that brings. But it is also tacitly or explicitly taken for granted that the large-scale role of these notions is the same as that of the concepts of natural science. Indeed, some discussion of the development of 'theory of mind' in children openly emphasizes the parallel between their progress and scientific theorizing (Wellman, 1990; Gopnik and Wellman, 1992). Others have questioned how far the parallel can be pressed. Is the child really a little scientist devising concepts and testing hypotheses? Should we not rather suppose psychological concepts to be innate or to be maturationally triggered? (See Segal (1996) for a way into this debate.) But behind this disagreement about how psychological understanding is acquired lies a deeper agreement on the nature of what is acquired. The disputants are agreed that grasp of psychological concepts equips a child to do *vis-à-vis* people what grasp of scientific or proto-scientific concepts equips it to do *vis-à-vis* the inanimate world: namely, predict, explain, and control.

Given this assumption about the nature of psychological concepts, there is, however, something prima facie odd about the privileging of joint attention in their genesis. We may put the oddness this way. Let us suppose that the mainstream assumption is correct, and that psychological concepts do have the shape and role sketched. Why should we then expect episodes of joint attention to be particularly significant in their acquisition? Why should such episodes provide the necessary scaffolding on which the understanding of other minds is elaborated, or the seed from which it grows? After all, mental states play their productive role in causing another's behaviour whenever that other is active. When a parent is making a bed, tidying a room, or struggling to fit all the shopping into a shopping bag, he or she provides eminently interesting observations which could serve to stimulate or trigger the child's understanding of notions like 'goal', 'perception', 'belief', and so forth. In order to have occasion to 'theorize' others' activities, all the child needs is plenty of such observable activities going on around him or her. Why should the behaviour involved in episodes of joint attention loom so large?

Clearly there are answers which a defender of the mainstream view could offer to that question. For example, she might suggest that during episodes of joint attention the behaviour of other persons (their gazing, pointing, vocalizing, etc.) is particularly prominent in the child's attention. Also it could be said that the child finds such episodes (for various reasons) notably enjoyable. So the child is motivated to seek such episodes, and is then likely to attend to others' behaviour during them in a cognitively fruitful way. Hence grasp of the central psychological concepts (for example, those of inner representational goal-directed or information-bearing states) is likely to be triggered or prompted in the child, as she seeks to understand why her carer gazes, points, or vocalizes during these enjoyable episodes. Our theorist admits that such a grasp could also be triggered or prompted when the child seeks to understand why her carer is, for example, making the bed, tidying the room, or packing the shopping. But (says the theorist) this is not the most usual route to acquisition of psychological concepts.

On this account, episodes of joint attention are allowed to be particularly prominent in the developmental story. Their prominence is, however, merely the upshot of the fact that episodes of joint attention offer rich and motivating occasions for psychological or proto-psychological cognition. It is not the upshot of the fact that engaging in joint attention itself calls on any conceptually distinctive structures which are foundational for grasp of the psychological. There is nothing in the nature of psychological concepts themselves which demands that they be elaborated on the basis of joint attentional interactions. As far as their conceptual structure and cognitive role are concerned, there is nothing to make it impossible for them to be developed solely on the basis of the child's observations of bed-making, tidying, or shopping.

This is what the 'theory of mind' conception of the nature of grasp of psychological notions requires us to say. But does this do justice to what theorists felt they had dimly perceived when they first suggested that the abilities engaged in joint attention behaviour are important precursors of grasp of the psychological? It seems possible that something has gone missing when we spell things out as above.

3. JOINT ATTENTION AND COMMUNICATION

We may contrast with the account just given another view of the centrality and role of joint attention. This second account centres on early language and communicative development. It is woven together from elements in a variety of discussions, but in general spirit it is closest to the ideas of those psychologists who first raised the topic of joint attention. (For example, it calls on the themes touched on by Bruner in his Foreword to Moore and Dunham, 1995; Tomasello (1995) also contributes elements to this story, as do many other authors.) We can tell this story without mentioning 'theory of mind' at all. Instead, we set matters out roughly as follows.

In the very early weeks and months of life we find carer and child attending intensively to each other—gazing into each other's eyes, smiling at each other, copying gestures, and the like. From about 6 months we note the appearance of outward-directed attention, occurring in situations where it is natural to think of three corners of a triangle: namely, carer, infant, and a part of the world to which both attend. First to appear is a tendency in the infant to follow the outward-directed gaze of the adult. Then there is development of more sophisticated variants, such as gaze-checking if the initial gaze-following does not easily identify something worth attending to. Bit by bit, yet more elaborations follow, such as attempts by the child to bring about joint attention by use of pointing gestures. These focusings of cognitive effort gradually become embedded in sequences of interlocking actions of growing length and complexity: for example, objects pointed at by the child are given to the child, who then plays with them. Such episodes of joint attention are also frequently occasions for adults to engage in linguistic behaviour ('Look at the pretty X', 'Oh yes, the Y has fallen over', 'Do you want the Z?', etc.), and are soon also the locus where the child produces utterances, first naming, then topic and comment and so on.

As these sophistications develop, we see that what is jointly attended to becomes more finely discriminated, and, relatedly, that the sequences of co-operative actions in which the joint attention is embedded also become more highly focused and differentiated. For example, parent and child are having a meal; the parent offers the child a choice, the child points at and remarks on what she would like next, and the parent gives it to the child. Or parent and child are jointly building a tower, each indicating various bricks to the other, remarking on whether they will fit or make the tower topple over. A further step is to find child or adult, in the course of their interactions, explicitly initiating joint attention to states of affairs which are not perceptually present or to actions which are merely possible ('There are some more bricks in the next room', 'Shall we put some more on this side?', etc.).

When we follow through this whole line of development, what we find at the end of it is fully-fledged adult language use, engaged in during social co-operative activity. It may well include use to secure joint attention to actual and possible situations which may be very distant in space and time, or may involve abstract and sophisticated concepts. So one thing we might find is a discussion in which words are uttered as a means of bringing it about that the attention of a group of philosophers and psychologists is jointly focused on the topic of joint attention, where contribution to this discussion is part of the pursuit of the shared project of finding answers to philosophical and psychological questions about that topic.

Words are, on this conception, an immensely delicate and useful way of pointing. Pointing itself is an elaborated way of focusing shared gaze. And what in turn grounds the whole enterprise is the sense of living together with another, a sense which perhaps shows itself already in the infant in those very early episodes when infant and carer smile at each other. Two presuppositions are implicit in this story. One is that joint attention is an early and vital staging post in the development of fully-fledged linguistic communication. The other is that communication itself is to be seen as an aspect of co-operative daily activity. Thus the significant cognitive structures which exist in such finely tuned and elegant form in developed language use are found already, in broad outline, in early gaze-following.

It is worth noting here that the idea of a commonality of basic cognitive structure in joint attention and linguistic communication is suggested also by the way in which the problem of mutual knowledge, and how to explicate it, forces itself on us in both contexts. Theorists of joint attention and communication have both struggled with how to make sense of the openness and mutuality characteristic of the situations they study without needing to invoke some sort of infinite regress. Despite many ingenious discussions, it appears that we still do not have a really satisfactory account of the matter.

4. A SPECULATION: FIRST, SECOND, AND THIRD PERSON

Here are two intuitions. One is that there is something helpful in the narrative just set out. It is illuminating to see language use as a refinement of a kind of sharing of thought which is already present in joint attention. So joint attention is foundational for development of communication. The other is that joint attention is an important precursor of fully-fledged grasp of the psychological, not just causally, but conceptually. The psychological configurations which develop into grasp of the nature of other minds show up at their earliest in ability to participate in episodes of joint attention. So joint attention is foundational for grasp of other minds.

I cannot say anything further here to substantiate these intuitions. It seems, however, that they may be shared by others, the first by those psychologists who initially discussed joint attention and language, and the second by those who carried on the debate by linking joint attention with psychological understanding. (So those who link joint attention with 'theory of mind' are on to something, even if the story they tell, as outlined in section 3, makes joint attention not conceptually, but merely contingently, important.)

How should we proceed if we are in sympathy with both intuitions and want to carry both forward? When we try, in the boldest and simplest way possible, to combine them, what we get is the following: to be aware of other people as minded beings is to be aware of them as beings with whom one may communicate and live a shared life. So full grasp of psychological concepts, and that ability to talk about oneself and others which it makes possible, is best seen as the cognitive aspect of what is needed for effectively carrying forward a communicative and shared life.

How different is this from the 'theory of mind' view of the nature of the psychological? The shift from one to the other need not be a total alteration of outlook. Rather it is like what happens on the turn of a kaleidoscope, where many familiar pieces can still be seen, but in an overall arrangement which makes a strikingly different impression. This is not the place for full-scale consideration of this question, but I shall point to just a few of the possible ramifications of the shift.

One notable contrast centres on the relative importance which will be given to first-, second-, and third-person uses of psychological concepts. The 'theory of mind' approach, as remarked above, takes for granted that grasp of psychological notions fills the same very broad role as grasp of physical concepts: namely, that of enabling us to predict and, sometimes, to control our environment. The mainstream view thus talks frequently of the need to understand and explain the difference between first- and third-person occurrences of psychological terms. Typically its questions are: 'What is it to grasp that he or she thinks, desires, or feels?' and 'Can we give an account of these matters which also explains what it is for me to grasp that I think, desire, or feel?' On this mainstream view, the second person—'you'—gets little explicit attention, so tends to be seen as variant of the third person. Relatedly, occasions on which I plainly do exercise psychological concepts in the second person—for example, occasions when I talk to you—are assimilated to actions having the same large-scale structure as my attempts to influence and control inanimate objects in my environment.

But if the first/third contrast is the primary one, it is in fact difficult to see how the second person ever gets in on the act. How are 'you' to be differentiated from 'it'? It might be thought that introducing some central concepts of the 'theory of mind' approach—for example, the concept of a representational state—would help deal with this question. But it is far from clear that it does, at least if the notion of a 'representational state' is spelt out in the causal and naturalistic terms which are found attractive in the framework of the 'theory of mind' view. How does the fact that I am acting on some object which I recognize to have internal 'representational states' in that sense make it appropriate to use the second person in my dealings with that object? How can theorizing a thing as having a particular kind of internal causal structure turn it from an 'it' into a 'you'?

On the alternative view we get clear of these problems in one bound, just by bringing the second person to prominence from the start. Since psychological notions have their central role in enabling us to live a shared and (at least partly) co-operative life, the basic subjects of psychological predicates will be us: viz. you and me. Given a grasp of 'you' and 'me', we do not find problems in explaining how 'he' and 'she' come on the scene. They are easily accommodated as other 'you's who are temporarily not present with us. Or perhaps they are beings who could be encountered as 'you's but have not yet been so encountered.

So the suggestion is that when we delve back to the conceptualizations or proto-conceptualizations from which fully-fledged psychological competence arises, what we find is not the infant with a sense of itself as contrasted with an external world, which then turns out to contain a variety of different kinds of things, animate and inanimate, with which the infant must learn to deal. Rather, the normal infant from the earliest moments has a sense of him or herself as part of an 'us', an 'us' whose shared life is already moving forward in the context of an external, spatial world. What the infant learns with growing conceptual sophistication is to play his or her part in that life. Playing that part requires mastering both the nature of the material world and the intricacies of the social world.

With this change of perspective, other more familiar debates in philosophical psychology take on a slightly different look. One concerns whether there is a link between thought and rationality. Both sides of this debate are represented within the mainstream view. Some take it that thoughts are items which provide explanation which is both causal and rationalizing (Lewis, 1983, chs. 7 and 8), while others urge that there can be items which are thoughts, in that they are representational, but which need not cohere rationally (Fodor, 1987, ch. 3; Fodor and Lepore, 1992, chs. 3 and 5).

On the view of the psychological that I am suggesting, we shall clearly come down on the side of those who link thought to rationality. But this link is not now grounded in the supposed predictive or causal-explanatory fruitfulness of a rationality assumption, or in the idea that there is good empirical evidence for allowing it, nor yet is it offered as just a basic a priori intuition. Rather, it is grounded in the facts that as a deliberator I must presuppose my own ability to respond to reasons, both practical and theoretical, and that I must extend this presumption to the collaborators with whom I jointly make decisions. Correlatively, being aware of others as having certain beliefs and desires will now be seen as important not primarily because it enables me to predict what they will do, but rather because it shows me what reasons they already acknowledge and what kinds of discussion and project it might be fruitful to engage in with them. To say this is not to deny the propriety of seeing the psychological explanations which we can give in terms of beliefs and desires as in some way 'causal'. But it is to stress that the way such causal explanation is construed must respect the primary communicative and rationalizing context of thought ascription.

It also seems highly likely that the view of the psychological which I am suggesting would reject the 'theory-theory' account of how we arrive at claims about the thoughts and feelings of others, and would favour instead the 'simulationist' account. In other words, it will deny that we possess some body of theoretical knowledge about the causes and effects of thoughts which enables us to work out how others' minds are functioning. And it will say instead that in arriving at our views about others' thoughts, we need to use imagination in re-creating at least some part of their outlook and thought processes.

With this issue, as with the thought and rationality question, it is true that philosophers holding the mainstream view appear on both sides of the debate. And again it is the case that a shift to the view of the psychological that I am recommending would supply a different kind of backing for the position it recommends. In the mainstream view, simulation is likely to be thought of as merely a heuristic which we use because we lack a full psychological theory. On the proposed alternative, simulation is seen as the only possible way of coming to grasp the thoughts of our fellow deliberators and agents. (See Davies and Stone, 1995*a* and *b*, and Carruthers and Smith, 1996, for an introduction to this literature. Some of the themes of these last paragraphs are developed in Heal, 1998.)

Although what I have called the mainstream analytic view has been very widely accepted in the last decades, it has not been the only philosophical account of psychological notions. Rival accounts, having much in common with the view I am recommending, have been articulated in the *Verstehen* tradition and by Wittgenstein and philosophers influenced by him (e.g., Collingwood, 1946; Wittgenstein, 1953). (For a recent treatment bringing out Collingwood's relevance to our issues, see Blackburn, 1995. For a good introduction to Wittgenstein's thought, see McGinn, 1997.) Perhaps psychologists who would like to see joint attention as crucial in acquisition of understanding of minds would do better to look to this philosophical tradition, rather than to the mainstream analytic view, for identification of the concepts and conceptual structures whose origins they seek. On this tradition, another person is a unified and (more or less) rational subject of experience, having a distinctive point of view on our shared world, and capable of expressing his or her thoughts and feelings about that world to us. We have already mentioned some of the further themes central to this conception: for example, the possibility of mutual knowledge, the contrast of first, second, and third person, and the way shared rationality enables co-operative discussion and action. Developmental psychologists have pursued their investigations into the learning of psychological concepts on the assumption that what needs explaining is the child's growing competence with a distinctive kind of causal-explanatory scientific theory. But pursuing them in the context of this other conception of what is involved in the fully-fledged adult competence might offer new materials and suggest new directions for thought.

REFERENCES

BARON-COHEN, S. (1995), 'The eye direction detector (EDD) and the shared attention mechanism (SAM): two cases for evolutionary psychology', in Moore and Dunham, 1995, 41–59.

BLACKBURN, S. (1995), 'Theory, observation, and drama', in Davies and Stone, 1995a, 274–90.

BLOCK. N. (1980), (ed.), *Readings in the Philosophy of Psychology*, i. Cambridge, Mass.: Harvard University Press.

CARRUTHERS, P., and SMITH, P. (1996), *Theories of Theories of Mind*. Cambridge: Cambridge University Press.

COLLINGWOOD, R. G. (1946), *The Idea of History*. Oxford: Oxford University Press.

DAVIES, M. (1995), 'The philosophy of mind', in A. Grayling (ed.), *Philosophy: A Guide through the Subject*. Oxford: Oxford University Press, 250–335.

—— and STONE, T. (1995a), (eds.), *Folk Psychology*. Oxford: Blackwell.

—— —— (1995b), *Mental Simulation*. Oxford: Blackwell.

FODOR, J. (1987), *Psychosemantics*. Cambridge, Mass.: MIT Press.

—— and LEPORE, E. (1992), *Holism: A Shopper's Guide*. Oxford: Blackwell.

GOPNIK, A. and WELLMAN, H. M. (1992), 'Why the child's theory of mind really *is* a theory', *Mind and Language*, 7: 145–71.

HEAL, J. (1998), 'Understanding other minds from the inside', in A. O'Hear (ed.), *Current Issues in Philosophy of Mind*. Cambridge: Cambridge University Press, 83–100.

Lewis, D. K. (1983), *Philosophical Papers*, i. Oxford: Oxford University Press.

McGinn, M. (1997), *Wittgenstein and the* Philosophical Investigations. London: Routledge.

Moore, C., and Dunham, P. J. (1995), (eds.), *Joint Attention: Its Origins and Role in Development*. Hove: Erlbaum.

Segal, G. (1996), 'The modularity of theory of mind', in Carruthers and Smith, 1996, 141–57.

Smith, P., and Jones, O. (1986), *The Philosophy of Mind: An Introduction*. Cambridge: Cambridge University Press.

Tomasello, M. (1995), 'Joint attention as social cognition', in Moore and Dunham, 1995, 103–30.

Wellman, H. M. (1990), *The Child's Theory of Mind*. Cambridge, Mass.: MIT Press.

Wittgenstein, L. (1953), *Philosophical Investigations*. Oxford: Blackwell.

3

What Chimpanzees Know about Seeing, Revisited: An Explanation of the Third Kind

Josep Call and *Michael Tomasello*

Joint attention is not just two individuals looking at the same thing at the same time. Joint attention requires that each of the individuals knows that the other is attending to the same thing as they are attending to; that is what makes it a joint, rather than merely a simultaneous, activity (Tomasello, 1995). To engage in joint attention, therefore, an individual must at the very least be able to understand that another individual may see or attend to something. Whereas that assumption is mainly uncontroversial in human infants over 12 to 18 months of age, there is currently some controversy about whether chimpanzees—as the closest primate relatives of human beings—know that others can see or attend to things. This is the question that we shall address in this paper.

EVIDENCE THAT CHIMPANZEES DO NOT UNDERSTAND SEEING

Chimpanzees perform surprisingly poorly in two experimental paradigms that involve an understanding of seeing. In the first they must understand that a communicative partner needs visual access to their gesture in order to respond to it appropriately. In the second they must understand that the gaze and gesture of others can help them to locate hidden food in a foraging task. We discuss each of these in turn.

First, Tomasello *et al.* (1985, 1989, 1994, 1997*b*) identified around three dozen gestures that young chimpanzees use to communicate with group mates in various contexts. For instance, they raise their arms to initiate play, extend their arms to beg for food, slap the ground or clap their hands to call attention to themselves, and touch their mother's side to request travel to a different location. These gestures fall within three basic sensory modalities: visual, auditory, and tactile. Thus, visual gestures rely solely on visual information (e.g. hand-beg, see Fig. 3.1); auditory gestures rely mainly on sound production (e.g. hand-clap, see Fig. 3.1); and tactile gestures depend mainly on establishing physical contact with the recipient (e.g. arm-on, see Fig. 3.1). Tomasello *et al.* (1994, 1997*b*) found that chimpanzees use gestures from the three sensory modalities differentially, depending on the

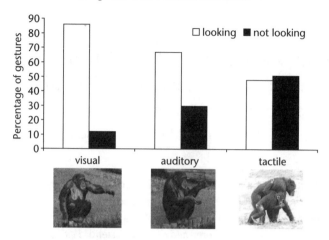

FIGURE 3.1. Percentage of gestures used by young chimpanzees in each of three sensory modalities (visual: hand-beg; auditory: hand-clap; tactile: arm-on) as a function of whether the recipient is looking at them.

spatial orientation of the recipient. In particular, young chimpanzees use gestures that are mainly auditory or tactile when their recipient is in all kinds of spatial orientations with respect to them, but they use visual gestures only when their recipient is facing toward them and therefore able to see them (see Fig. 3.1). One possible conclusion from these data is that chimpanzees know that if their visually based gestures are to work, others must see them.

But it is also possible that something simpler is at work, and indeed this is the conclusion of Povinelli and co-workers. In a series of fifteen experiments Povinelli and Eddy (1996a) tested seven 4- and 5-year-old chimpanzees' understanding of how humans must be bodily oriented for successful communication to take place (see also Povinelli *et al.*, 1999). They trained each of these seven juveniles to approach a Plexiglas barrier and extend their hand toward one of two human experimenters (each with a hole in the Plexiglas in front of them) to request food—with only the first gesture being responded to. In the critical test trials, one human stood behind each hole, and food was available on a table between them. The subjects thus had to choose which of these two humans to beg from. We will call this the Gesture Choice experimental paradigm (see Fig. 3.2).

Povinelli and Eddy began by presenting subjects with one human facing towards them and one facing away from them. The chimpanzees consistently gestured toward the human who was facing toward them, thus confirming the naturalistic findings of Tomasello *et al.* (1994, 1997b). In a number of other experimental conditions, however, chimpanzees did not seem to distinguish between more subtle differences between the humans. For example, they did not gesture differentially to a human who wore a blindfold over his eyes (as opposed

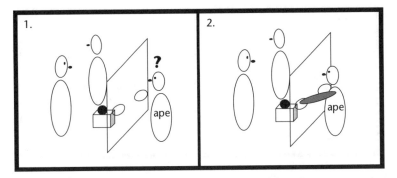

FIGURE 3.2. Gesture Choice paradigm (Povinelli and Eddy, 1996*a*). One of two human experimenters present in the room is facing the ape (1). The ape requests the food from one of the experimenters by extending her arm through a hole in the Plexiglas wall (2).

to one who wore a blindfold over his mouth), or to one who wore a bucket over his head (as opposed to one who held a bucket on his shoulder), or to one who held his hands over his eyes (as opposed to one who held his hands over his ears), or to one who had his eyes closed (as opposed to one who had his eyes open), or to one who was looking away (as opposed to looking at the subject), or to one whose back was turned but who looked over his shoulder to the subject (as opposed to one whose back was turned and was looking away). A number of control experiments ruled out possible artefactual explanations of these results. The investigators concluded that although these young chimpanzees had learned one or more cues that signal conditions conducive to communication with humans (e.g. bodily orientation facing toward, versus away from, the subject), overall they did not seem to understand very well precisely how visual perception works, especially the role of the eyes. These findings have recently been replicated by Reaux, Theall, and Povinelli (1999).

The second experimental paradigm that causes chimpanzees problems is in many ways even more surprising. In a number of different experiments from a number of different laboratories, chimpanzees have shown a very inconsistent ability to use the gaze direction of others to help them to locate food hidden under one of several objects; we will call this the Object Choice paradigm (see Fig. 3.3). For example, Call, Hare, and Tomasello (1998) presented chimpanzees with two opaque containers, only one of which contained food (with chimpanzees trained to know that they could choose only one). A human experimenter then looked continuously at the container with food inside. Not one of six chimpanzees used this cue to find the food. Tomasello, Call, and Gluckman (1997*a*) and Call, Agnetta, and Tomasello (1999) provided chimpanzees with several other types of visual gestural cues in this same paradigm and also found mostly negative results (the two individuals who sometimes tested above chance were both raised by

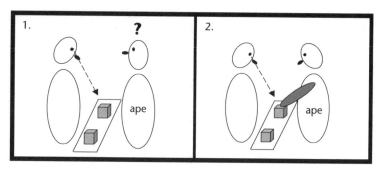

FIGURE 3.3. Object Choice paradigm (Call *et al.*, 1998; Itakura and Tanaka, 1998;
Povinelli *et al.*, 1999). A human experimenter is facing the ape and staring at one of
two containers (1). The ape selects one of the containers by touching it
through the fence (2).

humans—see next section). Povinelli, Bierschwale, and Cech (1999) found that
some young chimpanzees could learn to use gaze-direction cues in a similar
experimental situation, but they also showed in various ways that this was for
them only a learned behavioural cue, not an indicator of the visual experience of
others; for example, when the experimenter turned his head in the correct direction
of the baited container but looked to the ceiling and not at the baited container,
chimpanzees chose the correct container just as often as if the experimenter
looked directly at it. Itakura *et al.* (1999) used a trained chimpanzee conspecific to
give the gaze-direction cue, but still found negative results.

With one exception, the only positive results in this paradigm (other than with
human-raised chimpanzees) have come when the experimenter actually
approaches the correct container and actively inspects it, as if actually foraging for
food (Itakura *et al.*, 1999), or if he makes chimpanzee body movements or
vocalizations or noises in combination with gaze as cues (Call *et al.*, 1999;
Povinelli and Eddy, 1996*b*). In several different studies, even after an individual
chimpanzee subject has learned to be successful by using some other cue (e.g. the
'approach and forage' cue), when that same subject is later given the 'gaze only'
cue, they return to chance performance (Call *et al.*, 1998, 1999). The one exception
is the study of Itakura and Tanaka (1998) in which two chimpanzees (one of whom
was human-raised) performed reasonably well in this task. It is also interesting and
important to note that domestic dogs do much better in all versions of this task
than do chimpanzees (Miklósi *et al.*, 1998; Hare, Call, and Tomasello, 1998; Hare
and Tomasello, 1999). (And of course domestic dogs have extensive contact with
humans throughout their lives; see next section for a discussion of the role of
experience with humans as a factor in this task.)

Povinelli (1999) relates his history of growing scepticism as he tested his
chimpanzees in the Gesture Choice and Object Choice experimental paradigms in
many different studies over a several-year period, and we ourselves must admit to

being amazed at how poorly the chimpanzees in our laboratory continue to do in the Object Choice paradigm, returning to random performance on the 'gaze only' cue even after they have been successful on a cue that combines gaze with some other behaviour. The overall conclusion from these two experimental paradigms would thus seem to be: although chimpanzees show sensitivity to the bodily orientation of other individuals in communicating with them—in the sense that they do not attempt to use a visually based gesture to an individual who is facing away from them—most of them do not seem to understand that (1) visual perception depends on visual access for the eyes, or (2) the visual perception of others may be used as a cue to find hidden food whose location the looker, but not the chimpanzee subject, knows.

EVIDENCE THAT CHIMPANZEES UNDERSTAND SEEING

We have recently been engaged in another series of studies that give a much more positive picture of what chimpanzees understand about seeing. First, Tomasello, Call, and Hare (1998) conducted a very simple study, using chimpanzees in a semi-natural captive group (and four other primate species in captive groups). The basic idea was that a human experimenter waited until a pair of chimpanzees was spatially arranged so that one was facing toward him in the observation tower (the looker) and another was looking at that individual, with its back to the experimenter (the subject). He then held up a piece of desirable food, inducing the looker to look up at him (see Fig. 3.4). He then observed how the subject responded to the looker's looking behaviour. In control trials the experimenter displayed the food in an identical manner, but when the subject was alone. The results were very strong. Subjects reliably followed the gaze of conspecifics, looking

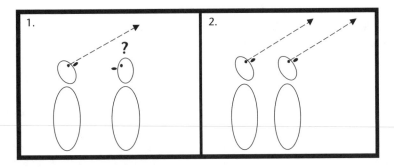

Figure 3.4. Gaze-following paradigm (Tomasello *et al.*, 1998). A non-human primate looks up at a piece of food held by a human experimenter (not shown in the drawing) while the subject is staring at her (1). The subject turns around to look at the experimenter (2).

to the food about 80 per cent of the time in experimental trials, as compared to about 20 per cent of the time in control trials (and this was found for the other primate species as well; see also Emery *et al.*, 1997).

It is interesting and important that chimpanzees also follow the gaze direction of human beings. They do this on the basis of eye direction alone, independent of head direction (Povinelli and Eddy 1996c), and they do this even when the target is located above or behind them (Call *et al.*, 1998; Itakura, 1996; Povinelli and Eddy, 1997). Call *et al.* (1998) also found that when a chimpanzee tracked the gaze of another individual to a location and found nothing interesting there, they quite often looked back to the individual's face and tracked their gaze direction a second time—'checking back' in this way being a much-used criterion in assessing human infants' understanding of the visual experience of others (Bates, 1979).

One possible explanation for simple gaze-following behaviour is that individuals learn, through experience, that when they look in the direction toward which another individual is visually oriented, they often find something interesting or important. The cognitive process might thus be: turn in the direction in which others are oriented, and then search randomly until you find something interesting. This is what Povinelli (1999) calls the 'low-level' explanation, since it is based on an individual learning what amounts to a conditioned discriminative cue: when another individual turns in a direction, you will quite often be rewarded for looking in that direction yourself. The 'high-level' explanation may be variously characterized, but in a loose formulation it consists simply in understanding that the other one is having a visual experience (perhaps similar to one's own).

Following a suggestive finding of Povinelli and Eddy (1996c), Tomasello, Hare and Agnetta (1999) effectively disproved the lower-level explanation of chimpanzee gaze following with two experiments. In the first experiment a chimpanzee watched as a human experimenter looked around various types of barriers (see Fig. 3.5). If chimpanzees simply look in the direction of others and then search randomly, as claimed by the low-level explanation, then they should either look at the barrier (if they find it interesting) or else look for something else in that direction. They did not do this, however. Instead, the chimpanzees actually moved themselves to new locations so that they could look around each of the barriers— seemingly to see what was behind it, where the experimenter (E) was looking (they did this much more than in a control condition in which E looked in another direction—so it was not just natural curiosity about what was behind the barrier). In the second experiment chimpanzees watched as a human experimenter looked to the top and back of their cage. As they turned to follow the human's gaze, a distractor object was presented. Again in this case, if chimpanzees simply look in the direction of others and then search randomly, as claimed by the low-level explanation, then they should look at the distractor (if they find it interesting) or something else in that direction. What they did, however, was to follow E's gaze all the way to the back of the cage, and they did this even though they

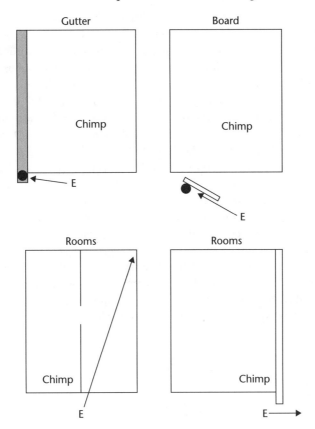

FIGURE 3.5. Basic layout of the four barrier situations used by Tomasello *et al.* (1999). Arrows indicate where the experimenter looked in the experimental condition (control to opposite side of the room). 'Chimp' indicates where the subject began each trial.

clearly noticed the distractor. Together, these two studies effectively disconfirm the low-level model of chimpanzee gaze-following, supporting instead the hypothesis that chimpanzees follow the gaze direction of other animate beings geometrically to specific locations in much the same way as human infants (Butterworth and Jarrett, 1991). These studies are of only limited helpfulness in assessing the degree to which chimpanzees interpret the gaze of others intentionally or mentalistically.

In none of these studies of gaze-following did chimpanzees have to use the information they gained by following the gaze of others. It is thus possible that the reason they do so well in tasks of simple gaze-following, but so poorly in the Object Choice paradigm is that this latter paradigm requires not just following gaze but then using that information to make a foraging choice. However, in a recent series of studies, Hare *et al.* (2000) have shown that in the right situation chimpanzees can use the gaze direction of others, in this case a conspecific, to make an effective foraging choice. They do this, however, not when that conspecific is attempting to inform them co-operatively of a hidden food's location, but rather when the conspecific is attempting to compete with them for food.

The basic set-up was as follows. In each of five experiments a subordinate and a dominant individual were placed in rooms on opposite sides of a third room. Each had a guillotine door leading into the third room which, when cracked at the bottom, allowed them to observe two pieces of food at various locations within that room—and to see the other individual looking under her door (see Fig. 3.6). After the food had been placed, the doors for both individuals were opened and they were allowed to enter the third room. The basic problem for the subordinate in this situation is that the dominant will take all of the food that it can see, and indeed in all the studies in which dominants had good visual and physical access to the two pieces of food, they took them both on most occasions (i.e. they went for one piece while staring at, and so intimidating, the subordinate from taking the other piece). However, in some cases we arranged things so that the subordinate could see a piece of food that the dominant could not see, for example, by placing it on the subordinate's side of a small barrier. The question in these cases was thus whether the subordinate knew that the dominant could not see a particular piece of food, and so it was safe for them to go for it.

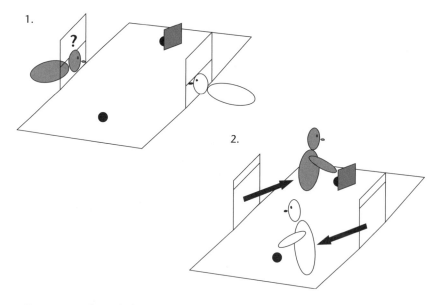

FIGURE 3.6. The occluder test (Hare *et al.*, 2000). Two pieces of food are placed inside a room with one subordinate (shaded) and one dominant (clear) chimpanzee facing each other through cracked doors. The subordinate is able to see both pieces, while the dominant animal can see only one of them due to occlusion (1). Subjects are released and select food pieces (2). In control tests, none of the two pieces is hidden behind an occluder.

The basic finding was that the subordinates did indeed go for the food that only they could see much more often than they went for the food that both they and the dominant could see. In some cases, the subordinate may have been monitoring the behaviour of the dominant, but in other cases this possibility was ruled out by giving subordinates a small head start and forcing them to make their choice (to go to the food that both competitors could see, or to go to the food that only they could see) before the dominant was released into the area. Moreover, we also ran two other control conditions. In one, the dominant's door was lowered before the two competitors were let into the room (and again the subordinate got a small head start), so that the subordinate could not see which piece the dominant was looking at under the door (i.e. it is possible that in the first studies the subordinate saw that the dominant was looking at the out-in-the-open food and so went for the other piece). The results were clear. Subordinates preferentially targeted the hidden piece. In the other control study, we followed the same basic procedure as before (one piece of food in the open, one on the subordinate's side of a barrier) but in this case we used a transparent barrier that did not prevent the dominant from seeing the food behind it. In this case, chimpanzees chose equally between the two pieces of food, seeming to know that the transparent barrier was not serving to block the dominant's visual access (and so her 'control' of the food) at all. The findings of these studies thus suggest that chimpanzees know what conspecifics can and cannot see and, further, that they use this knowledge to maximize their food intake in competitive situations.

The experiments previously described dealt with chimpanzees competing over food when all the relevant information was available at the time of choice. In the next series of experiments (Hare, Call, and Tomasello, 2001), we investigated whether chimpanzees were also able to take into account past information, such as whether the dominant had seen the baiting. For these experiments we used two barriers and one piece of food, and manipulated what the dominant saw. In experimental trials dominants had not seen the food hidden, or food they had seen hidden was moved to a different location when they were not watching (whereas in control trials they saw the food being hidden or moved). Subordinates, on the other hand, always saw the entire baiting procedure and could monitor the visual access of their dominant competitor as well. Subordinates preferentially retrieved and approached the food that dominants had not seen hidden or moved, which suggested that subordinates were sensitive to what dominants had or had not seen during baiting. In an additional experiment, we switched the dominant who had witnessed the baiting for another dominant who had not witnessed the baiting and compared it with a situation in which the dominant was not switched. Results indicated that subordinates retrieved more food when the dominant had been switched than when it was not switched, thus demonstrating their ability to keep track of precisely who had witnessed what. This result also ruled out the possibility that subordinates were using just the sequence of door opening and closing to decide which food to take.

More importantly, this whole second series of experiments ruled out the possibility suggested by Povinelli (2002) that subordinates are attracted to the food behind a barrier because in general they prefer to forage around barriers rather than grab food that is in the open. In other words, subordinates prefer the hidden food, Povinelli argued, not because they understand anything about the visual access of others, but simply because that's their natural foraging tendency. The foraging preference hypothesis, however, fails to account for the results of this second series of experiments, because subordinates are confronted with two barriers in all trials, and the only thing that changes across trials is whether the dominant animal has seen where the food is hidden. According to the foraging tendency hypothesis, subordinates should treat all trials with food behind the barrier equally, but they did not. They preferentially approached and took those pieces that the dominant animal had not seen hidden.

This series of experiments on chimpanzee gaze-following in more naturalistic and food competition situations thus reveals that in some situations chimpanzees know much more about seeing than is apparent in the Gesture Choice and Object Choice experimental paradigms. Discrepancies among the findings in the different situations could conceivably be due to methodological issues not related to chimpanzees' understanding of seeing *per se*, but this is extremely unlikely, since in all of the different studies the findings are extremely robust and replicable across variations of task design, laboratories, and subjects. So the theoretical challenge is to explain the apparently reliable yet different chimpanzee behaviours that emerge in the different observational settings, and to do so in a way that is revealing about the nature of chimpanzee social cognition.

SO WHAT DO CHIMPANZEES REALLY UNDERSTAND ABOUT SEEING?

The current review has shown that chimpanzees follow the gaze of conspecifics and humans, follow it past distractors and behind barriers, 'check back' with humans when gaze-following does not yield interesting sights, use gestures appropriately depending on the visual access of their recipient, and select different pieces of food depending on whether their competitor has visual access to them. Taken together, these findings make a strong case for the hypothesis that chimpanzees have some understanding of what other individuals can and cannot see. However, chimpanzees do not seem nearly so skilful in the Gesture Choice and Object Choice experimental paradigms. If these positive and negative findings are both reliable—and we believe that they are—one theoretical possibility is that chimpanzees' successful performance in the positive tasks is artificially high, in the sense that they are using some cue other than gaze direction. But the variety of lines of evidence and methods used (including both naturalistic and several different kinds of experimental observations), as well as the robustness of the findings in general, argues against this hypothesis.

Much more likely is the hypothesis that chimpanzees' poor performance in some task situations reflects the context-sensitive nature of their understanding of the gaze behaviour of others; that is to say, in some situations they simply do not understand the gaze behaviour of others, or they have a difficult time translating their understanding into action. We believe that this second hypothesis is the correct one, which means that we must look a bit more carefully at the two experimental paradigms in which chimpanzees do not perform skillfully on a consistent basis.

The Gesture Choice and Object Choice Paradigms

As emphasized by Tomasello (1996), the failures of the chimpanzees in the Gesture Choice paradigm may all be explained as failures to understand not visual perception in general, but rather the role of the eyes in particular in visual perception. Recall that just as in their naturalistic behaviour (as observed by Tomasello *et al.* 1994, 1997*b*), the chimpanzees in Povinelli and Eddy's (1996*a*) experiments were quite reliable in gesturing to the individual who was facing them as opposed to the one whose back was turned. What they could not deal with were situations in which they needed to know that the eyes are the organs of visual perception (e.g. in choosing between two people facing them, one with a blindfold), as opposed to situations in which they could use some more generic understanding that the front part of the body enables perception. It is salutary in this context to imagine how human beings would perform in a task in which they needed to know exactly which part of the eye—iris, pupil, or eyeball as a whole—is responsible for visual perception. If they failed in this task, it would not mean that they do not understand visual perception, but only that they do not know the precise mechanism through which it works. And so we believe quite simply that the Povinelli and Eddy findings tell us that chimpanzees do not understand the role of the eyes in visual perception—and that is all they tell us.

The Object Choice paradigm reveals something different—and potentially much more telling—about chimpanzees' skills of social cognition. Given that chimpanzees in this task quite often follow the gaze of the human experimenter but then do not choose the container being gazed at, one interpretation is that they can follow the gaze of others but do not know what this gaze means—its possible information value beyond leading them to a spatial location. That is to say, chimpanzees follow gaze to a location, but when they do not see food or anything else interesting at that location, they forget about the gaze and simply choose among containers randomly (Call *et al.*, 1998). Based on this kind of analysis, Tomasello *et al.* (1997*b*) hypothesized that chimpanzees' troubles in the Object Choice paradigm were due to the fact that they do not understand communicative intentions; they do not understand that in gazing at a container the human intends that they take his gaze as a communicative signal relevant to their searching activity (see also Tomasello, 1999). On this account, whatever chimpanzees may or may not understand about the intentions of others—a currently controversial topic—they do not understand embedded intentions such as those involved in communication: he intends something as regards my intentional (or attentional) state.

Two further facts are relevant to an interpretation of chimpanzee behaviour in the Object Choice paradigm. First, in the recent studies of Hare *et al.* (2000, 2001) reviewed above, chimpanzees were skilful at determining what the other individual could see in a competitive situation and then using this information to make a foraging choice—in this case going for the one that the other individual was not looking at or could not see. It would thus seem odd that in the Object Choice paradigm they do not then use the gaze of the other as a cue for which container they should choose—even if they do not understand communicative intentions *per se*—taking it simply as information. Said another way, in the competitive situation the individual simply sees the food, checks to see if the other can also see it, and if the other cannot see it, goes for it. The question is why they cannot then do something similar in the Object Choice paradigm, but in this case go for the food the other *is* looking at. But again the problem might revolve around communication versus competition. The situation in which another individual is trying to inform them about the location of food is clearly not the one chimpanzees normally experience, since they spend their whole lives competing with group mates for food. This is especially true when it is a monopolizable food item that the other individual could clearly take if it wished (Hauser and Wrangham, 1987). So the subject in this paradigm does not take the gaze of the other as an informative cue—'she is looking at something interesting so that must be where the food is'— because no individual would behave like that in the presence of food she could take for herself. So subjects in this experimental paradigm just do not know or care why the other is looking at one container and not another, because such behaviour does not suggest the presence of food—whereas in the same set-up foraging behaviour itself (as in Itakura *et al.*, 1999) does suggest food, and so is an effective cue. The basic idea is thus that the Object Choice paradigm is difficult because it involves either (i) understanding communicative intentions, or (ii) taking gaze behaviour in a co-operative, rather than a competitive, spirit.

The second important fact is that some individuals are at least somewhat skilful in this task. Several of the subjects in Povinelli *et al.*'s studies learned to use gaze cues; two subjects in the study of Itakura and Tanaka (1998) were skillful; and two subjects in Call *et al.* (2000) were skillful. Although it cannot account for all of the variation observed, one effective factor is very likely the amount and kind of experience these individuals have had with humans. The two skilful subjects of Call *et al.* (2000) had both been raised in infancy by humans, and one of the subjects of Itakura and Tanaka (1998) was human-raised as well. The other skilful subject in their study had also had much human experience, but not significantly more than some other subjects who never became skilful, so human experience is clearly not the whole story; there are very likely individual differences due to other sources as well. But to the extent that experience with humans is important, we would hypothesize that the key factor is that humans regularly attempt to communicate with and direct the attention of the other individuals with whom they interact. More specifically, chimpanzees who grow up with humans experience many attempts by others to direct their attention and behaviour, and after they respond in some way, they get feedback about their response. That is, humans respond to the chimpanzees' responses with praise and happiness when the chimpanzee succeeds in doing what the human intended her to do, but with something less positive when they do not respond in this way. By contrast, individuals who grow up with conspecifics do not have these learning opportunities, as chimpanzees rarely if ever try to direct the attention of conspecifics to outside objects.

There is much evidence for this interpretation in the direct comparison of enculturated (human-raised) and non-enculturated apes on a variety of social and communicative behaviours (see Call and Tomasello, 1996, for a review). Some especially relevant findings are that enculturated apes look more at humans than conspecifics in joint attentional interactions and in gestural communication with humans (Call and Tomasello, 1994; Carpenter *et al.*, 1995; Gómez, 1996). (On some accounts, to be effective, the process of human enculturation must begin at an early age: Rumbaugh and Savage-Rumbaugh, 1992). So it is not unreasonable to suggest that extensive experience in social and communicative interactions with humans from an early age is a reason for the superior performance of many, if not most, of the individual chimpanzees who are skilful in this task. It is also relevant in this regard to recall that domestic dogs—who have been bred phylogenetically and raised ontogenetically to be at tuned to human beings—are actually much better in the Object Choice task than are chimpanzees.

So our hypothesis is that chimpanzees in some situations do understand what other individuals can and cannot see. They do not understand, however, the role of the eyes in the process, and they do not understand when another individual is using gaze (or other gestures or cues) in an attempt to direct their attention—unless they have had relatively extensive previous experience in communicating with humans.

An Explanation of the Third Kind

Even if chimpanzees do indeed understand what other individuals can and cannot see in some situations, there are still multiple possibilities for the nature of this understanding, some more mentalistic than others. For example, the cognitively strongest hypothesis is that chimpanzees understand the visual perception and experience of others in much the same way as do humans. That is, an individual understands not only that others see things that she does not currently see (e.g. due to occlusion), but also that (i) others can *attend* to different aspects of things within a single visual field; (ii) others can have different *perspectives* on the same object she is now perceiving (e.g. from a different angle); and (iii) others' visual experience is *similar to her own* (i.e. she can simulate the visual experience of others by imagining how she would see it if she were in the other's place). By contrast, the cognitively weakest hypothesis is that chimpanzees' understanding of visual perception and experience of others is based on learned behavioural contingencies (or blind rules), accompanied by no understanding of the other's visual experience at all.

We do not believe that either of these extreme hypotheses is correct. First, we do not believe that chimpanzees understand visual perception in the same manner as humans (especially the analogy to the self), because they show no evidence of such understanding in a variety of other studies of social cognition (see Tomasello and Call, 1997, for a review). But we also do not believe that all that is involved is some form of non-cognitive behavioural conditioning. Our mixed hypothesis is that during their normal ontogenies, as they interact with others and attempt to predict their behaviour in many situations, individuals may learn many things about the relation of their group mates' visual access to things (i.e. both to themselves and to external objects) and their subsequent behaviour. For instance, individuals may learn about the visual access of others when occluders are present via situations in which they (i) notice and follow the gaze direction of another individual (and also notice its behaviour and emotions); (ii) see a barrier of some sort; and (iii) subsequently see the target of the other's gaze, behaviour, and emotions because the barrier moves, the target moves, or they themselves move around the barrier (Tomasello *et al.*, 1999). The basic idea is thus that through individual experience, chimpanzees come to know important things about the relationship between the visual access of others, its likely target (either the self or stimuli in the environment), and how this relates to their behaviour in a variety of different situations. It is important to emphasize that our mixed explanation is not equivalent to a behavioural conditioning, non-cognitive explanation. Even though it involves learning, it may be construed as a cognitive form of learning which leads to real understanding and insight, as expressed in knowledge flexibly displayed in behaviour in novel situations—as in our food competition experiments.

Within this third way it can be argued that there are still different types of understanding that can be distinguished. Indeed, one may be tempted to distinguish between more psychological versus more behavioural explanations. However, we do not think that this distinction is fully satisfactory. First of all, to some extent this distinction perpetuates the bipolar view between theory of mind and learned behaviour that we tried to eliminate in the first place. More importantly, we do not think that this distinction captures the essence of our third view. One problem is that the dichotomy psychological versus behavioural is misleading, because all levels in the third view are psychological, although we prefer to call them 'cognitive'. Calling some of them behavioural may confuse the issue, because they may be equated to the learned behavioural contingencies position. Yet, it is true that finer distinctions within this cognitive third view are possible, and indeed desirable. But those distinctions should be viewed as part of a continuum with more translucent constructs, such as the visual perception of others (i.e. seeing), at one end and more opaque constructs, such as knowledge states of others, at the other end of the continuum.

Similarly, we argue, the knowledge that individuals have about the visual perception of others affords various distinctions. One can distinguish between perceptual access (whether others can or cannot see something), perspective taking (how others perceive something from their vantage-point), or attention (what aspect of something others are focusing on; more on attention later). Currently, there is evidence suggesting that chimpanzees reach at least the first level of understanding the visual access of others, which corresponds to level 1 visual perspective taking in Flavell's (1985) account. In other words, they know what others can or cannot see. Whether or not they also possess the ability to take the perspective of others or know what others are attending to, remains an unresolved question that awaits further research. Likewise, we still know comparatively little about other mental states, such as intentions, knowledge, or beliefs. Although there is some evidence suggesting that chimpanzees may also be sensitive to the intentions or the knowledge states of others, other interpretations have not been ruled out yet, and therefore, unlike the research about visual access in others, it is still premature to draw solid conclusions.

Thus, we do not believe that the only explanatory alternatives for complex primate social behaviours are (1) behavioural conditioning or (2) theory of mind (e.g. Byrne, 1995, 1997; Heyes, 1998). Rather, following Tomasello and Call (1997), we prefer a third alternative: namely, that individuals may have insight into social problems in the same way that they have insight into physical problems such as tool use and spatial reasoning—with this insight in all cases depending to some degree on personal experience with the objects and activities involved (see also Call, 2001). It is hypothesized that the social cognition of chimpanzees (and other primates) is based in large part on a representational understanding of the behaviour of others, which permits them to do things like remember, foresee, and communicatively manipulate the behaviour and social relationships of others. This enables primates not only to react appropriately in social situations, but more importantly, to predict and influence their group mates' behaviour in novel situations as well. But—and this is what makes our explanation not about theory of mind—all of this understanding, prediction, and manipulation is of the behaviour, including visual behaviour, of others; it is not of the intentional or mental states of others. We call this an explanation of the 'third kind' because, unlike behaviouristic learning explanations, it involves complex cognitive processes such as understanding and perhaps even reasoning, and unlike theory of mind explanations, it concerns behaviour and perception, not intentional or mental states.

To give a concrete example, in our food competition experiments, the subordinate individual can see the dominant individual, and she can see the two pieces of food. She has learned from past experience that when there is an opaque barrier between another individual and an object, that individual does not behave towards that object in any way (showing no fear, attraction, or other emotional or behavioural response). To make her choice of which food to go for, she takes into account this knowledge and formulates a strategy accordingly. In this case, she approaches and takes the hidden piece of food. The most complex expression of knowledge of this type would involve the subordinate in attempting to actually manipulate the situation so as to make it favourable for her. In the current case, we would need to imagine a situation in which the subordinate had the ability to control the position of the barrier, so that it was either in place (blocking the dominant's view) or not before the trial began. An insightful social strategy—comparable in many ways to the anecdotal reports of primate deception (Whiten and Byrne, 1988)—would be for the chimpanzee to choose to place the barrier in its effective position before the trial began. We do not know of any experimental studies demonstrating the use of precisely this kind of strategy, but the main point in the current context is that the individual could formulate such an intelligent social strategy by reasoning about the behaviour and perception of the other individual, not its mental states.

And What about Attention?

If we claim that chimpanzees understand something about seeing in terms of the visual behaviour of others, but not the intentional or mental states of others, what does this imply about their understanding of the attention of others? Many authors basically equate an understanding that another sees something with an understanding that they are attending to something. We think that is a mistake. Attention is an intentional phenomenon in the sense that it involves the individual intentionally focusing on one aspect of their current experience to the exclusion of others. A person may see an apple and then choose to focus their attention either on its shape, its colour, its edibility, or any of an infinite number of aspects. To understand another individual's visual attention is to understand that they have made an intentional choice about what to include and what to exclude in their visual experience. This way of looking at attention links it inseparably to an understanding of intentionality in general (Gibson and Rader, 1979; Tomasello, 1995).

On this definition of attention, we do not know of any studies indicating that chimpanzees have any understanding of the attention of others. Admittedly, it is difficult to see how one would investigate this question directly without using language or some other symbolic system that embodies different communicative perspectives on things, and indeed it is possible that some enculturated apes may have learned to appreciate the attention of others as a result of their 'linguistic' interactions with them. But in the normal course of events, in their natural habitats, chimpanzees and other primates do not experience others attempting to manipulate their intentions or attention, and they do not understand or attempt to manipulate the intentions or attention of others either. So joint attention in the normal, human-based meaning of the expression, is simply not an issue.

Without going into detail, we should also mention at this point that one hypothesis is that human infants understand intentional and mental states such as attention from about 1 year of age, because they are able to make some kind of correspondence between their own experience and that of others (Tomasello, 1995, 1999). The reason why this ability does not emerge until around 1 year of age is that it is not until then that infants themselves control their own intentional behaviour and attention sufficiently to differentiate ends from means, and so to experience their own intentional and mental states as something separate from their behavioural expressions. In this basically simulation view, chimpanzees can learn a lot about the behaviour and perception of others, but they will always be looking at others from the 'outside in', because, without an identification of self and other, they will not be able to use the simulation processes (putting themselves in the 'cognitive shoes' of the other) on which adult human social cognition depends.

CONCLUSION

Our explanation of the third kind is difficult, because human beings have a difficult time imagining that other organisms can observe the behaviour of conspecifics or humans and not understand and describe that behaviour in intentional terms. What does it mean that a chimpanzee understands seeing if that does not mean on analogy to her own visual experience? What does it mean to understand perception but not attention? We do not currently know how to answer these questions at any deep level. But what we will say at this point is simply that it is an empirical fact that chimpanzees' behaviour in many socially complex situations is decidedly mixed. They behave very intelligently in some ways—seeming to understand and reason about others—but they still do not seem to understand some social interactions in the way that humans do. Our hypothesis is simply that they have the cognitive skills to recall, represent, categorize, and reason about the behaviour and perception of others, but not about their intentional or mental states—because they do not know that others have such states, since they cannot make a link with their own. Chimpanzees—and perhaps in a different way autistic children—are showing us the most intelligent way an individual can understand and interact with conspecifics in the absence of using one's own intentional and mental states as a model for those of others.

Human beings began their own evolutionary trajectory with these same skills, of course, but then at some point in their evolution (probably quite recently) they began to understand that their own experience could serve as some kind of model for that of other persons. This allowed for even better prediction and control of the behaviour of others, and better communication and co-operation with them as well, and so it was an adaptation with immediate beneficial consequences that ensured its survival. Its implications for the ontogeny of human social cognition and behaviour—and indeed the crucial role of this adaptation in the evolution of human culture—is only now being fully recognized.

REFERENCES

BATES, E. (1979), *The Emergence of Symbols: Cognition and Communication in Infancy.* New York: Academic Press.

BUTTERWORTH, G., and JARRETT, N. (1991), 'What minds have in common is space: spatial mechanisms serving joint visual attention in infancy', *British Journal of Developmental Psychology*, 9: 55–72.

BYRNE, R. W. (1995), *The Thinking Ape.* Oxford: Oxford University Press.

—— (1997), 'Machiavellian intelligence', *Evolutionary Anthropology*, 5: 172–80.

CALL, J. (2001), 'Chimpanzee social cognition', *Trends in Cognitive Sciences*, 5: 369–405.

—— and TOMASELLO, M. (1994), 'Production and comprehension of referential pointing by orangutans (*Pongo pygmaeus*)', *Journal of Comparative Psychology*, 108: 307–17.

—— —— (1996), 'The role of humans in the cognitive development of apes', in A. E. Russon, K. A. Bard, and S. T. Parker (eds.), *Reaching into Thought: The Minds of the Great Apes.* Cambridge: Cambridge University Press, 371–403.

—— AGNETTA, B., and TOMASELLO, M. (1999), 'Cues that chimpanzees do and do not use to find hidden food'. Manuscript submitted for publication.

—— —— —— (2000), 'Social cues that chimpanzees do and do not use to find hidden objects', *Animal Cognition*, 3: 23–34.

—— HARE, B., and TOMASELLO, M. (1998), 'Chimpanzee gaze following in an object choice task', *Animal Cognition*, 1: 89–100.

CARPENTER, M., TOMASELLO, M., and SAVAGE-RUMBAUGH, E. S. (1995), 'Joint attention and imitative learning in children, chimpanzees, and enculturated chimpanzees', *Social Development*, 4: 217–37.

EMERY, N., LORINEZ, E., PERRETT, D., ORAN, M., and BAKER, C. (1997), 'Gaze following and joint attention in rhesus monkeys (*Macaca mulatta*)', *Journal of Comparative Psychology*, 111: 286–93.

FLAVELL, J. H. (1985), *Cognitive Development.* Englewood Cliffs, NJ: Prentice-Hall.

GIBSON, E., and RADER, N. (1979), 'Attention: the perceiver as performer', in G. Hale and M. Lewis (eds.), *Attention and Cognitive Development.* New York: Plenum Press, 6–36.

GÓMEZ, J. C. (1996), 'Non-human primate theories of (non-human primate) minds: some issues concerning the origins of mind-reading', in P. Carruthers and P. K. Smith (eds.), *Theories of Theories of Mind.* Cambridge: Cambridge University Press, 330–43.

HARE, B., and TOMASELLO, M. (1999), 'Domestic dogs (*Canis familiaris*) use human and conspecific social cues to locate hidden food', *Journal of Comparative Psychology*, 113: 173–7.

—— CALL, J., and TOMASELLO, M. (1998), 'Communication of food location between human and dog (*Canis familiaris*)', *Evolution of Communication*, 2: 137–59.

—— —— —— (2001), 'Do chimpanzees know what conspecifics know and do not know?' *Animal Behaviour*, 61: 139–51.

—— —— AGNETTA, B., and TOMASELLO, M. (2000), 'Chimpanzees know what conspecifics do and do not see', *Animal Behaviour*, 59: 771–85.

HAUSER, M. D., and WRANGHAM, R. W. (1987), 'Manipulation of food calls in captive chimpanzees: a preliminary report', *Folia Primatologica*, 48: 207–10.

HEYES, C. (1998), 'Theory of mind in nonhuman primates', *Behavioural and Brain Sciences*, 21: 101–48.

ITAKURA, S. (1996), 'An exploratory study of gaze-monitoring in nonhuman primates', *Japanese Psychological Research*, 38: 174–80.

—— and TANAKA, M. (1998), 'Use of experimenter-given cues during object-choice tasks by chimpanzees (*Pan troglodytes*), an orangutan (*Pongo pygmaeus*), and human infants (*Homo sapiens*)', *Journal of Comparative Psychology*, 112: 119–26.

—— AGNETTA, B., HARE, B., and TOMASELLO, M. (1999), 'Chimpanzees use human and conspecific social cues to locate hidden food', *Developmental Science*, 2: 448–56.

MIKLÓSI, A., POLGÁRDI, R., TOPÁL, J. and CSÁNYI, V. (1998), 'Use of experimenter-given cues in dogs', *Animal Cognition*, 1: 113–21.

POVINELLI, D. J. (1999), 'Social understanding in chimpanzees: new evidence from a longitudinal approach', in P. D. Zelazo, J. W. Astington, and D. R. Olson (eds.), *Developing Theories of Intention*. Hillsdale, NJ: LEA, 195–225.

—— (2002), 'On what chimpanzees know about self'. Paper presented at the VI International Conference of the Association for the scientific study of Consciousness, Barcelona, May.

—— and EDDY, T. J. (1996*a*), 'What young chimpanzees know about seeing', *Monographs of the Society for Research in Child Development*, 61 (3): 1–152.

—— —— (1996*b*), 'Factors influencing young chimpanzees' recognition of "attention"', *Journal of Comparative Psychology*, 110: 336–45.

—— —— (1996*c*), 'Chimpanzees: joint visual attention', *Psychological Science*, 7: 129–35.

—— —— (1997), 'Specificity of gaze-following in young chimpanzees', *British Journal of Developmental Psychology*, 15: 213–22.

—— BIERSCHWALE, D. T., and CECH, C. G. (1999), 'Comprehension of seeing as a referential act in young children, but not juvenile chimpanzees', *British Journal of Developmental Psychology*, 17: 37–70.

REAUX, J. E., THEALL, L. A. and POVINELLI, D. J. (1999), 'A longitudinal investigation of chimpanzees' understanding of visual perception', *Child Development*, 70: 275–90.

RUMBAUGH, D. M. and SAVAGE-RUMBAUGH, E. S. (1992), 'Cognitive competencies: products of genes, experience, and technology', in T. Nishida, W. C. McGrew, P. Marler, M. Pickford, and F. B. M. De Waal (eds.), *Topics in Primatology*: Human Origins. Tokyo: University of Tokyo Press, 293–304.

TOMASELLO, M. (1995), 'Joint attention as social cognition', in C. Moore and P. Dunham (eds.), *Joint Attention: Its Origins and Role in Development*. Hillsdale, NJ: LEA, 103–30.

TOMASELLO, M. (1996), 'Chimpanzee social cognition', *Monographs of the Society for Research in Child Development*, 61 (3): 161–73.

—— (1999), 'Having intentions, understanding of intentions, and understanding of communicative intentions', in P. D. Zelazo, J. W. Astington, and D. R. Olson (eds.), *Developing Theories of Intention*. Hillsdale, NJ: LEA, 63–75.

—— and CALL, J. (1997), *Primate Cognition*. New York: Oxford University Press.

—— —— and GLUCKMAN, A. (1997a), 'The comprehension of novel communicative signs by apes and human children', *Child Development*, 68: 1067–81.

—— —— and HARE, B. (1998), 'Five primate species follow the visual gaze of conspecifics', *Animal Behaviour*, 55: 1063–9.

—— —— NAGELL, K., OLGUIN, K., and CARPENTER, M. (1994), 'The learning and use of gestural signals by young chimpanzees: a trans-generational study', *Primates*, 35: 137–54.

—— —— WARREN, J., FROST, G. T., CARPENTER, M., and NAGELL, K. (1997b), 'The ontogeny of chimpanzee gestural signals: a comparison across groups and generations', *Evolution of Communication*, 1: 223–59.

—— GEORGE, B., KRUGER, A., FARRAR, M., and EVANS, A. (1985), 'The development of gestural communication in young chimpanzees', *Journal of Human Evolution*, 14: 175–86.

—— GUST, D., and FROST, G. T. (1989), 'The development of gestural communication in young chimpanzees: a follow up', *Primates*, 30: 35–50.

—— HARE, B, and AGNETTA, B. (1999), 'Chimpanzees follow gaze direction geometrically', *Animal Behaviour*, 58: 769–77.

WHITEN, A., and BYRNE, R. W. (1988), 'Tactical deception in primates', *Behavioral and Brain Sciences*, 11: 233–44.

4

Joint Attention and the Notion of Subject: Insights from Apes, Normal Children, and Children with Autism

Juan-Carlos Gómez

In this paper I will address the problem of the cognitive mechanisms of Joint Attention (JA) with the help of the comparative study of apes, normal children, and children with autism. Let me start with a statement about what I believe is involved in JA and the main proposals I will be defending in this paper.

JOINT ATTENTION

I propose that JA can be analysed into two main components: *Attention following* (a subject attends to the same target of attention as another subject in response to the latter's attention) and *Attention contact* (two subjects mutually attending to each other's attention). Each component may appear independently, or they can be combined into what amounts to *referential communication*—claiming someone's attention to direct it to a target (Sperber and Wilson, 1986). Furthermore, both components can appear either in a comprehension mode (following the attention of another; detecting another's attention on oneself) or in a productive mode (making another follow one's attention to a particular target; calling another's attention upon oneself).

Attention following can be represented as $(A > [B > X])$, where A and B are subjects, X a target of attention, and '$>$' denotes the attentional link connecting subjects to objects (or other subjects). To follow B's attention upon X, subject A must be able to compute the direction of attention of B, and reorient its own attention to the same target.

The second component—Attention contact—is not a mere derivative of the first: it does not consist merely of two subjects attending to each other; for example, if I am looking at your feet and you are looking at my hands, this is not Attention contact. Attention contact occurs when two subjects are attending to

I am grateful to the editors of this volume for their insightful comments on the first version of this paper, which was written while enjoying a DGICYT grant (BSO2002-00161).

each other's attention; i.e. when the X in the formula (B > X) is not just another subject A, but A attending to B attending to A attending to B..., etc. Thus, if we try to describe Attention contact in the same terms as Attention following—[A > (B > (A > (B > A > ...]—we are confronted with a problem of infinite regression which is isomorphic with the problem of mutual knowledge (Smith, 1982; Gómez, 1994) for exactly the same reason: an intentional process—one that is about another—ends up having to be about itself being about another that is about itself.

One of my tenets is therefore that the Attention contact component of JA must be based upon a different kind of representation, say (A >< B), where '><' denotes a special kind of attentional link between two subjects. This is a *second-person representation* that supports second-person intentionality, in contrast with [A > (B > X)], which is a *third-person representation* supporting third-person intentions (Gómez, 1996a).

Joint attention upon an external target, as it happens, for example, in referential communication, consists of a combination of these two types of intentions and their underlying representations, giving rise to a new representation that could be described as, for example, (A > (X) < B), in which the attention of A and B to X is fused in an overlapping loop where they attend to each other's attention to X.

This is thus my first proposal: there are two different intentional components in JA which require different kinds of representational processes.

My second proposal is that these representational processes need not be (and in the case of second-person intentions, *cannot* be) meta-representations or second-order representations (i.e. representations of other subjects holding internal representations separable from their behaviour), but practical, first-order representations comparable to those dubbed 'sensorimotor' or 'practical' by Köhler (1921), Piaget (1936), Vygotsky (1930), and other early students of infant and ape intelligence (see Karmiloff-Smith, 1992, for a modern version of this idea). These practical representations of intentionality represent subjects as being connected to targets by relying upon external cues such as the directionality of body orientation and gaze.

The reason why young infants and, as we shall see, non-human primates can engage in JA behaviours is that, although in a certain analysis JA may appear to constitute a complex and abstract exercise in meta-representation, it can actually be achieved through these more primitive (in the sense of 'basic') intentional representations.

My plan in this chapter is to explore the nature of these sensorimotor representations of intentionality and the nature of the distinction between third-person and second-person representations with the help of comparative studies of their emergence.

JOINT ATTENTION IN INFANTS, AUTISM, AND APES

JA is commonly attributed to 1-year-old infants because they are capable of engaging in behaviours like following the gaze of others (Butterworth, 1991), participating in face-to-face interactions arranged around patterns of attention contact (Trevarthen, 1979), or, more importantly, using gestures to engage in pre-verbal referential communication (Bates *et al.*, 1975; Bruner, 1983). Although some of these patterns, specially those involving attention contact, may appear earlier, there are indications that representations of the kind (A > X) and (A > (X) < B) may be operative only from 12 months onwards (see Chapter 6).

Children with autism, by contrast, are considered to suffer from an impairment in JA and communication. They display, if anything, a limited repertoire of gestures, sometimes bizarre, such as taking the hand of people towards the objects they want them to manipulate; they typically lack spontaneous gaze-following and display a restricted set of communicative functions. Typical children engage in both 'proto-imperatives' (e.g. requesting an object) and proto-declaratives (showing things to people). By contrast, children with autism have been described as developing, if anything, only proto-imperative gestures (Baron-Cohen, 1989).

In Gómez *et al.* (1993) I and my colleagues proposed that, in relation to the use of JA in communication, anthropoid apes appear to be somewhere in between normal infants and children with autism. On the one hand, apes show striking superficial similarities to children with autism, such as a lack of proto-declarative gestures and a tendency to use contact gestures such as taking people's hands to objects; but, on the other, when executing their proto-imperative requests, apes use JA behaviours. Our suggestion was that apes display JA and engage in referential communication, but do so on the basis of a set of representations—what I will call in this paper a sensorimotor notion of subject—that is at the same time similar and different both from that of typical human infants and from the damaged version of children with autism. Moreover, we suggested that the differences between apes and normal infants are due not to the early onset in the latter of a meta-representational mechanism that takes control of JA functions (Leslie and Happé, 1989; Baron-Cohen, 1989), but to a differently organized sensorimotor system of practical representations of attention. Children with autism have problems with JA because their practical notion of subjects is damaged.

In the next sections I review some relevant evidence that appeared after the publication of our paper that, in my view, lends support to our original hypothesis, and more specifically to an analysis of JA in the terms that I have outlined in the first section above. I will start by discussing the ape evidence, which has been somewhat controversial during the past years.

JOINT ATTENTION IN NON-HUMAN PRIMATES

The bulk of our argument for apes possessing a genuine JA ability rested on the analysis of data from the longitudinal study of a hand-reared gorilla which developed a strategic use of eye contact behaviours when interacting with people (Gómez, 1990, 1991, 1992). For example, she would request someone to open a door by taking him by the hand towards the door while making occasional eye contact with him. Moreover, this and other hand-reared gorillas developed attention-getting procedures that they typically used before making a request; for example, they would pull the clothes of an inattentive human and make eye contact with him before engaging in any request (Gómez, 1992).

This led us to suggest that, underlying this behaviour, there was a 'practical' or implicit understanding of attention, i.e. one that did not represent attention as an *internal* mental state, but as an external property of certain behaviours (Gómez, 1990, 1991). In the terms I used in the first section of this chapter, the gorillas were using eye contact as a way of achieving Attention contact, and their peculiar 'leading' gestures[1] as a way of directing the attention of others to targets. This combination constitutes the essence of intentional referential communication (Gómez, 1998*b*).

This interpretation is supported by apparently similar uses of joint attention in combination with gestures in chimpanzees (Gómez *et al.*, 1996; Leavens and Hopkins, 1998) and orangutans (Bard, 1990) and by observational evidence about how apes appear to be sensitive to, and able to manipulate, the direction of attention of others (Menzel, 1973; Whiten and Byrne, 1988).

However, it appears to be in conflict with some experimental evidence, most notably Povinelli and Eddy's studies (1996*a* and *b*) of chimpanzees' (lack of) understanding of seeing and attention. For example, Povinelli and Eddy (1996*a*) reported that, in an extended range of experimental situations, captive chimpanzees addressed requests to humans independently of whether the humans were or were not attending to them. The chimps were asked to choose between humans who had their eyes open and oriented to the Plexiglas barrier separating them versus humans with their eyes closed, or looking aside, or with a blindfold, etc. If chimpanzees had any notion of, in Povinelli's (1996) words, 'seeing as attention', they should be able to select the humans oriented to them with open eyes. They did not (except in the most blatant case of inattention instantiated by a person with her back to the chimpanzee). Their results, therefore, would appear to disconfirm the suggestion that apes (at least chimpanzees) have an understanding of Attention contact.

However, a careful inspection of the experimental protocols used by these authors reveals that the supposedly attentive humans were actually not looking at the chimpanzees: in a first series of conditions, they were looking fixedly at an

---

[1] Gorillas also used non-contact gestures, such as extending the arm to the target object or offering objects from a distance.

imaginary point on the Plexiglas partition that separated them from the chimps, carefully avoiding eye contact with the subjects; in a second series, they were looking fixedly at the hole in the Plexiglas through which the chimpanzees had been painstakingly trained to put their arms as a way of getting a reward from the human. That is to say, in none of the conditions were the humans really attending to the chimpanzees themselves; on the contrary, they were carefully avoiding the very sign of attentional availability that in our studies with gorillas we identified as the key for engaging in communicative behaviours. From the point of view of Attention contact, in Povinelli and Eddy's experiments both humans were equally disconnected from the chimp. It should come as no surprise, then, that the chimpanzees chose their recipient at random.

Furthermore, in a less well-known continuation of the previous study, Povinelli and Eddy (1996*b*) found that, when the chimpanzees were offered a choice between humans who were showing actual signs of attention to them, such as eye contact, and humans who were passively looking at the hole in the Plexiglas, the results dramatically changed: the chimpanzees now systematically addressed their actions to the humans who were giving signs of Attention contact with them. Moreover, there was one condition that was even more powerful than eye contact in attracting requests from the chimps: one in which the humans were asked to perform movements with their head that, according to the authors, were typically displayed by their chimps when attending to something. This latter condition is specially interesting because the head movements associated with attention were effective even if the eyes of the human were closed. The authors interpret this as a sign that the chimps cannot be responding to attention, because in their view attributing attention presupposes the attribution of seeing. However, it can be argued that seeing and attention are distinct mental states, and it is possible to represent one without the other. Even in adult humans, attention can be detected and attributed independently by using cues other than eye direction (Langton *et al.*, 2000). The sensitivity of the chimps to the specific sign of attention associated with head movements in Povinelli and Eddy's study clearly rules out any simplistic explanation that chimpanzees choose people who are making eye contact with them because they like that, and points to a sensitivity of chimps towards attention as an overarching notion that can be instantiated in different ways.[2]

Provoking Attention Contact

A study I conducted with the specific aim of assessing chimpanzees' understanding of Attention contact supports these conclusions (Gómez, Teixidor, and Laá, 1996).

---

[2] It is difficult, however, to try to draw any firm conclusions from Povinelli and Eddy's experiments, because they present a number of methodological problems: extensive previous training of the chimps; artificiality of the request gesture, which is not addressed directly to the target; lack of a record of whether the chimps were or not looking at the human before making a request; etc. (See Gómez, 2004.)

Chimpanzees were confronted with a single human who in normal trials would be paying attention to them and not avoiding eye contact if the chimps looked at her eyes. She would bring a piece of food at the beginning of each trial and place it on a platform before starting to attend to the chimpanzee. In normal trials (of attentive human) we recorded whether the chimps looked at the eyes of the human when they requested the food. The results showed that they did so only in about half of the trials. The human always gave them the food when they requested it, independently of whether they had or had not made eye contact.

The experimental trials consisted of trials in which the human was inattentive for one of the following reasons: her eyes were closed, she was looking to one side, she was looking over the chimp's head, she was sitting with her back to the chimp, or she was looking at the food. The measure we took was not whether the chimps made a request to the inattentive human. We knew from the first phase that chimps do not always check the attention of the human before making a request: they could be simply taking their attention for granted (after all, the human has just walked with the food and sat in front of them). Our measure—based upon previous observations of spontaneous behaviours in gorillas and chimpanzees—was whether the chimps would or would not engage in any kind of *attention-getting* behaviour before repeating their request (if they had made one). Our rationale was that, if chimps understood the role of Attention contact as a causal link in interaction, they would seek to establish it when it was missing.

To make sure that any attention-getting behaviour was caused by the absence of Attention contact and not by the lack of response from the inattentive human, we introduced control trials in which the human was fully attentive but did not respond for 5 seconds. The prediction was that in these trials the chimpanzee would not use attention-getting behaviours, but merely repeat the request after checking that the human was attentive (a longer interval was not used, because a sustained failure to respond to repeated gestures could give rise either to an interpretation of inattention or to a variation in the requesting means that could be misinterpreted as attention getting).[3]

Three of the six chimpanzees we tested displayed attention-getting behaviours (e.g. touching, pulling the human, throwing straw) in all the inattentive conditions. In the control condition (no response for 5 seconds while attending), they merely repeated their request showing no signs of attention-getting procedures. Interestingly, these chimps appeared to interpret the condition in which the human was looking at the target as one more case of inattention. This underlines the importance that chimpanzees attach to Attention contact as a factor on its own, different from Attention following.

---

[3] This is probably what happened in a study by Theall and Povinelli (1999), vaguely inspired by our own, in which they instructed humans to wait for 20 seconds without reacting.

The other three chimpanzees did not show attention-getting behaviours in the inattentive trials. These three chimpanzees were those with less experience of humans in their early years. This could hint at some sort of enculturation effect (Tomasello, 1999), or simply the role of experience in developing representations of other subjects' attention.

In sum, available evidence suggests that chimpanzees can not only detect attention contact but also actively provoke it in a strategic way.

Associations and Understanding

One question that inevitably comes to mind, especially when there is evidence of experience playing a role in the development of an ability, is to what extent apes' and young infants' use of attention contact relies upon simple associative learning; i.e. they have learned that making eye contact makes other people more likely to give them food or toys.

Against this 'simple association' interpretation speak the following facts. First, in our longitudinal study of gorilla gestural development, we found that initially our subject used gestures without eye contact for a few months, getting about 50 per cent of her requests granted. The emergence of gesture/eye contact combinations did not have any impact whatsoever on the probability of getting a reward, which remained at about 50 per cent of all requests. Eye contact, however, did have an effect upon the kind of negative response given by the human: explicit refusals, instead of simple failures to respond (Gómez, 1992). For one thing, an explicit refusal (e.g. saying 'No, I cannot give you my pen' while looking at the gorilla and withholding the pen) may have the effect of showing that the lack of success is not due to a failure to convey your request, but to the unwillingness of the human to grant it (in whatever way a gorilla understands this; see Bruner *et al.*, 1982 for an analysis of the complexities of requesting behaviours in human children).

Secondly, gorillas and chimpanzees actively seek and provoke attention contact (or, in other situations, they actively avoid it (De Waal, 1982)). Our experiment with chimpanzees demonstrated that the successful ones not only refrain from making a request when someone is not attending, but also actively establish the missing attention contact.

These facts are consistent with an interpretation that apes may be representing Attention contact as a causal link that connects their behaviour with the behaviour of others.

Understanding Attention-Following

The studies I have just analysed support the idea that apes have an understanding of what I have called the Attention contact component of JA: a format of second-person intentionality specially useful in communicative contexts. What about the third-person component of JA: the one that implies attention-following, the understanding that another's attention can be about targets in the world other than oneself?

Numerous observations suggest that attention-following is a frequent spontaneous behaviour in apes and other primates (see Chapter 3). The doubt is whether this attention-following is just a limited reflex-like reaction, as suggested by Povinelli (1996), or is supported by intentional representations of the kind $(A > X)$, which establish a link between the subject and a target. A recent study by Tomasello *et al.* (1999) suggests that chimps appear to interpret others' gaze as being about targets, because they will actively seek such a target in the area where the person is looking, but not beyond barriers that would block the other's view. Furthermore, Hare *et al.* (2000) have found that chimps appear to take into account whether other chimps can or cannot perceive a target (a piece of food) before deciding to go for it themselves. In their innovative study they confronted dominant and subordinated chimps; the prediction was that subordinate chimps would refrain from trying to get food that could have been detected by the dominant but not food that could not be seen by him. They found that this was the case. Chimps acted as if they could represent not only actual connections between gaze and targets, but also possible ones (but see Karin-D'Arcy and Povinelli, 2002, for a criticism).

However, these clearly positive results about chimpanzees' ability to perceive gaze as directed to targets coexist with a number of paradoxical findings. When tested in an Object Choice paradigm, where they have to choose one of two inverted bowls only one of which contains food, chimps are surprisingly inept at following the 'advice' of a human who actively looks at the baited bowl (see Chapter 3 for a detailed description). They may even follow the gaze of the human to the correct bowl, but then choose at random. Call and Tomasello suggest that this may be due to an inability to understand the communicative intention of the human ('the food is in *that* bowl'). One possible explanation is that chimpanzees use their gaze-following skills only in competitive situations, rather than in these artificial co-operative settings that do not resemble their intraspecific patterns of behaviour. However, when tested with barriers and tubes such that the human who gives the attentional cue can actually see the hidden food, chimpanzees do choose the correct location. This suggests that the chimpanzees' problem in this particular task may indeed consist of combining their third-person representation of gaze directed at a target with a second-person representation of communicative intentionality. Be that as it may, this is a failure to use attention-following representations to support other behaviours. This could be a difference with human infants, who from very early appear to be capable of recruiting their attention-following skills for other tasks (e.g. learning the meanings of words; see Chapter 8).

All in all, the available data suggest that chimpanzees can compute third-person and second-person intentional relations between other subjects and targets on the basis of external behavioural cues. These findings are consistent with the original notion I advanced in 1990 of apes using a sensorimotor notion of subjects, one of whose key components is the ability to produce practical representations of attention. In the next sections, I address the issue of what is meant by a subject notion, and how different species may have different subject notions.

THE NOTION OF SUBJECT

Several authors have explored non-meta-representational ways of accounting for mentalism—for example, by using a notion of *intersubjectivity* (Trevarthen, 1979; Hobson, 1989; see Gómez, 1998b). Their idea is that subjects can co-ordinate their 'subjectivities' (i.e. their mental processes) with other creatures' subjectivities through affective and emotional processes without having to use explicit representations of these.

One problem with these approaches (including my own) is the difficulty of going beyond an intuitive characterization of notions like 'intersubjectivity' into a more precise description of the mechanisms and representations that would be responsible for this form of knowing other minds. Indeed, some authors (e.g. Trevarthen) prefer to completely dispense with the very notion of representation and knowledge (and certainly with the term 'theory of mind') in their account of intersubjectivity.

In my view, however, notions like intersubjectivity are not incompatible with the idea that young infants (and apes) form and use representations of other people as *subjects* and, therefore, as endowed with *subjective* properties. Without such representations, early intersubjective interactions, including JA, would just be behaviours supported by 'instinctive', reflex-like mechanisms, perhaps enriched by some learned associations and 'spiced up' with emotional stimuli, but not involving any real understanding and flexibility of action. On the contrary, I propose that intersubjective behaviours rest partly upon representations that capture a number of external 'subjective' properties characteristic of other subjects and integrate them with plans of action and interaction. (In this, I believe, my proposal is closer to Peter Hobson's views; Hobson, 1989, and Chapter 9.)

One way of trying to understand the nature of these 'subjective' representations is to compare them with Piaget's (1936) sensorimotor or practical notions, or, in more recent developmental literature, procedural/implicit representations (Karmiloff-Smith, 1992). In short, the idea is that, as there is a sensorimotor notion of object with associated notions of space and mechanical causality, so too there is a sensorimotor notion of subject with associated notions of social relations and social causality (Gómez, 1990).

A sensorimotor notion of subject consists of a network of perception–action schemas that are applied to a certain class of entities characterized by 'subjective' properties like being animate (self-propelling), intentional (target-directed), and expressive (showing emotions). A fundamental component of any subject notion is attention—the state of being oriented to potential targets of action. Unlike other mental states, like belief or knowledge, attention can be (and typically is) displayed overtly in characteristic patterns of behaviour. This opens up the possibility of developing a practical notion of attention by representing the invariants present in external expressions of attention (eye, head, body orientations, and their accompanying facial/bodily expressions). One of these invariants is the presence of environmental targets 'at the other end' of the attentive behaviours displayed by primates. Primates may possess some innate priming for detecting 'directionality' in faces, i.e. a tendency to look in the direction to which the face is oriented (third-person orientation) when it is not looking directly at themselves (second-person orientation) (see Farroni *et al.*, 2002; Myowa-Yamakoshi and Tomonaga, 2002). This could act as a spring-board for building representations of others as attending to targets (A > X) or to oneself (A >< B).

These attentional representations would undoubtedly be part of a wider network in which the subsequent actions of subjects upon the targets of their attention (approach, grasp, avoidance, etc.) and their perceived and experienced emotions (Hobson, 1989) would also be represented. In this network of practical representations, attentional behaviours would be understood as a causal link connecting subjects with other subjects and objects, rather than as an index of internal mental states that are the actual cause behind the expressions and the actions, as a meta-representational theory of mind would have it. In the same way that apes seem to understand—in a practical or sensorimotor way—that when using a stick to retrieve an object they must establish physical contact between the tool and the object, they also understand—in a similarly practical or sensorimotor way—that to exert an influence upon other organisms, they must first establish 'attention contact' with them, or that, in order for an organism to act upon a target, an attentional link must first be established between the organism and the target.

Are these sensorimotor representations of attention mentalistic? To some extent the answer to this question is arbitrary. We could decide to limit the term 'mentalistic' to notions of mental states as internal, unobservable processes that cause their external manifestations but remain detachable from them (e.g. Povinelli, 2000). However, I argue that representations of attention (and other mental states like emotions and intentions) as external states can indeed be mentalistic.

The Evolution of Aboutness

Representing someone attending to X goes beyond representation of a behaviour and an object, to that of a *relationship* between the behaving organism and a target.

To do so, we need not invoke an internal, invisible representation of the object inside the organism, to which the latter is attached by means of an internal, invisible link (a propositional attitude); rather, the relationship of 'attending' can be *perceived* between the actual organism and the actual target True, this relationship itself is not visible (not present), but is a way in which subjects *re-present* the available information. The visual system of primates and other animals is known to go beyond the information given in many other areas: for example, in visual illusions or the perception of occluded figures as complete figures (Fujita, 2001).

Now, the ability to represent subjects and objects as connected by attentional behaviours captures a fundamental property of the mental—*aboutness*. An organism's behaviour is represented as being *about* a target. In some traditions, aboutness is the trademark of intentionality and mentalism (Lycan, 1999). Do we imagine this aboutness as something that occurs inside the organism? Or do we rather perceive and represent it as a particular Gestalt configuration that occurs *between* subjects and objects?

The evolutionary history of primates can be understood as a trend towards developing explicit displays of the aboutness of their behaviour. Primates are characterized, among other features, by having evolved the most complex faces of the animal kingdom (Huber, 1931). Primate faces are the result of an extraordinary combination of features, among them a frontal convergence of the eyes and a differentiation of facial musculature that allow them to produce an extraordinary variety of facial expressions of emotions (this is specially true of the ape lineage to which humans belong; see Gómez, 2004). This remarkable combination allows them to express a variety of emotions at the same time as they express the target of these. The evolution of these systems of communication and interaction was probably accompanied by evolution of ways of representing others as *being about* particular targets by using the rich visible information provided by primate faces and bodies.

There is no doubt that humans have evolved more elaborate ways of representing the intentionality that emanates from primate bodies, among them metarepresentational theories of mind. However, the emergence of these new forms of mentalism may have occurred in the context of an already sophisticated system of representing others' behaviour that could be fairly considered to be mentalistic, in that it uses as a corner-stone the representation of aboutness.

Evolving Different Notions of Subjects

A key aspect of my proposal is that the subject notions of human infants and apes are different. Probably further differences among primate species can be found, but I will concentrate here on the comparison of apes and children in relation to Joint Attention behaviours.

An interesting possibility is that the JA systems of apes and humans may emphasize different aspects of the social world. For example, as we have seen, gorillas and chimpanzees reared in interaction with humans use 'contact gestures' to request actions from others (e.g. taking the hand of someone towards an object). Contact gestures are also occasionally used by normally developing children, and apes also use distal gestures like extending their hands; however, in hand-reared apes, contact gestures appear to play a more central role in regulating interaction than in typically developing children (although a proper quantitative comparison remains to be made). One possible explanation is that actions may be at the core of the apes' sensorimotor representation of social events. The referential systems that apes develop to interact with humans may revolve around schemas of *actions upon objects*, whereas their schemas of *attention upon objects* remain subordinated to the former.

A radical interpretation would be that, although apes check attention contact, they do not combine this attention-checking with attention-following in requesting situations; i.e. once her attention is secured, they would exclusively seek to direct the *actions* of the person upon the target without caring about her attention. The attention-following skills of primates would remain confined to the domain of competitive interactions (Hare, 2001), in both the productive and the comprehension modalities (remember chimpanzees' difficulties in using gaze to detect hidden targets). However, the flexibility exhibited by some apes in orchestrating their requests, and their use of gaze alternation between the target and the addressee, speak in favour not of an absence, but of a subordinated role, of third-person representations of attention in these co-operative situations.

Be that as it may, the primary aim of the communicative gestures used by anthropoids does not appear to be to direct the *attention* of others upon a target, but rather to direct their *action* upon the target. Acting on the attention of the other person is a means of getting him to act in the way they want. This is not incompatible with attributing to apes an understanding of the role of attention in communication, both attention contact (in recruiting her help) and attention-following (in directing her to the target).

This would also explain why apes do not normally produce proto-declarative gestures, whose goal appears to be concentrated on the attentional/expressive reaction of a subject, not on an executive response.

There can be other differences in the way in which apes and young humans represent others as subjects of attention. For example, they may have a different understanding of the relation between the states of seeing and attention. They may not understand the difference between them, or their understanding of the conditions that make seeing possible may be different (e.g. they may not understand the precise role of the eyes in granting access to visual information, as suggested by Call and Tomasello in Chapter 3).

Be that as it may, apes display an ability for engaging in joint attention that appears to rest upon the use of practical representations of attention that are at the same time similar and different from the joint attention system of humans. One might be tempted to enter into a discussion of whether these differences make of the apes' system a less 'genuine' JA. The following analogy may be useful in this context. Are chimpanzees who occasionally walk bipedally engaging in *genuine* bipedal walking? Their bipedal excursions are occasional, relatively inefficient, and subserved by an underlying mechanical dynamics that is not exactly like that of humans. However, it would seem extremely arbitrary to say that they are not really 'walking on their feet'. Apes can walk bipedally, even if humans were the ones who developed further adaptations that made of bipedalism a fundamental way of life; the structures that make bipedalism possible in apes are perhaps primarily selected and used for slightly different locomotor and postural behaviours (e.g. there is the hypothesis that some of the adaptations that led to human ground bipedalism may have emerged for assisted arboreal bipedalism, a paramount example of which is provided by current orangutans: Crompton, 2000), but locomotion and posture remain the main purposes, and a substantial part of the underlying mechanical apparatus and dynamic operations are shared, even if others are not, and perhaps the whole system works slightly differently.

Something similar may occur with JA: the scope of JA in non-humans is more limited than in humans. Some of its underlying mechanics and mental operations may be different, and, specially in adult humans, JA may be working in collaboration with a number of other systems (e.g. language, meta-representation) not available to apes. But apes still show genuine JA, in the sense that both some of the functions and part of the machinery may be common or closely related.

In summary, I have argued that an understanding of attention and other mental states can be achieved through representations based upon their external manifestations, and that these representations could be considered as mentalistic in the sense that they capture at least one of the fundamental properties of the mind—aboutness. However, the ways in which these representations are organized in apes and humans may differ. We turn now to what happens when JA mechanisms fail in humans.

JOINT ATTENTION IN AUTISM

Deficits in joint attention are one of the earliest and most characteristic features of autism (Mundy *et al.*, 1993). Children with autism typically do not spontaneously follow the gaze of other people. This might appear to indicate that their gaze-following skills are damaged. However, surprisingly many children with autism who do not engage in spontaneous gaze-following are perfectly able to answer the question 'Where is A looking at?' by looking in the same direction and finding the target of A's attention (Leekam *et al.*, 1997; see also Chapter 10). It is the *spontaneity* of the gaze-following response that typically appears to be altered in autism.

As to the attention contact component of Joint Attention, there is also evidence that children with autism typically fail to look at the eyes of other people in ambiguous situations (Charman, 2003), although, contrary to early clinical impressions, they do not appear to avoid eye contact and can readily show it in face-to-face interactions involving physical games, such as tickling.

In relation to their ability to use JA in communication, as already mentioned, children with autism are typically unable to produce proto-declarative gestures, but they may produce proto-imperatives, sometimes with contact gestures similar to those we have discussed for apes (Baron-Cohen, 1989; Mundy *et al.*, 1993). However, early descriptions of proto-imperative gestures in autism did not take into account whether the gestures were or were not accompanied by attention-checking behaviours (Gómez *et al.*, 1993).

In a simple test modelled after the gorilla study reported above, Phillips *et al.* (1995) allowed young children with autism to request an out-of-reach target from a person, and recorded if they looked at the eyes of the person at any point. To enhance the probability of eliciting attention-checking behaviours, the experimenters did not immediately answer the requests of the children. The result was that 60 per cent of the children with autism made their requests without seeking to make eye contact with the person at any point. This difference was significant when compared to the use of eye contact by normal and mentally retarded children in the same situation. However, contrary to the clinical impression, children with autism did not show a significant tendency to use more contact gestures than children with other learning difficulties.

In a pilot study using the same 'inattentive states' design as in Gómez *et al.*'s (1996) study with chimpanzees discussed in the previous section, we found that young children with autism typically ignored the attentional state of the person, except in the case of 'being with the back to them', in which some of the children showed some sensitivity by refraining from making requests when the human had his back to them (Gómez and Lopez, 1996). However, even in this condition there was a failure to actively elicit the attention of the person. The failure to take attention into account was especially conspicuous in those children with autism whose favourite requesting technique involved taking the hand of the person to the desired object. These children never engaged in procedures of hand 'pre-request' like those I found in gorillas (Gómez, 1992).

Phillips *et al.* (1992) reported that normal toddlers and mentally retarded children, when challenged with an unexpected action like suddenly withdrawing an object that was being handed to them, reacted by making instant eye contact with the person who was teasing them. However, most children with autism failed to do so. When we tried this with the same chimpanzees who participated in our study about understanding inattention, all of them instantly looked at the eyes of the person (Gómez, Teixidor, and Laá, unpublished data).

Autism, Apes, and Children

As mentioned at the beginning of this paper, in a superficial analysis children with autism and hand-reared apes may appear to share some remarkable peculiarities in their JA behaviours (absence of proto-declaratives and use of contact gestures). However, when one considers the whole picture, the differences outnumber the similarities. If we define proto-imperative communication as requiring a co-ordination of JA and gestures, then a majority of children with autism are not making full-fledged requests, because they fail to engage and monitor the attention of people. That component of JA that I have called 'Attention contact' appears to be damaged or not recruited for communication about external targets. Furthermore, as mentioned before, many autistic children have difficulty with spontaneous attention-following, whereas this behaviour has been consistently reported in anthropoid apes and monkeys (see Chapter 3). Finally, many children with autism use pointing gestures (perhaps not co-ordinated with attention-checking) (Baron-Cohen, 1989), whereas pointing, at least in its 'extended index finger' morphology, is a rare behaviour in apes.

It is difficult, however, to draw any firm conclusions about autism and JA, as there seem to be important individual differences. For example, 40 per cent of the children in Phillips *et al.*'s (1995) study did show some attention-checking during requests. Certainly our measure was very simple—a single instance of eye contact would count as using JA—and perhaps a more detailed analysis of their JA patterns would reveal differences from typical children. On the other hand, different subgroups of children with autism have different degrees of JA skills (Leekam and Moore, 2001; Chapter 10; Charman, 2003).[4]

Be that as it may, this pattern of results would not be compatible with a simplistic view of children with autism being like apes in terms of their JA abilities, or there being a monolithic JA ability that one either has or has not got. The distinction between Attention contact and Attention-following components of JA may help us understand the autistic deficit. It is conceivable that children with autism have special problems activating representations of Attention contact even when they engage in eye contact. For example, in Phillips *et al.*'s (1995) study the experimenter reported a subjective impression that those children with autism who made eye contact were taking information from her but not giving

---

[4] A similar note of caution could be made in relation to apes. Individual differences are known to be important among them, especially when it comes to their performance in human-like tasks. Not all apes engage systematically in attention contact behaviours with humans in relation to external targets (Gómez *et al.*, 1996).

her information, in contrast with normal and mentally retarded children (Phillips, personal communication). One possibility is that the children with autism were not activating a second-person representation [(A <> B)], but just checking the direction of gaze of the person [A > (B > X)], perhaps to check if she was or was not starting to respond. They might have learned that the orientation of people is a good predictor of their imminent action. If this were the case, then their eye contact could have been purely accidental and would not imply Attention contact. Moreover, the failure to elicit spontaneous gaze-following in autism despite evidence of an intact geometric mechanism may be due to a failure of the Attention contact component to trigger Attention-following.

In summary, some aspects of the typical JA deficits detected in children with autism could be understood in terms of the distinction between Attention-following and Attention contact mechanisms. Children with autism may have special problems with Attention contact and its articulation for regulating interaction with others even in merely requesting contexts. In this respect, the autism impairment would affect not so much meta-representational mechanisms as some of the components of their practical notion of subjects (see Hobson, 1989, and Chapter 9 for a similar approach).

CONCLUSIONS

I started this paper by proposing that JA can be achieved with representations that are not mentalistic in the sense of meta-representational, but none the less capture an essential component of mental states: intentionality or aboutness. I dubbed these representations sensorimotor to emphasize their first-order nature. I also proposed that these representations encode two different kinds of intentionality: a third-person one that in JA is expressed as Attention-following and a second-person intentionality that is best described as Attention contact.

The sensorimotor nature of these representations establishes some limitations on the sorts of communication and JA that can be achieved with them, but at the same time it confers on them the possibility of doing things that meta-representations would be unable to do, most notably computing the state of Attention contact and its derivatives—ostension and mutual knowledge: Sperber and Wilson, 1986—an impossible task for a meta-representational system, but an easy one for a mechanism that represents attention as an external mental state (Gómez, 1994).

In apes we may find a rudimentary version of what the combination of these two kinds of JA representations can achieve: a primitive, but genuine, sort of referential communication. In normal human infants of 12 to 18 months of age we find an evolutionarily different version, in which action coding and attention coding are well separated, and the latter can be pursued as an end in itself.

Moreover, a specialized means for distal reference—pointing—has been provided by evolution. In children with autism, we find a disturbance of this system, whose characterization is as yet incomplete. In achieving a more complete understanding of the autistic JA deficit, the distinction between second-person and third-person representations may be useful, as well as the notion of sensorimotor representations of subjects, which are prior to and independent of meta-representational understanding.

I have explored some insights about JA derived from this approach: for example, how attention can be understood not as the mentalistic, inner counterpart of seeing or looking, but as an autonomous mental state that can be attributed independently of the attribution of seeing. In our everyday life as adult human beings, these sensorimotor representations of subjects work in close interaction with meta-representations (which sometimes may provoke the illusion that we are using only the latter), but the most basic functions of JA may be performed by sensorimotor representations of others as 'subjects'. Moreover, although humans may have evolved more complex forms of mentalism (e.g. the ability to compute meta-representations), these not only coexist with more basic forms of social cognition, but the latter already imply a mentalistic way of representing the world. The mind shows up in the intentional texture of behaviour, and this is especially evident in the domain of Joint Attention.

REFERENCES

BARD, K. A. (1990), ' "Social tool use" by free-ranging orangutans: a piagetian and developmental perspective on the manipulation of an animate object', in S. T. Parker, and K. R. Gibson, (eds.), *'Language' and Intelligence in Monkeys and Apes: Comparative Developmental Perspectives*. Cambridge, Mass.: Cambridge University Press, 356–78.

BARON-COHEN, S. (1989), 'Perceptual role taking and protodeclarative pointing in autism', *British Journal of Developmental Psychology*, 7: 113–27.

BATES, E., CAMAIONI, L., and VOLTERRA, V. (1975), 'The acquisition of performatives prior to speech', *Merrill–Palmer Quarterly*, 21: 205–26.

BRUNER, J. S. (1983), *Child's Talk: Learning to Use Language*. Oxford: Oxford University Press.

—— ROY, C., and RATNER, N. (1982), 'The beginnings of request', in K. E. Nelson (ed.), *Children's Language*, iii. Hillsdale, NJ: Lawrence Erlbaum Associates, 91–138.

BUTTERWORTH, G. (1991), 'The ontogeny and phylogeny of joint visual attention', in A. Whiten (eds.), *Natural Theories of Mind*. Oxford: Blackwell, 223–32.

CHARMAN, T. (2003), 'Why is joint attention a pivotal skill in autism?', *Philosophical Transactions of the Royal Society, Biological Sciences*, 358: 315–24.

CROMPTON, R. (2001), 'The evolution of bipedalism', *School of Psychology Seminar Series, University of St Andrews*.

FARRONI, T., CSIBRA, G., SIMION, F., and JOHNSON, M. H. (2002), 'Eye contact detection in humans from birth', *Proceedings of the National Academy of Sciences*, 99: 9602–5.

FUJITA, K. (2001), 'What you see is different from what I see: species differences in visual perception', in T. Matsuzawa (ed.), *Primate Origins of Human Cognition and Behavior.* Berlin: Springer, 29–54.

GÓMEZ, J. C. (1990), 'The emergence of intentional communication as a problem-solving strategy in the gorilla', in S. T. Parker and K. R. Gibson (eds.), *'Language' and Intelligence in Monkeys and Apes: Comparative Developmental Perspectives.* Cambridge, Mass.: Cambridge University Press, 333–55.

—— (1991), 'Visual behavior as a window for reading the minds of others in primates', in A. Whiten (ed.), *Natural Theories of Mind.* Oxford: Blackwell, 195–207.

—— (1992), 'El desarrollo de la comunicación intencional en el gorila', (Ph.D. dissertation, Universidad Autónoma de Madrid).

—— (1994), 'Mutual awareness in primate communication: a Gricean approach', in S. T. Parker, M. Boccia, and R. Mitchel (eds.), *Self-Recognition and Awareness in Apes, Monkeys and Children.* Cambridge, Mass.: Cambridge University Press, 61–80.

—— (1996a), 'Second-person intentional relations and the evolution of social understanding', *Behavioral and Brain Sciences*, 19 (1): 129–30.

—— (1996b), 'Ostensive behavior in the great apes: the role of eye contact', in A. Russon, S. Parker, and K. Bard (eds.), *Reaching into Thought: The Minds of the Great Apes.* Cambridge, Mass.: Cambridge University Press, 131–51.

—— (1998a), 'Some thoughts about the evolution of LADs, with special reference to SAM and TOM', in P. Carruthers and J. Boucher (eds.), *Language and Thought: Interdisciplinary Themes.* Cambridge, Mass.: Cambridge University Press, 76–93.

—— (1998b), 'Do concepts of intersubjectivity apply to non-human primates?', in S. Braten (eds.), *Intersubjective Communication and Emotion in Ontogeny.* Cambridge: Cambridge University Press, 245–59.

—— (2004), *Apes, Monkeys, Children, and the Growth of Mind.* Cambridge, Mass.: Harvard University Press.

—— and LÓPEZ, B. (1996), *Applications of the Theory of Mind Approach to Assessment and Intervention of Children with Autism.* Fifth International Congress Autisme-Europe: Hope is not a dream, Barcelona, 3–5 May 1996.

—— SARRIÁ, E., and TAMARIT, J. (1993), 'The comparative study of early communication and theories of mind: ontogeny, phylogeny and pathology', in S. Baron-Cohen, H. Tager-Flusberg, and D. Cohen, (eds.), *Understanding Other Minds: Perspectives from Autism.* Oxford: Oxford University Press, 397–426.

—— TEIXIDOR, P., and LAÁ, V. (1996), 'Understanding the referential and ostensive functions of joint visual attention in young chimpanzees'. Paper presented at BPS Developmental Psychology Section Annual Conference, Oxford, 11–13 September 1996.

HARE, B. (2001), 'Can competitive paradigms increase the validity of experiments on primate social cognition?', *Animal Cognition*, 4: 269–80.

—— CALL, J., AGNETTA, B., and TOMASELLO, M. (2000), 'Chimpanzees know what conspecifics do and do not see', *Animal Behaviour*, 59: 771–85.

HOBSON, P. (1989), 'On sharing experiences', *Development and Psychopathology*, 1: 197–203.

HUBER, E. (1931), *Evolution of Facial Musculature and Facial Expression.* Baltimore: Johns Hopkins University Press.

KARIN-D'ARCY, M. R., and POVINELLI, D. J. (2002), 'Do chimpanzees know what each other see? A closer look', *International Journal of Comparative Psychology*, 15: 21–54.

KARMILOFF-SMITH, A. (1992), *Beyond Modularity: A Developmental Perspective on Cognitive Science*. Cambridge, Mass.: MIT Press.

KÖHLER, W. (1921). *Intelligenzprüfungen an Menschenaffen*. Berlin: Springer.

LANGTON, S. R. H., WATT, R. J., and BRUCE, V. (2000), 'Do the eyes have it? Cues to the direction of social attention', *Trends in Cognitive Sciences*, 4: 50–9.

LEAVENS, D., and HOPKINS, W. (1998), 'Intentional communication by chimpanzees: a cross-sectional study of the use of referential gestures', *Developmental Psychology*, 34: 813–22.

LEEKAM, S., and MOORE, C. (2001), 'The development of attention and joint attention in children with autism', in T. Charman, J. Burack, N. Yirimaya, and P. R. Zelazo (eds.), *Development and Autism: Perspectives from Theory and Research*. Mahwah, NJ: Lawrence Erlbaum Associates, 105–29.

—— BARON-COHEN, S., PERRETT, D., MILDERS, M., and BROWN, S. (1997), 'Eye-direction detection: a dissociation between geometric and joint attention skills in autism', *British Journal of Developmental Psychology*, 15 (1): 77–95.

LESLIE, A. M., and HAPPÉ, F. (1989), 'Autism and ostensive communication: the relevance of metarepresentation', *Development and Psychopathology*, 1: 205–12.

LYCAN, W. (1999), 'Intentionality', in R. Wilson and F. Keil (eds.), *The MIT Encyclopedia of the Cognitive Sciences*. Cambridge, Mass.: MIT Press, 413–15.

MENZEL, E. W. (1973), 'Leadership and communication in young chimpanzees', in E. W. Menzel (ed.), *Precultural Primate Behavior*. Basel: Karger, 192–225.

MUNDY, P., SIGMAN, M., and KASARI, C. (1993), 'Theory of mind and joint attention deficits in autism', in S., Baron-Cohen, H. Tager-Flusberg, and D. Cohen (eds.), *Understanding Other Minds: Perspectives from Autism*. Oxford: Oxford University Press, 181–203.

MYOWA-YAMAKOSHI, M., and TOMONAGA, M. (2001), 'Perceiving eye-gaze in an infant Gibbon (Hylobate agilis)', *Psychologia*, 44: 24–30.

PHILLIPS, W., BARON-COHEN, S., and RUTTER, M. (1992), 'The role of eye-contact in goal-detection: evidence from normal toddlers and children with autism or mental handicap', *Development and Psychopathology*, 4: 375–84.

—— GÓMEZ, J. C., BARON-COHEN, S., LAÁ, M. V., and RIVIÈRE, A. (1995), 'Treating people as objects, agents or "subjects": how young children with and without autism make requests', *Journal of Child Psychology and Psychiatry*, 36: 1383–98.

PIAGET, J. (1936), *La Naissance de l'intelligence chez l'enfant*. Neuchâtel: Delachaux et Niestlée.

POVINELLI, D. J. (1996), 'Chimpanzee theory of mind? The long road to strong inference', in P. Carruthers and P. K. Smith (eds.), *Theories of Theories of Mind*. Cambridge: Cambridge University Press, 293–329.

—— (2000), *Folk Physics for Apes*. Oxford: Oxford University Press.

—— and EDDY, T. J. (1996a), 'What young chimpanzees know about seeing', *Monographs of the Society for Research in Child Development*, 61 (3): 1–190.

—— —— (1996b), 'Factors influencing young chimpanzees' (*Pan troglodytes*) recognition of attention', *Journal of Comparative Psychology*, 110 (4): 336–45.

SMITH, N. V. (1982) (ed.), *Mutual Knowledge*. London: Academic Press.

SPERBER, D., and WILSON, D. (1986), *Relevance: Communication and Cognition*. Cambridge, Mass.: Harvard University Press.

THEALL, L. A., and POVINELLI, D. J. (1999), 'Do chimpanzees tailor their gestural signals to fit the attentional states of others?', *Animal Cognition*, 2: 207–14.

TOMASELLO, M. (1999), *The Cultural Origins of Human Cognition*. Cambridge, Mass.: Harvard University Press.

—— HARE, B., and AGNETTA, B. (1999), 'Chimpanzees follow gaze direction geometrically', *Animal Behaviour*, 58: 769–77.

TREVARTHEN, C. (1979), 'Communication and cooperation in early infancy', in M. Bullowa, (ed.), *Before Speech: The Beginnings of Human Communication*. Cambridge: Cambridge University Press, 321–47.

VYGOTSKY, L. (1930), 'Orudie i znak [Tool and sign in the development of the child]', in R. W. Rieber (ed.), *The Collected Works of L. S. Vygotsky, vi: Scientific Legacy*. New York: Kluwer/Plenum, 1–68.

WAAL, F. DE (1982), *Chimpanzee Politics: Power and Sex Among Apes*. London: Jonathan Cape.

WHITEN, A., and BYRNE, R. W. (1988), 'Tactical deception in primates', *Behavioral and Brain Sciences*, 11: 233–73.

5

Before the 'Third Element': Understanding Attention to Self

Vasudevi Reddy

Turn away thine eyes from me,
For they have overcome me

Song of Solomon, 6: 5

MUTUAL ATTENTION, JOINT ATTENTION, AND THE UNDERSTANDING OF ATTENTION

The perception of another person's attention upon oneself can lead to being overwhelmed by emotion: with love as in the Song of Solomon, or, in other contexts, with shame, sympathy, hate, adoration, anger, amusement, or pain. Gaze, although providing a particularly vivid example, is not the only medium for conveying attention—the touch or voice of another person can be equally powerful.

What does it take to experience these psychological phenomena in the perception of others' attention? What does it take to perceive the directedness of attention in others—the 'psychological spotlight', as Baldwin and Moses (1994) put it? When does it develop? Can young infants perceive it? In art, images abound of mothers and young infants gazing intently into each others' eyes, much as Solomon and his beloved presumably did. Do infants understand the directedness of the mother's attention, its focus and its emotional tone?

Current approaches to the development of the understanding of attention generally see it as synonymous with the achievement of 'joint attention', a term which has come to mean triadic attentional engagement. That is, understanding the attention of another person is believed to begin with the achievement of the (conscious) joining of two people's attention upon a 'third' element or target. Phenomena of mutual attention, where two organisms attend directly to each other without another target or topic of attention, are generally excluded from the study of the development of the understanding of attention. Why is this? After all, there is no doubt that even when there is no other topic or target of attention two people can attend to each other, and each can experience the other's attention. One might even argue that this is the most direct sharing of attention and the most powerful experience of others' attention that one can have. How has psychology reached a point where the most direct attentional engagements between organisms are disregarded when it comes to evidence of the understanding of attention?

This chapter attempts to explore some of the reasons for this neglect of mutual attention, and presents three reasons for attempting to redress it. An alternative look at the empirical evidence through the first year of infancy suggests that the developmental story is not one of the belated discovery of attention in others somewhere in infancy. Not only is the actual emergence of the object or 'third element' a gradual rather than a revolutionary achievement (as others such as Adamson and Bakeman, 1991; Bakeman and Adamson, 1984; and Bates *et al.*, 1976, have shown), but this achievement is not a signal of the beginning of the awareness of attention. I argue that the awareness of attention is not only already present in mutual attention, but that the experience of *being* the object of another's attention in mutual attention is vital for any further understanding of the nature and scope of attentionality.

THE CURRENT DISREGARD OF MUTUAL ATTENTION

There are many reasons for the current disregard of mutual attention as evidence of attention-understanding. For a start, one could argue that since, in mutual attention, the target of attention is actually different for each person—i.e. each is looking at the *other*—the attention cannot be said to be joint, and therefore relevant to an awareness of attention. As Bruner suggested, if the infant seeks or follows a joint focus of attention on the same target, it suggests a knowledge that what is in her awareness is also in the other's awareness, a 'belief' that she is experiencing the same world as others are (Bruner and Sherwood, 1983). However, if we are interested in the infant's understanding of others' attention, then it is not the joint focus upon a common target (i.e. the awareness of the sameness of the experience) that is crucial, but rather the awareness of the attention itself, even without the existence of a common target. As indicated earlier, the awareness of attention to the self may be the most direct and powerful experience of attention that is possible. While the study of mutual attention does not tell us anything about the infant's awareness of the other's awareness of the outside world, it *could* tell us about the infant's awareness of the other's awareness of the infant.

There may be methodological reasons for being cautious about accepting mutual attention as evidence of the understanding of attention. As Bakeman and Adamson (1984) put it, although the infant is engaged with the attention of others from the early months, this engagement is essentially expressive. There appears to be little evidence of the infant seeking to control or direct others' attention until near the end of the first year. But, as will be shown later, this lack of evidence may be more apparent than real; if one accepts the *self* as a possible target of others' attention, then evidence of directing and controlling others' attention is, in fact, available. In dyadic interactions, however, infant attention may appear to be 'confined to the process of interaction itself' (Bakeman and Adamson, 1984, p. 1278) rather than to attention *per se*. In a related vein, other authors often dismiss responses to mutual attention as 'biological' or 'social' or 'emotional' reactions, implying that social and emotional processes are separable from awareness, and that reacting emotionally or socially is separate from awareness of the attention being reacted to. This is an argument that we cannot separate infants' attention to the (other's) *attention* from their attention to the *interaction* itself. On the face of it, this argument seems logical. If you wish to put the infant's understanding of attention *per se* under a microscope, you need to separate out this feature from the myriad 'confounding' features that accompany it (e.g. emotion, interaction, warmth, dynamic actions, etc.), and you might do this a little more easily in triadic engagements. The argument raises questions, however, of whether separating attention from everything else is possible even in triadic situations (and there is reason to believe that it is not), and of whether an attempt to de-contextualize attention is the best way of studying the infant's understanding of attention. Quite apart from such questions, though, the point to be made here is that this argument is for methodological caution in interpreting mutual attention; it is not a reason for *discounting* mutual attentional phenomena altogether.

But the current exclusion of mutual attention is not based on methodological caution alone. It is not only a methodological criterion but very much an article of theoretical faith that until triadic attentional engagement is achieved in development, attention *cannot* be understood by the infant. It is now believed that it is *only* when the infant can understand the elsewhere-directedness of others' attention that he or she can be said to understand attention. Theories of 'mind-knowledge' argue that triadic attentional engagements and the onset of reference, occurring at the very earliest at the end of the first year, are caused by an underlying conceptual change in the understanding of people (e.g. Tomasello, 1995). So these accounts make it a theoretical, not a methodological, requirement that mutual attention not be considered a suitable datum for the understanding of attention.

This theoretical commitment to triadic attentional engagement is probably an agenda (and some assumptions) from a historical legacy. As part of the quest for the roots of skills (believed to be uniquely human), such as language, reference, and symbolism, interest settled on the emergence of the independent 'object' as the key developmental milestone. Werner and Kaplan's (1963) organismic theory of the emergence of the symbolic capacity, for instance, has been enormously influential in turning modern cognitive-developmental thought towards triadic engagements. They saw early dyadic interactions (the 'primordial sharing situation') as the ground for the differentiation of the separate object in the development of reference and the symbolic capacity. Their emphasis on dyadic engagement as central to further development has been only partially adopted by developmental psychology. Their conception of the differentiation of the object (or topic of reference), however, has become very much part of mainstream theorizing today, as has their distinction between *action upon* and *contemplation about* an object or topic (also a theme in Brentano, 1874, cited in Perner, 1991). From this point on, developmental psychology has travelled down a path on which differentiating the independent object or topic has come to be seen not only as criterial for language and reference, but also as criterial for communication in general, and indeed for any kind of intersubjectivity or perception of mentality in others. Understanding attention in others, therefore, has come to be viewed as dependent on the capacity to represent another person's representation of an independent object, and mutual attention has not been seen as informative for this enterprise. Current theories seem to assume not only that an object or topic is necessary for joint attention to occur, but that it must be external to and spatially distinct from the persons involved. This assumption, as I will show, makes it actually very difficult to explain the understanding of the aboutness of attention at all.

Even if one were to accept the need for an external object (or 'third element': Bates *et al.*, 1976) as criterial in the understanding of attention, the idea of an object or topic is itself problematic. Where does an object begin and end? Is one's own foot an 'object' separate from the self? Is the movement of one's foot an object? Is one's face or one's smile an object? Is the ongoing interaction an object? When you hold another's hand, is one of the hands an object? Any answers to these questions will inevitably be tentative and contextual. However, in current research in this area the focus on infant–other–object attentionality has generally emphasized the visual modality over the haptic or auditory, and the spatial over the temporal delineation of the object. Certain forms of attentional engagement, as well as certain kinds of objects, are precluded in this approach: the self, actions by the self, decoration of the self, another person, and tactile acts or events, for instance, do not count as legitimate 'objects' for the pre-verbal engagement of attention. Avoiding this visual basis is vital: triangulation of attention in other modalities may suggest a very different developmental scheme (see Rattray, 2000), as would considering an other person as the third element (see Fivaz-Depeursinge and Corboz-Warnery, 1999), or when the third element is an ongoing event not distal from the self.

'Mutual attention' is not an unfamiliar term in the literature on attention understanding. Bruner, for instance, speaks of mutual attention as 'a harmony or "intersubjectivity"' (Bruner and Sherwood, 1983, p. 40), and refers to 'simple eye-to-eye joint attention' as different from the 'the more complex interaction entailed in sharing attentional focus on a common object' (Bruner, 1995, p. 1). He describes children's attempts to seek joint attention with others as initially being 'through direct eye contact' (p. 11) and later through resorting to topics. However, in terms of the other minds issue, he focuses little on eye-to-eye contact, choosing instead the knowledge that there is a common experience as being the critical phenomenon.

Defining sharing broadly as 'acting in concert with responsive partners', Adamson and Bakeman (Bakeman and Adamson, 1984; Adamson and Bakeman, 1991) differentiated two forms of shared attention: *mutual attention* (focused on a social partner) and *joint attention* (focused on objects). Interested principally in the development of joint involvement with objects, they suggested that brief periods of 'shared alertness' in the neonatal period (possibly led by endogenous organization for 'windows' for shared attention) allow a transformation to intricately patterned episodes of shared 'interpersonal engagement' by about 2 months. From 6 months until the end of the first year, joint object involvement shows a gradual increase in co-ordination and many opportunities for accessing the world with people. However, what does the infant understand of the other's attentionality during this or earlier periods? What do the younger infant's limited co-ordinative acts tell us about her understanding of aspects of adult attentionality? These questions are not addressed directly in the literature, or by Adamson and Bakeman, except to offer negative answers by default.

Trevarthen has been a lone voice suggesting that dyadic attention in the early months directly implies an understanding of attention and (along with Adamson and Bakeman) that triadic attentional interactions are its 'developmental heir' (Trevarthen and Hubley, 1978). The shift from dyadic to triadic interactions, which Trevarthen and Hubley were among the first to describe, involves the mother becoming 'an interesting agent, whose own motives become something of an object or topic in themselves' (Trevarthen, 1980). Whereas for many recent writers this shift is one of a new ability and a new *awareness*, Trevarthen argues that it is a shift in the infant's *interests*. Even prior to this, according to his theory, there must be an (albeit non-focused and non-reflective) awareness of mentality in order for the infant to influence action and development in dyadic engagement. However, while often used to support descriptions of early mutual engagement, this theory and these data are rarely discussed in the context of attention-understanding or early mind-knowledge.

Baron-Cohen (1995) suggests that there is a mechanism called the eye-direction detector (EDD) which functions (much like the bug detector in frogs and the hawk detector in rabbits) to detect eyes turned towards (and away from?) the self. By at least 4 months of age, he suggests, the EDD builds representations of the relation between seer and seen which presume, in the organism, both a concept of seeing and a concept of itself seeing. The extreme modularity of this theory and its assumption of conceptual skills in early infancy make it an unusual and not widely accepted contribution to the debate about mind-knowledge. It is an attempt to explain early mutual attentional phenomena in attentional terms, although it is difficult to determine whether Baron-Cohen is postulating that the 4-month-old infant understands that others are looking at her, or is merely building physicalistic links about gaze direction. None the less, Baron-Cohen, like many others, argues that the crucial module for understanding attention is SAM, a shared attention mechanism which comes into being at the end of the first year and allows triadic representations.

The research focus, then, has been on the 'third element', as Bates and her colleagues put it in 1976. Their ground-breaking study (focusing on the origins of the symbolic capacity and the emergence of language, rather than on attention and its understanding) suggested that this element begins to distance itself from the activities of the self from around 9 or 10 months of age. They suggest that infants may begin to act to obtain adult attention to themselves as a goal in itself at around the same time as they develop the ability to seek adult attention to things around them (Bates, Camaioni, and Volterra, 1976). In other words, they believed that the awareness of attention at around 9 or 10 months allows the simultaneous perception of that attention to self and to other objects. This achievement of the understanding of attention is today believed to occur at 12 months (Tomasello, 1995), at 18 months (Perner, 1991), or at 24 months (Moore, and D'Entremont, 2001), depending on the theory one chooses. Triangulation of attention is believed not only to allow us to detect the infant's awareness of attention, but to allow it to come into existence.

SOME RECENT EXPLANATIONS AND DEVELOPMENTAL TIMETABLES FOR THE UNDERSTANDING OF ATTENTION

Tomasello (1995, 1999) argues, in a manner reminiscent of Werner and Kaplan's (1963) idea of the concept of other as 'agent of contemplation', that infants engage in joint attentional interactions when they understand that people are intentional agents who choose to act in particular ways or attend to particular things. In his view, although there is a high degree of sociality evident in human infants from birth, it is not until the latter half of the first year that evidence begins to emerge that infants understand 'that other persons are psychological agents with their own interests and attention to outside entities' (Carpenter, Nagell, and Tomasello, 1998, p. 3). Two points are evident here: (1) that the understanding of intentionality is believed to precede and determine joint attentional engagements; and (2) that there is an unquestioned assumption that understanding attention must involve joint attention to 'outside entities'. Mutual or dyadic attentional engagements are considered as evidence of 'sociality' but not of understanding, implying that some 'instinctual' or 'other' basis must underpin those behaviours in contrast to the 'understanding' that underpins joint attentional behaviours. For Tomasello there is a world of difference between these two types of existence—separated by a socio-cognitive revolution at the end of the first year.

Perner (1991) argues that even triadic interactions at 9 and 12 months need not demonstrate an understanding of attention. The latter can be said to occur only when the infant can manage multiple mental representations of reality, and can imagine invisible entities such as attentional states. According to him, early triadic interactions—even that bastion of reference, proto-declarative pointing—may be underpinned by a form of conditioning—the infant realizes that the act leads to interesting reactions in others and thus repeats it. It is not until 18 months that the same actions can be underpinned by an understanding of attention.

Moore and colleagues take an alternative line. They see continuities rather than revolutions occurring in the space of the first two years. They argue that early joint attentional behaviours such as gaze-following, communicative gestures, and social referencing provide the ground for the infant to learn about people, rather than revealing any attribution of psychological (attentional) states to others. Contrary even to Tomasello's claim that such understanding begins at the end of the first year, Dunham and Dunham (1995), for example, explicitly argue that both the early dyadic reciprocating structures and triadic reciprocating structures affect development but involve no incipient understanding of the mental states of the adult partner. They argue that it is not until about 24 months that the infant attributes shared visual perceptual experiences to others. From this perspective too, early mutual or dyadic attentional engagements are 'social' engagements, evidencing infant interest in the reinforcements that obtain from engaging with other people, but not evidence of any awareness of their attentionality.

In general, then, current approaches within the field of early mind-knowledge adopt cognitive developmental explanations of the understanding of attention which make two central assumptions: (1) that attention is an invisible mental event not accessible to perception, and therefore only available to inference and conceptual deduction; (2) that knowing is a purely mental process separate from action, which, although it might provide data for the mental process, is a purely behavioural process. According to these views, the images of mothers and infants gazing into each others' eyes are invitations to romantic and unscientific interpretations of understanding on the part of the infant. It is acknowledged that others' gaze may be observed by the young infant, but as nothing more than a physical event (even if it is an 'attractive' one). Others' gaze may mean nothing to the infant in terms of the attention or psychological condition of the other; understanding of attention cannot occur until such a time as the infant or organism can imagine or deduce invisible entities, and this does not occur until much before the end of the first year.

REASONS TO DOUBT THE CURRENT DEVELOPMENTAL STORIES OF THE UNDERSTANDING OF ATTENTION

Is there any reason to doubt this developmental and metaphysical picture? I argue that there are three assumptions which are questionable in this picture: (i) assumptions regarding the nature of attention, (ii) assumptions regarding the nature of knowledge, and (iii) assumptions regarding the empirical story.

The Nature of Attention: Attention as an Invisible Mental State or as the Action of Attending?

It is a commonplace in current theories of theories of mind that attention (and mind in general) is characterized as an internal mental representation, which cannot be perceived or accessed except through other, inferential, mental representations (see e.g. Astington, 1993; Wellman, 1990; Gopnik, 1993). This metaphysical assumption of the invisibility of attention has powerful implications.

First, if attention as a psychological event has to be conceived, rather than perceived, then it can only be done after the organism can conceptualize non-visible and non-concrete entities and ideas—i.e. at a relatively intellectually advanced stage of development. Given this assumption, any evidence suggesting an understanding of attention before such a stage of cognitive advancement has to be wrong. The understanding must be of something else, not of attention. In other words, the assumption of invisibility of attention demands a developmental theory and criteria for identifying attention-understanding which rules out, as inadmissible, evidence from attentional engagements prior to the theoretically specified developmental 'stage'.

Second, it demands the drawing of a line between the mental and the behavioural aspects of attention. It requires that in order to obtain evidence that an organism is perceiving attention as a psychological event, one has to rule out the possibility that what the organism is actually doing is perceiving and responding merely to attention 'behaviour'. So, if an infant sees someone turn towards her and reacts by hiding her face, in order for us to demonstrate that the infant understands that the other is looking at her, we need first to show that the infant was not simply reacting to the turning behaviour, or to the physical appearance of the eyes, or to the length of time the eyes were turned on her, or to the shape of the eyes, etc., etc. At first, this might seem like a reasonable requirement. After all, some fish and birds react immediately to the appearance of certain kinds of eyes, even to the illusion of eyes marked on other parts of the body. And many animals, including human neonates, are capable of learning that certain movements—e.g. turning—may lead to other movements—e.g. a visual display (e.g. Siqueland and Lipsitt, 1966). Clearly we wish to rule out such reactions. However, this cannot be done by separating attention from attention-behaviour. To do this, we would need to ensure that an organism is responding in any given instance to 'pure' attention rather than to attention 'behaviour'; however, there can be no action upon or reaction to attention which could not also be interpreted as action upon, or reaction to, attention 'behaviour'. Attention 'behaviour' may be an undesirable contaminant within a theory which separates it from an idea of 'pure' attention *per se*. But it cannot be eliminated.

For example, it is widely accepted that pointing to external targets while checking the other's face is evidence of an awareness of the others' attentionality. However, as Josef Perner (1991) argued, even this evidence need imply no more than an awareness of behavioural reactions; it could be an attempt on the infant's part to experiment on or provoke merely behavioural reactions in the other person.

However bizarre the implication that an infant pointing to a passing train is actually experimenting on his mother's eye movements, we cannot both accept the premiss of the division of attention from attention 'behaviour' and deny Perner's argument. And it is not just in the case of non-verbal infants that we cannot rule out contamination from behavioural associations. For example, even children's verbal clarifications following miscommunications, usually accepted as evidence of an understanding of the other's lack of information (mental content), could be interpreted merely as the child's desire to manipulate the other's behaviour and achieve some goal—e.g. praise for obeying a conversational rule (Shatz and O'Reilly, 1990). If we accept the premiss of a fundamental separation between mental events and behavioural events, even adult verbal behaviour is suspect when it comes to watertight evidence excluding contamination from behavioural associations. By the logic of dualism we cannot—even if we talk about it—obtain evidence that we understand minds uncontaminated by behaviour.

Linked logically to the dualist premiss and the desire to exclude behavioural associations is a third implication: that if a response can be shown to be influenced by learning, then it undermines any claim that that response shows understanding. Indeed, the learning interpretation has often been used to criticize what one theorist feels is another's over-interpretation of an early developmental demonstration of mind-knowledge (e.g. see also Moore and D'Entremont, 2001). However, not even in adults can we show either an understanding of pure mental states without behaviour associated with them or pure 'understanding' without any learning involved in it. The argument from learning is a red herring, put in place by psychology's behaviourist history of deliberate exclusion of mind from behaviour.

In practice, therefore, both the insistence upon decontaminating attention from attention 'behaviour' and the insistence upon ruling out learning from understanding are simple expediencies—devices designed to allow the theorist of the day to interpret phenomena flexibly, in line with the constraints of a particular theory. The focus upon a mind–behaviour divide has concentrated our attention upon trying to establish the point in developmental time when the mental Rubicon is crossed. Perhaps its most negative consequence has been that, by making us distrust behavioural evidence, it has caused us to neglect what infants actually *do with attention* in others. An alternative conception of attention which views it as 'attending'—i.e. a non-dualist process involving action rather than mind + behaviour as two separate processes—offers us an opportunity to rethink our understanding of attention. It allows us to examine even young infants' actions upon others' attending without discrediting it automatically as non-consequential and 'merely' behavioural.

Knowing as Detached Contemplation or as Action in Engagement?

The assumption that knowing is a purely mental activity, perhaps fed by information gleaned from action, but existing as an independent process from the action itself, has been challenged many times in the backlash against cognitivism. When action has been admitted into the 'psychological stakes', it has been seen as at best a developmentally inferior level of ability (Costall *et al.*, 1996). As Samuel Alexander (1912) put it a long time ago, the problem of understanding knowledge always arises when we see it as existing as a separate process from doing. However, the problem appears to be alive and kicking in some of our interpretations of infants' reactions to others' attention. Questioning the mind–behaviour dualism in our approach to mentality has the necessary implication that we also question the dualism in the organism's actions with that mentality.

A related issue concerns the origins of knowing. It could be argued that knowing is not only inseparable from action as a process, but that it can develop only through direct action. Such an argument challenges the standard assumption of Western science that detachment and detached contemplation provide the only true source of knowledge. Martin Buber (1958) argues that mutuality is the basis of all knowledge. This does not mean simply that mutuality is the base from which knowledge springs, but that mutual relation is the primary form of knowledge. For Buber things are known first when we engage with them, in direct relation with them, with the thing being a *Thou* to one's *I*. Then they can be known in more detached fashion as an *It*, a relation in which one is not directly engaged with the thing as a *Thou*, but can see it as an *It*. Translated into modern psychological terms, this approach to knowing would suggest that mutual attentional engagement involves a direct and primary form of knowledge of the attention of the other. In contrast to twentieth-century preoccupation with objectivity and detachment as the sole route to knowledge, Buber's idea suggests that both for the adult and for the infant there is another form of knowing which may, developmentally and experientially, precede detached knowledge.

The Empirical Story: Delayed Onset of Attention-Understanding or Early Awareness of Attention?

Lastly, there is an empirical reason for questioning this picture: the evidence does not quite fit the story it is being forced into. Early mutual attentional engagements cannot in fact be explained away as biological or social reactions which are assumed to exclude 'understanding' of attention. A closer look at these mutual attention phenomena themselves, as well as at the continuities in development between them and later triadic attentional phenomena in typical development, suggests that attention *per se* is not a late-developing conceptual acquisition; it is perceived and begins to be understood *as attention* much earlier. Similarly, the evidence of attentional disturbances in children with autism, which has been used in support of the argument for a landmark with triadic engagements, is far from simple and supportive. As several authors are beginning to argue, the difficulties of children with autism in understanding attentionality in others may begin with dyadic engagements (see Adamson *et al.*, 1998; Hobson and Lee, 1998; and also Chapters 9 and 10 below), suggesting that whatever is going on in dyadic attentional engagements may indeed be critical, not just as a source of information and experience about attentional behaviour, or as a scaffold for the subsequent development of awareness of attention, but also as evidence of awareness of attention.

ANOTHER LOOK AT THE EMPIRICAL EVIDENCE ABOUT THE UNDERSTANDING OF ATTENTION

I will argue that infant understanding of attention in others is evident in dyadic as well as in triadic attentional engagements, and that the issue of attention-understanding needs to be considered separately from the issue of the development of the 'third element'. Our definition of the 'object' in interpersonal interactions might need to be broadened if we are to understand the infant's understanding of the simple directedness of the spotlight of others' attention. The data suggest that during the first year there is a gradual differentiation of the link between the attention of others and the targets to which it is directed, before the 'third element', as we know it, is spatially visible. In the second year this third entity undergoes further distancing from the self by moving away in time as well.

Table 5.1 shows a summary of the evidence discussed in the text and suggests that the directedness of another's attention is understood even in the first few months of life, provided its target is the infant. It may be the case that at each 'level' of object or topic the infant first shows evidence of perceiving and responding to others' attention, then evidence of seeking and directing it. That is, the developmental progression from responding to directing (see also Werner and Kaplan, 1963; Bates, Camaioni, and Volterra, 1976; Tomasello, 1995, 1999) may be repeated many times for different kinds of attentional engagement. This may well continue to be the case throughout life! Where a phenomenon may exist but there is not even anecdotal evidence to support it, a question-mark is used to indicate uncertainty. It is clear from Table 5.1 that there are many gaps in our knowledge. Such an 'object'-centred collection of the evidence available (and of that still needed) may help both to clarify our theorizing about the infant's understanding of attention and to highlight the places where there is need for further evidence.

In the section below, phenomena of mutual attention are organized into two main subsections which avoid the criterion of spatial isolation of the object: one in which the self is the object of attention and the other in which acts by the self and other events are the objects of attention.

TABLE 5.1. *Expanding awareness of the objects of others' attention: from self in engagement to events over time*

(From) Age	The object of the other's attention	Infant response to and action upon other's attention
2–4 months	Self	*Responding*: to others' gaze to self with interest, pleasure, distress, ambivalence, indifference, and co-ordinated expressions. *Directing*: making 'utterances', 'calling' attention to self, seeking face to face engagement.
6–8 months	Frontal events and targets	*Responding*: Following others' gaze to frontal targets; gaze alternation between target and attentive other person, with interest, pleasure, anxiety, indifference. *Directing*: No known evidence.
7–10 months	Acts by self	*Responding*: to others' attention to acts by self with pleasure, interest, anxiety. *Directing*: repetition of acts that elicit laughter/attention/praise, with gaze to others' faces.
9–11 months	Objects in hand	*Responding*: to others' gaze at objects in hand? Evidence unclear. *Directing*: Beginning of showing/giving objects in hand.
10–14 months	Distal targets	*Responding*: following others' gaze to distal targets. *Directing*: going across room to fetch objects to give; pointing to distant objects.
15–20 months	Past events, absent targets	*Responding*: attending to others' reports of past events and absent targets? Evidence unclear. Following gaze to targets behind the self. *Directing*: Discriminating absence of attention, reference to past events.

Understanding Others' Attention to Self

Interest in and Emotional Reactions to Others' Attention to Self

We know that human infants react emotionally to others' attention when it is directed to them. A wide range of studies of early infancy show that from birth human neonates are visibly interested in others' faces (Fantz, 1963; Johnson and Morton, 1991), are reported to look intensely and with knit brows into others' eyes within minutes of birth, and respond to verbal and tactile attention from others with bodily and facial expressions of responsiveness and pleasure (Brazelton, 1986).

We know that from at least 2 months of age infants smile when adults are looking at them rather than when they are turned away (Wolff, 1987), that they distinguish between adults who have their eyes open and those who have them shut or are looking elsewhere, and smile more to the former (Vecera and Johnson, 1995); and we know from personal engagements with 2-month-old infants that although smiling occurs at other times, the onset of mutual gaze is a powerful elicitor of smiles. In one study five 2–4-month-old infants were filmed in naturalistic interactions (with their parents) consisting of occasional breaks of 5 seconds or more in interaction and mutual gaze. In all five infants the first 5 seconds of onset of mutual gaze after a break produced more infant smiles (and possibly parent smiles, although no data are available) than either the second or the third 5 seconds (Reddy, 2000).

We also know that even at birth and in the early months, infants can react negatively to attention. As in adults, 'too much' direct attention from someone can lead to attempts to disengage from it, or to distress, if disengagement is not possible for reasons such as neurological immaturity or damage or the other person's repeated attempts to re-engage mutual gaze (Brazelton, 1986). More interestingly, as with adults, 2-month-old infants can respond to attention from others with ambivalence. The onset of mutual gaze is sometimes accompanied by positive shy or coy reactions involving a deepening smile accompanied by the aversion of gaze or head or both, and sometimes with arms raised to face in a stereotypical coy pattern (Reddy, 2000). Particularly interesting is the finding that these reactions are more common immediately following the onset of attention to self than later on, much like self-conscious reactions such as blushing in adults. Although the significance of the resemblance of these reactions to self-conscious reactions may be debated, here it is the fact that they are a response to mutual attention that is crucial. Infants can also be indifferent to others' visual attention, as anyone knows who, trying to engage a 2-month-old, has had the infant glance expressionlessly at them and turn away. These reactions are similar in range and tone to those in older children and adults, suggesting at least an emotional continuity in reaction to mutual attention.

Interest in others' attention by two to three months, therefore, is not a constant. It is not an automatic response even in alert and happy infants. It fluctuates predictably with mood and with other factors. Further, there is no single response to the attention of others even when there is interest; the responses can range from intense smiles, to sober gaze, to shy or coy ambivalent smiles, to distressed avoidance. It would seem, therefore, that the argument that these emotional reactions are 'merely' biological, or are so innately specified that there is no room for agency and awareness on the infant's part, cannot be maintained. Something in the attentive behaviour of others is clearly of interest to infants shortly after birth, and elicits a range of emotional reactions very similar to those in adults. It is evident that the infant's responsiveness to the attention of others is not limited to simple arousal to simple stereotypical 'stimuli' (including smiling, staring, turning away indifferently, repeatedly avoiding, crying without turning away, fussing, smiling with turning away briefly and turning back again, etc.), but is much more differentiated and flexible. Is it the case, however, that the infant is merely a passive reactor to others' attention, whatever he or she makes of it?

Actively Directing Attention to Self

Little research has focused directly on the question of whether infants in the early months actively seek others' attention. Anecdotal reports suggest that somewhere around 3 months, several weeks after the infant has been showing clear emotional and interested reactions to attention, infants start to 'call' the caregiver (with shrill or raised voice) when he or she is not perceivable. This calling is notably in a happy mood, and is distinct from fussing or crying or distressed indications of need for the presence of others. Although it seems very likely that the 'calling' ceases with the onset of attention to the self, we have no clear descriptions of such behaviour nor of the different conditions which elicit or terminate it. Indirectly, however, there is experimental evidence that infants of between two and three months actively seek to re-engage a parent's attention when it is artificially disrupted or distorted. 'Still-face' and double-video studies (Tronick and Cohn, 1989; Murray and Trevarthen, 1985; Nadel and Tremblay-Leveau, 1999) show that if within an active and successful engagement the adult's attention is disrupted, infants, along with other responses, seek intermittently to re-engage the attention. That is, if gaze is still directed to the infant but with a sudden and uncharacteristic inhibition of all other responses (still-face), or if gaze and other responses are still directed to the infant but the behaviour is out of synchrony with the infant's behaviour (video replay), then the infant responds with a suppression of smiles and positive behaviour and an alternation of visual avoidance and initiative towards the other.

Clearly, these infant attempts to call the adult to interaction or to re-engage following disruption may be directed not simply to gaze or to what we may variously term attention, but to the engagement as a whole. What the infant may be responding to when attention is appropriate is a Gestalt of positive/attentive/ engagement, and when attention is inappropriate, seeking the re-emergence of this Gestalt. What is evident also is that the Gestalt is sought by the infant to be directed not to specific features of the environment, nor to specific features of the self, not even to the self as a conceptual entity, but to the self-as-a-whole-in-engagement. How does this change in the next few months?

Understanding Attention to Events and to Acts by Self

Attentional Referencing

The phenomenon of *social* referencing, involving gaze alternation between an external object/person/location of an event and a nearby caregiver (Klinnert *et al.*,

1986), has been accepted by the developmental psychological community as a robust one occurring from around 7 to 8 months of age. However, its implications for the infant's understanding of attention have rarely been explicitly drawn (see Adamson and MacArthur, 1995), and are certainly not uniformly accepted by joint attention theorists as important or even relevant. Social referencing can be said to reveal merely the infant's need for the mother in the face of ambiguity and a global reaction to the emotional tone of the mother's expression rather than revealing any understanding of a psychological link between the mother's expression and the target object (e.g. Perner, 1991).

One could argue that when the stimulus is of negative or ambivalent emotional valence, it is harder to distinguish between a reaction to emotionality and a specific perception of emotion/attention to the target, than when the stimulus is of positive valence. Some authors consider social referencing as developmentally prior to joint attention, even as one of the signs of the emergence of joint attention (Adamson and MacArthur, 1995). On the other hand, there is also a view in the literature that positive affect sharing (looking around to an other's face when confronted with a positive or interesting stimulus) may in fact be developmentally simpler than social referencing or seeking information about negative or ambiguous stimuli (Hornik and Gunnar, 1988; Kasari *et al.*, 1995). However, evidence about the occurrence of gaze to the other's face in positive triadic situations before the development of social referencing is sparse.

Everyday life for infants can be just as, if not more, full of positive events/persons/objects as of negative or ambivalent ones. In one naturalistic study of 8-month-olds the following non-ambiguous and non-negative situations were observed to sometimes elicit immediate infant gaze to a caregiver's face: situations in which *events occurred which were outside the infant's control and unpredictable* in the circumstances; situations in which the events were *accidental actions* performed by the infant and also unpredictable in the circumstances; situations in which the events were *intentional actions* performed by the infant. Although there were no control situations to explore the nature of the events (unexpected or outstanding) that led to the gaze to face, and although we have no information about their frequency, the incidents in 8-month-olds in Table 5.2 illustrate some common everyday situations in which attentional referencing 'about' an object or event takes place before triadic joint attention is properly in existence.

In a striking experimental study still in progress, David Leavens and Brenda Todd (see Leavens and Todd, 2002) have observed that even 6-month-olds frequently engage in gaze alternation between target (a doll suddenly moving arms and legs) and nearby caregiver. The infants are usually happy and excited in response to this target event, whether at 6 months or 12 months (when the gaze alternations are likely to be accompanied by pointing towards the target). The younger infants did not differentiate between parent-attentive and inattentive conditions with different frequencies of referential looking. However, what is

TABLE 5.2. *Incidents of attention referencing in three different contexts at 8 months*

Following events out of infant control

Infant (JF) busy playing alone with toys on floor has not looked up for 2 minutes prior to incident at M or F sitting several feet away on one side of room or at researcher (R) behind camera. (Although M, F, and R occasionally speak to each other, they are generally attending to and smiling at JF when she looks up to engage with them.) The family cat makes a noise at other side of room (from M and F). JF looks at it, then turns and looks at F, then turns back to the cat, squeaks herself in imitation of the noise, and turns to look at camera/R. Everyone laughs. JF turns back to toys. Minutes later the cat makes a noise again, JF looks at cat, then turns round with an imitation of the sound to M and F, then back to toys again. Twelve seconds later cat makes noise again, and JF looks at it for several seconds. R laughs behind camera. JF looks at R, then turns to M and F with a smile and an imitation of the cat sound. . . .

Following accidental actions involving infant

Infant (AW) playing with toys on floor with M sitting about 2 feet away and attending to AW playing. R behind camera. AW playing alone with plastic toy mask, accidentally bumps self on face with the mask and looks up with an amused smile to M's face. M smiles back.

Infant (FDV) playing with toys alone with M sitting beside her and R behind camera. FDV accidentally produces a sound while doing something with a toy, turns to R with a smile, then leans back, shy, into M with a look and smile at M.

Following intentional actions by the infant

Infant (DD) is given a bell by R. DD manages to pick it up and ring it. DD laughs (at the success of her action or the sound itself or both), and turns to look at R with a smile.

Infant (MT) is presented with some blocks by R. With difficulty MT manages to hold a block in each hand, then turns and shows them (holds them up slightly), beaming, to R2 (who continues smiling at her), then waves blocks around, and still beaming and waving, looks at R1 and then at M.

striking in these studies is that before the infant actively directs attention to a distal target event by pointing to it, there appears to be triangulation of gaze by the infants between target and other person.

Directing Attention to Aspects of the Self

Another set of phenomena involving others' attention also emerges before infants begin to direct others' attention to distal targets by pointing to them. Infants begin to detect others' attention to aspects of the self, rather than to the self as a whole, and to make causal connections between these aspects and the eliciting or maintenance of others' attention. The aspects may involve *temporary features* of the body, such as a hat or a revealed tummy, or *acts* by the self, such as shaking the head, shrieking, screwing up the nose, clapping hands, etc. In two studies based on parental interviews and video-taped observations of naturally occurring interactions in the home, it was found that from about 7 to 8 months, infants not only appear to be appreciative of attention to themselves, and seek to elicit attention to the self as a whole, but also seek to elicit attention to these specific aspects of the self. When infants notice that, perhaps accidentally in the first instance, others' attention has been elicited by an aspect of self, they may repeat the showing of this aspect in order to re-elicit the attention (Reddy, 1991). Such attention seeking occurs in at least two ways: through *clowning* and through *showing-off*. The former involves the attempted re-eliciting of laughter, and the latter the attempted re-eliciting of positive attention or praise.[1]

The critic might argue, however, that when an 8-month-old shakes her head to re-elicit her father's laughter, she may be using the head-shaking to get attention to herself rather than seeking attention to the head-shaking. In other words, as was the case several months earlier, the global self (rather than the act itself) may still be the 'topic' to which the other's attention is sought.

However, there are crucial differences. When the 4-month-old 'calls', obtaining the other's attention to the self leads to cessation of the calling. In the case of clowning and showing-off, obtaining the other's attention usually leads to a repetition of the act, suggesting a clearer awareness of the link between the attention and the act. This does not, of course, mean that the self as a whole is not also a target. The other's attention may never be sought exclusively for an act even in adulthood—consider the case of the child repeatedly performing acrobatic manoeuvres for others' attention—the attention is clearly understood to be linked to the act, although it is also sought for the self. Similarly, the 8-month-old appears to be more conscious of the link between act and attention than is the 4-month-old, and more aware of attention to things other than the global self. However far the infant has yet to go in terms of elaborating and differentiating her understanding of attention, this linkage is clearly an advance upon the previous linkage between attention and the global self.

But what sort of link *does* the 8-month-old perceive? Perner (1991) suggested in the case of early proto-declarative pointing that in the infant's mind the link between pointing and maternal reaction might be no more than a mechanical, causal link. In other words, the infant may learn that pointing leads to exaggerated behaviour, and seek to elicit the latter. The same could be argued to be the case for clowning and showing-off. In other words, this criticism might accept that the 'topic' is the act rather than the self as a whole, but argue that the thing sought is not attention as a psychological state but merely a behavioural reaction. As has been argued before, however, such an argument assumes that attention as a mental state

---

[1] It is not always easy to distinguish between the two; laughter sometimes accompanies praise, and in any case always involves positive attention. However, it is the case that sometimes the two situations can be distinguished; praise for clapping or waving can be delivered without laughter, and amusement at a cheeky face can consist of laughter without praise for a skill.

is a representational entity which can only be known representationally. It sees any behavioural component as a contaminant which needs to be eliminated in order for the true knowledge to be grasped. With these premisses this argument would hold true for all gestural behaviour in children and adults, and lead to an empirical impasse in terms of proving knowledge of mind without behaviour. It might be more fruitful to see attention in an adualist manner, allowing us to trace the infant's dealings with others' attention as dealings with psychological rather than 'merely' behavioural phenomena.

Two other aspects of clowning and showing-off are relevant for understanding their relation to triadic attentional engagements. First, the incidence of clowning and showing-off is low in pre-school children with autism, as also is the incidence of proto-declarative pointing, in comparison with mental age-matched children with Down's syndrome (Reddy, Williams, and Vaughan, 2002). This is consistent with current knowledge of deficits in (triadic) joint attention in autism (e.g. Mundy and Sigman, 1989). Second, in both typically developing infants and pre-school children with autism or with Down's syndrome, the incidence of clowning and showing-off is related to the incidence of proto-declarative pointing. Over half of the typically developing infants showed either both (clowning/showing-off at 8 months and proto-declarative pointing at 11 months) or neither. None showed pointing before clowning or showing-off. Three-quarters of the children with autism showed either both or neither, and none showed pointing before clowning or showing-off. Almost all the children with Down's syndrome showed both or neither, and none showed pointing before clowning or showing-off.

This link between clowning/showing-off and proto-declarative pointing suggests that the two kinds of behaviour may be similar in terms of required skill and motivation, with the former being developmentally simpler than the latter. There is no evidence here to suggest an attention-understanding module of any kind—the relation between the occurrence of the two behaviours may be mediated by a variety of other factors. What seems clear, however, is that it does not make sense to consider the origins of reference to external objects without considering the occurrence of invitations to attend to aspects of the self. Nor can one understand such invitations without considering earlier invitations to attend to the self as a whole. The development here concerns changes in the infant's relation to the object of others' attention, rather than a radical change in the reaction to attention itself. It would also appear that these changes are in each case expansions and elaborations of an existing mutuality—that between self and other expanding to involve other 'topics', as discussed here, or that between child and object-in-hand expanding to involve other people (Werner and Kaplan, 1963; Bates Camaioni, and Volterra, 1976).

The argument that these phenomena display developmental continuity, and that the development concerns the nature of the object would be strengthened if the continuity extended beyond the mere onset of reference. Does the object continue to develop after the onset of reference to distal objects? Do the same infants who engage early or willingly in clowning/showing-off and proto-declarative pointing also engage more in reference to more complex objects? Although we do not have data about individual differences and continuities in relation to this question, the evidence below suggests that the development of the object (and therefore of attention-understanding) continues at least into the second year of infancy.

After 'Joint Attention': Further Developments

The distancing of the third element from the activities of the self (clowning/showing-off) to the object-in-hand (showing/giving) and then the distal object (pointing), continues even after conventional definitions of joint attention have been met. The object of reference can now become something that is not only spatially but also temporally distal—in the past or in the future. Further, the object of reference can become something that is distal for the partner in communication even if not for the self. Infants, for instance, may remember events from earlier in the day to tell interested (or even uninterested!) parties about significant events. They may even, very occasionally, deliberately plan to tell someone later—e.g. not letting the evidence of the use of the potty be thrown out in order to 'show Mummy when she comes home'!! In two studies, one naturalistic and one experimental, 18-month-olds were found significantly more often to point, show, demonstrate, or 'tell' adults about a toy or an event if the adults had not already witnessed it, than if they had (Reddy and Simone, 1995, in preparation). This is consistent with findings that infants at this age, in communication with others, are selecting information relevant to them (Greenfield, 1976), and with findings that from about two and a half years infants, when requesting objects, are selectively informing adults about the location of objects depending on the adults' knowledge (O'Neill, 1996).

The attention of others appears to be seen by the infant in the second year as something that can extend beyond the present (as memory of things witnessed or already known), and the infant's grasp of the targets of others' attention now extends to the past as well. The access to temporal distance in the target may be explained in many ways—e.g. by a Piagetian explanation of the beginnings of representational thought, or by an information-processing explanation of some kind based on increasing memory and other processing capacities. The importance of this in terms of the developing understanding of attention, however, is simply that it is the *object* of the other's attention that is becoming more complex in these exchanges, not the ways in which (or the fact that) attention itself is sought to things to do with the self.

The development of complexity in the 'object' or 'topic' of attention does not of course imply that simpler objects and topics disappear or become less important.

Emotional reactions to others' attention to the (global) self continue well beyond the first few months of life. From the second half of the first year, with the onset of stranger anxiety, the attention (whether through gaze or speech or approach) of the stranger to the self (globally) can lead to shyness or distress as well as pleasure. The onset of attention to self, especially if unexpected, can continue to lead to a variety of emotional reactions in childhood and adulthood. Similarly, children and adults also *seek* the attention of others to the global self.

AN ALTERNATIVE DEVELOPMENTAL STORY ABOUT THE UNDERSTANDING OF ATTENTION

In the face of the evidence described above, an alternative approach may be both more economical in explaining how the understanding of attention develops and more fruitful for the conceptualization of attention and other psychological phenomena. Attention is conceived here as attend*ing* (following Gibson and Rader, 1979, and Adamson and Bakeman, 1991)—as the process through which organisms attend to the world (including their own bodies), rather than as a 'purely' mental state that is both discrete and unavailable in action and interaction. The reason for this shift in emphasis is twofold. First, attention is not a discrete state but a continuous act. Although the targets to which one attends change (and therefore the boundaries of attention to specific targets can be identified), attention itself is a continuous process. 'Attending' conveys the sense of action involved better than does 'attention'. Second, attention is clearly not 'just' a mental act or state. Nor is it two acts, first a mental one, then a physical or behavioural one. The verbal form 'attending' conveys the meaning of a unitary act better than does the noun 'attention' in the particular history of the term in Western psychology.

The extent to which we consider attention to be an embodied or a disembodied phenomenon also bears on another crucial issue raised by Bruner (1995): the developmental relation between the knowledge *that* someone is attending to something and the knowledge of *what* is being attended to. One could simplistically argue for the primacy of the knowledge of attention (the *that*) over the knowledge of its targets (the *what*), thus making the case that early mutual attention reveals the infant's understanding of the *that*. However, one cannot understand attention without understanding that it is in fact directed somewhere—even if one doesn't quite know where. Attending cannot happen without a target or a direction, and therefore engagement with another's attending cannot happen without a connection with that target or that directedness of the other's attention. But this connection can be simply through *being* the target or *receiving* the directedness, rather than only through mentally representing the third element. If the (knowing of the) *what* were defined as a mental representation of the thing towards which attention is directed, then the infant would be considered not to know attention, since she has no mental representation (reflective awareness) of the self as the object of attention. This implausible conclusion would exist in the face of evidence that the infant could receive attention to the self, respond to it with appropriate emotion and actions, and seek to direct and manipulate it. It would also set up an implausible circularity: if one accepted participation as a central feature of developing an understanding of attention, infants could not participate with others' attention without mentally representing its objects, but also could not develop the mental representations of the objects without the participation.

Alternatively, viewing the directedness of attention as perceptually available allows actual participation in attentional engagements, and therefore the development of further knowledge of both the nature and the targets of attention. From within this shifted perspective the infant's engagement in mutual attention is crucial for three reasons: (i) it demonstrates a *capacity* for dealing with others' attention from very early in infancy; (ii) it demonstrates an *interest* in dealing with others' attention from very early in infancy; and (iii) it provides the infant with the *experience* necessary for further developments in the understanding of attention. The understanding of attention cannot therefore be said to emerge late in infancy. The idea that the understanding is a conception that can emerge at a single point (or series of points) in time is seriously questionable. It is more helpful to think of attention as being understood in engagement and as developing in continuity. It makes no sense to exclude mutual attentional phenomena from the realm of attention-understanding, and it makes no empirical sense to argue that mutual attentional engagement in human infancy is lacking in attentional understanding. To borrow another metaphor from Bruner (1994), we cannot give the infant a joint attention diploma at 9 or 12 or 18 or 24 months. Nor does offering a series of diplomas make the solution any more palatable.

SIX DEVELOPMENTAL CONCLUSIONS

1. The understanding of attention does not *begin* in late infancy with the emergence of the separate 'object' or referential topic. Before the existence of the 'third element' in interaction, even in mutual attention, others' attentionality already plays a serious role in the infant's psychological awareness and development. Over time (probably over the life span) there is a developing understanding of the scope and extendedness and limits of others' attention.

2. The 'object' or topic in attentional engagements has a gradual emergence. The object not only emerges over the course of months from within joint actions involving objects (as suggested by Werner and Kaplan, 1963; Bakeman and Adamson, 1984; Adamson and Bakeman, 1991; and others); and not only does it emerge as a distancing from actions (Bates, Camaioni, and Volterra, 1976), but emerges first

from *being* the object. The self is the first target of others' attention that the infant experiences, and it is from this experience of attention that others' attention to other topics can be understood. Infant responses to, and attempts to direct, attention (to the self, to actions by the self, and to distal targets) demonstrate a clear continuity in, as well as development of, the understanding of attention.

3. Consistent with predictions by Tomasello, Werner and Kaplan, and others, infant understanding of attention seems first to show itself in responding to others' attention and then to directing it. However, it seems likely that this shift from response to directing occurs for each level of 'object' of others' attention throughout the first year (and after), rather than at some point when attention is 'discovered'.

4. The early perceptual availability of the directedness of attention in others allows the infant to participate in actual attentional (rather than merely behavioural) engagements, and for this participation to lead to further knowledge of both the nature and the targets of attention.

5. Three kinds of participation or mutuality in engagement may form the basis for an expanding understanding: (a) between self and other, (b) between self and the actions of the self, and (c) between self and object. The third element appears to emerge emotionally, temporally, and spatially, respectively, from these three forms.

6. Emotions are bound up more closely with the understanding of attention than we have hitherto taken account of (see Adamson and Russell, 1999). Even in the first 2 months of life, emotional reactions to others' attention are subtle and varied. Emotional reactions to attention are a crucial indicator of the organism's understanding of attentionality, arising first and most powerfully in mutual attention, and probably mediating all further understanding of attention.

REFERENCES

ADAMSON, L., and BAKEMAN, R. (1991), 'The development of shared attention in infancy', in R. Vasta (ed.), *Annals of Child Development*, viii. London: Jessica Kingsley Publishers, 1–41.

—— and MACARTHUR, D. (1995), 'Joint attention, affect and culture', in C. Moore and P. J. Dunham (eds.), *Joint Attention: Its Origins and Role in Development*. Hillsdale, NJ: Lawrence Erlbaum Associates, 205–21.

—— and RUSSELL, C. (1999), 'Emotion regulation and the emergence of joint attention', in P. Rochat (ed.), *Early Social Cognition: Understanding Others in the First Months of Life*. Mahwah, NJ: Lawrence Erlbaum Associates, 281–97.

—— MCARTHUR, D., MARKOV, Y., and DUNBAR, B. (1998), 'Autism and resisting joint attention'. Poster presented at International Conference on Infant Studies, Atlanta, Georgia.

ALEXANDER, S. (1912), 'On relations; and in particular the cognitive relation', *British Psychological Society* 16: 305–28.

ASTINGTON, J. (1993), *The Child's Discovery of the Mind*. Cambridge, Mass.: Harvard University Press.

BAKEMAN, R., and ADAMSON, L. (1984), 'Co-ordinating attention to people and objects in mother–infant and peer–infant interaction', *Child Development,* 55: 1278–89.

BALDWIN, D. A., and MOSES, L. J. (1994), 'Early understanding of referential intent and attentional focus: evidence from language and emotion', in C. Lewis and P. Mitchell (eds.), *Children's Early Understanding of Mind: Origins and Development.* Hove: Lawrence Erlbaum Associates, 133–56.

BARON-COHEN, S. (1995), *Mindblindness: An Essay on Autism and Theory of Mind.* Cambridge, Mass.: MIT Press.

BATES, E., CAMAIONI, L., and VOLTERRA, V. (1976), 'Sensorimotor performatives', in E. Bates (ed.), *Language and Context: The Acquisition of Pragmatics.* New York: Academic Press, 49–71.

BRAZELTON, T. B. (1986), 'The development of newborn behavior', in F. Faulkner and J. M. Tanner (eds.), *Human Growth: A Comprehensive Treatise,* ii. New York: Plenum Press, 519–40.

BRUNER, J. (1983), *Child's Talk: Learning to Use Language.* New York: Norton.

—— (1994), Foreword, in C. Lewis and P. Mitchell (eds.), *Children's Early Understanding of Mind.* Hove: Lawrence Erlbaum Associates.

—— (1995), 'From joint attention to the meeting of minds: an introduction', in C. Moore and P. J. Dunham (eds.), *Joint Attention: Its Origins and Role in Development.* Hillsdale, NJ: Lawrence Erlbaum Associates, 1–14.

—— and SHERWOOD, V. (1983), 'Thought, language and interaction in infancy', in J. D. Call, E. Galenson, and R. L. Tyson (eds.), *Frontiers of Infant Psychiatry.* New York: Basic Books, Inc., 38–52.

BUBER, M. (1958), *I and Thou,* trans. R. G. Smith, 2nd edn., Edinburgh: T. & T. Clark.

CARPENTER, M., NAGELL, K., and TOMASELLO, M. (1998), 'Social cognition, joint attention and communicative competence from 9 to 15 months of age', *Monographs of the Society for Research in Child Development,* 63 (4).

COSTALL, A. *et al.* (1996), 'Unexplaining social development'. JPS conference paper.

DUNHAM, P. J. and X. DUNHAM, (1995), in C. Moore and P. J. Dunham, (eds.), *Joint Attention: Its Origins and Role in Development.* Hove: Lawrence Erlbaum Associates.

FANTZ, R. L. (1963), 'Pattern vision in newborn infants', *Science,* 140: 296–7.

FIVAZ-DEPEURSINGE, E., and CORBOZ-WARNERY, A. (1999), *The Primary Triangle.* New York: Basic Books, Inc.

GIBSON, E. J., and RADER, N. (1979), 'Attention: the perceiver as performer', in G. A. Hale and M. Lewis (eds.), *Attention and Cognitive Development.* New York: Plenum Press, 1–21.

GOPNIK, A. (1993), 'How we know our minds: the illusion of first person knowledge of intentionality', *Behavioural and Brain Sciences,* 16: 1–14.

GREENFIELD, P. M. (1976), *The Structure of Communication in Early Language Development.* New York: Academic Press.

HOBSON, R. P., and LEE, A. (1998), 'Hello and goodbye: a study of social engagement in autism', *Journal of Autism and Developmental Disorders,* 28 (2): 117–26.

HORNIK, R., and GUNNAR, M. R. (1988), 'A descriptive analysis of infant social referencing', *Child Development,* 59 (3): 626–34.

JOHNSON, M. H., and MORTON, J. (1991), *Biology and Cognitive Development.* Oxford: Blackwell.

KASARI, C., FREEMAN, S., MUNDY, P., and SIGMAN, S. (1995), 'Attention regulation by children with Down Syndrome: co-ordinated joint attention and social referencing looks', *American Journal on Mental Retardation*, 100 (2): 128–36.

KLINNERT, M. D., CAMPOS, J. J., SORCE, J. F., EMDE, R. N., and SVEJDA, M. (1983), 'Emotions as behaviour regulators: social referencing in infancy', in R. Plutchik and H. Kellerman (eds.), *Emotion: Theory, Research and Experience*, ii. New York: Academic Press, 57–86.

LEAVENS, D., and TODD, B. (2002), 'The development of socially mediated visual attention in late infancy'. Poster presented at the 13th Biennial International Conference on Infant Studies, Toronto, Canada, 18–22 April.

MOORE, C., and D'ENTREMONT, B. (2001), 'Developmental changes in pointing as a function of attentional focus', *Journal of Cognition and Development*, 2(2): 109–29.

MUNDY, P., and SIGMAN, M. (1989), 'The theoretical implications of joint-attention deficits in autism', *Development and Psychopathology*, 1: 173–83.

MURRAY, L. and TREVARTHEN, C. (1985), 'Emotional regulation of interaction between two-month-olds and their mothers', in T. M. Field and N. Fox (eds.), *Social Perception in Infants*. Norwood, NJ: Ablex, 101–25.

NADEL, J., and TREMBLAY-LEVEAU, H. (1999), 'Early perception of social contingencies and interpersonal intentionality: dyadic and triadic paradigms', in P. Rochat (ed.), *Early Social Cognition: Understanding Others in the First months of Life*. Mahwah, NJ: Lawrence Erlbaum Associates, 189–212.

O'NEILL, D. K. (1996), 'Two-year-old children's sensitivity to a parent's knowledge state when making requests', *Child Development*, 67: 659–77.

PERNER, J. (1991), *Understanding the Representational Mind*. Cambridge, Mass.: MIT Press.

RATTRAY, J. (2000), 'Dancing in the Dark: The Effect of Visual Impairment on the Nature of Early Mother–Infant Dyadic Interaction and Communication', (Ph.D. thesis, Department of Psychology, University of Dundee).

REDDY, V. (1991), 'Playing with others' expectations: teasing and mucking about in the first year', in A. Whiten (ed.), *Natural Theories of Mind*. Oxford: Blackwell, 143–58.

—— (2000), 'Coyness in early infancy', *Developmental Science*, 3 (2): 186–92.

—— and SIMONE, L. (1995), 'Acting on attention: towards an understanding of knowing in infancy'. Paper presented at the Annual Conference of the Developmental Section of the British Psychological Society, Strathclyde, Scotland.

—— —— (in preparation), 'Eighteen-month-olds' sensitivity to knowledge and ignorance: co-ordinating others' knowledge through proto-declaratives'.

—— Williams, E., and Vaughan, A. (2002), 'Sharing humour and laughter in autism and Down syndrome', *British Journal of Psychology*, 93, 219–42.

SCAIFE, M., and BRUNER, J. (1975), 'The capacity for joint visual attention in the infant', *Nature*, 253: 265–6.

SHATZ, M., and O'REILLY, A. (1990), 'Conversational or communicative skill? A reassessment of two-year-olds' behaviour in miscommunication episodes', *Journal of Child Language*, 17: 131–46.

SIQUELAND, E. R., and LIPSITT, L. P. (1966), 'Conditioned head-turning in human newborns', *Journal of Experimental Child Psychology*, 3: 356–76.

TOMASELLO, M. (1995), 'Joint attention as social cognition', in C. Moore and P. J. Dunham (eds.), *Joint Attention: Its Origins and Role in Development*. Hove: Lawrence Erlbaum Associates, 103–30.

—— (1999), 'Social cognition before the revolution', in P. Rochat (ed.), *Early Social Cognition*. Mahwah, NJ: Lawrence Erlbaum Associates, 301–14.

TREVARTHEN, C. (1980), 'The foundations of intersubjectivity: development of interpersonal and cooperative understanding in infants', in D. Olson (ed.), *The Social Foundations of Language and Thought: Essays in Honour of J. S. Bruner*. New York: Norton, 316–42.

—— and HUBLEY, P. (1978), 'Secondary intersubjectivity: confidence, confiding and acts of meaning in the first year', in A. Lock (ed.), *Action, Gesture and Symbol*. London: Academic Press, 183–229.

TRONICK, E. Z., and COHN, J. F. (1989), 'Infant–mother face-to-face interaction: age and gender differences in coordination and the occurrence of miscoordination', *Child Development*, 60: 85–92.

VECERA, S. P., and JOHNSON, M. H. (1995), 'Gaze detection and the cortical processing of faces: evidence from infants and adults', *Visual Cognition*, 2: 59–87.

WELLMAN, H. (1990), *The Child's Theory of Mind*. Cambridge, Mass.: MIT Press.

WERNER, H., and KAPLAN, B. (1963), *Symbol Formation*. Hillsdale, NJ: Erlbaum.

WOLFF, P. H. (1987), *The Development of Behavioural States and the Expression of the Emotions in Early Infancy*. Chicago: University of Chicago Press.

6

Infants' Understanding of the Actions
Involved in Joint Attention

Amanda L. Woodward

Joint attention plays a pivotal role in many aspects of development. This is because episodes of joint attention provide children with a great deal of information. To illustrate, imagine a mother and her young son at a family reunion. The mother turns to look at a newcomer to the party, smiles, points at her, and exclaims, 'There's Aunt Grace.' The child in this situation could infer from these actions that Aunt Grace is the name of the indicated person. He might further infer that his mother likes Aunt Grace and is likely to seek contact with her. That is, joint attention behaviors provide information not only about the objects at which they are directed, but also about the dispositions and mental states of the person who performs them.

The child's ability to extract this information rests on his understanding of attentional behaviors such as looking and pointing. It is possible to respond to the attentional behaviors of another person apparently appropriately, yet not understand the meaning of these behaviors for the person who performs them. To illustrate, the child in the above example might shift his attention to Aunt Grace in response to his mother's gaze and pointing, without yet understanding that his mother is attending to Aunt Grace. In this case, the significance of these behaviors would be largely lost on the child. He would have no basis for making inferences about his mother's utterances, epistemic states, emotional reactions, or likely next behaviors.

In investigating the development of joint attention, therefore, it is critical to distinguish between children's orienting responses to gaze and pointing and their understanding of these behaviors as involving attention on the part of the person who performs them. There is now a wealth of evidence concerning the first of these abilities. As George Butterworth's work elegantly documented, by 6 months of age, infants respond to shifts in gaze by shifting their own gaze at least in some situations, and by 18 months of age, infants are skilled at following both gaze and points with precision (Butterworth, 1995; Butterworth and Cochran, 1980; Butterworth and Grover, 1988; Butterworth and Jarrett, 1991). These findings

The research described in this chapter was supported by grants from the John Merck Fund, the Robert R. McCormick Tribune Foundation, and NIH (FIRST grant # R29-HD35707). I am grateful to Catharine Seibold and Anneliese Hahn for their assistance in completing the studies, and to the parents and infants who participated.

indicate that gaze and pointing direct infants' attention from early in life. However, there is as yet little evidence concerning infants' understanding that these behaviors involve an attentional connection between a person and an object.

Adults understand many aspects of attentional behaviors. For example, we understand the likely phenomenological experience of a person who looks at something—we can imagine what he or she sees. We can also predict the effects that this experience will have on his or her epistemic states, emotional reactions, and other mental processes. We know that when someone points to an object, she is aware of it, and she likely wishes to make someone else aware of it as well. Finally, we also understand the implications of looking and pointing for a person's subsequent behavior. For example, people tend to move toward and act on the objects of their gaze. Underlying all of this knowledge is the fundamental insight that there is a connection between a person and the object of her gaze and pointing. That is, like many other intentional actions, gaze and pointing are object-directed. If infants lacked an understanding of gaze and pointing as object-directed, it would be impossible for them to interpret these behaviors as anything more than a series of motions, like sneezing or jumping, or as signals to orient in a particular direction.

The work I describe below investigates this most basic insight about joint attention behaviors. This approach provides a new view of infants' comprehension of points and gaze. Until now, researchers have generally used orienting responses as measures of infants' comprehension of points or gaze. The assumption has been that infants' propensity to orient in response to another person's gaze or point is an indicator of their underlying understanding of these actions as implying a psychological relation between the person and the object. As one illustration, in a recent review chapter, Bruner concluded that in order to understand gaze-following in young infants, 'All that is needed...beyond a shared knowledge of space...is knowing that another is looking and experiencing something in the visual world' (Bruner, 1995, p. 7). The work described below will suggest that this assumption is not always correct.

INFANTS' APPRECIATION OF ACTOR–OBJECT RELATIONS

Many actions that adults understand as intentional instantiate a relation between an actor and some object; that is, they are object-directed. This is true for attentional actions such as gaze and pointing, as well as for physical actions such as grasping. In mature systems of knowledge, many aspects of the relation between actor and object are represented. As discussed above, adults understand the specific psychological and behavioral implications of gaze and pointing, and they also understand these aspects of grasping and other physical actions (e.g. adults understand that an actor who grasps a toy probably wants it, is likely to bring it closer to herself, etc.). In order to develop this rich understanding of intentional actions, children must at least understand the object-directed nature of these actions. Prior work from my laboratory has shown that by 6 months of age, infants understand at least one intentional action as involving a link between actor and object (Woodward, 1998, 1999). These studies focused on grasping, an action that is commonly performed both by the agents whom infants observe and, after 4–5 months, by infants themselves. Because these studies provide a model for our later work on gaze and pointing as well as an informative point of comparison, I will review them here.

When infants see a person reach for and grasp an object, there are many ways in which they could represent this event. They might focus on the 'surface' of the event, encoding the path of motion taken by the actor's arm, the angle at which the arm is extended, the position of the object relative to the person and other objects in the scene, etc. On the other hand, infants might represent this event primarily in terms of the relation between the person and the object which she grasps. This would be like adults' construal of such events as object-directed ('She grasps the bear' or, perhaps, 'She wants the bear').

The visual habituation paradigm provides a way to test which of these two con-struals infants apply. In a series of studies completed in my laboratory (Woodward, 1998), infants were first shown an event in which a person reached for and grasped one of two toys which sat side by side on a small stage (see Fig. 6.1). To habituate infants to this event, it was repeated on subsequent trials

Habituation event

New-path test event   New-toy test event

Figure 6.1. Sample events for the studies of grasping (based on Woodward, 1998).

until the infant's attention to it declined to half its initial level. Then, the positions of the toys were reversed, and infants saw two test events in alternation. In one (the new-toy event), the actor reached to the same location as during the habituation phase, this time grasping a different toy. In the other (the new-path event), the actor reached to the other location, grasping the same toy as during the habituation phase. Following habituation, infants will look longer at stimuli which are less similar to the habituation stimuli, and less long at those which are more similar to the habituation stimuli. Therefore, infants' level of looking on the two kinds of test trials provides evidence as to how they represented the habituation event. If infants represented the habituation event mainly in terms of the physical properties of the reach, then they would be expected to look longer on new-path trials. Alternatively, if infants represented the habituation event mainly in terms of the relation between actor and object, then they would be expected to look longer on new-toy trials. The results were that 6- and 9-month-olds looked longer on new-toy trials than on new-path trials, suggesting that at these ages, infants understand the human grasp as an object-directed action.

Additional findings indicated that young infants' propensity to construe actions as object-directed is specific to human actors and, initially, specific to the act of grasping. First, when infants observed a mechanical claw move toward and grasp a toy, they looked equally at new-toy and new-path test events, suggesting that they did not construe this event in terms of the relation between the claw and the toy (Woodward, 1998). Second, when infants observed an actor contact the toy with the back of her hand, they did not construe this action as object-directed (Woodward, 1999).

Before accepting this evidence as strong support for infants' understanding the object-directed nature of human grasps, however, it was critical to rule out an alternative explanation for the findings. It was possible that infants' responses to the new-toy and new-path test events derived from the spotlighting effects of hands that grasp. Perhaps infants have a bias to orient attention to hands that grasp and the objects they hold, but lack such a bias for claws and inert hands. If this were the case, infants' patterns of response to the grasping events could be driven by the fact that a new object is being spotlighted on new-toy trials but not on new-path trials. To explore this possibility, we coded the videotapes of each infant's test trials frame by frame to determine how long they looked at the toy that was the target of the action versus the other toy. This coding revealed that the grasping hand, claw, and inert hand were equally effective at drawing infants' attention. Regardless of which of these contacted the toy, infants spent more time staring at the toy that was contacted than at the other toy.

This result is important for two reasons. First, it rules out one possible explanation for the findings of the habituation experiments. Because the grasping hand, claw, and inert hand were equally effective at directing infants' attention, spotlighting cannot account for infants' differential responses to these three actions. Second, it indicates that infants' encoding of actor–object relations can be distinguished from their propensity to orient in response to actions. It is possible to draw infants' attention to an object in many ways, including grasping it with one's hand, grasping it with a mechanical claw, and laying one's hand on top of it. Only for human grasps, however, do young infants represent the action in terms of the relation between actor and object.

The findings from these studies suggest a strategy for investigating the distinction between infants' orienting responses to pointing and gaze and their understanding of these actions as object-directed. Specifically, infants' novelty responses to changes in the relation between actor and object can serve as a measure of their understanding of the object-directed nature of an action, and infants' attention to the individual objects in the events can serve as an index of their propensity to orient in response to the action. The studies I describe below pursued this strategy.

INFANTS' DEVELOPING UNDERSTANDING OF GAZE AS AN OBJECT-DIRECTED ACTION

Like grasping, gaze is ubiquitous in infants' environments. Moreover, young infants are sensitive to eyes and eye direction from the first few months of life. Infants as young as 2 to 6 months show preferential attention to eyes over other aspects of the face (Caron *et al.*, 1973; Haith, Bergman, and Moore, 1977; Maurer and Salapatek, 1976). Young infants respond to shifts in gaze direction (Hains and Muir, 1996; Symons, Hains, and Muir, 1998; Vecera and Johnson, 1995), and direct their own attention based on another person's gaze by 6 months or perhaps even younger (Butterworth and Jarrett, 1991; D'Entremont, Hains, and Muir, 1997; Hood, Willen, and Driver, 1998; Scaife and Bruner, 1975).

Given that gaze serves as an attentional spotlight for young infants, do infants also understand gaze as an action that links a person to some object? In a recent series of studies (Woodward, 2003), I used the habituation paradigm described above to ask this question. The first experiment tested twenty infants at each of two ages, 7 and 9 months. Infants saw events in which an actor turned to look at one of two toys (see Fig. 6.2). At the start of each trial the experimenter made eye contact with the infant, said 'Hi. Look!' as she turned to look at one of the toys. She then held still until the infant looked away for 2 seconds to end the trial. Infants saw the same event on subsequent trials until they had habituated to it. Then, the positions of the toys were reversed, and infants saw two kinds of test events. On new-toy trials, the actor turned to the same side as during habituation, this time looking at a new toy. On new-side trials, the actor turned to the opposite side as during habituation, to look at the same toy as during habituation. If infants attend to the relation between a person and the object of her gaze, then they would be expected to look longer on new-toy trials, in which this relation is altered.

Habituation event

New-toy test event

New-side test event

FIGURE 6.2. Sample events for the studies of looking (based on Woodward, 2003).

If infants respond instead to surface features of the event, such as the physical motion of the actor, they might look longer on new-side trials.

A preliminary question was whether infants oriented in response to the actor's gaze. If they did not, then they would have had no chance to note the relation between actor and object. Given the findings from studies of gaze-following described earlier, it was predicted that the infants in this experiment would follow the actor's gaze to the toy, and they did. As in the earlier studies of grasping, we coded the test trials for the amount of time infants spent looking at the same toy as the actor versus the other toy: 81 percent of the 7-month-olds and 94 percent of the 9-month-olds spent more time looking at the same toy as the actor than at the other toy.

The question of interest was whether infants at either age responded to the change in relation between the actor and the object, as evidenced by longer looking on new-toy trials than on new-side trials. In spite of the fact that they responded systematically to the actor's shift in gaze by orienting to the same toy, infants at neither age responded to the change in the relation between actor and object. Both 7- and 9-month-olds looked equally on new-toy and new-side test trials. In fact, infants at both ages failed to show a reliable increase in looking from the end of habituation on either kind of test trial. It is as if 7- and 9-month-olds identified the visible objects (the bear, the ball, and the actor) as being the same as during habituation, without considering the relations between them.

One concern about these findings is that the method may have been insensitive to infants' representations of object-directed action. Although we had used this paradigm successfully with 6- and 9-month-old infants, in our prior work the actor's face was never visible. Since the measure was looking time, anything that might contribute to longer or shorter looking times overall could add noise to the data. The addition of a human face, known to be a highly attractive stimulus for infants, could have had such an effect. To investigate this possibility, a second group of infants at each age was shown events that were identical to those in the first experiment, with one exception—as she turned to look at the toy, the actor also grasped it. Thus, in this study infants saw an action that they understand as object-directed—namely, grasping—in the presence of a potentially distracting human face. Given prior findings, if the current paradigm was sensitive to infants' representations of action, we would expect infants at both ages to look longer on new-toy trials than on new-side trials. This is precisely what was found. Infants at both ages looked longer on new-toy trials than on new-side trials, and infants at both ages recovered from habituation on new-toy but not new-side trials. Taken together, the findings indicate that 7- and 9-month-olds understand grasping, but not looking, as an object-directed action.

A final question is the age at which infants begin to represent the relation between looker and object. A third experiment addressed this question by testing 12-month-old infants using the events from the first study, in which the actor looked at but did not grasp the toy. Like the younger infants, 12-month-olds responded to the actor's shift in gaze by looking at the same toy as she did: 84 percent of the babies looked longer at this toy than at the other toy. In contrast to the younger infants, 12-month-olds also showed evidence of noting the relation between actor and object. They looked reliably longer on new-toy trials than on new-side trials, and recovered from habituation on new-toy trials but not new-side trials. Therefore, the results suggest that infants begin to understand the object-directed nature of looking between 9 and 12 months of age.

To summarize, when they saw a person turn toward and look at a toy, 7- and 9-month-old infants did not organize their representations of the event around the relation between the actor and the toy. In contrast, 12-month-olds did. The failure of the younger infants to attend to the relation between actor and object is remarkable given that they systematically responded to the actor's gaze by shifting their own gaze to the object at which she looked. Thus, at one level, 7- and 9-month-olds were quite attentive to the experimental events, but at another level, they missed a critical aspect of these events. As was the case in our earlier studies of grasping by hands versus claws, therefore, there is evidence for a dissociation between infants' propensity to orient in response to an action and the representations that they derive from witnessing the action. Infants begin to orient in response to gaze shifts several months before they appreciate the relation between a person who looks and the object of her gaze.

These findings support two conclusions. First, at the earliest stages, infants' gaze-following seems not to reflect knowledge of gaze as object-directed.

Therefore, researchers should be careful in drawing conclusions about infants' understanding of seeing or attention based only on infants' propensity to follow gaze. However, this is not to say that there is never a relation between gaze-following and infants' understanding of the object-directed nature of gaze. From the end of the first year onward, infants become more skilled at following gaze and negotiating joint attention episodes. For example, infants become able to follow gaze to objects outside their own field of view and to locate the object of an adult's gaze when there are several objects in the same region (Butterworth and Jarrett, 1991). In addition, at the end of the first year, gaze-following becomes embedded in rich joint attention interactions, in which infants actively seek to manipulate the attention of others, and seem to check to see whether their efforts have been successful (Bates *et al.*, 1979; Carpenter, Nagell, and Tomasello, 1998; Schaffer, 1984). These later developments may rest on an emerging understanding of the link between a person and the object of her gaze. Additional investigations are needed to explore this possibility.

The second conclusion derives from a comparison of infants' understanding of grasping and gaze. Even though gaze, like grasping, draws young infants' attention to an object, infants do not seem to understand gaze as an object-directed behavior until several months after they begin to understand grasping as object-directed. These findings indicate that infants do not begin with a propensity to construe all human actions as object-directed. Instead, they seem to discover actor–object relations at different points in development for different kinds of actions. This finding contributes to a more general pattern emerging from the work in our laboratory (Guajardo and Woodward, in press; Sommerville, 2002; Woodward, 1999; Woodward, Sommerville, and Guajardo, 2001), suggesting that the earliest stages of intentional understanding are grounded in experience with particular actions and particular actors. This apparent specificity is at odds with several recent proposals that infants are endowed with relatively abstract and general notions of intentionality (Baron-Cohen, 1995; Csibra *et al.*, 1999; Premack, 1990).

Discovering the Link between Looker and Object

In discovering the relation between a person and the object of her gaze, there are at least two kinds of evidence on which infants might draw. First, infants might note the behavioral regularities associated with gaze—that is, the ways in which gaze is related to the other actions a person performs. For example, people tend to move toward and act on objects that are the targets of their gaze rather than objects that have not been the targets of their gaze. These behavioral regularities are a critical aspect of the adult's understanding of gaze. Because we understand these aspects of gaze, we seamlessly infer that an opponent on the soccer field will veer in the direction in which her eyes are pointed and that a curious toddler will reach for the attractive coffee mug he has just spied. For adults, these behavioral regularities provide evidence of underlying psychological states, such as intentions, interests, or desires. Infants may understand the looker–object link at a behavioral level, without yet making inferences about the underlying psychological link between looker and object. It is also possible that behavioral evidence provides one source of infants' understanding of the psychological link between looker and object. As Whiten (1994) has proposed, a detailed behavioral understanding of human action could provide the basis for an insight about the underlying psychological causes of action.

Another route into the understanding of the link between looker and object may be provided by a second source of evidence available to infants—the evidence provided by their own eyes. Infants might reflect on their own experience of seeing, and in some way map this experience onto the gaze behavior of other people. This mapping would provide infants with information about the internal, psychological aspects of attention. This process might occur directly, based on an innate ability to link facial actions of self and other, as hypothesized by Meltzoff and Gopnik (1993). Alternatively, the experience of orienting in response to the gaze of another person could set up the conditions for associating the experience of seeing a particular object with observing the gaze of another person. This mechanism has been proposed by Moore and Corkum (1994) to contribute to the development of joint attention.

Each of these kinds of evidence likely plays a role in children's developing understanding of gaze at some point, and considering each of these kinds of evidence can help to explain the developmental lag in infants' understanding of gaze as object-directed compared to their understanding of grasping as object-directed. To start with, the behavioral information concerning the relation between actor and object may be less clear for acts of looking than for acts of grasping. Whereas grasps involve a physical connection between the actor and the object, gaze involves a relation at a distance. The demands posed by relating entities separated in space may make it more difficult for infants to learn about gaze. In addition, in everyday life, grasping is often accompanied by concrete cues to the actor's underlying intentions, and such cues may be more limited or even absent for gaze. For example, grasping often results in the object being moved closer to the actor, and this could help infants to infer that the actor had the goal of obtaining the object. In contrast, gaze itself has no effect on the object, and the consequences of gaze for the actor are not always obvious. In addition, if infants draw on their own experience of seeing, and seek to relate this to the behavior of other people, the demands of doing this may be greater for gaze than for grasps. Infants can observe their own grasps, but not their own gaze. Although there is evidence that infants can note the correspondence of oral gestures produced by themselves and others (Meltzoff and Gopnik, 1993), there is as yet no evidence as to whether they can do this for the actions of their eyes.

INFANTS' DEVELOPING UNDERSTANDING
OF POINTING AS AN OBJECT-DIRECTED ACTION

For adults, pointing, like gaze, serves as a spotlight to direct the observer's attention, and also implies an attentional link between the actor and an object. Most of the time in natural interaction, points, like gaze, specify an object at some distance from the actor. Infants begin to orient in response to points later than they do so for gaze. At about 12 months, or perhaps even later, babies begin to follow points at a distance; before 12 months infants are likely to ignore points or look at the pointing hand itself (Butterworth and Jarrett, 1991; Desrochers, Morissette, and Ricard, 1995; Lempers, 1979; Leung and Rheingold, 1981; Murphy and Messer, 1977).

When points occur in physical contact with the referent object, or quite close to the object, they may function as spotlights of attention for younger infants. For example, some researchers report that points very near to an object lead infants as young as 9 months of age to look at the object (Lempers, 1979; Murphy and Messer, 1977; but see Butterworth and Grover, 1988; Desrochers *et al.*, 1995). This instance of spotlighting may not be specific to points, since, as our prior work has shown, contacting an object with an inert hand or mechanical claw also serves to draw young infants' attention to the object (Woodward, 1998, 1999).

Jose Guajardo and I (Woodward and Guajardo, 2002) adapted the habituation paradigm described above to investigate infants' appreciation of pointing as an object-directed action. Given the findings just summarized, we were concerned that infants under 12 months might not follow a point at a distance to the referent object. If this occurred, then infants would have no hope of noting the relation between actor and object. Therefore, in the experimental events, we had the actor touch the toy with her index finger as she pointed. We expected that contact between the actor's hand and the toy would be sufficient to direct infants' attention to the toy.

In our first experiment, we tested 9- and 12-month-old infants. There were forty infants at each age. Half the infants at each age saw events that were very similar to the grasping events, in that only the actor's arm was visible (see Fig. 6.3, panel A). The other half saw events that more closely resembled naturalistic points. The actor was fully visible from the waist up; she made eye contact with the infant and greeted him or her, and then turned to look at and point to the toy (see Fig. 6.3, panel B). We thought that these additional cues might provide further evidence that the point was directed toward the object, and therefore that infants in this condition might respond to the relation between actor and object more strongly than those who saw only the actor's arm. In each condition, infants were habituated to one pointing event. Then the positions of the toys were reversed and infants saw new-toy test events (in which the actor moved her arm in the same way to point at the other toy) and new-path test events (in which the actor moved her arm through a different path in order to point at the same toy).

A. Hand only event   B. Fully visible event

FIGURE 6.3. Sample for the studies of pointing (based on Woodward and Guajardo, 2002).

Our first question was whether we had been successful at directing infants'
attention to the toy to which the actor pointed. To address this question, as in
prior studies, we coded the amount of time during test trials that infants looked
at the object indicated by the actor versus the other object. This coding confirmed
that both 9- and 12-month-olds oriented toward the object at which the actor
pointed: 92 percent of 12-month-olds and 95 percent of 9-month-olds looked for
longer at the indicated object than at the other object during test trials.

The next question was whether infants at either age attended to the relation
between the actor and the object of her point, as indicated by their overall levels
of looking on new-toy and new-path test events. Counter to our intuitions about
the additional information provided when the actor was fully visible, there were
no reliable differences between the patterns shown by infants who saw the actor's
face versus those who saw just the actor's arm. The main finding was that infants
at the two ages responded differently to the two kinds of test events. The
12-month-olds looked longer on new-toy trials than on new-path trials, indicating
that they noted the change in the relation between actor and object. In contrast,
the 9-month-olds as a group looked equally at the two test events. Further analyses indicated that for 9-month-olds the results varied as a function of the test trial
type given first. Infants at this age looked longer at the event they saw first, regardless of whether it was a new-toy or a new-path event. In contrast, 12-month-olds
looked longer on new-toy events whether they came first or second. Thus, by
12 months, infants seem to understand pointing as an object-directed action. As
is the case for gaze, therefore, infants appear to discover the object-directed nature
of points between 9 and 12 months of age.

The finding that 9-month-olds did not show evidence of understanding pointing as object-directed is noteworthy in comparison to the findings from earlier
studies indicating that infants 9 months of age and younger understanding grasping as object-directed (Woodward, 1998, 1999; Woodward *et al.*, 2001; see also
Wellman and Phillips, 2001). Pointing is similar to grasping in several respects: it
is a manual action, involving motion in the direction of an object, coordinated

motions of the digits, and, in our studies, physical contact between the actor and the toy. Nevertheless, 9-month-old infants represented the grasping and pointing events differently. These findings lend further support to the conclusion that infants begin with relatively specific understandings of object-directed action, and that they enrich this understanding by discovering the link between actor and object for new actions one at a time.

Discovering the Link between Pointer and Object

How do infants discover the object-directed nature of pointing? One possibility is that infants discover this link based on behavioral evidence during interactions with adults who point. Murphy and Messer (1977) found that when mothers point during interactions with their infants, they almost always look at the object of their point, and the onsets of the point and glance co-occur within a very narrow time window. Infants may note this co-occurrence and infer that, like looking, pointing also relates an actor to some object. It is also possible that in parents' behavioral repertoires pointing is probabilistically linked with other behaviors such as approaching, grasping, and handling, and that infants use these behavioral linkages as further evidence about pointing.

In addition to this source of evidence, the timing of the onset of point production, as well as the nature of the first points, suggests another possible contributor to the development of the understanding of points as object-directed. Researchers report the onset of object-directed points as early as 9 months of age (Bates *et al.*, 1979; Lempers, 1979; Murphy and Messer, 1977). Index finger extensions appear much earlier (Fogel and Hannon, 1985), but it is not until about 9 months that points appear to be directed at objects. A number of observers have reported that infants' first object-directed points appear not to be communicative in nature, but rather seem to be an expression of the infant's own attention and interest (Bates *et al.*, 1979; Desrochers *et al.*, 1995; Schaffer, 1984; Werner and Kaplan, 1963).

The appearance of object-directed points beginning at about 9 months of age suggests a means by which infants might learn about the relation between pointer and object: Specifically, infants might draw on their own experience of pointing as an expression of interest to infer that the points of others reflect a similar internal state. That is, infants may seek to relate their own internal experiences and actions to the observable actions of other people, and thereby gain an understanding of the attentional link between a person who points and the object of her point. If this account is correct, then infants' first insight into the object-directed nature of points may arise outside the communicative arena. That is, infants may first understand pointing as object-directed, and only later come to use and understand the gesture in acts of communication.

One prediction of this account is that there should be a correlation between infants' use of object-directed points and their understanding of the link between another person and the object of her point. In a first exploration of this possibility, Guajardo and I (Woodward and Guajardo, 2002) tested forty-eight infants between the ages of 8.5 and 11 months in the same procedure as in the first experiment, except that all infants saw the events from the 'fully visible' condition. In addition, we gathered two kinds of data on infants' own pointing behavior. First, by means of a short questionnaire, we asked parents whether they had observed their infants pointing at objects and also whether their infant seemed to use pointing to communicate. Second, we coded the videotape from each habituation session for the incidence of object-directed pointing. Much of the time the two sources of evidence agreed, but for some infants one but not the other provided evidence of object-directed pointing. We used these two sources of evidence together to determine whether there was any evidence that an infant pointed in an object-directed manner and whether this object-directed pointing was also communicative.

There were eighteen infants for whom there was evidence of object-directed pointing (henceforth, the pointers), and thirty for whom there was no evidence of object-directed pointing (henceforth, the nonpointers). Of the eighteen pointers, eight were rated by their parents as also using points to communicate, and ten were not. Thus, like previous observers, we found evidence for the existence of early, noncommunicative, object-directed pointing. Interestingly, pointing status was not related to age in the group we studied. The pointers were 9 months, 21 days, of age on average (those who used points communicatively had an average age of 9 months, 20 days, and those who did not had an average age of 9 months, 22 days), and the nonpointers were 9 months, 18 days, on average.

Our main finding was that pointing status was related to infants' responses to the habituation events. The nonpointers looked equally on the two kinds of test trials, thus showing no evidence of having noticed the relation between the actor and the object of her point. The pointers looked significantly longer on new-toy trials than on new-path trials, indicating that they noted and responded to the change in relation between the actor and the object of her point. This was true whether or not the infant also pointed communicatively. That is, the critical aspect of pointing behavior seemed to be the production of object-directed points and not the communicative use of points. This finding was not accounted for by differences in overall levels of engagement: pointers and nonpointers did not differ in the number of trials they took to habituate, or the total amount of time they spent watching the test events. Thus between 9 and 11 months, those infants who produced object-directed points also understood points produced by others as object-directed, whereas those who did not produce object-directed points seemed not to understand points as object-directed.

Of course, the existence of a correlation does not provide evidence as to the direction of causality. Infants may begin to produce object-directed points because they have learned about the object-directed nature of this gesture in others; or, as we hypothesize, they may discover the significance of the pointing gesture in other people based on their own use of the gesture. Until further evidence is gathered, our hypothesis remains a speculation. However, we believe some of the existing evidence supports it. Specifically, infants seem to understand the object-directed nature of points before they use or respond to them in the course of social interactions. Our findings suggest that infants become sensitive to the object-directed nature of others' points between 9 and 11 months. As reviewed above, it is not until after 12 months that infants systematically follow the points of social partners in the laboratory. This ordering of events is inconsistent with the possibility that insight into the object-directed nature of points results from observing the (socially produced) points of adults. If laboratory findings are an accurate reflection of point-following in the wild, then it is possible that infants' propensity to follow points results from their earlier discovery that pointing is an object-directed action.

Our preliminary findings indicate the need for further studies, particularly studies investigating the ontogeny of noncommunicative object-directed points. Because of a preoccupation with finding evidence for the intentional, communicative use of pointing, noncommunicative points have been neglected in the literature. In fact, some researchers report the onset of pointing as relatively late, 12 months or later, because they only count points that are accompanied by evidence of the intent to communicate such as gaze alternation (e.g. Carpenter *et al.*, 1998).

DISCUSSION

Infants develop in a sea of human action. This sea is packed with information critical for myriad aspects of development. Simply swimming in the sea is not sufficient for infants to gain full access to this information. Beyond just soaking it in, infants must be able to derive well-structured representations of the intentional actions they observe. This is particularly true for attentional and referential actions, such as gaze and pointing. In principle, observing these actions in others could inform infants about the properties of objects (e.g. which things are dangerous, or disgusting, or pleasing), the functions of cultural artifacts, and the meanings of words, as well as information about the behavioral propensities and internal states of the person who performs them. Children's ability to extract this information is dependent, in part, on their understanding that there is an attentional relation between the person and the object of her gaze and/or point.

It has long been known that infants in the first and second year of life respond to gaze and pointing by orienting to the relevant piece of the world. But until recently, little evidence has been available concerning infants' understanding of attentional relations. The findings reviewed in this chapter provide initial insights into this aspect of social cognition. They indicate that infants are not adrift in the sea of action, but rather, that they have begun to analyze the actions of others in terms of their intentional structure. Our findings suggest three initial conclusions, each of which motivates continued investigation.

1. Infants discover the relational structure of different actions at different points in development. Our findings suggest that infants become sensitive to the relational structure of different actions at different points in development. Although infants understand grasping as object-directed by 6 months of age, they do not seem to understand gaze and pointing as object-directed until near the end of the first year of life. Despite the fact that the pointing and grasping events we showed infants were in many ways similar, infants encoded them differently, suggesting that they attend to the fine details of actions. It is not the case that infants begin by encoding all human actions, or even all manual actions, as relational. Rather, infants seem to accrue knowledge about particular actions gradually during the first year of life.

These findings offer an initial foothold into infants' action knowledge, but they leave much of the terrain unexplored. There are many aspects of a mature understanding of pointing, and gaze that are not represented in the simplest construal of these actions as object-directed. The work reported here focuses on the way in which grasping, pointing, and looking are the same—they center on a relation between actor and object. In doing so, it leaves unaddressed infants' understanding of the ways these actions differ from one another, including both the unique mental correlates of each action and the unique behavioral regularities associated with each action. Progress has been made in investigating these issues in older children (see Flavell and Miller, 1998). A critical direction for future investigation is to explore these issues still earlier in ontogeny (Flavell and Miller, 1998).

2. Infants' propensity to orient in response to an action is distinct from their relational encoding of the action. There are multiple levels at which infants respond to the actions they observe. At one level, infants may respond to the actions of other people by orienting to specific aspects of the environment. At another level, infants may interpret these actions as instantiating a relation between the person and the object at which his or her actions are directed. Our findings indicate that these two levels of response are not always linked in development. Infants orient in response to a range of events and actions, only some of which they encode as object-directed. Moreover, in the case of gaze, infants show strong orienting responses many months before they become sensitive to the relation between looker and object.

One conclusion from these findings is that infants' orienting responses are not a simple reflection of their underlying comprehension of joint attention behaviors. These findings have strong implications for the approach of inferring infants' comprehension of an action based on their orienting responses. This approach runs the risk of over- or under-attributing comprehension to infants, and it may entirely miss important components of action knowledge. More generally, our findings suggest that it is misguided to seek a single measure of action 'comprehension'. Both orienting and relational encoding are intelligent responses to the actions of social partners, and these two responses do not exhaust the behavioral propensities or levels of interpretation that infants or young children might engage in.

3. *There are varied developmental relations between these two levels of response.* Considering our findings in the context of the broader joint attention literature suggests that there can be varying developmental relations between orienting responses to and relational encoding of particular actions. In particular, the relation between these two levels of response appears to be different for gaze than for pointing. Infants orient in response to gaze by 3 to 6 months of age, but our findings indicate that it is not until 9 to 12 months that infants understand gaze as an object-directed action. By contrast, infants seem not to follow points at a distance until 12 months at the earliest, around or just after the period when they begin to encode pointing as object-directed.

An important direction for further study will be to verify these patterns within a single population, and in so doing investigate the ways that orienting and relational encoding may impact one another during development. It is possible that in some cases, orienting responses set up the conditions for infants' extracting information about the object-directedness of the action to which they are responding. This may be the case for gaze. Alternatively, in other cases, infants may not spontaneously orient in response to an action until they have gleaned insight into its object-directedness. It is possible that this is true for pointing.

CONCLUSION

Although infants' responses to gaze and pointing initially follow different developmental pathways, our findings suggest that these pathways converge to yield a more general insight about attentional relations between 9 and 12 months of age. It is at this point that infants begin to construe two distinct actions, one done with the hands and the other with the eyes, as involving a connection between actor and object. This insight would enable infants to extract the rich and multi-faceted information that referential actions can provide. Indeed, recent findings indicate that in the months following their first birthdays, infants do just that. By 12 to 14 months, infants use gaze to predict a person's subsequent actions (Phillips, Wellman, and Spelke, 2002), interpret a person's emotional expressions as being about the object at which she gazes (Moses *et al.*, 2001; Repacholi, 1998), and interpret the words a person utters as naming the object at which she directs referential behaviors (Woodward, 2004).

REFERENCES

Baron-Cohen, S. (1995), *Mindblindness: An Essay on Autism and Theory of Mind.* Cambridge, Mass.: MIT Press.

Bates, E., Benigni, L., Bretherton, I., Camaioni, L., and Volterra, V. (1979), *The Emergence of Symbols: Cognition and Communication in Infancy.* New York: Academic Press.

Bruner, J. (1995), 'From joint attention to a meeting of minds: an introduction', in C. Moore and P. J. Dunham (eds.), *Joint Attention: Its Origins and Role in Development.* Hillsdale, NJ: Erlbaum, 1–14.

Butterworth, G. (1995), 'Origins of mind in perception and action', in C. Moore and P. J. Dunham (eds.), *Joint Attention: Its Origins and Role in Development.* Hillsdale, NJ: Erlbaum, 29–40.

—— and Cochran, E. (1980), 'Towards mechanisms of joint visual attention in human infancy', *International Journal of Behavioral Development,* 3: 253–72.

—— and Grover, L. (1988), 'The origins of referential communication in human infancy', in L. Weiskrantz (ed.), *Thought without Language.* Oxford: Clarendon Press, 5–24.

—— and Jarrett, N. (1991), 'What minds have in common is space: spatial mechanisms serving joint visual attention in infancy', *British Journal of Developmental Psychology,* 9: 55–72.

Caron, A. J., Caron, R. F., Caldwell, R. C., and Weiss, S. J. (1973), 'Infant perception of the structural properties of the face', *Developmental Psychology,* 9: 385–99.

Carpenter, M., Nagell, K., and Tomasello, M. (1998), 'Social cognition, joint attention and communicative competence from 9 to 15 months of age', *Monographs of the Society for Research in Child Development,* 63 (4).

Csibra, G., Gergely, G., Biro, S., Koos, O., and Brockbank, M. (1999), 'Goal attribution without agency cues: the perception of "pure reason" in infancy', *Cognition,* 72: 237–67.

D'Entremont, B., Hains, S. M. J., and Muir, D. W. (1997), 'A demonstration of gaze following in 3- to 6-month-olds', *Infant Behavior and Development,* 20 (4): 569–72.

Desrochers, S., Morissette, P., and Ricard, M. (1995), 'Two perspectives on pointing in infancy', In C. Moore and P. J. Dunham (eds.), *Joint Attention: Its Origins and Role in Development.* Hillsdale, NJ: Erlbaum, 85–102.

Flavell, J. H., and Miller, P. H. (1998), 'Social cognition', in W. Damon, D. Kuhn, and R. S. Siegler (eds.), *Handbook of Child Psychology,* ii: *Cognition, Perception and Language.* New York: John Wiley and Sons, 851–98.

Fogel, A., and Hannon, T. E. (1985), 'Manual actions of nine- to fifteen-week-old human infants during face-to-face interaction with their mothers', *Child Development,* 56: 1271–9.

Guajardo, J. J., and Woodward, A. L. (in press), 'Is agency skin-deep? Surface attributes influence infants' sensitivity to goal-directed action', *Infancy.*

Hains, S. M. J., and Muir, D. W. (1996), 'Infant sensitivity to adult eye direction', *Child Development,* 67: 1940–51.

Haith, M. M., Bergman, T., and Moore, M. J. (1977), 'Eye contact and face scanning in early infancy', *Science,* 198: 853–5.

Hood, B. M., Willen, D., and Driver, J. (1998), 'Adult's eyes trigger shifts of visual attention in human infants', *Psychological Science,* 9: 131–4.

LEMPERS, J. D. (1979), 'Young children's production and comprehension of nonverbal deictic behaviors', *Journal of Genetic Psychology*, 135: 95–102.

LEUNG, E. H. L., and RHEINGOLD, H. L. (1981), 'Development of pointing as a social gesture', *Developmental Psychology*, 17: 215–20.

MAURER, D., and SALAPATEK, P. (1976), 'Developmental changes in the scanning of faces by young infants', *Child Development*, 47: 523–7.

MELTZOFF, A., and GOPNIK, A. (1993), 'The role of imitation in understanding persons and developing a theory of mind', in S. Baron-Cohen, H. Tager-Flusberg, and D. J. Cohen (eds.), *Understanding Other Minds*. Oxford: Oxford University Press, 335–66.

MOORE, C., and CORKUM, V. (1994), 'Social understanding at the end of the first year of life', *Developmental Review*, 14: 349–72.

MOSES, L., BALDWIN, D. A., ROSICKY, J. G., and TIDBALL, G. (2001), 'Evidence for referential understanding in the emotions domain at 12 and 18 months', *Child Development*, 72: 718–35.

MURPHY, C. M., and MESSER, D. J. (1977), 'Mothers, infants and pointing: a study of a gesture', in H. R. Schaffer (ed.), *Studies in Mother–Infant Interaction*. London: Academic Press, 325–54.

PHILLIPS, A. T., WELLMAN, H. M., and SPELKE, E. S. (2002), 'Infants' ability to connect gaze and emotional expression to intentional action', *Cognition*, 85, 53–78.

PREMACK, D. (1990), 'The infant's theory of self-propelled objects', *Cognition*, 36: 1–16.

REPACHOLI, B. M. (1998), 'Infants' use of attentional cues to identify the referent of another person's emotional expression', *Developmental Psychology*, 34 (5): 1017–25.

SCAIFE, M., and BRUNER, J. S. (1975), 'The capacity for joint visual attention in the infant', *Nature*, 253: 265–6.

SCHAFFER, H. R. (1984), *The Child's Entry into a Social World*. London: Academic Press.

SOMMERVILLE, J. A. (2002), 'Means–end Reasoning: Infants' Developing Ability to Interpret and Perform Intentional Actions (unpublished Ph.D. diss., University of Chicago).

SYMONS, L. A., HAINS, S. M. J., and MUIR, D. W. (1998), 'Look at me: five-month-old infants' sensitivity to very small deviations in eye-gaze during social interactions', *Infant Behavior and Development*, 21 (3): 531–6.

VECERA, S. P., and JOHNSON, M. H. (1995), 'Gaze detection and the cortical processing of faces: evidence from infants and adults', *Visual Cognition*, 2: 59–87.

WELLMAN, H. M., and PHILLIPS, A. T. (2001), 'Developing intentional understandings', in B. Malle, L. Moses, and D. Baldwin (eds.), *Intentionality: A Key to Human Understanding*. Cambridge, Mass.: MIT Press, 125–48.

WERNER, H., and KAPLAN, B. (1963), *Symbol Formation*. New York: John Wiley and Sons, Inc.

WHITEN, A. (1994), 'Grades of mind reading', in C. Lewis and P. Mitchell (eds.), *Children's Early Understanding of Mind*. Hillsdale, NJ: Erlbaum, 47–70.

WOODWARD, A. L. (1998), 'Infants selectively encode the goal object of an actor's reach', *Cognition*, 69: 1–34.

—— (1999), 'Infants' ability to distinguish between purposeful and non-purposeful behaviors', *Infant Behavior and Development*, 22: 145–60.

—— (2003), 'Infants' developing understanding of the link between looker and object', *Developmental Science*, 6: 297–311.

WOODWARD, A. L. (2004), 'Infants' use of action knowledge to get a grasp on words', in D. G. Hall and S. R. Waxman (eds.), *Weaving a Lexicon*. Cambridge, Mass.: MIT Press, 149–72.

—— and GUAJARDO, J. J. (2002), 'Infants' understanding of the point gesture as an object-directed action', *Cognitive Development*, 17: 1061–84.

—— SOMMERVILLE, J. A., and GUAJARDO, J. J. (2001), 'How infants make sense of intentional action', in B. Malle, L. Moses, and D. Baldwin (eds.), *Intentions and Intentionality: Foundations of Social Cognition*. Cambridge, Mass.: MIT Press, 149–69.

7

Infant Pointing: Harlequin, Servant of Two Masters

Fabia Franco

INTRODUCTION

In this chapter I want to examine one specific aspect of joint attention: that is the production of the pointing gesture by infants. In particular, I will report my own work on this topic and discuss it in a broader joint attention context. I will try to argue that pointing, like Harlequin,[1] serves two masters: social cognition and language development. It is in providing the link, and informing one domain with the other, that pointing presents a uniquely powerful tool in communication and language development.

Some babies start pointing around 9 months of age, and most babies do so by their first birthday (Blake, O'Rourke, and Borzellino, 1994). In shops, parks, or at traffic lights it is very common indeed to see toddlers in pushchairs pointing at interesting things and vocalizing. In most cases, they point *to show* all these amazing things to the companion of their trip.

The pointing gesture emerging around the end of the first year of life involves the extension of both arm and index finger towards an object, person, or visual event. It is often co-ordinated with other communicative behaviours such as vocalizations, and it is intentionally addressed. In the pre-verbal infant, this is shown by gaze alternation between referent and addressee, a criterion vastly agreed upon in developmental psychology (among others, see Golinkoff, 1983; Tomasello, 1995).

As is often apparent when we look at human development closely, this well-formed ability does not appear suddenly, although an individual baby may have never pointed with the finger before today. When it does happen, there may be the

This chapter is dedicated to the memory of two developmental psychologists: George Butterworth, with whom some of the work reported here was conducted, and Gabriele Di Stefano, who taught me, but died at the time I began to write this chapter.

S. Arcati, A. Gagliano, P. Perucchini, C. Raneri, and A. Tasso collaborated with the collection and analysis of data reported here. The studies were carried out under two grants from the Economic and Social Research Council of Great Britain to G. Butterworth and F. Franco, and grants from the Italian National Research Council, the Italian Ministry of University & Scientific Research and NFFR/Middlesex to F. Franco.

[1] In the Italian *commedia dell'arte*, Harlequin is a comic character whose troubles often arise from serving two masters.

subjective impression of having entered a new era in the relationship with the baby. Years ago I used to give checklists of communicative behaviours and simple diaries to fill to friends who had babies. One such friend was a philosopher of language, who did not become an assiduous observer, contrary to my hopes—until his baby daughter began to point. Suddenly, it was interesting, there was great excitement: the basis for the triangle of reference had been established. Not all fathers are as interested as my friend in reference *per se*, but the changes in communication at this stage of development are important enough to justify the label 'revolution' used by Tomasello (1995, 1999*b*) to describe them: that is, the passage from dyadic to triadic interaction.

The magnitude of the subjective experience in the above anecdote is matched by the attention paid to the pointing gesture in classical or early theoretical accounts of psychological development which concerned themselves also with language. A brief summary of such accounts will show how one of the central questions related to pointing is its communicative function. For instance, both Werner and Kaplan (1963) and Vygotsky (1926) ascribed great importance to pointing, although for different reasons. Werner and Kaplan thought that pointing was special because it marks the first, pre-verbal form of reference characterized by a 'contemplative stance'. For that pointing would later develop, functionally, into naming. By contrast, for Vygotsky early pointing was associated with the instrumental (rather than 'contemplative' or, we would say, declarative) function, and its importance lies in replacing the request reaching gesture (as a failed attempt to grasp an out-of-reach object) with a proper symbol. Pointing would then play a crucial role in the development of the symbolic function, which is essential for language.

Although the above views stress different aspects of pointing, what is implicitly common between the two proposals is the referential nature of the pointing gesture, its singling out of a target against a background and making of this a shared referent for communication. In this respect, pointing is perhaps the most obvious realization of triadic communication.

More specifically, the pointing gesture appears to be the very embodiment of joint attention initiated by the infant, as the example in Fig. 7.1 shows. Here, an 18-month-old girl points first to her mother's eyes and then to her own target of interest, hence drawing a line which connects mother's eyes and referent. Thus, pointing could be considered a symbol of extended attention or of the deployment of attention.

It is, however, the question of the more general pragmatic meaning of pointing that has attracted a great deal of attention recently. In this respect, it is important to distinguish between the pointing gesture as such and communicative acts[2] involving pointing. On its own, the former is a directive for someone's attention: something like 'Look at that' or, as illustrated by the example in Fig. 7.1, 'Turn your eyes

---

[2] For the notions of communicative acts as a form of pre-verbal speech acts and of 'primitive speech acts', see Dore, 1975, 1976.

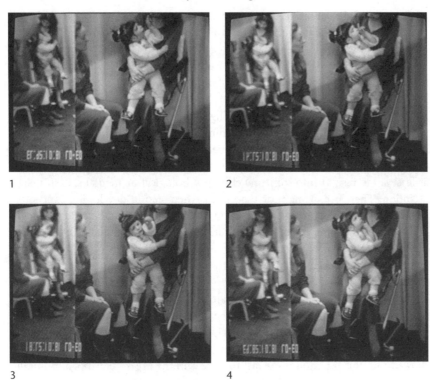

FIGURE 7.1. An 18-month-old girl draws a line with her pointing finger between her mother's eyes and an interesting target.

over there'. Nevertheless, *communicative acts* involving pointing can be declarative as well as imperative.[3] Babies point because they want to share attention with someone about some object/event (proto-declarative: 'That/X is interesting!'), or because they want someone to do something for them about some object/event (proto-imperative: 'Give me that/X', for instance). However, young children with autism appear to have significant difficulties with joint attention in general (Mundy, Sigman, and Kasari, 1990), and in particular with proto-declarative pointing (Baron-Cohen, 1989; Carpenter and Tomasello, 2000). Furthermore, primates have been shown to produce gestures (sometimes even finger, point-like gestures) having proto-imperative but not proto-declarative function (e.g. Gomez, 1991; Leavens, Hopkins, and Bard, 1996). Therefore, proto-declarative and proto-imperative communicative acts involving pointing are unlikely to be variants of the same script. Although they are both intentionally addressed (gaze

---

[3] In the developmental literature, the terminology proto-declarative/imperative has been used more often than assertive/directive, hence it will be adopted here.

alternation) and referential (clear, shareable target), the former appears linked to the developing understanding of the mind, the latter to an understanding of action. In other words, the social partner is attributed physical agency (agent of her action) in proto-imperative acts, but mental agency in proto-declarative acts (e.g. agent of her own attention) (see also Tomasello, 1995, 1999*a*). More specifically, pointing acts specialize in proto-declarative communication.

This general picture has two interesting sides, which I will attempt to illustrate with experimental data: the first concerning social cognition, the second concerning language development. If we consider the development of social cognition, pointing, particularly in a proto-declarative communicative act, appears to imply at least some insight into someone else's psychological or mental states, such as attention. Therefore, it may correspond to a first step in developing conceptual knowledge about people, in the direction of what later would be called a 'theory of mind'. On the other hand, the implications relevant for language development derive not only from the referential component intrinsic to pointing, but also from the link between certain declaratives and linguistic expression. Generally speaking, the goal of an assertion is that of passing on some information to the addressee which would change their state of knowledge. Halliday (1975) distinguished simple declarations (in which the information passed on to the addressee is not necessarily new to them) from declarations conveying information which is *new to the addressee*. He called the latter pragmatic function 'informational' and showed that this function is the last to appear in the pre-verbal epoch of human development, coinciding with the appearance of systematic verbalizations in the second half of the second year of life. As we will see, pointing appears to have specific use in realizing informational acts when language is still very limited.

In this chapter, I will report my own work, beginning with an analysis of the emergence of the pointing gesture and its pragmatic meanings in infancy, then moving on to implications for social cognition and joint attention, and finally exploring the link with language.

THE POINTING GESTURE

The emergence of pointing as a gesture around the end of the first year of life is prepared by developments in cognition, emotion, and motor control. To begin with, I will analyse various aspects concerning the pointing posture, whereas in the second part of this section I will discuss our first studies and issues related to the communicative functions (also referred to as pragmatic meanings) of pointing.

Babies as young as three months have been reported to produce a pointing hand posture, which is not a pointing gesture for morphological and functional reasons: it lacks the arm extension typical of pointing, and is not directed to any meaningful aspect of the environment. The context of occurrence is face-to-face interaction, during what has been called 'proto-conversation' (Fogel and Hannan, 1985; Trevarthen, 1977). Arm extensions become systematically successful in reaching movements aimed at grasping an object between 4 and 5 months of age, and the index finger is used consistently to explore details and contours of objects between 8 and 10 months.[4] Finally, in the last trimester of the first year most infants achieve the pincer grip and produce pointing gestures. My own research begins here, with the advent of canonical pointing.

Canonical pointing is a gesture involving the extension of both arm and index finger, with the other fingers curled under. In our studies we observed how this particular posture might be considered the core prototype of a wider (and fuzzier) category. Infants produce a number of other manual gestures with indicative function, which lack either the conventional hand posture for pointing or the extension of the arm (see also Lock *et al.*, 1990). In the latter case, we have small points characterized by the extension of the index finger only (not the arm); the hand may be at rest (e.g. on a table) or may be being used for something else (e.g. holding something). Finger points have also been observed in the context of adult gesticulation accompanying speech (McNeill, 1987). However, the more variable category is the former, when the arm is extended, but the hand assumes all sorts of postures (see Fig. 7.2), such as the following: fist-shaped postures (e.g. Fig. 7.2c); fingers other than the index finger stretched towards the target (e.g. the middle finger or the little finger); a flat open hand with fingers extended and set very apart, or a flat hand with all fingers extended but tightly close to one another as in the Roman salute (e.g. Fig. 7.2a), and so on.

In babies, perhaps the aspect in common between these indicating gestures is that they appear somewhat 'rushed': that is, they are gestures not necessarily of shorter duration, but ones that somehow have a sudden and very quick start in comparison to canonical pointing. For the rest, they are typically accompanied by neutral to positive facial expressions and a sitting back posture (see also Lock *et al.*, 1990), hence supporting the idea that they are indeed serving the same referential function as pointing. The proportion of these gestures remains fairly stable well into the third year of life (see Franco and Gagliano, 2001). Finally, infants under 18 months were observed to produce indicating gestures with other parts of the body: for instance, head-pointing (when the head is suddenly directed and raised in the direction of the target) or foot-pointing (when the leg is suddenly extended from a sitting posture with the foot directed toward a target). Again, forms of indicating with non-pointing hand postures or with other parts of the body have been observed also in adults and in other cultures—for instance, the conventional lip-pointing amongst the Guatemalan San Blas Cuna (Sherzer, 1973).

---

[4] Already Shinn (1900) had suggested a link between the index finger explorations of fine details of objects (typical at the end of the first year) and the emerging pointing gesture, in that both are exploratory in function: the former of proximal space, the latter of distal space.

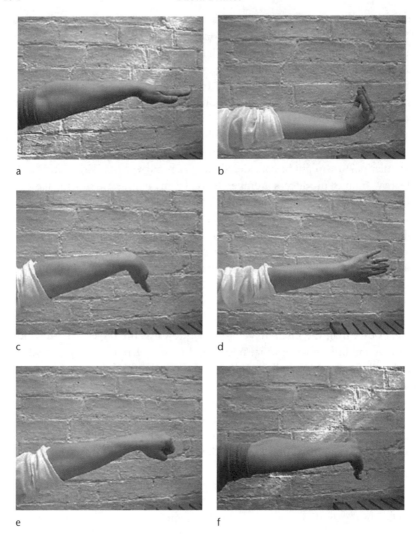

FIGURE 7.2. Examples of some hand postures observed in infant indicating gestures (here performed by an adult).

In sum, indicating referential acts can be performed by using a variety of hand and body postures. Amongst them, conventional pointing has acquired prototypical status, and is the most frequently used also by babies. If imitation accounts for the general posture (arm and hand), something else must be invoked to explain why 3-month-old infants produce hand-only pointing postures during face-to-face interaction with an adult (Trevarthen, 1977; Fogel and Hannan, 1985). As mentioned earlier, such finger points are typically produced during what have been called 'proto-conversations' (i.e. instances of vocal turn-taking) while baby and adult are engaged in mutual gaze, positive affect, and vocalizing. And of course, such finger points have no referential meaning, as they are not directed anywhere coinciding with the simultaneous or temporally adjacent deployment of visual attention by the baby. In other words, such pointing hand postures happen to be produced in the process of *mutual attention* associated with vocal communication in young babies. In this context, the index finger does not have just one-fifth likelihood of being extended: the other fingers do not enter a specific posture anywhere near as often as the index finger does. It is therefore possible that the pointing hand posture is part of a specialized (species-specific) repertoire linked to instrumental and symbolic behaviour associated with socialization and tool use (Butterworth and Franco, 1993). In fact, it is the index finger again that is involved in the pincer grip (a species-typical grip) that babies develop in the last trimester of their first year while handling and exploring objects. However, the very same posture (pincer grip) is exercised non-functionally (i.e. in the lack of any object) by young babies. Similarly to finger points, it is the index finger that is mostly involved in such grips (see anecdotal photographic evidence in Fig. 7.3).

If the development of the postural aspects involved in the pointing gesture appears relatively clear, the development of pointing communicative functions has been debated. Therefore, in the first studies we tried to address the issue of the core meaning (in terms of pragmatic function) of pointing, as this appeared to be the key to the developmental story. As mentioned earlier, classical theories (Werner and Kaplan, 1963; Vygotsky, 1926) and more recent contributions (e.g. Bates, Camaioni, and Volterra, 1975; Bruner, 1975) offered different predictions. Following Vygotsky, one would expect pointing to emerge in request contexts, as a symbolic replacement of reaching gestures. Differently, following Werner and

FIGURE 7.3. Examples of infants (3-week-, 3-month-, and 7-month-old, respectively) producing the hand posture later used in precision pincer grips.

Kaplan, one would expect pointing to emerge as a referential-declarative gesture, independently from reaching and requests.

Research around this had been scarce and, by and large, lacking sufficient experimental control to answer the questions convincingly. For instance, Leung and Rheingold (1981) did introduce various interactional contexts in order to analyse gesture production in infancy, but then their count of gestures was collapsed across contexts. In this way information about the communicative function of gestures (based on production contexts) was lost. Hence their support for Vygotsky's hypothesis on the grounds that there appears to be more reaching in younger babies and more pointing in older babies was flawed by having confounded the gestures' symbolic meanings with their communicative functions. In other words, their results were perfectly compatible with the idea that perhaps younger babies would produce more requests than declarations, but pointing would emerge in declarative contexts. Older babies would perhaps produce more declarations and use pointing with both request and declarative functions.

A systematic analysis of typically developing infants' gestures in controlled contexts appeared timely, therefore. In our studies (Butterworth and Franco, 1993; Franco and Butterworth, 1996), rather than just registering pointing production contexts in spontaneous interaction, and interpreting them as 'request' or 'declaration' (the typical analysis at the time), we decided to go experimental and introduce control over production contexts. By manipulating objects—baby distance and type of object, we created two contexts designed to facilitate different communicative intents: either the desire to get hold of a toy and manipulate/play with it (request), or the desire to share attention/comments about a novel event with someone (declaration). Perhaps a neater experimental design would have not confounded distance and type of object. But what we aimed at in the first place was to create ecologically valid contexts, natural enough for a baby to produce requestive or declarative gestures, rather than be distracted or bored by some odd (however meaningful for a draconian experimentalist) aspect of the context.[5] We used average-size toys (e.g. a toy telephone) near the baby to facilitate acts of request (Request-Facilitating, REQ-F henceforth) and large doll manikins on stands (Fig. 7.4), which could be animated via remote control, far from the baby, to facilitate declarative acts (Declarative-Facilitating, DEC-F henceforth). Near and far were defined as follows: near was just out of reach for the baby, and far was at the other end of the room, about 250 cm away. The 'treatment' to induce requestive acts included the experimenter demonstrating two toys (both producing effects such as movement of some internal part and noise or sound), whereas the 'treatment' to induce declarative acts involved the animation of the two dolls according to a pre-established sequence of movement and pause.

---

[5] However, systematic target–baby variations of distance were investigated later in the referential-declarative context (Franco, 1995, 2002).

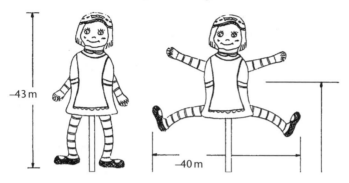

-43 m

-40 m

FIGURE 7.4. Animated objects used in the experiments.

The two contexts were considered the strongest feature on which to base our interpretation of the pragmatic meaning of a gesture, at least in the absence of contradicting signs. For instance, a point produced in the DEC-F context was assumed to have a declarative function. A gesture produced in the REQ-F context was assumed to have a request function if associated with serious to negative facial expression, but a declarative function if associated with a smile (another indicator would be, for example, a leaning forward versus sitting back posture, or the quality of associated vocalizations). Analogously, hand-open gestures such as reaching, produced in the DEC-F context while leaning forward with a serious to negative facial expression and rhythmic, harsh vocalizations, would not be taken as a declaration.[6] Eventually, this detailed analysis of gestures did not prove necessary, because the large majority of gestures produced in the DEC-F context were points accompanied by neutral to positive facial expression, sitting back posture, and often excited vocalizations (hence prototypical declarative). On the other hand, in the REQ-F condition there were more reaches than points, and the majority of points was associated with positive facial expression or sitting back postures, hence still suggesting a comment rather than a request (Table 7.1). Therefore, we felt reasonably confident in seeing pointing as typically declarative, and reaching as typically requestive, in our experimental conditions, at least in the age range considered here (10–19 months) (Franco and Butterworth, 1996).

[6] Such reaching gestures are the first type of request gesture typically emerging in human development; they are often produced in a ritualized form, with the hand opening and closing rapidly as if grasping an object, while looking at the social partner (among others, Bates, Camioni and Volterra, 1975, which refers to these gestures as 'proto-imperative'). Although their origin is likely to be in failed attempts to grasp an object, the action corresponding to the aim of the gesture (grasping) is used with a signal function when addressed to someone, in order to act on the addressee so that he or she will provide the desired, out-of-reach object. Later, the same communicative goal is achieved by using a variety of gestures, including pointing and 'give-me' (open hand, palm up, oriented towards the desired object), and language.

TABLE 7.1. *Average incidence of pointing and reaching by 12–19-month-olds in Declarative- and Request-facilitating contexts*

		Declarative-facilitating	Request-facilitating
Experiment 1	Pointing	8.0	6.7
	Reaching	0.3	10.7
Experiment 2	Pointing	10.5	6.5
	Reaching	0.5	8.0

Source: Franco and Butterworth, 1996.

Another aspect of the setting that was novel was that we controlled carefully the relative position of baby and social partner. The sitting arrangements were such that the baby had to turn 90 degrees to her left or right in order to see the adult's face. That meant that every baby's look directed to the adult's face required a voluntary movement, different from what happens in face-to-face interaction where the participants' eyes may meet by chance. Capitalizing on all the previous work on communication development and the issue of intentionality, we knew that for pre-verbal communication to be considered intentional, the gesture or vocalization would have to be associated with a look directed to the addressee. The conventional indicator (conservative as it might be) of intentionality therefore involved gaze alternation between referent and social partner (e.g. Golinkoff, 1983).

Finally, in a first experiment we asked the infant's mother to be the social partner, while in a second experiment an experimenter was used. The social partner was supposed not to point or direct the baby's attention, but she could be spontaneous in responding to the baby's initiatives or sustaining the baby's interest in the objects with vocal and facial behaviour. In other words, we wanted to keep the interaction as natural as possible, while leaving to the baby the task of initiating. Remarkable individual differences were observed amongst the mothers, with some being very or even too active and others being so quiet they hardly smiled or said a word. We worried that this might introduce a confounding element, and switched to an experimenter for social partner in the second experiment, in order to give all participants the same type and amount of response/support. Of course the issue that we so carefully avoided (maternal individual differences and their impact on infant's communicative style) is tremendously important and would deserve to be addressed in its own right. However, the results of the two experiments were very similar.

The results showed that in the condition designed to facilitate declarative communication (DEC-F) the majority of gestures produced were pointing, whereas reaching was restricted to the condition designed to induce requests (toys just out of reach, REQ-F). As pointing was produced with a declarative function even by the youngest participants (12 months) in two experiments, we later tested a younger group of 10-month-olds in order to check the primary meaning issue at the level of pointing emergence (proto-imperative versus proto-declarative first). The younger the babies, the fewer of them were producing any pointing at all, at least in the laboratory; for many of them, the parents did not think pointing was yet in their repertoires. However, those 10-month-olds who were able to point did engage in proto-declarative pointing—fewer points than older babies produced in the DEC-F context, but they were none the less declarative gestures. Thus, the declarative function is there right from when pointing begins. Other studies have suggested that infants younger than 12 months tend to produce more imperative than declarative pointing, but the evidence showing a primacy of requesting over declaring in the ontogenesis of pointing behaviours is limited (Carpenter, Nagell, and Tomasello, 1998; Perucchini, 1997).

However, the possibility still existed that requesting precedes declaring at a microgenetic level, that is, within a session or episode. One of our experiments therefore included order of presentation of the requesting- and declaring-inducing conditions as a factor. The results indicated that this did not affect the distribution of gestures within conditions. In other words, there was no evidence of a greater production of imperative gestures in the first than in the second part of the session, or of a greater production of pointing in the REQ-F context if this was presented first (Franco and Butterworth, 1996).

In sum, the results of these first experiments supported the hypothesis that pointing emerges as a specifically declarative component of communication. Interestingly, around their first birthdays, babies begin to produce a number of other gestures, such as 'all-gone' (both hands palm up), which are used within declarative communicative acts. However, these other gestures have a much lower frequency of occurrence, probably because they include some further constraint to their meaning with respect to pointing, at least in the contexts we used. For example, while the pointing gesture just singles out a referent, a gesture as 'all-gone' involves a referent and its disappearance, which is a much less frequent event. In other words, whereas a baby can point to a variety of things/events, including the door behind which someone has disappeared, he or she will only be able to produce an 'all-gone' gesture in the latter context. Furthermore, one could argue that pointing is almost a materialization of attention in space *per se* (spotlight), whereas in other gestures with a declarative function the referential component is instrumental to convey some other meaning (e.g. 'gone'). Therefore, pointing is not only a proto-declarative gesture, but a gesture whose meaning is mainly focused on the deployment of attention. And when such a gesture is socialized (i.e. intentionally addressed to another person, as shown by gaze alternation between referent and addressee), it becomes the quintessential tool for initiating joint attention.

POINTING AND GAZE

In our first studies, what I think was the most important finding concerned visual checking associated with gestures. We had set up our layout in such a way that babies had to turn 90 degrees to the left or right if they wanted to look into the addressee's eyes/face. The purpose of this arrangement was for us to be able to monitor voluntary head turns aimed to establish eye contact or check on the social partner's direction of attention. In this way we were able to assess whether there was evidence of intentional communication for the gestures observed. In other words, only if there is evidence of the gesture having an intended recipient (as suggested, for example, by gaze alternation between referent of the gesture and addressee) can we consider it as a means to convey some kind of meaning *for* some social agent/recipient. In this respect, the possibility exists that pointing is produced by the younger infants mostly in an 'egocentric' way—that is, without looking at the social partner to check if they are attending (as suggested by Bates, Camaioni, and Volterra, 1975).

More than half of the gestures in our studies were socialized (i.e. accompanied by visual checking with the adult). There did not appear to be large differences in the overall proportion of socialized gestures between the various types of gestures (pointing, indicating, reaching, etc.), although this proportion tended to be higher for pointing. However, a significant difference emerged in the way the pattern of visual checking associated with pointing (declarative) versus reaching (imperative) developed across age-groups, as illustrated below.

In order to produce a fine-grained analysis of the co-ordination between gestures and looks to the addressee, we considered a time window from 2 seconds before gesture initiation to 2 seconds after gesture completion. We then classified gesture/gaze combinations into discrete categories based on the timing of the occurrence of the first look to the addressee (gaze before, during, or after gesture). We also counted the proportion of gestures that were accompanied by two or more looks (e.g. during and after gesture: *multicheck*).

For the proto-imperative gesture of reaching, the timing of checking was almost invariably *during* gesture execution, and the occurrence of *multicheck* was low in the age range considered (10–19 months). For pointing the pattern was very different, with the younger babies (10- and 12-month-olds) visually checking with the social partner mostly *after* or *during* the point, 13–15-month-olds typically checking *during* pointing (gaze alternation between referent and adult), and 16–19-month-olds checking *before* pointing and then again (increasing use of *multicheck*) (Franco and Butterworth, 1996). Thus there was a shift in the timing of checking associated with pointing: the older the babies, the earlier the look. Specifically, pointing at 16–19 months was typically associated with an *anticipatory* look to the adult.

The pattern of visual checking with reaching, mostly during the gesture, is what one would expect from the definition of an 'intentional gesture', typically characterized by gaze alternation between addressee and referent (e.g. Golinkoff, 1983). More recently, it has been suggested that such developments are part of the '9 month revolution', hence involve the attribution of physical agency to others (Tomasello, 1995, 1999*b*). Indeed, the very same pattern also characterizes pointing until about 16 months of age, as well as all other gestures considered in our studies (Franco, 2002). Thus, it appears that irrespective of both a gesture pragmatic function (e.g. proto-declarative versus proto-imperative) and symbolic content (e.g. pointing versus all-gone), visual checking tends to occur *during* the gesture. But, besides this common basis, the development of pointing/gaze co-ordinations presents some specific and quite unique features. In particular, the later development of anticipatory looks to the addressee associated specifically with pointing highlights an insight into social cognition: namely, that persons are agents not only of their own actions but also of a mental state such as attention. The following paragraphs will analyse in detail the development of pointing/gaze co-ordinations and their significance.

In our experimental conditions, the youngest babies (aged 10 months) either would not point or would do so to a lesser extent than even 12-month-olds (see previous section). However, those 10-month-olds who did point did so (a) in proto-declarative contexts, and (b) clearly addressing the social partner—that is, turning to look towards the adult, usually after the completion of the gesture, or during it. This temporal frame (look 'after') is where infants come from; that is, it is the typical sequence characterizing emerging joint attentional (triadic, intersubjective) behaviours, such as the following:

1. *Event*: an interesting event happens (whether distal or proximal—e.g. the baby discovers a new object or new properties of an object, etc.), in the presence of a social partner;
2. *Referential look*: after (1) the baby turns to look at the social partner (often vocalizing and/or producing some facial expressions other than poker face) and then returns to the event/object (see D'Odorico and Levorato, 1990, among others).

This pattern of behaviour is certainly typical around 9 months. We can speculate that pointing is initially simply added to this basic triadic interaction, included in the pay-attention-to-event part of the sequence described above. The trouble is, this is not a straightforward operation, as it involves one more element getting into the sequence, and this element is a new scheme. As we have seen, although index finger extensions do occur in 3–4-month-olds, arm extensions as in the typical pointing gesture are not observed at that age. For one thing, various components of the gesture need to be co-ordinated (simultaneous arm and finger extension, aiming at the target, etc.). Imitation may play a role in achieving the conventional pointing gesture. Moreover, in Piagetian terms, we are witnessing the development of the creative combination of two (or more) motor schemes: organizing a specialized action (pointing gesture) and co-ordinating it with looking and, very often, vocalizing.

In our studies, we had the luck to catch a few 10-month-old babies in the very working out of this co-ordination (or dissociation and re-co-ordination). Once an interesting visual event had happened, the infant would first produce a point towards the objects involved in the event and *then* turn to look at the mother, as is quite typical in this age-group. However, the pointing hand/arm would also move from the target to the mother as if following the eyes; that is, the target for gaze and point was the same (object first, then social partner). Behaviourally, this means pointing and looking at the event, then turning to look at and point to the adult (often going back with gaze and point to the event, and so on). If we consider this, even the more typical gaze alternation between referent and addressee *during* pointing or other gestures appears a great achievement in flexibility, keeping in mind also that vocalizations are to be integrated in this behavioural sequence.

Within the next 6 months of development, however, another element would be added to the sequence in the case of proto-declarative pointing: an anticipatory look to the social partner, just *before* initiating the gesture. Although this behaviour occasionally happens with other gestures too, it becomes systematic only for pointing (Franco, 2002; Franco and Butterworth, 1996; Franco, Perucchini, and Butterworth, 1992; Franco and Wishart, 1995). Furthermore, such anticipatory looking is likely to be a generalized behaviour in communicative acts involving pointing only temporarily (between 18 and 24 months). In the third year of life, it appears to be used 'strategically',—that is, specifically in contexts where joint attention is more difficult to achieve (see next section and Assanelli, Salerni, and Franco, 2001; Franco, 1995; Franco and Gagliano, 2001). Figure 7.5 presents a summary of the evolving pointing/gaze relation.

Visual checking before pointing, as seen in an 18-month-old, appears to involve some hierarchical thinking and the seed of mentalizing. In the attempt to explain this achievement, we must keep in mind that with proto-declarative pointing, the main goal is to bring someone else's attention to the referent object or event that the infant finds interesting. Once this is realized, some exchange of information concerning the referent may take place—for instance, identity ('This is a X'), properties ('Big', 'Red', 'Fast'), actions ('Moved', 'Stopped'), or the self (['I FIND THIS'] 'Interesting', 'Funny', 'Scary', 'Novel', etc.). Pointing is highly associated with infant vocal behaviour, and the majority of points would be accompanied by at least some vocalizing. Thus, the comment following a pointing gesture may be conveyed by vocalizations and (later) words, facial expression, or other gestures (such as, for example, 'all-gone', because the puppets have stopped) combined in a sequence. Particularly with younger babies, the adult may contribute to, interpret, or acknowledge (vocally, verbally, or expressively) this comment—for instance, with utterances such as (mirroring the categories above) 'The doll!'/, 'It's quick isn't it?'/, 'Jumping again!'/, 'Amazing!' plus exaggerated surprise facial expression/.

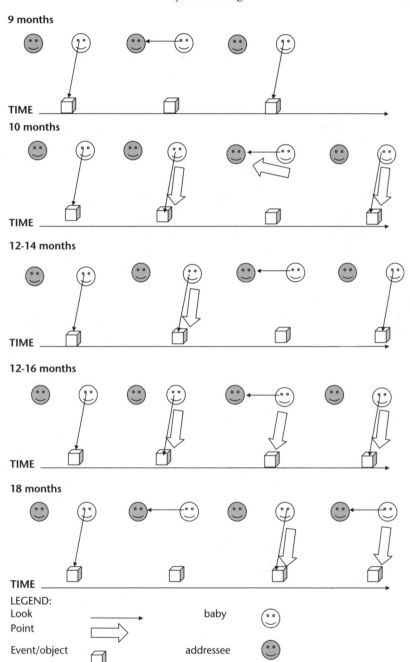

FIGURE 7.5. Summary of the evolving pointing/gaze relationship.

To summarize, at the earlier stages of communicative acts involving pointing we observe a two-step plan:

1. achieve joint attention about referent with social partner (i.e. direct addressee's attention to relevant object/event) by pointing,
2. exchange comment about referent with social partner.

This means being able to keep in mind and postpone the achievement of goal (2) while executing goal (1), which is a pre-condition. Looks during or after pointing are likely to have the function of checking that the message is being received.

The great shift at 16–18 months concerns the addition of one more, crucial step to the sequence, which develops into:

1. establish mutual attention (verify social partner is attending),
2. achieve joint attention about referent with social partner,
3. exchange comment about referent with social partner.

The addition of the first step (anticipatory look to social partner) suggests that the baby does not take for granted that the adult is paying attention (hence recognizing agency at a basic mental level). On the contrary, there appears to be awareness that visual attention is a requirement for successful non-verbal communication: if my addressee does not look at me, he or she will not see my pointing, hence joint attention and meaning exchange about my target will not be achieved (Franco, 1997). It is here that hierarchical thinking or planning are involved, and that the relationship between looking and seeing is, if not fully understood, at least considered implicitly.

In fact, in the kind of interactional context described here, involving physical proximity and no other task for the social partner, adults monitor the baby most of the time, precisely in order to facilitate or maximize joint attention. This is clearly the way things work with younger babies. For example, when a 14-month-old points to something interesting and turns to look at the social partner, typically the adult will have been following what the baby is doing and will be there to meet the baby's eyes, from there to move on to the baby's target, and so on. Thus, the achievement of joint attention around 1 year of age still relies heavily on the adult's contribution. Differently, the anticipatory look observed when an 18-month-old points is a clear indication that babies of this age do take responsibility for securing joint attention. In terms of attentional implications, pointing by an 18-month-old is not dissimilar to our behaviour when driving a car in front of someone who does not know the way. Before making a turn, we check that another car has not come between us and that our friend in the car behind is still in a position to see us or our car indicator, etc.

The understanding that if you want the addressee to be able to receive your message, you had better have her or his attention first, as shown by anticipatory visual checking, would clearly be beneficial for other gestures too. It then remains to be explained why the behavioural marker of such understanding (anticipatory checking) does not appear to be as strongly associated with other gestures as it is with pointing (Franco, 1995, 2002; Franco and Butterworth, 1996). Exact figures vary slightly from one study to another, but the proportion of anticipatory checking with other gestures is between a third and a quarter of that observed with pointing (e.g. Franco, 2002). One possibility that we cannot rule out at present is that the quality and structure of our experimental situations were such that pointing would be facilitated much more than other gestures. The lower incidence of other gestures might then produce an unrepresentative sample of associated behaviours. However, consideration of the core function (declarative) of pointing may support an alternative explanation. The social partner's attention is pivotal for pre-verbal declaratives, in that it is the bridge between mutual and joint attention that establishes shared reference, hence a topic. Thus, it is perhaps the fact that the other's attention is part of the communicative goal itself that drives the infant's attention to focus first of all on the pre-conditions for achieving this goal. As Bates, Camaioni, and Volterra (1975) suggested, in terms of means–end relations (baby uses X in order to achieve Y), proto-imperatives can be described as 'baby uses adult in order to get the object', while proto-declaratives would imply that 'baby uses object to get the adult's attention/response'. Therefore, the other's attention is at the very core of the meaning of pointing, whereas it is less so for other gestures.

POINTING AND UNDERSTANDING ATTENTION

The question left open by the above studies and the interpretations proposed is: what do babies actually understand about attention? Do they understand the relationship between the action of looking and the state of seeing? Indeed, such a relationship identifies attention, which is considered a mental state. In an attempt to find answers to such questions, I studied the production of pointing in contexts in which joint attention was more difficult (or impossible) to achieve. The rationale was that if toddlers have a grasp of attention as the state defined by the relationship between looking and seeing, then specific adjustments of communication should appear when this relationship is obstructed or interrupted, so that joint attention with a social partner is hard or impossible to achieve.

Toddlers aged 18–36 months were tested with an adult social partner (a female experimenter) in the context that was previously found to facilitate proto-declarative communication (DEC-F). However, this time some manipulations were introduced in order to create conditions differing as to the visibility of target objects. Two remotely controlled clown manikins at a distance of 250 cm from participants were activated according to a pre-established sequence of movement/pause. First, two types of task were used (Franco and Gagliano, 2001), in which the manipulation concerning object visibility differed as follows.

Visibility Obstructed by Distal Obstacle: Whereas both clowns were visible to toddlers throughout this task, there were three conditions varying the number of

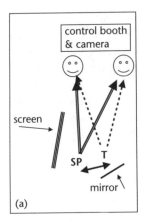 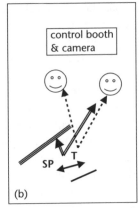 

FIGURE 7.6. Three conditions varying the number of targets visible to a toddler's social partner by using a distal obstacle to joint attention. SP = social partner; T = toddler.

targets visible to the social partner (see Fig. 7.6a, b, c): *both* clowns (Two henceforth), *one* colwn only (ONE henceforth), and *none* of them (NONE henceforth). These three conditions were created by changing the orientation of a large screen between targets and adult, so that the screen would or would not be an obstacle along the adult's line of sight towards the target objects. Eye contact between child and adult was always possible, but this involved a 90 degree head turn for the child.

Visibility Obstructed by Spatial Obstacle: Child and adult sat face to face. A clown manikin was positioned behind each interactant. In this way the child and the experimenter each had one target fully visible in front of them (CHILD's target and EXPERIMENTER's target henceforth), and one target not visible because located behind them (i.e. the target visible to the social partner). In order to see the latter, a 180 degree head turn was necessary (see Fig. 7.7).

The results from the two tasks were very consistent. When visibility was obstructed by the screen (distal obstacle), in condition NONE (no objects visible to the addressee) we recorded the highest frequency of pointing; the highest proportion of pointing associated with visual checking in general and, in particular, with anticipatory checking (from 24 months) and *multiple checking* (when a gesture is accompanied by more than one look at the experimenter, e.g. *before* and *after*); the highest incidence of vocalizations and words accompanying pointing, and the highest incidence of isolated language (i.e. not accompanying gestures). In contrast, in condition TWO (both objects visible to the addressee), pointing, visual checking, vocalizations, and language were least frequent. Interestingly, in condition ONE (a conflict condition, where toddlers had the choice between one target visible and one invisible to the addressee), responses were not randomly distributed: over 70 per cent of pointing was directed to the target *not* visible to the experimenter.

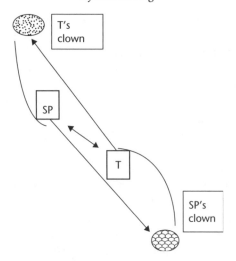

FIGURE 7.7. A condition creating a spatial obstacle to joint attention: toddler and social partner sit face to face each with one object visible. SP = social partner; T = toddler.

Besides the predictable sharp increase of words (either alone or accompanying gestures) in the older age-group, there were a few significant age differences. The older children (30–36 months) showed the highest incidence of pointing in condition ONE (rather than NONE) and produced nearly twice as many words accompanying pointing in condition ONE as in the other two conditions, but showed the highest incidence of isolated language in condition NONE. In other words, children younger than 30 months produced more vocalizations, words accompanying pointing, and isolated language when the addressee had no or limited access to the visual targets; but older children would produce more words accompanying pointing in condition ONE and more isolated language in condition NONE.

When visibility is obstructed because of the spatial arrangements (the second type of task used by Franco and Gagliano, 2001), most pointing was directed to the CHILD's target at 18–23 months, but to the EXPERIMENTER's target at 24–29 months, while it was equally distributed in the older children. The proportion of gestures associated with visual checking of the social partner was higher when pointing was directed to the CHILD's target (i.e. the one that the experimenter could *not* see). This was determined by a higher rate of checking *before* pointing when gestures were directed to the CHILD's target, in all age-groups. There was a very low incidence of pre-verbal vocalization in this task, but most of it accompanied pointing to the CHILD's target. Finally, more words were used when pointing to the CHILD's target.

To sum up, in general this pattern of results clearly indicates heightened communicative efforts from 18 months of age when joint attention is obstructed, suggesting at least some awareness of the social partner's situation. It also shows a persistent attempt to achieve joint attention with the available means. For the younger age-groups, there was a mainly *quantitative* difference between the different visibility conditions. Their available repertoire is still mostly non-verbal or heavily reliant on deictic gestures, and they simply produced more of everything (tried harder) when joint attention with the social partner could not be achieved. The older children, however, also showed *qualitative* differences between the three visibility conditions. In disambiguation contexts (i.e. THIS, *not that*: condition ONE) they specifically increased pointing plus language, but language alone increased when a verbal signal could specify reference (and related comments) while a point could not do so equally well (condition NONE).

In order to elucidate the relationship between the various components of an act of joint attention, further control conditions were run with thirty-two toddlers aged 18–23, 24–30, 31–36 months old in the same environment. The incidence of pointing and associated behaviours when there was a distal obstacle (screen) between social partner and targets was then compared with other contexts interfering with the visibility of referents in the different, following ways.

Sound: the interesting event was a sequence of sounds produced by objects which were invisible. In this case there is a potential target to share, but both toddler and adult have no visual access to it.

Proximal obstacle (PROX-OB henceforth): joint attention was obstructed by a proximal (a dark green cotton bag over the head of the social partner) rather than distal (screen) obstacle. In this case also mutual gaze and attention to the toddler are precluded, as the adult cannot see the toddler, in addition to not seeing the objects. Again, both visual and auditory events were used. In the latter case, the proximal obstacle prevented only mutual attention, as there was no object to be seen.

As this was an experiment, all conditions lasted the same amount of time. The general impression was that children found these control conditions more awkward than those previously described with distal obstacles and looked a bit puzzled. However, some useful results were obtained.

The frequency of pointing was lower in each of the three conditions (auditory target, PROX-OB/visual target, PROX-OB/auditory target) than in the distal obstacle conditions. However, while children older than 30 months virtually stopped pointing, toddlers younger than 23 months pointed very little only in the bag/auditory target condition (Fig. 7.8). This suggests that the older participants would not point unless there was some visible object to direct attention to, whereas the younger ones point to an auditory event as much as they do to a visible one. Moreover, the younger children would point only marginally less in the PROX-OB/visual target condition, in spite of having tried the bag on themselves (thus having experienced temporary blindness to the room). This may indicate a still uncertain understanding of seeing and attention in this age-group.

However, we cannot rule out at this stage an alternative hypothesis: that is these younger toddlers may find it hard to inhibit the only (or the most efficient)

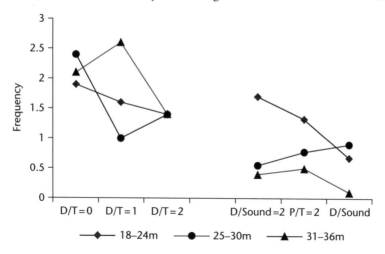

FIGURE 7.8. Frequency of pointing in conditions involving distal and proximal obstacles to joint attention.

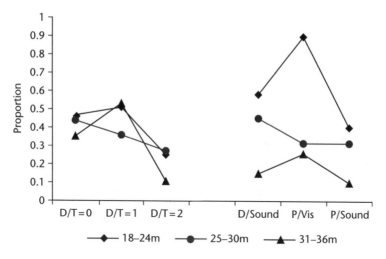

FIGURE 7.9. Proportion of pointing gestures associated with gaze to the social partner in conditions involving distal and proximal obstacles to joint attention.

response available to them to try and achieve joint attention with the blindfolded partner. Such an explanation is supported by the fact that the proportion of pointing associated with visual checking doubles and reaches 90 per cent in this condition and age-group only (Fig. 7.9). Furthermore, the highest proportion of anticipatory visual checking observed in the younger age-group is found in the PROX-OB conditions (Fig. 7.10).

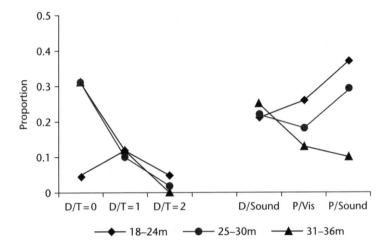

FIGURE 7.10. Proportion of pointing associated with gaze before gesture in conditions involving distal and proximal obstacles to joint attention.

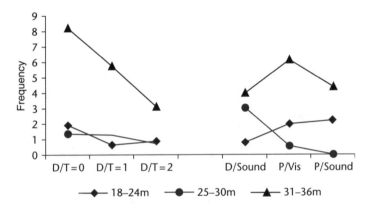

FIGURE 7.11. Frequency of words (isolated language) in conditions involving distal and proximal obstacles to joint attention.

Taken together, these data may be interpreted as a reflection of the poverty of other means of communication in this age-group. In fact, the older children *speak* in the PROX-OB conditions as much as when there is a screen between social partner and objects (Figs 7.11 and 7.12). Interestingly, however, these older children stop pointing when the addressee cannot see *them*. The pattern for pre-verbal vocalizations is similar, except that they increase in all age-groups in the PROX-OB conditions; this again suggests that vocal communication is understood as more appropriate when gestures cannot be seen (Fig. 7.13). The problem for the under 2-years-olds is that their language may be still too poor to sustain a solely linguistic act of communication.

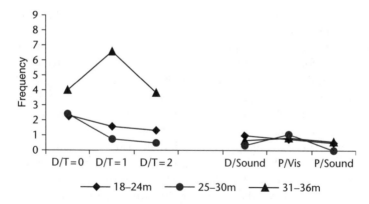

FIGURE 7.12. Frequency of words with pointing in conditions involving distal and proximal obstacles to joint attention.

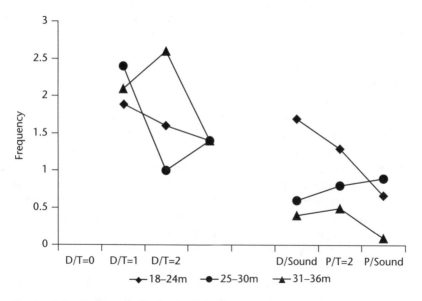

FIGURE 7.13. Frequency of isolated vocalizations in conditions involving distal and proximal obstacles to joint attention.

POINTING AND LANGUAGE

If we consider general trends between the average age at which pointing emerges and 2 years of age, in the type of context used to facilitate proto-declarative communication, pointing frequency increases up to 16–18 months, then it remains stable and does not decline throughout the third year (Franco, 2002). Other gestures appear to be produced less frequently, and this trend is even more evident as age increases. This does not mean that the production of other gestures decreases with age, but simply that pointing becomes more and more the typical gesture in joint attention contexts.

Although more data are required in this area, there is a general preference for the right hand for pointing in infancy, hence suggesting early lateralization. In a context such as the distal, animated DOLLS, this is shown by pointing with the right hand both to ipsilateral targets and to targets across the midline, at least to some extent. It is revealed also in conflict conditions, when two targets are presented, one left and one right; the target to the right is more likely to be pointed at, and with a shorter latency. Girls appear to achieve this lateralized pattern earlier than boys, around 15 months, which is consistent with a sex difference in the rate of lateralization linked to speech production (Butterworth *et al.*, 2002).

It has been argued that there is a special link between pointing and language acquisition: as pointing is a pre-verbal form of reference, it would promote the development of verbal reference, hence naming. It is therefore useful to compare how vocalizing and early language production relate to pointing and other gestures. If pointing has a special link with language, then some difference should emerge in the pattern of evolution of gesture/word combinations between pointing and other gestures.

Specific investigations should address this issue. However, data from sixty-five infants aged 12–26 months, together with the data from Franco and Gagliano (2001), may begin to answer this question. Between 12 and 16 months, pre-verbal vocalizations are produced more frequently in association with pointing than other gestures (Fig. 7.14a). Subsequently there is a general decline in the production of pre-verbal vocalizations (including isolated vocalizations) and no more differences between pointing and other gestures in the frequency of associated vocalizations. However, approaching the second birthday, there is again a difference between pointing and other gestures, but this time it is in their association with words. In joint attention contexts, significantly more words are associated with pointing than other gestures around 2 years of age (Fig. 7.14b), and this continues to be true in the third year of life (Franco, 2002).

Thus, pointing and other gestures are equally associated with words up to the end of the second year, and the association between pointing and language appears stronger at the age when children begin to produce multi-word utterances than during the single-word stage. As the last part of the second year is characterized by a very rapid vocabulary growth (the 'vocabulary spurt'—see also the Isolated Words data in Fig. 7.14b), the higher association of pointing with language in the third year may simply be the reflection of an increased vocabulary, rather than being part of the 'engine' (process) developing it. However, pointing does appear to have a unique developmental path.

1. Until 18 months approximately, it has a higher association with pre-verbal vocalizations than other gestures, and is associated with gaze to the addressee more often than other gestures.

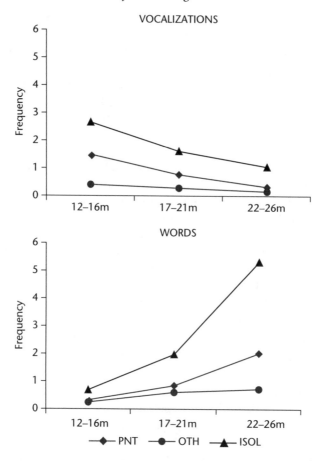

FIGURE 7.14. Frequency of vocalizations and words produced by 12–26-month-olds isolated (ISOL) or with pointing (PNT) and other gestures (OTH) in joint attention contexts.

2. From around 18 months (but not earlier) it is characteristically associated with checking before the gesture and multiple checks with the addressee, a shift not observed in other gestures (Franco and Butterworth, 1996).
3. Finally, in the third year, a specific association with language appears.

To sum up, with respect to other gestures, pointing appears specifically linked to vocalizing under 18 months, to visual checking associated with the gesture between 18 and 24 months, and to language after 24 months. Although all these data were collected in the same general communicative context, it is always hazardous to combine data from different studies in order to tell one story. In fact, only a longitudinal investigation can adequately address issues of causality and developmental relationships. None the less, it is tempting to speculate that the steps described above do identify a unique path (at least in production) in which pointing is the link between joint attention and language development. Proto-declarative pointing is produced from its inception with accompanying vocalizations. Checking before initiating pointing shows awareness of the addressee's attention; once the links looking-seeing and seeing-knowing are established, the referent/word match becomes systematic (Baldwin, 1995), and pointing may become a powerful tool for recruiting and trying out items for a fast-growing vocabulary. In turn, a larger vocabulary allows multi-word combinations (Bates and Goodman, 1997; Elman *et al.*, 1996); this or the combination between pointing and words may then allow children to complete the declarative act (originally attempted with vocalizations) with the communication of relatively complex meanings.

Halliday (1975) suggested that only towards the end of the second year of life do we observe the emergence of the most accomplished form of declaration: that is, when the speaker passes on some information that is novel or not accessible to the addressee. After thirty more years of research we have a much better appreciation of how important a transition this is, one involving some understanding of the attention and knowledge state of another person. We can clearly see this transition with pointing, if we compare the following cases.

(1) Point to doll and say 'DOLL' with the doll in full view for both interactants.
(2) Point to doll and say 'JUMP' with the doll in full view for both interactants.
(3) Point to doll and say 'JUMP' with the doll not visible to the addressee.
(4) Just say 'DOLL JUMP' with the doll not visible to the addressee.

Act (1) is declarative but not informational. Act (2) is not informative about the environment either, although it may implicitly inform about the pointer: what he or she is paying attention to at the moment. Acts (3) and (4) instead are truly informative, and they can be so because the addressee's attention has been taken into account.

Communication about something that the addressee does not know/cannot see must be a very important step in opening the door to communicating about various classes of things and events which are invisible in a variety of ways: because internal, such as feelings and states, because temporally disjointed, such as past and future or spatially dislocated. From a motivational point of view, I cannot imagine a more powerful reason to learn conventional language: so that we can share the invisible (see also Bloom and Tinker, 2001, for an intentional/motivational model of language acquisition).

EXTENSIONS TO OTHER SOCIAL CONTEXTS AND ATYPICAL POPULATIONS

The results described in the previous sections were supported and extended by studies showing that, in our communicative context designed to facilitate proto-declaratives, babies point for age mates (Franco, Perucchini, and Butterworth, 1992), but pointing virtually disappeared in the absence of a social partner (Franco and Butterworth, 1990). This means that pointing is intentionally produced to affect a social partner, and that what is expected of such a social partner is simply sharing attention—that is, a co-ordination of views in order to make communication possible.

What is communicated when the two interactants are pre-verbal babies is not clear. In an infant–adult interaction, the adult invariably verbalizes something about the object or event they are jointly attending. Also, whatever vocalizations a baby produces in association with pointing are likely to be interpreted in meaningful ways by the adult. In contrast, another baby does not provide such 'scaffolding', and the interaction between two pre-verbal peers sounds very quiet in comparison to when one of the partners is an adult. Figure 7.15 shows a sequence of interaction between two 14-month-olds: Baby 1 initiates joint attention by pointing to the animated DOLLS and turns to check what Baby 2 is doing. While Baby 1 is still pointing, Baby 2 turns to meet the eyes of Baby 1 (mutual gaze), after which Baby 1 redirects his point to another target, and Baby 2 follows. Once the pointing event is over, the two babies look at each other again. We can at least hypothesize that they want to signal the occurrence of an event (topic) and possibly share some epistemic or affective state/reaction about it (predicate). The partner's verbal support is not necessary, and is not the reason for a point to be produced (for instance, to get the label for the object/event singled out by the point).

However, the presence of another person is the most important catalyst for infant pointing. In the same type of condition used in our other studies (e.g. DEC-F), if babies are left alone, gesture production decreases in general, but pointing virtually disappears. What is interesting is that pointing is suppressed, not just the more obviously social behaviours such as visual checking towards the social partner. This is true also at 12 months of age and cannot be imputed to separation anxiety: most babies were watching with interest the dolls' movements, often with positive facial expressions (e.g. smiles) and sometimes vocalizing or (the older participants) calling 'MUM!' excitedly, for the mother to come and join them. Figure 7.16 shows four participants on reunion with the experimenter or mother (whoever walked back in the lab first). As can be seen, we witness a pointing explosion accompanied by smiles and vocalizations within seconds of hearing the door open. These proto-declarative acts are invariably produced while alternating gaze between the targets and the social partner.

Finally, one last extension of my work on pointing concerns atypical or at risk populations. Baron-Cohen (1989) suggested that young children with autism appear to have specific difficulties in both comprehension and production of proto-declarative pointing. In general, it has been confirmed that children with autism have specific difficulties with joint attention (e.g. Stone *et al.*, 1997) and that toddlers showing severe limitations in their joint attention skills at 18 months

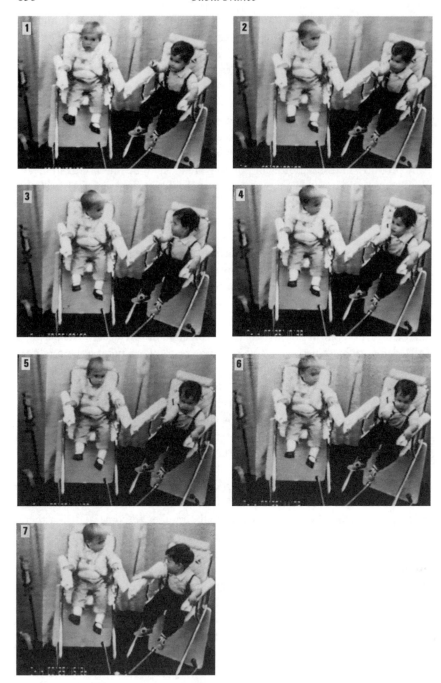

FIGURE 7.15. Sequence of joint attention between two 14-month-old babies.

Examples of reunion after the "baby alone" condition.

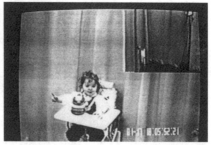

17 ms old: no pointing when alone: latency of first point=10 secs. (only when also mother appears: then she says "Mum!" and points)

18 ms old: no pointing when alone; latency of first point at reunion = 2 secs.

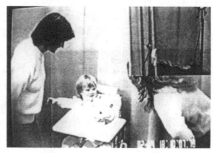

14 ms old: when alone, points to exit and loud vocalizations; latency of first point = 6secs.

17 ms old: no pointing when alone; latency of first point = 5 secs.

FIGURE 7.16. Pointing for a social partner who has not witnessed an interesting event.

are more likely to receive a diagnosis of autism at 30 months. It has been argued that this is consistent with the idea that joint attention in general, and proto-declarative communication in particular, is specifically related to the development of social cognition (understanding people). More recently, Charman and colleagues (2000) have shown that some joint attention behaviours, such as gaze alternation between referent and addressee at 20 months, do predict theory of mind ability at 44 months.

Consistently, young children with Down's syndrome, who are significantly delayed in their cognitive development but are not impaired in social relatedness, produce proto-declarative pointing in order to communicate both with an adult and with a peer (Franco and Wishart, 1995). Furthermore, the pattern of visual checking is similar to that observed in typically developing babies, including the most advanced forms such as the anticipatory check before pointing. The results with Down's syndrome are interesting, because language development lags behind cognitive development in this syndrome. The picture emerging is one in which, thanks to relatively intact capacities to relate to persons as such, joint attention appears to develop along with cognitive development in Down's syndrome. In fact, joint attention skills appear to compensate for the particularly poor language skills, for instance supporting non-verbal communication as highlighted by the very competent use of pointing, particularly in proto-declarative contexts.

The way in which cognition, language, and intersubjectivity are related with joint attention is still relatively fuzzy. We know that it is in contexts of joint attention that adults provide labels and children learn words (Baldwin, 1995; Kessler-Shaw, 1992; Tomasello and Farrar, 1986). Baldwin's studies in particular have shown a specific relationship between understanding joint attention and the possibility of associating labels with referents: only towards the end of the second year of life do children systematically check the attentional focus of the speaker in order to identify a label's referent. By then children already have a vocabulary of some dozens of words on average, accumulated thanks to episodes of shared attention occurring by chance or orchestrated by an adult partner. What changes around the middle of the second year is that toddlers take responsibility for securing joint attention in production (Franco and Butterworth, 1996) and comprehension (Baldwin, 1995). This happens to coincide with the beginning of the period often associated with dramatic gains in vocabulary (variously called 'vocabulary spurt', 'naming insight', etc.), thus suggesting that joint attention may have a prerequisite (or co-requisite) function in language development. In other words, only certain advances in joint attention may allow for the big push in language development—that is, the rapid growth of lexical items, which is the very basis of multi-word combination. It has been shown that multi-word utterances do not appear unless the vocabulary has reached, statistically, around 200 words at least (Bates and Goodman, 1997; Elman *et al.*, 1996); the correlation between early grammar (multi-word utterances) and vocabulary is so high as to suggest that they measure the same thing. Thus, the relationship between joint attention and language appears to involve two steps: a first level of joint attention skills, JA1, linked with establishing reference (hence single words), and a further joint attention level, JA2, linked with the development of multi-word utterances. The two joint attentional levels are based on the infant developing social cognition, as JA1 includes the working out of intentionality, hence the attribution of physical agency to people (as shown for example by gaze alternation with requestive behaviours), and JA2 the attribution of mental agency (albeit elementary, such as in attentional states). In the same perspective, Tomasello (1999*a*) speaks of an extension of joint attention from the visible to the represented world, respectively. Primates appear to lack the JA2 type of abilities (e.g. Povinelli and Eddy, 1996, among others), and although they can learn lexical items in certain circumstances, their vocabulary remains ≤ 200 words (critical mass), and they do not develop a grammar. As a result of the development of the JA2 type of abilities, for example, human infants may accelerate their lexical acquisition rate, thereby reaching (and going beyond) the critical mass statistically associated with the production of multi-word utterances.

In order to support this hypothesis further, the next step is to study developmental paths leading to specific language deficits. If our reasoning above is correct, then interference with the development of joint attention (JA2 in particular) may compromise vocabulary extension, which in turn would be responsible for a slow and poor development of grammar. With colleagues at the universities of Milan and Padua, we have therefore started to look at the development of joint attention (pointing and associated behaviours in particular) in 'late talkers'—that is, children who are below the tenth percentile in their vocabulary growth as measured by the McArthur CDI. Many of these children will catch up, but some may develop specific language impairment (SLI). SLI children may have the average vocabulary of a 2-year-old at 4 years of age, and it has been suggested that this very slow growth in the lexicon is responsible for the impaired grammar characteristic of these children (Conti-Ramsden, 2000; Leonard, 2000). Thus, we need to adopt a prospective study approach to the problem, and to monitor joint attention skills as early as a child can be identified as a 'late talker' with subsequent follow-ups of the child's language development. The results of the pilot phase of this study seem to suggest that 'late talkers' are also showing pointing and looking patterns characteristic of younger babies. In general, there appear to be subtle but pervasive differences in the use of pointing, looking, and vocalizing by 'late talkers', a result which encourages further investigation until follow-ups at later ages are possible (Assanelli, Salerni & Franco, 2001).

CONCLUDING REMARKS

In this chapter, the emergence and development of the pointing gesture in human infancy has been analysed in the function of initiating joint attention with a social partner in a variety of contexts. We have seen how pointing begins to be used towards the end of the first year of life as part of the psychologically profound transformation involved in what has been described as the passage from dyadic to triadic, referential interaction. Furthermore, although pointing is a gesture embodying the displacement of attention on to a target object or event, communicative acts involving pointing are produced with either a declarative or an imperative pragmatic meaning. It is the declarative pragmatic function, however, which is characteristically associated with pointing. In other words, pointing is typically produced in order to share attention with somebody about something and exchange comments about it. In this respect, the joint attentional component of pointing is instrumental in identifying the referent or topic.

With development, proto-declarative acts involving pointing become 'informational' (Halliday, 1975), in that they support meaning including information which is new to the addressee. Awareness of the state of attention and knowledge of the social partner, albeit elementary, is shown both by the 'informational' nature of some communicative pointing acts and by the pattern of visual checking exhibited with pointing. Specifically, by 18 months of age toddlers seek mutual attention as a pre-condition for initiating joint attention acts with a social partner. In the short time between about 12 and 18 months, infants appear to progressively master the link between looking and seeing, and seeing and knowing. This insight is of fundamental importance for language development.

Proto-declarative acts involving pointing are associated more frequently than other gestures with pre-verbal vocalizations until about 18 months, and with language from the end of the second year. The systematic use of anticipatory gaze to check the addressee's attentional state just before pointing characterizes proto-declarative pointing in the second half of the second year. It is tempting to speculate that this is indeed the pivotal mechanism whereby items are recruited to the infant vocabulary and replace earlier vocalizations.

Later, in the third year, children have vocabularies of a few hundred items, and use multi-word utterances. Then pointing and anticipatory visual checking are used strategically—that is, in contexts where it is more difficult to establish joint attention and language is not yet developed enough to support solely verbal communication.

Thus, in development, communicative acts involving pointing do have a Harlequin function in providing a juncture between social cognition and language acquisition. As psychologists, we are interested in causality issues (what causes what), but seldom are there definitive answers. Tentatively, it can be suggested that although pointing emerges as a gesture first as a behavioural 'symptom' of newly acquired socio-cognitive competence, it later becomes a powerful tool for communication and language development. In turn, language will provide representational tools on the basis of which further developments in social cognition will be possible (e.g. aspects of 'theory of mind'). We have seen how developments in joint attention skills of toddlers show the progressive elaboration of notions of agency, such as those of a physical or mental agent involved in some communicative acts. One can speculate that at the same time semantically related notions develop, such as that of experiencer (of bodily or other kinds of experience). Such distinctions are then found in language, where verbs involving agency are related to different kinds of inferences with respect to verbs involving states (e.g. inspect versus recognize, help versus love; among others, Brown and Fish, 1983; Franco *et al.*, 2000).

In concluding this chapter, I would like to mention a few issues that I have not discussed so far, simply because they are beyond the scope of my own work until now. First of all, the issue of social interaction. The developments described in this chapter do not take place in a social void, but are the results of hundreds of hours of social interaction between babies and caretakers. It is of course important to investigate the contribution of the adult to the process of developing joint attention in particular, and social cognition in general. An avenue for this type of work is the study of individual differences amongst parents; comparison of different types of social partner by role or age; and experimental manipulations targeting specific hypotheses.

A second issue which deserves further investigation is the relationship between gesture and speech. This is not a new topic, but one that needs constant readjustment in light of theoretical developments in either the language or the gesture field. For instance, deictic gestures were typically analysed together as a group, whereas we may now want to look at pointing separately from other gestures because of the implications that this gesture has shown for social cognition, and the link between social cognition and language.

Finally, we need to understand more clearly what is the function of the pointing gesture for the person who points. Here I refer more generally to models such as McNeill's (1987, 1992), claiming that gesture and speech actually convey different parts of the underlying (common) meaning. In particular, I am thinking here of how difficult it is to suppress pointing even in situations where it does not make much sense to point (e.g. some of the manipulations used in the studies reported above, such as when the social partner is blindfolded), or when there are specific instructions not to point (e.g. to the mothers or social partners in our studies). Also, pointing is widely used by adults in communication (including art), but is not used by the congenitally blind (Iverson and Goldin-Meadow, 1997). Instead, other gestures are observed in blind children (Iverson and Goldin-Meadow, 1997), which suggests that, irrespective of the early pointing hand posture observed at 3 months of age, pointing develops in strong association with visual experience and visual attention, including following someone else's line of regard or point, and mutual attention.

REFERENCES

ASSANELLI, A., SALERNI, N., and FRANCO, F. (2001), 'Linguistic delay and gestural communication', in *ELA 2001 Proceedings* (CD ROM), *Early Lexicon Acquisition Conference*, Lyon, December.

BALDWIN, D. A. (1995), 'Understanding the link between joint attention and language', in C. Moore and P. J. Dunham (eds.), *Joint Attention: Its origins and Role in Development*. Hillsdale, NJ: Erlbaum, 131–58.

BAREN-COHEN, S. (1989), 'Perceptual role-taking and protodeclarative pointing in autism', *British Journal of Developmental Psychology*, 7: 113–27.

BATES, E., and GOODMAN, J. (1997), 'On the inseparability of grammar and the lexicon: evidence from acquisition', *Language and Cognitive Processes*, 12 (5/6): 507–84.

—— CAMAIONI, L., and VOLTERRA, V. (1975), 'The acquisition of performatives prior to speech', *Merril–Palmer Quarterly*, 21: 205–26.

BLAKE, J., O'ROURKE, P., and BORZELLINO, G. (1994), 'Form and function in the development of pointing and reaching gestures', *Infant Behavior and Development*, 17: 195–203.

BLOOM, L., and TINKER, E. (2001), 'The intentionality model and language acquisition', *Monographs of the Society for Research in Child Development*, 66/4, serial no. 267.

BROWN, R., and FISH, D. (1983), 'The psychological causality implicit in language', *Cognition*, 14: 237–73.

BRUNER, J. (1975), 'The ontogenesis of speech acts', *Journal of Child Language*, 2: 1–20.

BUTTERWORTH, G., and FRANCO, F. (1993), 'Motor development: communication and cognition', in L. Kalverboer, B. Hopkins, and R. H. Gueze (eds.), *A Longitudinal Approach to the Study of Motor Development in Early and Later Childhood*. Cambridge: Cambridge University Press, 153–65.

—— —— McKENZIE, B., GRAUPNER, L., and TODD, B. (2002), 'Dynamic aspects of visual event perception and the production of pointing by human infants', *British Journal of Developmental Psychology*, 20: 1–24.

CARPENTER, M., and TOMASELLO, M. (2000), 'Joint attention, cultural learning, and language acquisition: implications for children with autism', in A. M. Wetherby and B. M. Prizant (eds.), *Communication and Language Issues in Autism and Pervasive Developmental Disorders: A Transactional Developmental Perspective*, Baltimore: Brooks, 31–52.

—— NAGELL, K., and TOMASELLO, M. (1998), 'Social cognition, joint attention, and communicative competence from 9 to 15 months of age', *Monographs of the Society for Research in Child Development*, 63, serial no. 255.

CHARMAN, T., BARON-COHEN, S., SWETTENHAM, J., BAIRD, G., COX, A., and DREW, A. (2000), 'Testing joint attention, imitation, and play as infancy precursors to language and theory of mind', *Cognitive Development*, 15: 481–98.

CONTI-RAMSDEN, G. (2000), 'The relevance of recent research on SLI to our understanding of normal language development', in M. Perkins and S. Howard (eds.), *New Directions in Language Development and Disorders*. London: Kluwer/Plenum, 7–12.

D'ODORICO, L., and LEVORATO, M. C. (1990), 'Social and cognitive determinants of mutual gaze between between mother and infant', in V. Volterra and C. J. Erting (eds.), *From Gesture to Language in Hearing and Deaf Children*. Berlin: Springer-Verlag, 9–17.

DORE, J. (1975), 'Holophrases, speech acts and language universals', *Journal of Child Language*, 2: 21–40.

—— (1976), 'Conditions on the acquisition of speech acts', in I. Markova (ed.), *The Social Context of Language*. New York: Wiley, 87–111.

ELMAN, J. L., BATES, E. A., JOHNSON, M. H., KARMILOFF-SMITH, A., PARISI, D., and PLUNKETT, K. (1996), *Rethinking Innateness: A Connectionist Perspective on Development*. Cambridge, Mass.: MIT Press.

FOGEL, A., and HANNAN, T. E. (1985), 'Manual actions of 2- to 3-month-old human infants during social interaction', *Child Development*, 56: 1271–9.

FRANCO, F. (1995), 'Variation of physical distance in interaction: what does it show about declarative communication in infants?'. Paper read at 1995 Child Language Seminar. Bristol, April.

—— (1997), 'The development of meaning in infancy', in S. Hala (ed.), *The Development of Social Cognition*. Hove; Psychology Press, 95–160.

—— (2002), 'Infant pointing: linking communication and social cognition'. Paper presented at Euroconferences on Brain Development and Cognition in Human Infants: The

Emergence of Social Communication: Hands, Eyes, Ears, Mouths. European Science Foundation, Maratea, June.

—— and BUTTERWORTH, G. (1990), 'Effects of social variables on the production of infant pointing'. Paper presented at the *IVth European Conference on Developmental Psychology*. Stirling, August.

—— —— (1996), 'Pointing and social awareness: declaring and requesting in the second year', *Journal of Child Language*, 23: 307–36.

—— and GAGLIANO, A. (2001), 'Toddlers' pointing when joint attention is obstructed', *First Language*, 21: 289–321.

—— and WISHART, J. (1995), 'The use of pointing and other gestures by young children with Down syndrome', *American Journal of Mental Retardation*, 100(2): 160–82.

—— LEVORATO, C., TASSO, A., and RUSSELL, J. (2000), 'Cross-linguistic developmental evidence of implicit causality in visual perception and cognition verbs', in M. Perkins and S. Howard (eds.), *New Directions in Language Development and Disorders*. New York: Plenum, 189–98.

—— PERUCCHINI, P., and BUTTERWORTH, G. (1992), 'Pointing for an age mate in 1 to 2 year olds'. Paper presented at the VIth European Conference on Developmental Psychology. Seville, September.

GOLINKOFF, R. (ed.) (1983), *The Transition from Prelinguistic Communication*. Hillsdale, NJ: LEA.

GOMEZ, J. C. (1991), 'Visual behaviour as a window for reading the mind of others in primates', in A. Whiten (ed.), *Natural Theories of Mind*. Oxford: Blackwell, 195–207.

HALLIDAY, M. A. K. (1975), *Learning How to Mean*. London: Arnold.

IVERSON, J. M., and GOLDIN-MEADOW, S. (1997), 'What's communication got to do with it? Gesture in children blind from birth', *Developmental Psychology*, 33 (3): 453–67.

KESSLER-SHAW, L. (1992), 'Maternal object and action references in response to infant gestures and other attention-indicating actions'. The City University of New York, Graduate School report.

LEAVENS, D. A., HOPKINS, D. W., and BARD, K. A. (1996), 'Indexical and referential pointing in chimpanzees (Pan troglodytes)', *Journal of Comparative Psychology*, 110 (4): 346–53.

LEONARD, L. B. (2000), 'Theories of language learning and children with specific language impairment', in M. Perkins and S. Howard (eds.), *New Directions in Language Development and Disorders*. London: Kluwer/Plenum, 1–5.

LEUNG, E., and RHEINGOLD, H. (1981), 'The development of pointing as a social gesture', *Developmental Psychology*, 17: 215–20.

LOCK, A., YOUNG, A., SERVICE, V., and CHANDLER, P. (1990), 'Some observations on the origin of the pointing gesture', in V. Volterra and C. J. Erting (eds.), *From Gesture to Language in Hearing and Deaf Children*. Berlin: Springer-Verlag, 42–55.

McNEILL, D. (1987), *Psycholinguistics: A New Approach*. New York: Harper & Row.

—— (1992). *Hand and Mind: What Gesture Reveals about Thought*. Chicago: University of Chicago Press.

MUNDY, P., SIGMAN, M., and KASARI, C. (1990), 'A longitudinal study of joint attention and language development in autistic children', *Journal of Autism and Developmental Disorders*, 20: 115–28.

PERUCCHINI, P. (1997), 'Sviluppo delle funzioni richiestiva e dichiarativa del gesto di indicare', *Giornale Italiano di Psisologia*, 24/(4): 813–29.

Povinelli, D. J., and Eddy, T. J. (1996), 'What young chimpanzees know about seeing', *Monographs of SRCD*, 61, serial no. 3.

Sherzer, J. (1973), 'Verbal and nonverbal deixis: the pointed lip gesture among the San Blas Cuna', *Language & Society*, 2: 117–31.

Shinn, M. (1900), *The Biography of a Baby*. Boston: Houghton Mifflin.

Stone, W. L., Ousley, O. Y., Yoder, P. J., Hogan, K. L., and Hepburn, S. L. (1997), 'Nonverbal communication in two- and three-year-old children with autism', *Journal of Autism and Developmental Disorders*, 27 (6): 677–96.

Tomasello, M. (1995), 'Joint attention as social cognition', in C. Moore and P. J. Dunham (eds.), *Joint Attention: As origins and Role in Development*. Hillsdale: Erlbaum, 103–30.

—— (1999a), *The cultural Origins of Human Cognition*. Cambridge, Mass.: Harvard University Press.

—— (1999b), 'Social cognition before the revolution', in P. Rochat (ed.), *Early Social Cognition*. Mahwah, NJ: Erlbaum, 301–14.

—— and Farrar, M. J. (1986), 'Joint attention and early language', *Child Development*, 57: 1454–63.

Trevarthen, C. (1977), 'Descriptive studies in infant behaviour', in H. R. Schaffer (ed.), *Studies in Mother–Infant Interaction*. London: Academic Press, 227–70.

Vygotsky, L. S. (1926), *Thought and Language*. English trans.: Cambridge, Mass.: MIT Press, 1962.

Werner, H., and Kaplan, B. (1963), *Symbol Formation: An Organismic Developmental Approach to Language and the Expression of Thought*. New York: Wiley.

8

Understanding the Role of Communicative Intentions in Word Learning

Mark A. Sabbagh and *Dare Baldwin*

SOCIAL COORDINATION AND JOINT ATTENTION

In the classic 1989 film, *When Harry Met Sally*, one of the most touching and intimate moments shared by the two main characters comes not in a face-to-face interaction, but over telephone lines. Harry, unable to sleep, sits up in bed and telephones Sally at her apartment. We discover that she too cannot sleep and is in bed watching the end of *Casablanca* on television. He asks Sally for the channel, and tunes into the film himself. Harry and Sally then sit in their respective beds in different New York apartments and watch the end of *Casablanca* 'together'. They go on to use their shared experience to ground a long conversation about love, men and women's notions of the ideal person, and the ideal partner.

Such technologically enhanced feats of social coordination are familiar in our present age of telecommunications, email attachments, and the Internet. A core aspect of these interactions is the ability to establish 'joint attention', which is central to social coordination of all sorts, including, of course, linguistic communication. Interlocutors work cooperatively to ensure that they and their conversational partners share a common point of attentional focus.

Coordinating joint attention can provide both cognitive and motivational benefits to communication. In the cognitive realm, joint attention provides a natural way of grounding topics of conversation. After establishing joint attention, utterances can be both understood and designed with respect to the aspect of the world on which interlocutors are jointly focused. In fact, much of the architecture of language structure seems oriented toward assisting interlocutors to achieve shared focus on a topic (Clark, 1996).

On the motivational side, joint attention makes possible a 'meeting of minds', which humans seem inherently to value. For example, even 15- to 18-month-olds seem to enjoy sharing attentional focus with a social partner and seek opportunities for shared engagement with others (Bakeman and Adamson, 1984; Trevarthen, 1980). Thus, achieving joint attention is inherently motivating, and it benefits social coordination of all forms. Social coordination and joint attention are central to language learning as well as to the communicative enterprise more generally. We offer word learning as a case in point. To learn the appropriate meanings of new words, parents and children must somehow coordinate their attention so that they are focused on the same aspects of the world when children hear words. Perhaps not surprisingly, then, evidence indicates that high degrees of social coordination benefit word learning. For example, children of parents who typically provide labels in episodes of joint attention have larger productive vocabularies than their age-matched counterparts (Harris *et al.*, 1986; Tomasello and Farrar, 1986).

Although researchers generally agree that joint attention and social coordination are important for word learning, there is as yet no clear consensus about the skills that infants and young children bring to the achievement of such social coordination. Below, we review several plausible hypotheses and argue that even infants actively pursue joint attention, and hence social coordination, and do so because they appreciate that others' attentional focus gives information about their referential intentions.

Speaker-Aided Covariation Detection

A classical hypothesis regarding children's word learning is that it simply involves the ability to detect regular covariation between linguistic utterances and the world (L. Bloom, 2000; Schafer and Plunkett, 1998; Samuelson and Smith, 2000; Whitehurst, Kedesdy, and White, 1982). That is, children learn words by associating the sound patterns they hear with the aspects of the world they are attending to at that time. On this proposal, parents and other adults play a central role in children's word-learning success—adults must make sure that the words children hear bear the appropriate relation to the things that occupy children's attention. Critically, if adults fail to take such care and children hear words at a time when they are focused on an inappropriate thing, children will be prone to establishing incorrect associations.

This proposal has a rich intellectual history, dating back at least to Locke (1964/1690), who observed that adults, when talking with young word-learners, take great pains to make sure that words are uttered in close contiguity with the presentation of the objects and substances they are meant to name.

Following Locke's intellectual lead, a number of researchers began to suggest that joint attention might be effective because it provides an especially transparent environment for covariation detection (Bruner, 1983; Ninio and Bruner, 1978). These researchers noticed that a considerable amount of early parent–child linguistic interaction takes place within highly routinized everyday activities, and that in these activities, joint attention episodes are natural and common. These routines provide both the motivational and the cognitive foundations for reliable covariation detection. First, these familiar activities hold children's interest and attention, thereby establishing ideal conditions for learning. Second, children's familiarity with these settings may provide the foundation for strong and reliable hypotheses about the meanings of the words used in these contexts (Tomasello and Farrar, 1986). Thus, joint attention episodes provide just the right conditions for children's mechanisms of covariation detection to operate with maximum efficiency.

The covariation detection hypothesis runs into problems, however, when one considers both the true character of parents' speech to children and the nature of children's word learning. First, in everyday language, covariation between word and object frequently violates the word–referent relations children need to learn. In the case of object naming, for example, an estimated 30 to 50 percent of parents' utterances refer to things that do not occupy their children's attention (Collis, 1977; Harris, Jones, and Grant, 1983). Second, Scheiffelin (1985, 1990) notes that among the Kaluli, object labels are rarely provided in ostensive labeling situations like the ones described first by Locke, and subsequently by Bruner and colleagues. Thus, children in such cultures frequently hear words without clear indication of the relevant referent. Given such 'noisiness' of the covariation between words and objects in the language children hear, we might expect children to be especially prone to errors. Interestingly, however, there is no evidence to suggest that errors occur with any regularity. Happily, it would appear that children often do not establish word–referent links on the basis of simple covariation detection alone.

Perhaps, however, children avoid errors that would arise through covariation detection in difficult, or 'noisy', circumstances by learning words over many trials as they wait for a reliable signal to emerge from the 'soup'. However, this kind of strategy does not seem to reflect the relative rapidity with which children learn words. In many situations, children appear to confidently learn names for objects following very minimal exposure; sometimes, just one exposure is sufficient (Carey and Bartlett, 1978; Heibeck and Markman, 1987; Nelson and Bonvillian, 1973). Importantly, as we will describe later, hearing the label and perceiving the object do not have to be temporally contiguous, nor even immediately consecutive events, for rapid word learning to occur (Baldwin, 1991; Tomasello and Barton, 1994). These findings about children's word learning seriously call into question the covariation detection hypothesis about children's word learning. Furthermore, they call into question the extent to which joint attention settings provide their benefits to word learning by simplifying and clarifying covariation for the child. We turn now to an alternative hypothesis of how joint attention might benefit word learning.

The 'Communicative Intentions' Account of Joint Attention

In adult conversations, establishing joint attention is critical, because it provides a basis for both understanding and designing utterances in conversation. This fact links joint attention to the domain of pragmatics, where understanding the meaning of utterances is linked to an understanding of how speakers use language in various contexts. Grice (1975) and others since (e.g. Clark, 1996; Gibbs, 1999) have noted that a central aspect of pragmatics is the ability to understand speakers' 'communicative intentions'. Although there is currently debate about the extent to which adults explicitly draw inferences about communicative intentions in conversation, it does seem clear that inferences about communicative intentions are especially important when conventional communicative routines do not apply (Keysar and Barr, in press). For young children learning words, there are few such conventional communicative routines, and so any information that could clarify speakers' communicative intentions, and in particular, their intended referents, would be invaluable. As it happens, speakers' attentional focus is generally a good guide to their intended referent. Perhaps, then, children seek joint attention in order to make appropriate and reliable inferences about speakers' referential intentions.

An initial test of the communicative intentions hypothesis comes from research looking at children's performance when they find themselves in situations in which their own attention diverges from that of a speaker. Baldwin (1991) presented 16- to 19-month-old infants with a novel word in one of two conditions. In the 'follow-in' condition, she presented the label while looking at a novel toy on which the child was likewise focused. In the 'discrepant' condition, by contrast, she presented the label while peering into an opaque bucket just as the child was focused on a different toy. Two results from this experiment are important. First, in the discrepant condition, none of the age-groups showed a significant tendency to mismap the novel label to the object on which they themselves had been focused at the time of the labeling. This finding demonstrates that covariation detection alone was not the force behind children's formation of new word–object links. Second, children of 18–19 months consistently linked the novel word with the object that the *experimenter* was attending to when she uttered the label— even though that object was out of view at the time of labeling. In other words, on hearing a novel label, children spontaneously disengaged their attention from their own object, actively sought information about the speaker's focus of attention, and used that information to guide the formation of a new word–object link. Children seemed to understand that words should be linked with the referent intended by the *speaker*, and actively gathered relevant information, such as gaze direction, body posture, and the like, to determine the speaker's referential intentions.

Additional evidence that children appreciate others' intentions as relevant to word learning comes from Baldwin and colleagues (Baldwin *et al.*, 1996). In these studies, 18- to 20-month-olds were seated beside an experimenter and presented with a novel toy in one of two conditions. In the 'coupled' condition, an experimenter (who was seated in view of the child and jointly focused on the novel toy) uttered a novel word. In the contrasting 'decoupled' condition, an experimenter seated behind a sound-conducting rice-paper screen uttered the novel word. From the adult point of view, the novel word in the decoupled condition emanated from a speaker whose attentional focus was unlikely to be the novel toy, since the barrier prevented the speaker from seeing the toy. In question was whether this violation of joint attention—so obvious to adults—would likewise strike infants' notice, and whether infants would take the attentional discrepancy into account in their word learning. It is important to note that in both of the conditions, the experimenter uttered the novel word while the child was focused on the target novel object. However, infants in these studies displayed word learning only in the coupled condition. In the decoupled condition, infants responded unsystematically to comprehension questions, indicating that they had not established any stable link between the new word and the novel object they had been focused on at the time they heard that word. This pattern of results confirms again that covariation between word and object is not the sole driving force behind children's word learning. Children apparently want evidence that a speaker is attending to—and hence intends to talk about—an object before linking a word with that object. At least in face-to-face conversation, children respect the importance of joint attention when determining whether to establish initial word–referent links.

These findings demonstrate that joint attention episodes are not engineered solely by parents attempting to create the best conditions for their children's covariation detection mechanisms. Instead, joint attention episodes can be the product of children's information-gathering efforts, carried out in the service of making appropriate inferences about speakers' referential intentions. Of course, imputing such high-level motivation and understanding to 18-month-old children raises a number of red flags for researchers in psychology. A chief concern arises regarding the cognitive complexity of inferences about referential intentions. A genuine appreciation of others' referential intentions requires skilled inferences made on the basis of a variety of observable cues in the environment. Although having the skill to make these appropriate inferences may be highly effective, it may also be quite costly in terms of the cognitive processing and knowledge required (Horton and Keysar, 1996; Saylor, Baldwin, and Sabbagh, 2004). Given the general limitations of children's cognitive processing skills, we might expect that their inferences about referential intentions would be at best slow and inaccurate, and at worst nonexistent. In addition to this general concern, a number of theoretical and empirical approaches have highlighted the power and efficiency of both simple heuristics and general cognitive processing biases that could achieve a high degree of efficiency in word learning, even without an understanding of referential intentions (L. Bloom, 2000; Samuelson and Smith, 1998, 2000). In what follows, we address these challenges on both theoretical and empirical grounds.

REPRESENTATIONAL THEORY OF MIND:
NOT REQUIRED, NOT HELPFUL

By attempting to understand children's word learning in terms of their abilities to draw appropriate inferences about communicative intentions, we highlight a potential connection between language development and developments in another domain—'theory of mind' (see Papafragou, 2002, for related discussion). Theory of mind refers to our everyday understanding of how people's external and observable actions are motivated by, and understood in terms of, underlying mental constructs such as belief, desire, and intention. Intentional inference is a foundational aspect of theory of mind as it captures the human propensity to interpret behavior in terms of mentalistic goals.

Within the theory-of-mind literature, there has been an especially concentrated effort to characterize the process by which a child comes to appreciate the *representational* nature of mental states (e.g. Perner, 1991). To clarify, representational understanding entails an understanding of mental states as subjective, idiosyncratic, relativistic construals of an objective situation. Consider, for example, the controversial American Abstract Expressionist Jackson Pollack. Through his revolutionary technique of thinning paint to a flowing viscosity and dripping it onto canvasses to create abstract forms, he elicited a diverse range of responses from the critical community. Though they were all looking at the same paintings, some thought it a brilliant innovation, while others thought it a travesty of the creative spirit. Intriguingly, as often happens with historical figures who break with a particular tradition, the diversity of critical opinion seemed to be offered in the service of trying to figure out what Pollack 'was trying to do'—in other words, to figure out what his goals and intentions were (see P. Bloom, 1998, for related ideas). Appreciating that his actions were consistent with an infinite number of possible intentions requires a representational theory of mind.

The first signs of children's understanding of a representational theory of mind are typically marked by their passing the 'false belief' task (e.g. Wimmer and Perner, 1983; Moses and Flavell, 1990), which requires children to make judgments about unwitting characters' beliefs in the face of changing real-world affairs. This task taps a representational theory of mind because, to pass the task, children must understand that the character thinks the world is one way, though they know it is another. Numerous variations in this task have been conducted, and the results are remarkably consistent: the ability to think about mental states as representations typically emerges between children's third and fourth birthday (Wellman, Cross and Watson, 2001).

The question relevant to the present discussion concerns whether infants' early intentional inferences, such as the ones that might support joint attention episodes, require a representational theory of mind. While there are some who might think this likely (e.g. Fodor, 1992), most researchers are inclined against. Specifically, infants might succeed on tasks tapping an understanding of intentions, such as Baldwin's, with a *nonrepresentational* level of understanding (see Baldwin, 1991, for relevant discussion). Specifically, what seems called for is simply an understanding of intentions that encompasses a naïve, implicit belief that humans are mentally motivated to act in ways that help them to attain observable goals. This kind of understanding is distinctly mentalistic—it entails recognizing that something other than physical phenomena are involved—but it need not be representational.

What does a nonrepresentational understanding of intention 'look like'? Perhaps the most vivid demonstration of an early appreciation of intention comes from children's understanding of goal-oriented action. Gergley and colleagues (1995) found that even 12-month-old infants were willing to attribute goals to shapes that showed signs of being animate (i.e. capable of self-propelled motion). Along these same lines, Woodward (1998) has demonstrated that young infants construe the actions of humans as goal-directed, though they do not apply the same construal to the motions of inanimate objects. Still more convincingly, Meltzoff (1995) found that 18-month-olds reenacted events that correspond with an actor's likely goals and intentions, even when those actions are not explicitly modeled. Across these studies and others (e.g. Carpenter, Akhtar, and Tomasello, 1998), very young infants demonstrate an impressive level of sensitivity to the fact that others' actions are motivated by internal mental states. However, these young infants would fail even the simplest tasks designed to tap a representational understanding of mental states, such as the false belief task (Wellman *et al.*, 2001). Thus, 18-month-olds clearly understand behavior in a distinctly mentalistic manner, but it is probably a mistake to ascribe a concomitant representational appreciation to these same children at such an early age.

The distinction between a nonrepresentational and a representational appreciation of intentions can be fruitfully related to Flavell's (1988) notion of Level 1 versus Level 2 perspective taking (see Flavell *et al.*, 1981). Children with Level 1 perspective-taking abilities appreciate that two individuals can be looking at different things—they understand, for example, that they themselves are focused on an object that differs from that of another person's focus. Where 18-month-olds are limited is in their Level 2 abilities—they cannot consider the fact that when two people are focused on the same object, they can have different perspectives with respect to that object. Though Level 2 perspective-taking may be important for language-relevant developments (see Doherty and Perner, 1998; Happé, 1994; Sabbagh, 1999; Sabbagh and Baldwin, 2001), it does not seem to be required for simple inferences about communicative intentions of the kind exemplified by the Baldwin research described earlier. The only perspective-taking ability required is the appreciation that two people can be looking at (and thus, attending to) different objects in the world.

In the case of inferences about others' intentions, Level 2 understanding enables one to grasp that the same action could be motivated by different intentions. For instance, two people boxing could harbor intentions to play, or intentions to harm. Recent research by Baird and Moses (2001) demonstrates that even 4-year-olds are still struggling to grasp the complexity of relations between actions and intentions. Their deficits in Level 2 intentional understanding lead them into difficulty in some situations, as an understanding of intentional diversity is important for certain forms of everyday reasoning (e.g. assigning responsibility for an unfortunate event). Paradoxically, however, young children's deficits in understanding intentional diversity may actually *benefit* word learning. As many theorists have noted, the task of interpreting novel words presents a complex inductive problem because, logically speaking, any given word could mean any of an infinite set of possible things (Markman, 1989; Quine, 1960). Put another way, a speaker's use of a word could be motivated by any number of possible communicative intentions. If 18-month-old word-learners were 'Level 2 capable', they would be at risk of actually considering this large and befuddling forest of multiple possible communicative intentions for each and every utterance they encounter. Fortunately, young children's limitations with respect to representational diversity serve naturally to constrain the hypothesis space regarding others' communicative intentions, making such inferences tractable.

Thus, 18-month-olds' important but limited abilities to make judgments about others' intentions are, in some sense, just right for helping them to establish reliable word–referent mappings quickly. These abilities are sophisticated enough to enable them to realize that the speaker might not be talking about the thing that they themselves are looking at when the label is used. At the same time, these abilities are not so sophisticated that they lead children to consider the possibility of multiple mental motivations for the labeling act, which might massively increase the inductive complexity of word learning.

CAN SIMPLE HEURISTICS CARRY THE DAY?

We believe, then, that intentional inferences need not (and better not) be unduly complex if they are to optimize children's formation of appropriate initial word–object links. However, this belief does not constitute evidence that children are indeed drawing such intentional inferences in the service of word learning. Simple intentional inferences may well be within the range of young children's cognitive capabilities, but may still not be recruited to the task of word learning. Perhaps other factors enable children to avoid the errors we might otherwise expect if left to the mercy of covariation detection in a noisy linguistic environment. Below, we address several alternatives that we think provide a serious challenge to the communicative intentions account of existing data, and discuss some additional data that favors the communicative intentions hypothesis (see Baldwin and Moses, 2001, for related discussion).

Simple Heuristics 1: Orient-Follow-Associate

Recall that children avoided mapping errors when faced with discrepant labeling (Baldwin, 1991, 1993). Their ability to do so suggests that they spontaneously monitor which objects speakers intend to refer to, and use this information to guide new word–object links. However, children's performance in such discrepant labeling scenarios could feasibly be driven by the joint functioning of two lower-level cognitive propensities: (1) orienting to the speaker because he or she has just made a loudish noise, and then (2) reflexively following the speaker's gaze direction. These two mechanisms, combined with a Lockian predisposition to associate novel words with novel referents available at the time of labeling, might account for children's skillful word learning in discrepant labeling studies.

In some ways, this 'orient-follow-associate' proposal is an elegant one. Through recourse to nonstrategic cognitive propensities, children circumvent the discrepant labeling problem that at first seemed fatal for an associationist account of word learning. Instead of viewing children as stock-model associators, children are viewed as turbo-charged ones, replete with a rich array of biases that serve to focus them on the appropriate aspects of the environment at just the right times (L. Bloom, 2000; Samuelson and Smith, 2000). Furthermore, these models require little, if anything, in the way of inference, thereby requiring few cognitive resources. Can such low-level strategies account for children's apparent success in the discrepant labeling paradigms? Fortunately, this is readily testable.

If a simple orienting mechanism alone is at the heart of children's gaze-checking on hearing novel labels, then gaze-checking should occur any time a novel label—an appropriate orienting stimulus—is uttered. As it turns out, however, infants of both 12 and 18 months are significantly more likely to orient to some utterances involving novel labels than others: those uttered in contexts in which the speaker's intended referent is ambiguous. Baldwin, Bill, and Ontai (1996) report, for example, that infants hearing a novel label in the presence of two novel objects were more likely to check the speaker's gaze than those hearing the same novel label in the presence of just one novel object. Clearly, reflexive orienting is not all that happens when infants check a speaker's gaze on hearing a novel label.

Reflexive gaze following? While children's orienting behaviors demonstrate that they orient more when the context requires social information for the resolution of ambiguity, a separate question is whether they understand the intentional relevance of the information they get. In other words, is their tendency to *follow* gaze direction during word learning simply a reflex, or does it reflect an appreciation of the speaker's intentional states?

On a logical level, one might argue that following gaze direction requires some knowledge of its informational content. Just as there is nothing about the physical stimulus of someone pointing that necessarily compels one to follow the gesture to the target (try it with a 6-month-old and note how they look at your hand), nothing about the eyes transparently signals an agent's attention to a particular target. Instead, we follow gaze because we understand it to be informative about others' attentional and intentional states.

Despite this logical argument, though, there has been some empirical evidence to suggest that gaze-following may emerge in advance of children's abilities to make simple intentional attributions. For instance, Hood, Willen, and Driver (1998) used an attentional cuing task to show that even 3-month-olds attended to locations that were cued by gaze direction. Demonstrating sensitivity to gaze projections in these young infants is impressive, given that the earliest signs of a genuine appreciation of intentions do not reliably emerge until somewhere between 12 and 18 months. Comparative research has also found evidence for gaze-following in the absence of measurable conceptual knowledge. Notably, Tomasello *et al.* (1998) found evidence for gaze-following in five non-human primates, and even in domestic dogs (Hare and Tomasello, 1999), despite the fact that these species' appreciation of the intentional information which gaze direction imparts is demonstrably impoverished (see Povinelli and Eddy, 1996; Tomasello, 1999). It is easy to see how a predisposition to follow gaze could have an evolutionary basis; following gaze can improve detection of the location of food, danger, threat, and other survival-critical aspects of the social and nonsocial worlds (Whiten, 1997; Hare and Tomasello, 1999). Moreover, all of these benefits could be conferred without the higher-level understanding of the intentional and attentional states signaled by gaze direction.

The notion that a propensity to follow gaze is part of our biological heritage has also received support from recent research in the domain of basic neuroscience. Specifically, Perrett and colleagues have identified cells in parietal and temporal cortex of macaques that seem to be especially responsive to gaze direction (Perrett *et al.*, 1992). Findings such as these suggest the intriguing possibility that our primate heritage predisposes us toward sensitivity to gaze.

Taken together, these disparate lines of evidence lead to the question: Is children's use of gaze information in word learning best attributed to an orienting reflex, or to a conceptually driven information-gathering strategy? If children really do follow gaze to gain information about word–referent links, we would expect them to follow gaze to a potential target object when speakers produce utterances with an intention to refer (i.e. labeling), but *not* follow gaze when the speaker's utterance is similarly noisy but devoid of referential intent (i.e. a sigh). By contrast, if gaze following is reflexive, we would expect children to follow gaze regardless of whether the speaker is intending anything referential. In one study examining these questions, Baldwin, Bill, and Ontai (1996) report that infants of 12 and 18 months showed equivalent levels of orienting to the speaker's eyes in response to hearing a sigh as in response to hearing a novel label. However, infants showed high rates of *following* the speaker's gaze direction only in the case of the referential utterance—the novel label. These findings thus provide yet further evidence that the pursuit of joint attention is more than simple reflexive behavior on infants' part.

Simple Heuristics 2: 'When I hear a novel label...'

A second type of simple heuristic that children might use to negotiate the referentially noisy world would be to employ simple, nonconceptual rules to guide their information gathering upon hearing novel labels. For instance, perhaps they establish word–referent links on the basis of a rule along the lines of 'When I hear a novel label, I should associate the label with the thing being intercepted by the speaker's gaze trajectory'. Generally speaking, this strategy could be quite valuable, and in particular it would help to negotiate successfully the standard case of discrepant labeling. Nevertheless, this simple strategy might lead children into either error or confusion any time a speaker's gaze direction failed to pick out a single referent at the time the novel label was offered. Research by Tomasello and his colleagues militates against this prediction.

First, Tomasello and Barton (1994) provided 24-month-olds with a novel label in the context of an object-finding game. That is, without a novel object present, an experimenter suggested, 'Hey, let's go find the *toma!*' The experimenter then went on to search for an object. After establishing joint attention with a first object, the experimenter replaced the object and continued searching. After doing the same thing in two successive locations, the experimenter finally pulled a fourth item out of a location and said, 'Aha!' The impression which this procedure created for adults was that the first three attempts to find the *toma* were unsuccessful, and thus, more searching was required. If children were relying primarily on a rote strategy such as 'associate the novel word with the object that intercepts the speaker's gaze trajectory', we might have expected that children would either be confused or associate the word with the first thing the speaker proffered. Contrary to this prediction, results indicated that children regularly linked the novel word with the toy that ended the experimenter's search, regardless of whether the relevant toy was the first or last object attended to. These findings indicate that children's word learning is not a simple product of the 'associate with intercept' strategy.

Perhaps children use a different, but equally simplistic, strategy. Specifically, children might treat gaze direction as just one indicator of 'positive engagement', and treat positive engagement as the important factor dictating the establishment of new word–object relations. In some circumstances, like the discrepant labeling paradigm, gaze direction signals positive engagement, but it might be less salient than, say, playing with the toy. In the research by Tomasello *et al.* just described, playing with the toy that was the object of the search may have been a more powerful cue than gaze direction, so children may have selected this as the referent. To test whether children use a rule along the lines of 'When I hear a novel label,

I should associate it with the first thing the actor positively engages after having produced the novel label', Akhtar and Tomasello (1996) tested 24-month-old children in an object-finding game paradigm very similar to the one used by Tomasello and Barton (1994). The difference was that after the experimenter said to the child, 'Hey, let's go find the *toma!*', the experimenter went to retrieve the toy from a barn that was locked. Thus, the intended referent of the novel word was inaccessible at the time of labeling. Instead of stopping, however, the experimenter frowned and then proceeded to another location and removed a novel toy. If children were simply linking novel words to referents that speakers 'positively engaged', they would have mapped the word *toma* to the object that the experimenter played with. Surprisingly, however, results indicated that children reliably linked *toma* to the toy that eventually emerged from the barn, and not to the referents that were both accessible and recipients of positive affect at the time of labeling. These findings lend still more weight to the possibility that children are not using simple rote strategies to capitalize on social information when establishing new word–referent links.

Simple Heuristics 3: It's What's Salient to the Child

Perhaps the strongest challenge to the communicative intentions hypothesis is one that has emerged in a recent paper that emphasizes the role that general cognitive processes, such as attention and memory, play in guiding children's word learning (L. Bloom, 2000; Samuelson and Smith, 1998, 2000). Specifically, these researchers maintain that children are *fundamentally* egocentric word-learners—they are interested in matching novel words they hear to aspects of the world that are most salient when the novel word is presented. The core of this argument is that all of the razzle-dazzle that experimenters have gone through to insure that children are making word–referent links on the basis of communicative intentions has simply served to make the target object more salient at the time of labeling. Importantly, on this proposal, the role that salience plays in guiding word learning is thought to be independent of any understanding of speakers' intentions on children's part.

To illustrate, Samuelson and Smith (1998) offer an alternative interpretation of data presented by Akhtar, Carpenter and Tomasello (1996), which purported to give compelling evidence of young children's flexible use of intentional cues in the word-learning arena. In brief, Akhtar *et al.* (1996) familiarized children with four novel objects, three of which were made familiar to two experimenters, and the third of which was presented in the absence of one experimenter as well as the child's parent. When the absent experimenter and parent returned, all four toys were collected in a clear plastic box, at which point the experimenter and parent (both of whom had been absent) provided a novel label ('Look, there's a gazzer in here!'). Results suggested that children were more likely to link the novel word with the toy that had been introduced in the experimenter's and parent's absence.

Akhtar *et al.* (1996) interpreted these findings as evidence that children understand the pragmatic principle that speakers talk about things when they are relevant; children assumed that since the speakers only uttered the novel word the first time they saw the novel toy (and not when they had seen the other three toys), then they could only have intended the word to refer to the toy new to them.

Samuelson and Smith (1998) claimed that an intentional account is not necessary to make sense of the Akhtar *et al.* findings. Recall that in order to make the target toy novel to the speaker, Akhtar *et al.* had the speakers leave the room when the toy was initially brought out. Samuelson and Smith note that this results in two encoding contexts: (1) speaker present, within which all of the distractor toys were presented; and (2) speaker absent, within which only the target toy was presented. When the speaker returns, after children have been introduced to the novel toy, the context is actually more like the speaker-present context, within which the distractors were presented. In this 'modified' speaker-present context, the distractor toys were more familiar than the target toy that was introduced in the speaker-absent context. This fact may simply have made the target toy more salient at the time of labeling, and thus more likely to be selected as the target of the absent experimenter's and parent's labeling utterances.

Samuelson and Smith (1998) tested this alternative explanation by developing an experiment that included similar contextual shifts but did so without manipulating the speakers' knowledge. That is, the speaker was present when the target toy was introduced, though it was introduced separately and in a different context (on a separate table with a special tablecloth) from the distractors. Their results were similar to those of Akhtar *et al.* (1996), thereby raising the possibility that the dynamics of memory and attention led to the increased salience of the target toy for the child, and thus served as the basis for word learning.

While this argument is persuasive in its parsimony, there is some reason to doubt whether it can account even for Samuelson and Smith's own data. In addition to the experimental condition, both groups of researchers conducted a control condition in which no novel label was provided until the comprehension test. In this control condition (as in the experimental condition), the comprehension test context was most similar to the first labeling context. Here, the toy that was introduced in the second labeling context should have been contextually novel, and thus salient, at the time of the test even though the object had not been labeled. In line with Samuelson and Smith's proposal, this should have led to the target object being selected in the comprehension test. However, neither group of researchers reported systematic selection of the target object in their control conditions. This diminishes the possibility that contextual novelty alone is sufficient to support children's word learning.

In addition, Samuelson and Smith noted that they could not rule out alternative explanations of their findings in terms of referential intentions. For instance, perhaps playing with the target toy separately and in a different location may have indicated to the child that the toy was special to the speaker, and thus the most likely focus of her referential intent. Samuelson and Smith claimed that this interpretation was not favored, since it was *post hoc*. Nevertheless, the fact that inferences about referential intentions could have been at work makes it difficult to argue from these data that children's word learning is driven by salience alone. For a strong argument to be made either way, an effort to separate out the effects of salience from those that can be attributed to socio-pragmatic factors is required.

Three studies have attempted to do just this. Baldwin (1993, study 2) familiarized children with two toys and then placed each in an opaque bucket. Then the experimenter proceeded to idly manipulate the lid of one of the buckets while looking directly at the children and saying 'I'll show you a *modi!*' The experimenter's lid manipulation was shown to enhance infant's attention to that bucket. Following this nonreferential labeling, the experimenter removed a toy, either the one from the bucket with the manipulated lid or the one from the other bucket, and presented it to the child. Comprehension test results showed that children did not systematically link the novel label to the toy in the bucket with the manipulated lid. In contrast, Baldwin also found in a first study that infants readily established a new word–object link when labeling was accompanied by referential action such as manipulating the lid in order to gaze into the bucket. Together, these findings strongly suggest that, in children's view, just any highlighting action on an object by a speaker is not sufficient to make the object a candidate referent for a novel word. Rather, the action by the speaker must clearly indicate referential intent for children to license a new word–referent link.

Another set of studies carried out by Moore, Angelopoulos, and Bennett (1998) suggests that when referential and salience cues are pitted against one another in a word-learning situation, 24-month-olds ignore salience and link words with referents in accordance with referential cues. In their study, children were presented with a novel word for two potential targets, one that moved when the word was said and one that did not. The experimental manipulation concerned the referential cues provided by the speaker: half the time the speaker looked at the moving (and thus more salient) toy, and half the time he looked at the stationary toy. In this paradigm, 24-month-olds were more likely to link the word with the toy indicated by the speakers' referential intentions regardless of whether the toy was independently salient. A similar pattern of findings has been demonstrated in research using a slightly different training and testing paradigm (Hollich *et al.*, 2000; Hirsh-Pasek, Golinkoff, and Hollich, 2000). These findings join others in showing that referential cues take precedence over salience cues when children form hypotheses about word meaning.

Finally, Diesendruck *et al.* (2004) have recently reported compelling evidence favoring an intentional understanding account of children's word learning over the Samuelson and Smith account. They presented children with novel labels across contexts that were balanced for contextual novelty but differed with respect to the speakers' intentionality. For example, in one case, the speaker intentionally treated one novel object differently from others, while in the other case one novel object was accidentally treated differently. Children linked the novel label to the highlighted object only when it had been singled out intentionally by the speaker. These findings speak strongly for children spontaneously interpreting new words in light of their analysis of speakers' intentions.

Researchers have not yet put all conceivable simple heuristics to the test. Thus, it remains possible that children indeed possess some powerful 'when I hear a label...' heuristics that guide their word learning without recourse to inferences about communicative intentions. Nonetheless, all of the simple rules that have been tried can be ruled out, thereby leaving the communicative intentions hypothesis the leading candidate.

Although there is strong reason to believe that genuine intentional inferences play a role in children's early word learning, the emergence of such understanding remains very much in question. That is, it is unclear precisely when children begin to appreciate the intentional quality of others' references and use this understanding to guide inferences about word meaning, and it is also unclear how they come by this understanding. With respect to the *when* question, several recent studies employing techniques like those described earlier indicate that infants as young as 13–17 months are already operating with a genuine appreciation for others' referential intentions (e.g. Moses *et al.*, 2001; Namy and Waxman, 2000; Woodward, 2000). For example, Woodward (2000) found that 13-month-olds readily learned a novel label for a toy to which they attended at the time of labeling, but only if the speaker was providing evidence that she intended to label that toy, indicating that infants were taking the speaker's referential intentions into account. On the other hand, based on a series of studies investigating infants' ability to track intentional clues to avoid mapping errors, Hollich and colleagues concluded that 12-month-olds fail to recognize the import of intentional clues and instead operate like covariation detectors (e.g. Hollich *et al.*, 2000). In particular, in two studies 12-month-olds showed some signs of linking labels with the object salient to them regardless of what the speaker actually intended to refer to.

Thus, as yet it remains uncertain whether infants at the earliest phases of language learning can draw on intentional understanding to guide word learning, or whether simple heuristics jump-start initial word learning and are gradually replaced by genuine intentional understanding during the second year of life. The interest of the latter possibility is that children's dawning language understanding might itself play a role in promoting the emergence of intentional understanding. This raises the second outstanding question: *how* intentional understanding arises in children's development. As yet there is virtually no hard evidence that speaks to this most interesting of questions (see Baldwin and Baird, 2001, for a consideration of the available evidence), leaving plenty of elbow room for the pleasures of rampant speculation. Suggestions run the gamut from strongly constructivist (e.g. Carpenter, Nagell, and Tomasello, 1998) to robustly nativist (e.g. Baron-Cohen, 1995; Premack and Premack, 1995), while others opt for an intermediate, epigenetic account (e.g. Baldwin, in press; Baldwin and Baird, 2001). Gaining evidence that speaks to these possibilities is at the heart of research that we, and others, have recently initiated (e.g. Baldwin *et al.*, 2001; Brand, Baldwin, and Ashburn, 2002).

Summary of the Evidence

Claims regarding children's use of high-level inferential skills in any domain must naturally be supported by strong evidence supporting the necessity of granting such skills to children. We have offered one such claim here: that young children's language learning benefits from the ability to draw appropriate inferences about speakers' referential intentions. Clearly, it is up to us to demonstrate that children's apparent skills in this domain cannot be attributed to simpler, but potentially powerful, heuristics. Above we have reviewed three classes of such heuristics and argued that, at least as yet, empirical evidence favors inferences about communicative intentions over the operation of these heuristics. Given the current state of the evidence, then, it seems very likely that genuine inferences about speakers' referential intentions enhance word learning even during the early phases of semantic acquisition.

CONCLUDING WITH PSYCHOLOGY

Recent research provides a sound empirical and theoretical basis for suggesting that an ability to make appropriate inferences about others' intentions immeasurably benefits children's word learning. Nonetheless, there is a sense in which this is a somewhat unsatisfying claim, because little is known about the cognitive mechanisms that underlie these inferences which we claim are so crucial. The mysterious nature of the skill is underscored by the fact that it is sometimes given the term 'mind-reading' (e.g. Baron-Cohen, 1995). In some ways, this concern echoes a wider philosophical concern regarding the enterprise of imputing mental states to others (Wittgenstein, 1997/1953). Specifically, how can we as adults—much less infants—ever truly know what another person is thinking? We take these important challenges very seriously. Fortunately, a number of research programs have emerged from diverse areas within the field of psychology, each dedicated to understanding the cognitive, conceptual, and neurobiological underpinnings of our ability to attribute intentions to others in everyday settings (see Mallé, Baldwin and Moses, 2001). We are optimistic that these programs will ultimately reveal that the human capacity to understand others' intentions is not a mysterious or magical ability. Instead, skill at discerning intentions is made possible by a powerful complement of cognitive skills that humans can martial, beginning in infancy, to make sense of human behavior.

REFERENCES

AKHTAR, N., and TOMASELLO, M. (1996), 'Two-year-olds learn words for absent objects and actions', *British Journal of Developmental Psychology*, 14: 79–93.

—— CARPENTER, M., and TOMASELLO, M. (1996), 'The role of discourse novelty in early word learning', *Child Development*, 67: 635–45.

BAIRD, J. A. (2000), 'Young Children's Understanding of the Relation between Actions and Intentions' (unpublished dissertation, University of Oregon).

—— and MOSES, LOUIS J. (2001), 'Do preschoolers appreciate that identical actions may be motivated by different intentions?', *Journal of Cognition & Development*, 2 (4): 413–48.

BAKEMAN, R., and ADAMSON, L. B. (1984), 'Coordinating attention to people and objects in mother–infant and peer–infant interaction', *Child Development*, 55: 1278–89.

BALDWIN, D. A. (1991), 'Infants' contribution to the achievement of joint reference', *Child Development*, 62: 875–90.

—— (1993), 'Early referential understanding: infants' ability to understand referential acts for what they are', *Developmental Psychology*, 29: 832–43.

—— (in press), 'Discerning intentions: characterizing the cognitive system at play', in B. Homer and C. Tamis-LeMonda (eds.), *The Development of Social Cognition and communication*. Hillsdale, NJ: Lawrence Erlbaum.

—— and BAIRD, J. A. (2001), 'Discerning intentions in dynamic human action', *Trends in Cognitive Sciences*, 5: 171–8.

—— and MOSES, L. J. (2001), 'Links between early social understanding and word learning: challenges to current accounts', in A. Imbens-Bailey (ed.), special issue of *Social Development*, 10: 309–29.

—— BAIRD, J. A., SAYLOR, M., and CLARK, M. A. (2001), 'Infants parse dynamic human action', *Child Development*, 72: 708–17.

—— BILL, B., and ONTAI, L. L. (1996), 'Infants' tendency to monitor others' gaze: is it rooted in intentional understanding or a result of simple orienting?' Paper presented at the International Conference on Infancy Studies, Providence, RI.

—— MARKMAN, E. M., BILL, B., DESJARDINS, R. N., IRWIN, R. N., and TIDBALL, G. (1996), 'Infants' reliance on a social criterion for establishing word–object relations', *Child Development*, 67: 3135–53.

BARON-COHEN, S. (1995), *Mindblindness: An Essay on Autism and Theory of Mind.* Cambridge, Mass.: MIT Press.

BLOOM, LOIS (2000), 'Pushing the limits on the theories of word learning', *Monographs of the Society for Research in Child Development*, 65 (3): 124–35.

BLOOM, P. (1998), 'Theories of artifact categorization', *Cognition*, 66: 87–93.

BRAND, R., BALDWIN, D. A., and ASHBURN, L. (2002), 'Evidence for "motionese": modifications in mothers' infant-directed action', *Developmental Science*, 5: 72–83.

BRUNER, J. (1983), *Child's Talk: Learning to Use Language.* New York: W. W. Norton.

CAREY, S., and BARTLETT, E. (1978), 'Acquiring a single new word', *Proceedings of the Stanford Child Language Conference*, 15: 17–29.

CARPENTER, M., AKHTAR, N., and TOMASELLO, M. (1998), 'Fourteen- to 18-month-old infants differentially imitate intentional and accidental action', *Infant Behavior and Development*, 21: 315–30.

CARPENTER, M., NAGELL, K., and TOMASELLO, M. (1998), 'Social cognition, joint attention, and communicative competence from 9 to 15 months of age', *Monographs of the Society for Research in Child Development*, 63: (4).

CLARK, H. (1996), *Using Language*. Cambridge: Cambridge University Press.

COLLIS, G. M. (1977), 'Visual co-orientation and maternal speech', in H. R. Schaffer (ed.), *Studies in Mother–Infant Interaction*. (London: Academic Press, 355–75).

DIESENDRUCK, GIL, MARKSON, LORI, AKHTAR, NAMEERA, and REUDOR, AYELET (2004), 'Two-year-olds' sensitivity to speakers' intent: an alternative account of Samuelson and Smith', *Developmental Science*, 7 (1): 33–41.

DOHERTY, M., and PERNER, J. (1998), 'Metalinguistic awareness and theory of mind: just two words for the same thing', *Cognitive Development*, 13: 279–305.

FLAVELL, J. H. (1988), 'The development of children's knowledge about the mind: from cognitive connections to mental representations', in J. W. Astington, P. L. Harris, and D. Olson (eds.), *Developing Theories of Mind*. New York: Cambridge University Press, 244–67.

—— EVERETT, B. A., CROFT, K., and FLAVELL, E. R. (1981), 'Young children's knowledge about visual perception: further evidence for the Level 1–Level 2 distinction', *Developmental Psychology*, 17: 99–103.

FODOR, J. A. (1992), 'A theory of the child's theory of mind', *Cognition*, 44: 283–96.

GERGLEY, G., NADASDY, Z., CSIBRA, G., and BIRO, S. (1995), 'Taking the intentional stance at twelve months of age', *Cognition* 56: 165–93.

GIBBS, R. (1999), *Intentions in the Experiencing of Meaning*. Cambridge and New York: Cambridge University Press.

GRICE, H. P. (1975), 'Logic and conversation', in P. Cole and J. Morgan (eds.), *Syntax and Semantics, iii: Speech Acts*. New York: Academic Press, 41–58.

HAPPÉ, F. G. E. (1994), 'Communicative competence and theory of mind in autism: a test of relevance theory' *Cognition*, 48: 101–19.

HARE, B., and TOMASELLO, M. (1999), 'Domestic dogs (*Canis familiaris*) use human and conspecific social cues to locate hidden food', *Journal of Comparative Psychology*, 113: 173–7.

HARRIS, M., JONES, D., BROOKS, S., and GRANT, J. (1986), 'Relations between the nonverbal context of maternal speech and rate of language development', *British Journal of Developmental Psychology*, 4: 261–8.

—— —— and GRANT, J. (1983), 'The nonverbal context of mothers' speech to infants', *First Language*, 4: 21–30.

HEIBECK, T. H., and MARKMAN, E. M. (1987), 'Word learning in children: an examination of fast mapping', *Child Development*, 58: 1021–34.

HIRSH-PASEK, K., GOLINKOFF, R. M., and HOLLICH, G. (2000), 'An emergentist coalition model for word learning: mapping words to objects is a product of interaction of multiple cues', in R. M. Golinkoff, K. Hirsh-Pasek, L. Bloom, L. B. Smith, A. L. Woodward, N. Akhtar, M. Tomasello, and G. Hollich (eds.), *Becoming a Word Learner: A Debate on Lexical Acquisition*. Oxford: Oxford University Press, 136–64.

HOLLICH, G. J., HIRSH-PASEK, K., GOLINKOFF, R. M., BRAND, R. J., BROWN, E., CHUNG, H. L., HENNON, E., and ROCROI, C. (2000), 'Breaking the word learning barrier: an emergentist coalition model for the origins of word learning', *Monographs of the Society for Research in Child Development*, 65.

HOOD, B., WILLEN, J. D., and DRIVER, J. (1998), 'Adults' eyes trigger shifts of visual attention in human infants', *Psychological Science*, 9: 131–4.

HORTON, W. S., and KEYSAR, B. (1996), 'When do speakers take into account common ground?' *Cognition*, 59: 91–117.

KEYSAR, B., and BARR, D. J. (in press), 'Coordination of action and belief in conversation', in J. C. Trueswell and M. K. Tanenhaus (eds.), *World Situated Language Use: Psycholinguistic, Linguistic and Computational Perspectives on Bridging the Product and Action Traditions*. Cambridge, Mass.: MIT Press.

LOCKE, J. (1964/1690), *An Essay Concerning Human Understanding*. Cleveland: Meridian Books.

MALLÉ, B. F., MOSES, L. J., and BALDWIN, D. A. (2001), *Intentions and Intentionality: Foundations of Social Cognition*. Cambridge, Mass.: MIT Press.

MARKMAN, E. M. (1989), *Categorization and Naming in Children*. Cambridge, Mass.: MIT Press.

MELTZOFF, ANDREW N. (1995), 'Understanding the intentions of others: re-enactment of intended acts by 18-month-old children', *Developmental Psychology*, 31 (5): 838–50.

MOORE, C., ANGELOPOULOS, M., and BENNETT, P. (1998), 'Word learning in the context of referential and salience cues', *Developmental Psychology*, 35: 60–8.

MOSES, L. J., and FLAVELL, J. H. (1990), 'Inferring false beliefs from actions and reactions', *Child Development*, 61: 929–45.

—— BALDWIN, D. A., ROSICKY, J. G., and TIDBALL, G. (2001), 'Evidence for referential understanding in the emotions domain at 12 and 18 months', *Child Development*, 72: 718–35.

NAMY, L. L., and WAXMAN, S. R. (2000), 'Naming and exclaiming: infants' sensitivity to naming contexts', *Journal of Cognition & Development*, 1 (4): 405–28.

NELSON, K. E., and BONVILLIAN, J. (1973), 'Concepts and words in the two-year-old: acquisition of concept names under controlled conditions', *Cognition*, 2: 435–50.

NINIO, A., and BRUNER, J. S. (1978), 'The achievement and antecedents of labeling', *Journal of Child Language*, 5: 1–15.

PAPAFRAGOU, A. (2002), 'Mindreading and verbal communication', *Mind & Language*, 17: 55–67.

PERNER, J. (1991), *Understanding the Representational Mind*. Cambridge, Mass.: MIT Press.

PERRETT, D. I., HIETANEN, J. K., ORAM, M. W., and BENSON, P. J. (1992), 'Organization and functions of cells responsive to faces in the temporal cortex', *Philosophical Transactions of the Royal Society of London*, B, 335: 23–30.

POVINELLI, D. J., and EDDY, T. J. (1996), 'Factors influencing young chimpanzees' (Pan troglodytes) recognition of attention', *Journal of Comparative Psychology*, 110: 336–45.

PREMACK, D., and PREMACK, A. J. (1995), 'Intention as psychological cause', in D. Sperber and D. Premack (eds.), *Causal Cognition: A Multidisciplinary Debate*. Symposia of the Fyssen Foundation. Oxford: Clarendon Press, 185–99.

QUINE, W. V. O. (1960), *Word and Object*. Cambridge, Mass.: MIT Press.

SABBAGH, M. A. (1999), 'Communicative intentions and language: evidence from right-hemisphere damage and autism', *Brain and Language*, 70: 29–69.

—— and BALDWIN, D. A. (2001), 'Learning words from knowledgeable versus ignorant speakers: links between preschoolers' theory of mind and semantic development', *Child Development*, 72: 1054–70.

SAMUELSON, L. K. and SMITH, L. B. (1998), 'Memory and attention make smart word learning: an alternative account of Akhtar, Carpenter, and Tomasello', *Child Development*, 69: 94–104.

SAMUELSON, L. K. and SMITH, L. B. (2000), 'Grounding development in cognitive processes', *Child Development*, 71: 98–106.

SAYLOR, M. M., BALDWIN, D. A., and SABBAGH, M. A. (2004), 'Converging on word meaning', in D. G. Hall and S. R. Waxman (eds.), *Weaving a Lexicon*. Cambridge, Mass.: MIT Press, 509–31.

SCHAFER, G., and PLUNKETT, K. (1998), 'Rapid word learning by fifteen-month-old infants under tightly controlled conditions', *Child Development*, 69: 309–20.

SCHEIFFELIN, B. B. (1985), 'The acquisition of Kaluli', in D. Slobin (ed.), *The Cross-Linguistic Study of Language Acquisition*. Hillsdale, NJ: Erlbaum, 525–93.

—— (1990). *The give and take of everyday life: Language socialization of Kaluli Children*. Cambridge: Cambridge University Press.

TOMASELLO, M. (1999), 'Having intentions, understanding intentions, and understanding communicative intentions', in P. D. Zelazo and J. W. Astington (eds.), *Developing Theories of Intention: Social Understanding and Self-Control*. Mahwah, NJ: Erlbaum, 63–75.

—— and AKHTAR, N. (1995), 'Two-year-olds use pragmatic cues to differentiate reference to objects and actions', *Cognitive Development*, 10: 201–24.

—— and BARTON, M. (1994), 'Learning words in non-ostensive contexts', *Developmental Psychology*, 30: 639–50.

—— and FARRAR, J. (1986), 'Joint attention and early language', *Child Development*, 57: 1454–63.

—— CALL, J., and HARE, B. (1998), 'Five primate species follow the visual gaze of conspecifics', *Animal Behaviour*, 55: 1063–9.

TREVARTHEN, C. (1980), 'The foundations of intersubjectivity: development of interpersonal and cooperative understanding in infancy', in D. Olson (ed.), *The Social Foundations of Language and Thought: Essays in Honor of J. S. Bruner*. New York: Horton, 316–42.

WELLMAN, H. M., CROSS, D., and WATSON, J. K. (2001), 'Meta-analysis of theory-of-mind development: the truth about false belief', *Child Development*, 72: 655–84.

WHITEHURST, G. J., KEDESDY, J., and WHITE, T. G. (1982), 'A functional analysis of meaning', in S. A. Kuczaj II (ed.), *Language Development*, i: *Syntax and Semantics*. San Diego: Academic Press, 397–427.

WHITEN, A. (1997), 'The Machiavellian mindreader', in A. Whiten and R. W. Byrne (eds.), *Machiavellian Intelligence II: Extensions and Evaluations*. New York: Cambridge University Press, 144–73.

WIMMER, H., and PERNER, J. (1983), 'Beliefs about beliefs: representation and constraining function of wrong beliefs in young children's understanding of deception', *Cognition*, 13: 103–28.

WITTGENSTEIN, L. (1997/1953), *Philosophical Investigations*. Oxford: Blackwell.

WOODWARD, A. L. (1998), 'Infants selectively encode the goal object of an actor's reach', *Cognition*, 69: 1–34.

—— (2000), 'Constraining the problem space in early word learning', in R. M. Golinkoff, K. Hirsh-Pasek, L. Bloom, L. B. Smith, A. L. Woodward, N. Akhtar, M. Tomasello, and G. Hollich (eds.), *Becoming a Word Learning: A Debate on Lexical Acquisition*. New York: Oxford University Press, 81–114.

9

What Puts the Jointness into Joint Attention?

R. Peter Hobson

INTRODUCTION

In this chapter I shall explore what 'joint attention' means, and attempt to characterize some of the conditions that make the development of joint attention possible. I shall do this with reference to the special case of autism, where abnormalities in the emergence of joint attention promise to reveal a great deal about the sources and the developmental implications of triadic person-to-person-to-world relatedness.

It will be apparent from the title of the chapter that one of my concerns is how an infant comes to *share* a focus of attention with someone else. Everyone would agree that for an instance of infant social engagement to count as joint attention, it is not enough that the infant attends to some object or event that just happens to be at the focus of someone else's attention. Critically, the infant needs to be aware of the object or event *as* the focus of the other person's attention—and in addition, for full 'jointness', he or she should share awareness of the sharing of the focus, something that often entails sharing an attitude towards the thing or event in question. (To take an example from adulthood: when a friend and I shared our wonder and joy at a late cut by David Gower in a Lord's Test Match, I do not know whether the onset of my blissful smile was before or only when my eyes met those of my friend.) But this apparently straightforward formulation disguises many less-than-straightforward issues about the nature and content of such awareness. For example, is the infant aware that she is aware? Does she *think* the other person is attending? What exactly is she aware *of*? Does she already have a concept or pre-concept or percept or whatever... of *attention*?

Which brings me to the second of my concerns: what we mean by 'attention'. 'Attention' is a term that comes easily to our lips. We seem to know what it means—or at least, we seem to be more comfortable with the notion of attention than with other consciousness-invoking psychological terms. Often we take it that attention is basic to conscious awareness. Therefore it seems perfectly reasonable to suppose that attention is what infants come to be aware of when they start to engage in triadic person–person–world transactions towards the end of the first

I thank Jessica Meyer for her comments, and especially for her point about sharing awareness of a shared focus, and Johannes Roessler for his helpful editorial nudges.

year of life. It is joint attention that they achieve (one supposes), and this involves being aware of another person's attentiveness to the world.

It is interesting that the word 'attentiveness' has somewhat different connotations to the word 'attention'. If we imagine a state of attentiveness in an animal or a child, we probably envisage a set of bodily expressed attitudes as much as an inner mental state. Attitudes are mental as well as physical, of course. But attitudes/attentiveness are manifest in bodily expressions, orientations, and actions; they are visible, not hidden in cognitive processing procedures deep inside the skull. I am going to presume that one part of the meaning of someone paying attention to something is that the someone might manifest their attentive relatedness to the world; and so, on the basis of seeing someone showing attentiveness, we can say that the person is paying attention. I am also going to suppose that attention/attentiveness is a feature of attitudes, and that attitudes are bodily-cum-mental orientations that often, if not always, have an emotional component. These suggestions have a developmental point, of course, in that a child might need to get to the idea of attention through reacting to perceptible signs of attentiveness, and signs of attentiveness may comprise a family of expressions and actions that have a special (emotional) effect on the observer.

It seems to me that the concept of attention does its job by capturing something common to a range of conscious mental states. Attention is, as it were, a lowest common denominator for such states. Partly for this reason, it is a rather colourless idea. It is like a stage without actors. Or it would be, if one really thought in terms of a kind of spotlight of consciousness, in the abstract. In fact, we do not think like that. We know that you cannot *just* attend to something—the 'attention' is merely one amongst several qualities of your psychological engagement with whatever you are attending to. You are feeling attentively, or thinking attentively, or doing attentively, or whatever. Or again, you cannot attend but attend to nothing. The description of you as attending implies that there is something you are attending to. In other words, the concept of attention is not one that refers to a state of being in an isolated individual. In the typical case, at least, attention is a concept that refers to one particular quality of the relation between an individual and the world-as-experienced.

Now whatever object or event is the focus of someone's attention falls under a particular description for the person who attends. In other words, the person attends to it as a such-and-such. This leads to questions about the degree of jointness of joint attention when what two people 'see' in the same object or event is radically different. If I see the man in the water waving to me, and you see the man drowning, do we attend to the same thing? In such a case you would not shout, 'No, look over there', but you might cry, 'No, look at him this way'. You would still be drawing my attention to something; and once I saw what you meant, the 'jointness' of our experience would be substantially increased.

My main point is this. We psychologists and philosophers are perfectly entitled to think with the abstract concept of attention, and for certain purposes we may be well advised to do so. On the other hand, we need to be careful not to assume that what we have abstracted as a basic property of consciousness is also foundational for an infant's developing understanding of mental states. It could easily be the case that, on the contrary, the infant first has to register and respond to blood-and-guts qualities expressed in the behaviour of others. Perhaps it is only much later that he or she might be said to pick up diagnostic clues (as it were) to the person's degree of attention. If this is so, then we can begin to explore how it is that *through* registering and responding to another person's expressive behaviour, the infant comes to an increasingly elaborated (and ultimately, articulated) understanding of people as having subjective orientations. In other words, we might accept that one end-point of development in understanding the mind is to grasp the concept of attention as (a) referring to an 'internal' quality common to a variety of conscious mental states that (b) includes the idea of someone having a selective psychological focus, so that something is attended to under a description for that person, and even (c) sometimes may be applied to people and animals for whom/which it is difficult or impossible to discern what their state or focus of attention is (for example, for a person sitting motionless with her eyes closed). But at the same time, we might want to explain how a child acquires such a concept in terms that are more behaviourally and perhaps emotionally anchored than those we tend to use in thinking about attention. In other words, we may need to see how the concept of attention is abstracted from an infant's experiences of other people, rather than suppose that infants acquire an awareness of attention and then have to link it up with more specific qualities in other people's behaviour and/or expressions of feeling.

A SIMPLE SCHEME FOR THE DEVELOPMENT OF JOINT ATTENTION

How is joint attention possible? How can a child, and a very small child at that, come to register that something with which she is psychologically engaged is also a focus for someone else? Or that something on which someone else is focused could be of interest to herself? Or, perhaps at a more basic level, that she and the other can share experiences of the world?

To begin to address these questions, I want to reframe attention as psychological engagement. Immediately we realize that there are different forms of psychological engagement; for example, to feel about something is not the same as to intend to act upon it. Now the issue arises: In what ways can 'jointness' be said to characterize one person's forms of engagement with another person's forms of engagement with the world? For example, I might be able to detect and look towards the focus of a robot's 'actions' or 'sensors', and come to have new intentions or feelings towards that object or event as a result; but I would not be in a state of joint attention *with* the robot except in a sense that is derivative from my experiences of sharing a focus of attention with a person. Or, to take a complementary example, when children with autism get another person to *do* something to an object (for example, reach for a jar of cookies), we should not assume how far they experience 'jointness' even when they establish interpersonally co-ordinated behavioural relations with that object.

I believe that an infant's awareness of *sharing* a subjective orientation with someone else is founded on early-developing propensities to identify with the bodily expressed attitudes of others—a special form of interpersonal engagement involving feelings—such that by the end of the first year of life, the infant has become aware of the potential linkage between his or her own and the other's engagement with a shared focus. Often, but not always, the infant is in a position to perceive the particular attitudes of the other on a given occasion of joint attention; at other times, as in showing someone an object, the infant seems to be aware at the outset that such attitudes, and the sharing of attitudes, is a potential feature of the ensuing interpersonal exchange; or at yet other times, the infant might (say) read the intentions of the other person towards something, but only in the background have awareness that the other's relations can involve attitudes that may come to assume centre-stage. In the story of the development of joint attention, the interpersonal co-ordination of attitudes is critical; the interpersonal co-ordination of actions (or intentions) is not sufficient. Nor, perhaps, does the concept of 'social orientation' (as in Leekam's excellent Chapter 10 below) get an adequate purchase on interpersonal linkage in experience to explain where joint-ness comes from—it does not, as it were, get below the skin of the two individuals involved—despite its value as a behavioural pointer towards developmentally critical social processes.

Joint attention, then, occurs when an individual (say, P_1) is psychologically engaged with someone else's (P_2's) psychological engagement with the world. The nature of P_1's engagement has to be that she relates to P_2's relation to the world; in other words, she has to encompass the state of P_2 as this is directed to something that P_1 also experiences from her own vantage-point. Moreover, for P_1 to be aware (at whatever level we suppose this happens) of P_2's awareness of the world, it must be the case that P_1 can register P_2's separateness from herself not only physically, but also psychologically. Jointness implies differentiation as well as co-ordination. Finally, there is the matter of sharing awareness of shared experiences of the world.

In my view, joint attention develops in three stages.

1. The infant engages with someone else.
2. The infant engages with someone else's engagement with the world—and is 'moved'.
3. The infant achieves a new level of awareness that she is engaging with some-one else's engagement with the world (in part through the process of being engaged with the other's engagement with herself).

I am going to concentrate on the second of these phases, although in order to do so, it will be necessary to consider the first phase as well. There are two critical issues that I am not going to discuss. The first is the pivotal developmental significance of infants sharing experiences in one-to-one interpersonal transactions during the early months of life (Hobson, 1989; and Heal, Chapter 2 above, for a related perspective). The second is the transition from a 12-month-old's ability to *register* someone else's attitude to the world, to the 18-month-old's ability to *conceptualize* another person as having a subjective orientation (Hobson, 1993a). All I want to stress here is that, in achieving joint attention, what an infant registers/perceives is more (and less) than objectively characterized behaviour, in so far as the infant is *affected* in such a way that his or her attitude may be aligned with or otherwise influenced by that of the other person. The most obvious examples come from contexts of social referencing, where a child's attitude to an object or event is altered by another person's attitude to that same object or event. But I think it is a feature of all proto-declarative joint attention. And recall that it is not enough simply to be 'moved', as one might be moved to a new orientation by any emotion-rousing event; nor is it enough simply to 'read' or 'diagnose' from an external and uninvolved vantage-point that the other person is having relations of such-and-such a kind with something in the world. It also requires that the child's movement in psychological stance is accompanied by awareness (which may be intermittent) that this is occurring through the child's responsiveness to another person, just as the child's experience of sharing is accompanied by awareness of being in relation to a person. A point I shall return to later is that joint attention entails more than merely recognizing another person's attitude—it also means feeling connected with the person as the source of the attitude. This might lead one to wonder whether the prehistory of such jointness includes not only co-ordinating, but also intending to communicate, attitudes—a matter I shall gloss over for now.

My approach is to consider some recent evidence from children with autism, in order to focus on the kind of interpersonal engagement that seems to be missing in this disorder. I hope that this will suggest why joint attention is deficient in autism (which I shall take as a given at this stage, but give some evidence later; and again see Leekam, Chapter 10)—and correspondingly, why joint attention becomes so central for children who do not have autism.

PERCEIVING AND RELATING TO OTHERS

The background hypothesis is that children with autism are unusual in their relative failure to become emotionally engaged with the emotional states of other people. In their relations with others, both they and the people with whom they interact lack the experience of interpersonally co-ordinated and patterned exchanges of feeling. Or, to be more precise, the children with autism lack the experience, and the people with whom they interact experience the lack. Put simply, this limitation in the children's experience of intersubjective contact and reciprocal engagement with others is a fundamental impediment to growth in their understanding of what it is to have a subjective mental orientation. *En route*, I shall be arguing, it is a fundamental impediment to their engaging in joint attention.

A problem with arguing this case is that 'intersubjectivity' does not lend itself to conventional scientific measurement. Among the approaches that colleagues and I have adopted to highlight autistic children's difficulties is to investigate their efforts to read emotional meanings in the bodily gestures and facial and vocal expressions of other people (Hobson, 1991, 1993*b*). One of several problems with this approach is that if one takes a narrow view of perception, the studies seem to reduce to tests of skill in 'emotion recognition'. In our own view, perception is relational, and to perceive a smile as a smile (to take the simplest example) is to respond with feeling, in such a way that *through* the smile one apprehends the emotional state of the other (Wittgenstein, 1980). In other words, there is a mode of feeling perception that is critical for establishing intersubjective relations between people, and it is a kind of perception that establishes a special quality of relatedness between the individual and what is perceived—in most natural circumstances, a person. One might choose to view intersubjective engagement as involving specific tendencies to action, or as involving a form of cognition (since it amounts to a powerful kind of categorization). What one cannot do is to *reduce* such engagement to action or cognition, however. I think the best way to think of it is as a form of relatedness of which psychological components of emotion, cognition, and conation become somewhat more differentiated (or separable for theoretical purposes) as development proceeds.

In order to illustrate our methodology, but also in order to make a point about the specificity of perceiving and becoming engaged with bodily expressed attitudes in other people, I shall describe our most recent—and quite possibly, our last—experiment in this programme of research (Moore, Hobson, and Lee, 1997). To restate the relevance for joint attention: in order to engage in joint attention, one needs to have a certain kind of psychological engagement with another person, and this kind of engagement begins and develops over the earliest months of life. It is an emotional engagement, and it can be described as involving a species of perception as well as a species of emotional responsiveness.

Our experiment was in three parts. The first part was designed to test whether children with autism could perceive appropriately configured moving dots of light as human people (point-light presentations first devised by Johansson, 1973, and reported to have meaning even for infants by Bertenthal, Proffitt, and Cutting, 1984). The second part was to test how they would respond when asked to comment on what they perceived was happening in sequences of point-light human displays. Here we predicted that the children with autism would spontaneously see and comment on the actions of the point-light people, but, unlike control participants, not remark on the emotions portrayed. The third part was to test a further prediction that there would be a group difference when children with and without autism were specifically asked to identify particular actions and particular feelings in the point-light displays.

It may be worth adding a brief word about our reasons for employing point-light displays. In previous studies, we had found evidence that, at least on occasion, children with autism appeared to be able to name bodily expressed emotions, for example in faces, but by employing unusual perceptual/cognitive strategies that might not reflect full experience and understanding of what the expressions signify for a person's feelings (e.g. Hobson, Ouston, and Lee, 1988; Hobson, 1991). Our aim now was to present emotionally expressive bodily forms that would be immediately apprehended by most people (and even by infants, as noted above), but were also outside the kinds of conventional bodily appearances such as stylized photographs of faces which children with autism might have learned to classify in a superficial manner using relatively 'non-emotional' strategies. The importance of this is that conventional tests of 'emotion recognition' might seriously underestimate the difficulties encountered by children with autism when it comes to entering into and sharing the feelings of others. So here we were trying to key into our participants' natural modes of apprehending feelings in bodily gestures, but with unfamiliar task materials.

The groups we tested for most of the tasks were thirteen children and adolescents with autism and thirteen children and adolescents of the same age and level of verbal ability who were not autistic. We also included a group of matched typically developing children, who, as it turned out, performed like the non-autistic mentally retarded participants, so will not be considered further.

Our first aim was to determine whether the children in each group were able to see moving points of light as people, even when the displays were presented only for very short periods of time. The results were that almost all the participants in each group were able to recognize objects *and* people in the point-light displays, and there was not a group difference. Many of the children needed exposure times of as little as 200 thousandths of a second to tell that the dots were stuck to a person, which was less than the time required to recognize most of the objects. There was therefore no doubt that in this very basic aspect of person recognition, the children with autism could read our moving dots without difficulty.

In the second part of the study, we presented separate 5-second sequences of the point-light person enacting gestures of surprise, sadness, fear, anger, and happiness in turn. For example, the surprised point-light person was seen to walk forward, suddenly check his stride and pull backwards with his arms thrown out to the side, and finally give a sigh. Or in the case of the sad figure, the point-light

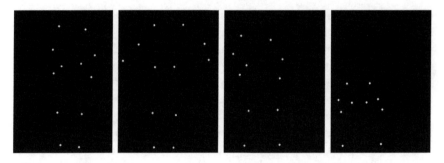

FIGURE 9.1. Still images from moving point-light display of sadness.

person walked forward with a stooped posture, paused, sighed, lifted his arms slowly, and then dropped them to his sides, and finally seated himself in a slumped posture and slowly put his head in his hands (four stills from this videotape sequence are shown in Fig. 9.1). We checked that adults who saw the videotapes were 100 per cent accurate in judging the expressions.

Before each videotape sequence, the children were told: 'You're going to see some bits of film of a person moving. I want you to tell me about this person. Tell me what's happening.' We took care to phrase the instructions and any prompts we gave in terms of 'what was happening' and made no reference to feelings nor actions.

The results were that all but one of the non-autistic children made a spontaneous comment about the person's emotional state on at least one occasion during the presentations. The majority of this group referred to emotions in two or more out of the five sequences. By contrast, ten of the thirteen children with autism *never* referred to emotional states (whether correctly or incorrectly). Yet *all* the children in both groups saw meaningful content in each and every presentation, and commented on this. In the case of the children and adolescents with autism, it was the person's movements and actions rather than feelings that were reported. For example, they described the sad figure as 'walking and sitting down on a chair', 'walking and flapping arms and bent down', and 'walking and waving his arms and kneeling down...hands to face'. The scared figure was said to be 'standing up and moving backward', 'standing on tip-toe...walking backwards', and 'moving backwards...sort of jumping'. The angry figure was 'dancing to some music...clapping a little bit', 'walking and jogging and shaking his arms', and 'walking and nodding'. There is a striking absence of emotion in these descriptions.

The final part of the task was designed to explore how accurately the children and adolescents could name actions and emotions when explicitly asked to do so. For this part of the study, we added five new emotionally expressive sequences to the five already described: these showed the point-light person in states of itchiness, boredom, tiredness, cold, and hurt. When these sequences were shown, one by one, we said: 'I want you to tell me what the person is feeling.' Alongside this test involving emotions and other attitudes, there was a test for the recognition of non-emotional actions: lifting, chopping, hopping, kicking, jumping, pushing, digging, sitting, climbing, and running. Here the instructions were: 'I want you to tell me what the person is doing.'

Before we analysed the results, we excluded items that yielded results with ceiling or floor effects (namely, kicking and jumping, and surprise and boredom, respectively). When these items were excluded, the two sets of items—of emotional and other attitudes, on the one hand, and of actions, on the other—were equally difficult for the non-autistic participants.

The results are illustrated in Fig. 9.2. On the actions task, the participants with autism were not significantly different from the control participants. On the emotions and attitudes task, on the other hand, they were markedly less successful, scoring a mean of only 2 out of 8 correct. Once again, they seemed to have real difficulty in reading the subjective states of the person depicted, a difficulty that did *not* extend to their judgements of actions. For example, when one child was asked what the 'itching' person was feeling, he said: 'scratching…lots of fleas'. This vivid description captures the action component of what was happening, but the emphasis is on the 'scratching', not the feeling which might have prompted the person to scratch.

If the experiment just described captures something of the abnormal way in which individuals with autism perceive other people, is this indeed (as I have suggested) just one perspective on a more complex and far-reaching limitation in their intersubjective engagement with others? What about the individuals' actual relatedness to others?

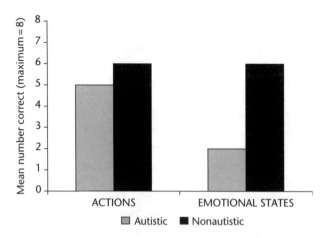

FIGURE 9.2. Judgements of actions and feelings in point-light displays.

There is something a bit odd in asking this question about children with autism, because by definition they relate to other people in ways that are strange. Yet it has been surprisingly difficult to pin down wherein the strangeness lies, and more specifically, to explore whether it may have anything to do with intersubjectivity. We tried to capture something of this in a study of greetings and farewells (Hobson and Lee, 1998). We simply videotaped a group of twenty-four children and adolescents with autism and a group of matched non-autistic individuals in a standardized situation in which they were introduced to, and subsequently departed from, a stranger seated across the room.

Compared with control participants, there were about half as many participants with autism who gave spontaneous expressions of greeting, and a substantial proportion of those with autism failed to respond when the stranger said 'Hello'. Whereas all the young people without autism made eye contact, and no fewer than seventeen smiled, a third of those with autism never made eye contact, and only six smiled. The results for the farewell episode were broadly similar. Half the individuals without autism, but only three of those with autism, made eye contact and said a goodbye. Of these, nine of the non-autistic individuals but not a single autistic individual also smiled.

We were keen to use this study to get just a bit closer to the kind of interpersonal lack of connection that is a prominent feature of clinical descriptions of children with autism, but that tends to be sidelined in theoretical accounts of the condition. We wanted to resist the slide towards seeing our study as a count of 'behaviours'. So we also asked the raters of our videotapes to make the following judgement about the greeting episode: 'Over this period and prior to sitting down, to what degree did you feel that the child engaged with Peter, (the stranger)?' The categories of response were either strongly engaged, somewhat engaged, or hardly, if at all, engaged. It turned out that different judges who made these ratings independently were in good agreement with each other. The results were that fourteen of the twenty-four non-autistic children were judged to be strongly engaged, and only two hardly, if at all, engaged. In contrast, only two of the twenty-four children with autism were judged to be strongly engaged, and thirteen of them seemed hardly, if at all, engaged. These judgements more or less (but not quite) mapped on to the behavioural ratings.

These studies illustrate something about interpersonal engagement and the relative lack of such engagement in individuals with autism. Yet they involved participants who were in late childhood or early adolescence. Therefore one cannot presume that the findings indicate some basic or 'primary' abnormality in autism. Obviously, the children might have become unengaged because of early and more fundamental psychological impairments. In order to address this possibility, we need to investigate much younger children. Turning now to such studies, I shall try to illustrate links between primary intersubjectivity and 'triadic' interpersonal relations—including joint attention—in young children with and without autism.

FROM PRIMARY INTERSUBJECTIVITY TO
TRIADIC INTERPERSONAL RELATIONS

One approach to studying the early natural history of autism is to ask parents of children who have the disorder what the children's infancy and early development were like. A recent study by Wimpory *et al.* (2000) overcame some of the limitations of previous studies, such as eliciting parents' accounts when their children were long past infancy, and when the parents were aware of the diagnosis of autism and many of its implications. Wimpory interviewed parents when their children were still very young (between 2½ and 4 years), and before a diagnosis had been made. The parents were each given an intensive guided interview focused upon developments in the infant's social engagement over the first 2 years of life (a period that had ended between 6 and 24 months before the interview, so that the events recalled were relatively recent). The comparison was between parental accounts of ten children who turned out to have autism and ten who did not have autism but had developmental delays, and were similar in age and cognitive ability.

The results indicated two kinds of group difference. First, there were items on which the children with autism were reported to have lacked person-to-person communicative expressions (essentially, manifestations of limited primary intersubjectivity) in the first 2 years of life: greeting the parents and waving, raising the arms to be picked up, frequency and intensity of eye contact, socially directed feelings of anger and distress, pre-verbal turn-taking and using noises communicatively, sociability in play with or without toys, and enjoying and participating in lap games. Secondly, there were items on which the children with autism were reported to have shown deficits in person–person–object ('triadic') interactions: the referential use of eye contact, offering and giving objects to others, showing objects to others, pointing at objects and following others' points. Looking at the results overall, it was the case that at least half the infants in the control group *but not a single infant with autism* were said to show the following during the first 2 years: normal eye contact, turn-taking and using noises communicatively, referential use of eye contact, offering and giving objects to others, and pointing at objects and following others' points.

Here was evidence that indeed, from very early in life—at least during the first 2 years—infants with autism were failing to display not only signs of joint attention, but also signs of deficient one-to-one interpersonal engagement. Lord *et al.* (1993) also reported that parents of young children with autism gave accounts in which their children were abnormal across a range of socio-emotional and communicative behaviour, and were also less likely than learning-disabled control subjects to babble in a socially directed way. In a study involving systematic history-taking and direct observation, Lord (1995) concluded that 2-year-olds with autism differed from children with developmental disorders in specific aspects of social reciprocity, such as failure to greet and lack of seeking to share enjoyment, as well as in communicative behaviour such as their lack of response to another person's voice, absence of pointing, and failure to understand gesture. Although the findings from other research are not entirely consistent, suggestive evidence from retrospective reports (Dahlgren and Gillberg, 1989) and from videotape studies of infants (e.g. Baranek, 1999; Osterling and Dawson, 1994) point to abnormalities in social orientation early in the children's lives.

A recent approach to studying the social impairments of infants with autism has been to identify infants who are candidates for the full syndrome when older. Building on an earlier study (Baron-Cohen, Allen, and Gillberg, 1992), Baron-Cohen et al. (1996) distributed a screening questionnaire (the Checklist for Autism in Toddlers) to general practitioners and health visitors in relation to 16,000 infants. Ten of the twelve children who failed to show proto-declarative pointing, gaze-monitoring and pretend play at routine 18-month developmental check-up later received the diagnosis of autism. The same research group were able to test 20-month-old children with autism, children with developmental delays, and typically developing children, and reported that infants with autism failed to use social gaze in empathy and in the context of switching gaze between an ambiguous toy and an adult, and were also specifically impaired on tests of imitation and prompted symbolic play (Charman et al., 1997). These results extended findings from earlier observations (e.g. Loveland and Landry, 1986; Mundy et al., 1986; Wetherby and Prutting, 1984) and more recent work (Leekam, Chapter 10 below) that there is a specific deficit in joint attention in children with autism.

To conclude this section, it may be appropriate to give a slightly more detailed illustration of what failures of joint attention mean in terms of autistic children's lack of engagement with others. Sigman et al. (1992) studied groups of thirty children with autism, thirty children without autism but with other developmental delays, and thirty typically developing children. The mean age of the former two groups was about 3½ years. These children had the same level of intellectual ability as the comparison group of normal children, who were only 1½ years old.

In one situation, an adult (who was the experimenter on one occasion and the child's mother on the other) was showing the child how to use a wooden toy hammer, when she appeared to hurt herself by hitting her finger. For half a minute she showed distress in her face and voice, then she settled, and finally she showed that her finger did not hurt any more. The question was how the children would react.

Videotapes revealed that the children with autism differed from the children of both other groups in taking longer to look at the distressed adult. They also looked at her for a significantly shorter time. Six of them did not look at all towards their unhappy parent, something that was never observed in the non-autistic children. Not surprisingly, then, the children with autism were rated as showing less concern than children in the other groups. Mostly they went on playing with toys instead of attending to what was happening to the other person.

In a second scenario, the adult who had been playing with the child pretended to be slightly ill for a minute by lying down on a couch, closing her eyes, and expressing discomfort. Half the children with autism did not seem to notice this was happening, whereas only a small minority of the other children failed to look at the adult. Having said this, half the children with autism did look at the person when it was their mother, and there were even some who touched her in a way that might have indicated they were affected by what was happening.

A final part of the study employed a small remote-controlled robot that moved towards the child and stopped about 4 feet away. For 30 seconds the parent and the experimenter, who were both seated nearby, made fearful facial expressions, gestures, and vocalizations. Almost all the non-autistic children looked at an adult at some point during this procedure, but fewer than half the children with autism did so, and then only briefly. The non-autistic children looked toward an adult for between 2½ and 6 seconds. For those with autism, the average time was just over half a second.

The other important question addressed in this study was how the children's attitudes towards the robot were affected by the adults' fear towards it. The children with autism were not only less hesitant than the mentally retarded children in playing with the robot; they also played with it for substantially longer periods of time (approximately 6 seconds, compared with 1½ seconds for the non-autistic retarded children). It seemed that they were less influenced by the fearful attitudes of those around them.

In summary, children with autism appear to lack a specific cluster of social abilities. In particular, they do not seem to share the world with other people, and they do not relate to the world-according-to-the-other. They rarely show things to someone else, they rarely point things out, and they rarely adjust their own behaviour in accordance with the attitudes of others. They are not easily 'moved' by the feelings of other people.

HOW DO CHILDREN WITH AUTISM ENGAGE WITH OTHERS' ENGAGEMENT WITH THE WORLD?

Thus far we have been concerned with the ways in which children with autism fail to engage with the subjective states of other people, in contexts of both primary and secondary intersubjectivity. The evidence has come from experiments in which participants perceive aspects of people, from parental accounts of very young children's modes of interpersonal exchange, and from observational and quasi-naturalistic studies of social responsiveness in young children. Although there is certainly suggestive evidence in all of this that children with autism are not 'moved' to the psychological position of the other in the course of early non-verbal affective-communicative transactions, the case is far from watertight. My colleague Tony Lee and I wanted to tackle this issue from a new direction: the study of imitation.

The literature on imitation in autism is remarkable for its lack of consensus. Some workers read the evidence as suggesting a very basic deficit in imitation in autism (e.g. Meltzoff and Gopnik, 1993; Rogers and Pennington, 1991); others have reported that some aspects of imitation are relatively intact (e.g. Charman and Baron-Cohen, 1994; Morgan, *et al.*, 1989). Partly on the basis of our own findings from the point-light experiment described above, we hypothesized that children with autism may be able to perceive and copy the actions of other people—a very important ability, and one that would mean that they can transpose the perceived actions of others into plans for their own action—but that they do not appropriate another person's mode of action *through identifying with the other person*. In other words, even when the child with autism copies the strategy by which a goal is achieved (something that appears to be beyond non-human primates), this is accomplished not by moving to the position of the other and appropriating the person's style and mode of dealing with the problem, but rather by 'watching from outside' and adopting the requisite strategies to achieve a goal.

What we did was to test sixteen children and adolescents with autism aged between 9 and 19 years, and sixteen children and adolescents without autism who were similar in age and in verbal ability. In a preliminary session a week before the testing proper, we gave each set of our task materials to the children, and asked them to 'use this'. In the event, not a single participant performed an action that was similar to what we were intending to demonstrate.

For the demonstration session, the child was seated across the table from the experimenter, who produced a pipe-rack (a wooden stand with slots in a ledge that used to hold the stems of my pipes) and a wooden stick and said 'Watch this'. He put the pipe-rack to his shoulder and drew the stick along its slotted edge three times, making a staccato sound. Then he put these materials away, brought out a bean-filled cloth frog and a wooden roller and repeated his instruction: 'Watch this'. He proceeded to wipe his brow with the frog in three brief movements, and flattened it with the roller. Next he used a hand-held stamp that was pressed down on an ink-pad and transferred to a piece of paper; and finally, he pressed down the head of a plastic toy policeman to make it move forward. Note that the children were not informed that they were going to be given the materials to use at a later point. They were simply told to 'Watch this'.

In each of these demonstrations, the experimenter employed two different styles of action. Half the children in each group saw him strum the pipe-rack in a harsh way, making a staccato sound, and half saw him use a graceful and gentle strumming action. Half the children saw him wipe the frog across his brow with abrupt, harsh movements, and half saw him use gentler, caressing movements.

Half saw him bring the stamp down upon the ink-pad and then the paper in a forceful way, and half saw him employ a careful rolling motion. Finally, in the rolling policeman task, half saw him use two outstretched fingers to depress the top of the policeman, and half saw him use the front of his cocked wrist. Over the series of demonstrations, each participant saw a mixture of harsh and gentle versions of the actions (or in the case of the policeman, one or other of the styles of pressing down), although they were shown only one version of any one action.

There was then a period of 10 minutes when the children were given a language test that was not related in any way to imitation. After this break, the experimenter produced the pipe-rack and stick and gave them to the child, saying merely: 'Use this'. Participants were given time to use the materials in whatever way they chose.

The videotapes of the experiment were edited so that we could give excerpts to judges, who assessed the styles of the children's responses without knowing which style had been modelled. Our prediction was that the children and adolescents with autism would be able to copy the goal-directed actions, but would not imitate the style in which those actions were performed.

The results were that nearly all the children of each group applied the stick to the pipe-rack to make a sound. They used the stamp-and-pad to transfer an imprint to the paper. And they depressed the head of the policeman in order to make him move. (I shall come to the case of brow-wiping with the frog in a moment.) This established that almost everyone taking part was attentive to what the experimenter was doing and was interested and motivated to achieve the goals in each task.

When it came to imitating the different styles of action, the large majority of the non-autistic children performed each action in the same way that the experimenter had done. Eleven out of sixteen adopted the same harsh or gentle strumming of the stick on the pipe-rack, for example, and thirteen of them pressed the head of the toy policeman in just the manner they had seen the experimenter adopt. This last test was perhaps the most striking, because it was often with great care that a child cocked back his wrist before pressing it down on the policeman's head, even though it was totally unnecessary to use this unnatural posture. These children and adolescents seemed to have an investment in performing the action exactly as the experimenter had done, almost always without the need for prompting.

In the case of the children with autism, the results were quite different. Only a small minority of these children and adolescents imitated the style with which the actions had been demonstrated. This was so, even though they were perfectly able to copy the strategy needed to achieve a goal. For example, only two out of sixteen children with autism strummed the pipe-rack in the harsh or gentle way that had been demonstrated, and only four imitated the style of action in depressing the head of the policeman. A majority of the children with autism pressed down the policeman's head in the simplest way possible, by using the palm of the hand.

They did not need to copy the style of the actions to achieve the goal of setting the policeman in motion, and so they ignored it.

How do we understand these results? The children without autism were imitating the *person* of the experimenter, and in so doing they assumed his style as well as his approach to accomplishing each goal. The children with autism watched and imitated the *action* rather than the person doing the action.

There was one additional finding. Two of the actions involved an orientation to the body of the person who was acting. The experimenter positioned the pipe-rack against his own shoulder before strumming the stick against it. He also wiped the frog against his own brow. Only if the participant identified with the experimenter, would he subsequently place the pipe-rack against *him* self, or wipe his *own* brow. It is only through such role-taking that the child would adopt the experimenter's self-orientated action as something he could now perform in relation to a quite different body, namely his own. In this case, he would imitate not only the action but also the self-orientation of the action. Someone who was only copying the action would not notice or bother with the self-orientation part of it.

The results were that a majority of the non-autistic children copied the experimenter's self-orientation in the pipe-rack task and again in brow-wiping, by orienting the actions to their own bodies. Yet only two of the sixteen children and adolescents with autism held the pipe-rack against their own neck or upper arm, compared with ten of those in the control group. Even when prompted, there were only three others who held the pipe-rack against their own bodies at all (and not in the way the experimenter had done). In the brow-wiping task, fourteen of the sixteen non-autistic children, but only five of the sixteen children with autism applied the frog to their own brows. Even more startling in the case of brow-wiping, where not only the action but also the goal of the action was self-orientated, was the fact that only nine of the children with autism (as against fifteen of the non-autistic children) took hold of the frog at all—and this despite the fact that all but one proceeded to flatten the frog with the roller. It was as if the self-orientated brow-wiping did not register with the autistic children, even though they had no problem in copying the other actions.

In two respects, then, the children with autism were not moved to adopt the orientation of the person they were watching. They did not adopt the style with which the experimenter executed the actions, nor did they identify with him and copy his self-orientated actions so that these actions became orientated towards themselves. On the other hand, they were perfectly able to perceive and copy the strategies by which he achieved the goals in each demonstration. So they were able to learn something from watching what the experimenter did. They were also motivated to use what they had learned when their own turn came round. Yet what they learned seemed to be available from their position as a kind of detached observer of actions and goals. They were not 'moved'.

SO...WHAT PUTS THE JOINTNESS INTO JOINT ATTENTION?

The answer to this question: intersubjective engagement.

One can only have joint attention if one has the capacity to 'join' another person—which means that one needs to be able to share experiences with others, registering intersubjective linkage—and at the same time remain separate. If my thesis is correct, to begin with, an infant joins with another person's subjective state through sharing or otherwise co-ordinating feelings in contexts of one-to-one primary intersubjectivity. Another person's feelings, as expressed through bodily manifestations such as facial expressions, bodily gestures, and emotionally toned vocalizations, have the power to affect an infant, as well as an older child, as well as an adult. This is a fact of human psychology. The joining goes deeper than this, however—it is a linkage that exists in what can only be called *identification*. Identification is not reducible to imitation, any more than a subjective orientation can be reduced to intention or action. It involves appropriating something of *the psychological orientation* as well as the actions of the other person. In the case of our study of imitation, identification meant that non-autistic participants assumed the style and the self-anchoredness that was intrinsic to the other person's stance-in-acting. Most of the children with autism did not.

Therefore identification involves potential *movement* in psychological orientation. This is paradoxical, in so far as appropriation implies that the movement is virtual, and by no means complete. In one sense it is to the position of the other, but in another sense it is from the other person into oneself—a case of interiorizing what takes place in the interpersonal domain (Vygotsky, 1978).

So jointness comes with being moved just enough to sense the psychological orientation of the other in oneself, but as the other's. This happens through intersubjective engagement that is emotional in source and emotional in quality. I have not laboured the message that we receive from the study of autism—that these children's specific forms of limitation in joint attention can be traced to specific forms of limitation in interpersonal relatedness, especially those based on the co-ordination of feelings between people—because I hope the investigations I have described convey this idea without further elaboration. Autism reveals what happens to joint attention if intersubjective engagement is lacking.

Neither children with autism nor non-human primates have the degree of intersubjective engagement to identify with others as non-autistic humans do—although it is important to note that some children with autism may be less affected than others in this respect. This is the reason why, by and large, neither children with autism nor non-human primates show things to others just for the sake of showing things. They have not registered others' attitudes in themselves, such that they seek to elicit and re-register the kind of connectedness that sharing entails. I have argued that this is also the reason why many children with autism and perhaps all non-human primates fail to employ symbols with the creativity and flexibility that is characteristic of *homo sapiens* (Hobson, 2000, 2002). But that is another story.

What I have offered here is an account of certain necessary but not sufficient conditions for joint attention. It is important that the conditions I have outlined lead an infant towards a grasp—at first a grasp in attitude, and only later an intellectual grasp—of what the focus of attention is apprehended-as by the other. This is simply because the infant's reading of 'attention' is a reading of attitude, and attitudes have qualities that betray something of what the world means to the person expressing the attitudes. In joining with another person in joint attention, therefore, one may also assume the other's stance towards whatever is at the focus of the other's attention, and this involves a shift in apprehending-as (cf. social referencing) that will be vital for the subsequent development of the child's understanding of what it means to perceive-as, to construe-as and, much later, to believe-as.

Yet it is also critical that the infant be able to read the outer-directedness of attitudes (and actions). Vision is the most important channel by which this reading is achieved. Studies of congenitally blind children have revealed a strikingly high prevalence of features of autism in the children (Brown, *et al.*, 1997; Hobson, Lee, and Brown, 1999), and I have argued that the blind child's lack of co-reference with others may be critical in this respect. For example, one can understand how congenitally blind children show echolalia and abnormalities in personal pronoun usage on the basis of their difficulties in identifying with a locus of separate psychological orientation in which linguistic utterances are anchored (Hobson *et al.*, 1997; Hobson, 2002). Again, the crux is the children's difficulty in responding to and identifying with another separate person who is perceived to relate to a shared world. It is a world that comes to have meanings-according-to-the-other.

So if intersubjective engagement and identification provide the 'interpersonal link' component of jointness, there is a complementary developmental account of what establishes the differentiation among one person, another person, and the world to which they jointly attend.

REFERENCES

Baranek, G. T. (1999), 'Autism during infancy: a retrospective video analysis of sensory-motor and social behaviors at 9–12 months of age', *Journal of Autism and Developmental Disorders*, 29: 213–24.

Baron-Cohen, S., Allen, J., and Gillberg, C. (1992), 'Can autism be detected at 18 months? The needle, the haystack and the CHAT', *British Journal of Psychiatry*, 161: 839–42.

—— Cox, A., Baird, G., Swettenham, J., Nightingale, N., Morgan, K., Drew, A., and Charman, T. (1996), 'Psychological markers in the detection of autism in infancy in a large population', *British Journal of Psychiatry*, 168: 158–63.

BERTENTHAL, B. I., PROFFITT, D. R., and CUTTING, J. E. (1984), 'Infant sensitivity to figural coherence in biomechanical motions', *Journal of Experimental Child Psychology*, 37: 213–30.

BROWN, R., HOBSON, R. P., LEE, A., and STEVENSON, J. (1997), 'Are there "autistic-like" features in congenitally blind children?', *Journal of Child Psychology and Psychiatry*, 38: 693–703.

CHARMAN, T., and BARON-COHEN, S. (1994), 'Another look at imitation in autism', *Development and Psychopathology*, 6: 403–13.

—— SWETTENHAM, J., BARON-COHEN, S., COX, A., BAIRD, G., and DREW, A. (1997), 'Infants with autism: an investigation of empathy, pretend play, joint attention, and imitation', *Developmental Psychology*, 33: 781–9.

DAHLGREN, S. O., and GILLBERG, C. (1989), 'Symptoms in the first two years of life', *European Archives of Psychiatry and Neurological Science*, 238: 169–74.

HOBSON, R. P. (1989), 'On sharing experiences', *Development and Psychopathology*, 1: 97–203.

—— (1991), 'Methodological issues for experiments on autistic individuals' perception and understanding of emotion', *Journal of Child Psychology and Psychiatry*, 32: 1135–58.

—— (1993a), *Autism and the Development of Mind*. Hillsdale, NJ: Erlbaum.

—— (1993b), 'Understanding persons: the role of affect', in S. Baron-Cohen, H. Tager-Flusberg, and D. J. Cohen (eds.), *Understanding Other Minds: Perspectives from Autism*. Oxford: Oxford University Press, 204–27.

—— (2000), 'The grounding of symbols: a social-developmental account', In P. Mitchell and K. J. Riggs (eds.), *Children's Reasoning and the Mind*. Hove: Psychology Press, 11–35.

—— (2002), *The Cradle of Thought*. London: Macmillan.

—— BROWN, R., MINTER, M., and LEE, A. (1997), ' "Autism" revisited: the case of congenital blindness', in V. Lewis and G. M. Collis (eds.), *Blindness and Psychological Development in Young Children*. Leicester British Psychological Society, 99–115.

—— and LEE, A. (1998), 'Hello and goodbye: a study of social engagement in autism', *Journal of Autism and Developmental Disorders*, 28: 117–27.

—— —— and BROWN, R. (1999), 'Autism and congenital blindness', *Journal of Autism and Developmental Disorders*, 29: 45–56.

—— OUSTON, J., and LEE, A. (1988), 'What's in a face? The case of autism', *British Journal of Psychology*, 79: 441–53.

JOHANSSON, G. (1973), 'Visual perception of biological motion and a model for its analysis', *Perception and Psychophysics*, 14: 201–11.

LORD, C. (1995), 'Follow-up of two-year-olds referred for possible autism', *Journal of Child Psychology and Psychiatry*, 36: 1365–82.

—— STOROSCHUK, S., RUTTER, M., and PICKLES, A. (1993), 'Using the ADI-R to diagnose autism in preschool children', *Infant Mental Health Journal*, 14: 234–52.

LOVELAND, K. A., and LANDRY, S. (1986), 'Joint attention and language delay in autism and developmental language delay', *Journal of Autism and Developmental Disorders*, 16: 335–49.

MELTZOFF, A. N., and GOPNIK, A. (1993), 'The role of imitation in understanding persons and developing theories of mind', in S. Baron-Cohen, H. Tager-Flusberg, and D. Cohen (eds.), *Understanding Other Minds: Perspectives from Autism*. Oxford: Oxford University Press, 335–66.

MOORE, D. G., HOBSON, R. P., and LEE, A. (1997), 'Components of person perception: an investigation with autistic, non-autistic retarded and typically developing children and adolescents', *British Journal of Developmental Psychology*, 15: 401–23.

Morgan, S. B., Cutrer, P. S., Coplin, J. W., and Rodrigue, J. R. (1989), 'Do autistic children differ from retarded and normal children in Piagetian sensorimotor functioning?', *Journal of Child Psychology and Psychiatry*, 30: 857–64.

Mundy, P., Sigman, M., Ungerer, J., and Sherman. T. (1986), 'Defining the social deficits of autism: the contribution of nonverbal communication measures', *Journal of Child Psychology and Psychiatry*, 27: 657–69.

Osterling, J., and Dawson, G. (1994), 'Early recognition of children with autism: a study of first birthday home videotapes', *Journal of Autism and Developmental Disorders*, 24: 247–57.

Rogers, S. J., and Pennington, B. F. (1991), 'A theoretical approach to the deficits in infantile autism', *Development and Psychopathology*, 3: 137–62.

Sigman, M., Kasari, C., Kwon, J., and Yirmiya, N. (1992), 'Responses to the negative emotions of others by autistic, mentally retarded, and normal children,' *Child Development*, 63: 769–807.

Vygotsky, L. S. (1978), 'Internalisation of higher psychological functions', in M. Cole, V. John-Steiner, S. Scribner, and E. Souberman (eds.), *Mind in Society: The Development of Higher Psychological Processes*. Cambridge, Mass.: Harvard University Press, 52–7.

Wetherby, A. M., and Prutting, C. A. (1984), 'Profiles of communicative and cognitive-social abilities in autistic children', *Journal of Speech and Hearing Disorders*, 27: 364–77.

Wimpory, D. C., Hobson, R. P., Williams, J. M. G., and Nash, S. (2000), 'Are infants with autism socially engaged? A study of recent retrospective parental reports', *Journal of Autism and Developmental Disorders*, 30: 525–36.

Wittgenstein, L. (1980), *Remarks on the Philosophy of Psychology*, ii, ed. G. H. von Wright and H. Nyman, trans. C. G. Luckhardt and M. A. E. Aue. Oxford: Blackwell.

10

Why do Children with Autism have a Joint Attention Impairment?

Sue Leekam

Ask any clinician to describe the earliest and most significant impairments in autism, and the chances are that they will put joint attention at the top of the list. Ask them to explain *why* children with autism have this impairment, and they will be less likely to give you a straightforward answer. The truth is that, despite advances in our knowledge of autism over the last twenty to thirty years, we still have contradictory interpretations for one of the most robust and predictive behavioural indicators of autism. In this chapter I look at these contradictions and outline an analysis that focuses on the relationship between the development of attention and the development of joint attention. This account attempts to deal with some of the questions that still remain unexplained, and in doing so re-examines the way that we think about the joint attention impairment.

1. WHAT IS IMPAIRED?

What do we mean when we say that a child with autism has a joint attention impairment? What is 'joint', and what is 'attentional' about it? At a clinical level, the joint attention problem in autism is commonly described in terms of an absence or poverty of behaviours such as gaze-following, pointing, or showing objects to others, but is there an underlying psychological impairment that prevents these behaviours from appearing? In this section I review some traditional ideas about the underlying joint attention impairment in autism. Although ideas about this impairment have changed in recent years, the key questions about the role of experience and development still remain. In our own research work I and my colleagues began with a hypothesis that children with autism may have a very basic low-level attentional impairment that would have a critical impact on the ability to follow others people's gaze. In the sections that follow I describe a series of experimental studies we carried out to investigate this hypothesis. To put our research into context, I first describe two traditional accounts of the joint attentional difficulty in autism. These are the meta-representational account and the

The research reported in this chapter was supported by Wellcome Trust grant 043022 and ESRC grant R000223447.

interpersonal-affective hypothesis, often presented as two polarized accounts of joint attention. The comparison of these two accounts raises some key questions about the conceptual boundaries of the joint attention impairment and questions about the role of experience and development.

The 'meta-representational account of joint attention' (Leslie, 1987; Baron-Cohen, 1995) views the absence of joint attention behaviours as a representational problem. This is a cognitive account, and the notion of 'intentionality' (Brentano, 1970/1874) is central to it. The key idea is that children not only perceive and represent objects in their world; they also come to understand that other people have representations that are directed towards particular objects or states of affairs. It is this recognition of other's mental states that first reveals itself in the autistic child's lack of triadic (child–other–object) joint attention behaviours such as gaze-following and declarative pointing. Absence of these behaviours in children with autism is thought to indicate damage to the cognitive mechanism responsible for constructing 'triadic' representations which specify self and other attending to the same object (Baron-Cohen, 1995). This is a modular account. The argument is that there is damage to selective mechanisms within a cognitive 'mindreading' system that specifically impairs the ability to form mentalistic interpretations of other's actions. Children are therefore unable to represent another person's inner state of 'attention' or 'interest', and fail to engage in acts of joint attention. The result is impairment in symbolic skills of pretence, language, and theory of mind.

In contrast, the interpersonal-affective account of autism (Hobson, 1993, 2002) views the absence of behaviours such as gaze-following and pointing as rooted in an affective problem. The issue to be explained here is not the representation of another person's attention but the shared nature of experience, the 'jointness' of joint attention. Central to this account is the child's early difficulty with interpersonal engagement. Key behavioural indicators of this impairment include not only triadic (child–other–object) exchanges such as pointing, showing, and gaze-following, but also difficulty with face-to-face interaction, mutuality of gaze, and patterning of behaviour within interactions. The origin of this difficulty is affective rather than cognitive. Children with autism lack the capacity to engage in affective, intersubjective experiences with others, and without these experiences they are unable to perceive the directedness of the other's attitude and relate to events as shared. The lack of this experience also has consequences for the child's ability to use symbols and to develop concepts of mind.

These two accounts demonstrate that people can be talking about quite different things when they talk about the joint attention impairment in autism. So what kind of thing *should* we be talking about? What kind of account of joint attention best describes the problems of children with autism? To answer this question it may help to look at some of the assumptions that are raised by these different accounts of joint attention.

1.1 A Dyadic or a Triadic Impairment?

An important difference between the meta-representation account and the interpersonal account is the predictions they each make about impairments in social interaction that are of a dyadic rather than a triadic nature. Although both accounts predict triadic difficulties, only the interpersonal account considers dyadic difficulties as being central to autism. The proposal that dyadic interaction difficulties precede triadic difficulties is consistent with the prediction one would expect from knowledge of typical development (Trevarthen and Hubley, 1978). Yet evidence for an account of this kind has become apparent only relatively recently. Diagnostic criteria include difficulties in eye-to-eye gaze amongst the behavioural features of autism, but what has not been clear is whether these difficulties are specific to autism rather than found amongst other groups with disabilities. Early research findings focusing on the joint attention impairment initially emphasized a specific impairment in triadic interactions rather than dyadic interactions. These studies indicated that some dyadic social interaction behaviours were intact, and that the behaviours specifically impaired in autism relative to other developmental disabilities were those involving triadic interactions (Mundy *et al.*, 1986).

Recently, however, the tide has begun to turn. Several studies show group differences in dyadic interaction between children with autism and those with other developmental delays. This difference in dyadic interaction is found particularly in children with low IQ and mental age (Mundy, Sigman, and Kasari, 1994; McEvoy, Rogers, and Pennington, 1993). Other research, involving the retrospective analysis of home videos taken on the child's first birthday, points to the hypothesis that difficulties with dyadic social interaction might be present very early in development. This research shows that certain measures of dyadic interaction predict diagnosis of autism several years later (Osterling and Dawson, 1994; Baranek, 1999).

1.2 An Affective or Cognitive Impairment?

The recent evidence of dyadic as well as triadic behavioural difficulties in autism suggests that, on the face of it, Hobson's account is the one that best describes the behavioural problems of children with autism. But does the absence of either dyadic or triadic behaviours conclusively demonstrate that the origin of this difficulty lies in the lack of capacity for affective, interpersonal engagement?

The question of whether cognitive or affective deficits are primary in autism has been a central issue for many years (Fein *et al.*, 1986), in relation not simply to joint attention but to the syndrome of autism as a whole. One reason why this issue might be unresolved relates to the notion of 'primacy'. A deficit is usually considered to be primary when it plays a key function in the onset and course of a disorder. The issue of primacy is difficult to settle in the case of developmental disorders because factors that might be considered primary early on in development might be different from the factors that subsequently come to have a central role in later development.

There is another reason why this issue might be unresolved, and it concerns the assumed separateness of cognition and affect. The extent to which cognition and affect are separate domains, especially early in development, is debatable. An argument for a combined cognitive and affective impairment in autism would be supported by recent neurological and brain imaging studies showing that there are reciprocal connections between parts of the brain that predominantly serve either emotional functions or cognitive functions (Allison, Puce, and McCarthy, 2000; Schultz, Romanski, and Tsatsanis, 2000). In line with such evidence, Mundy and colleagues have proposed that joint attention deficits in autism could be a combination of developmental disturbance in both affective and cognitive processes (Mundy and Sigman, 1989). In recent work Mundy and colleagues (Mundy, 1995; Mundy and Neal, 2001; Mundy, Card, and Fox, 2000) have attempted to provide neurological evidence for their claim, speculating that, early on, motivational factors may serve to prioritize perceptual inputs that are most significant to development.

1.3 An Impairment of Early Experience?

So far I've looked at questions relating to the conceptual boundaries of joint attention. But there are other unresolved questions concerning its origin and development. One question concerns the role of experience. How important is experience for the onset and course of joint attention ability? Most people would agree that experience is essential to activate the capacity for joint attention, but there is disagreement about the type and nature of this experience. According to the interpersonal-affective view, the capacity for joint attention is the result of social and affective experiences, whereas according to the meta-representational view the capacity for joint attention is the result of an innate maturational mechanism. So what kind of experience is needed for joint attention to be possible?

Although little is said about experience in Baron-Cohen's account, it appears that sensory input is essential to activate the proposed 'eye-direction' and 'share-attention' modules. Exposure to social stimuli therefore seems to be a basic requirement for the capacity for joint attention. This input would include exposure to conspecific information—e.g. faces and human movement. A question is then whether initial sensitivity to conspecific information arises out of interactive experience or whether it is already in-built. Even if initial sensitivity takes the form of an in-built bias to attend to, say, faces or eyes, it is still possible that the ability to engage in higher-level joint attention is built on interactive experiences with others. Given the evidence for early sensitivity to dynamic contingencies of interaction in the first months of life (Murray and Trevarthen, 1985), it is difficult to believe that the mechanisms controlling later joint attention simply spring into action on exposure to stimuli alone, without dynamic or contingent experiences being important. Despite a strong research tradition from both Vygotskian and attachment theory, we still know surprisingly little about the experiential basis for a joint attention impairment in terms of its social-cultural and social-emotional roots in atypical, as opposed to typically developing, children.

1.4 An Impairment of Development?

Autism is a developmental disorder, yet we know little about the way in which the joint attention impairment actually *develops*. Some research shows that younger children, especially those with low IQs, are more affected by a joint attention impairment than older and more able children (Mundy *et al.*, 1994; Leekam, Hunnisett, and Moore, 1998; Leekam, Lopez, and Moore, 2000). The lack of longitudinal research in this area means, however, that we still need to learn why it is that some individuals with autism, and not others, come to engage in joint attention. We also need to know how the capacity for joint attention changes, why age and ability level (IQ) make a difference, and whether these factors affect the course of joint attention differently for children with autism than for other children.

Related to the issue of how joint attention develops is the issue of joint attention as a precursor of other types of later development, particularly symbolic development. The reason why joint attention is considered to be so important in theories of autism is because of its critical 'gatekeeper' role for later development. According to theories of both typical development and autism, the appearance of joint attention opens the door to symbolic developments of language, pretend play, and theory of mind. Developmental psychologists are cautious about the way we should describe this relationship, however, reminding us that evidence for a precursor relationship should not be over-interpreted as evidence for a causal relationship. Nevertheless, joint attention has long been considered to play a 'John the Baptist' role, to borrow Gómez, Sarriá, and Tamarit's (1993) phrase. It announces the coming of symbolic developments, including language and theory of mind. While it may be difficult to settle the question of what specifically *causes* symbolic functioning, therefore, it may still be possible to trace the 'developmental pathway' between joint attention and symbolic development.

A critical stage in the development of symbols, according to several theorists (e.g. Bates *et al.*, 1979; Tomasello, 1999), is the development of communicative intention. There is some disagreement about what 'communicative intention' consists of. However, it is generally regarded to involve the child's awareness that a sign is understood both by the child him or herself and also by a recipient. According to Tomasello (1999), communicative intention occurs when a child understands another person's intention to the child's attentional stance. Joint attention behaviours, particularly those including looking, checking, and smiling, are thought to be crucial for conveying this idea of communicative intention. However, it is not clear whether communicative intention is even a necessary condition for understanding symbols, at least in some less social domains such as mathematics or physics. Therefore the role of joint attention and communicative intention in the child's acquisition of different types of symbol systems still remains to be established.

These, then, are the issues that seem to lie at the heart of the joint attention impairment. In the next part of the chapter I draw on evidence from our own experimental and observational studies in an attempt to explore some of these issues. In the following section I describe the questions and conceptual analysis we started with, our experimental method, and the results we found. I then turn to the revised view of joint attention that evolved from this research.

2. INITIAL QUESTIONS

The empirical work I am going to talk about focuses on one kind of joint attention difficulty, the problem of gaze following. Our research attempts to account for this problem in terms of an attentional orienting impairment. Before discussing this research, I want to explain why we chose gaze following as our candidate behaviour and why we chose attentional orienting as our candidate psychological mechanism.

2.1 Why Gaze-Following?

We chose gaze-following (looking where someone else looks) for several reasons. First, because it is the earliest joint attention behaviour to appear in normal development, emerging some months before the onset of other joint attention behaviours, and therefore offering insights into the developmental trajectory of joint attention. Second, we chose gaze-following because it can be analysed at both triadic and dyadic levels of interaction. Traditionally it has been considered to be a 'triadic' interaction, as it appears to involve a situation in which one person is attending to another person who is attending to an object. However, a dyadic component is also involved, as in a gaze-following situation the child first looks at the person who subsequently looks away.

Finally we chose gaze-following because it seemed to present such an intriguing puzzle for the traditional cognitive and affective interpretations. Taking first the traditional cognitive view, joint attention is proposed to rely on a 'shared attention mechanism' that represents the relations between self, object, and other. But an alternative analysis is that one can simply track head or eye orientation to interesting places without representing another person's mental state. This alternative analysis is supported by the fact that non-human primates follow head direction, but do not use higher-level acts of pointing and showing (Povinelli and Eddy, 1997). It is also supported by the fact that gaze-following is found early in typical development (as young as 3–6 months) when there are interesting objects in the baby's field of view (Moore, 1999), appearing well before the triadic forms of joint attention. The alternative explanation, then, is that gaze-following is a form of information-extracting exercise in which another's head turn provides directional information about events such as food or threat.

If gaze-following presents a challenge to the traditional cognitive account, how does it fit with the interpersonal engagement account? Possibly it presents a challenge to that view also. It can be argued that gaze-following occurs without sharing of attention in an affective sense, since what is critical for gaze-following is to follow another's head or eyes directed away from oneself. The averting of head or eyes may be the critical criterion for gaze-following, rather than face-to-face interpersonal engagement.

The puzzle, then, is this: If gaze-following can work at both a non-mentalistic and a non-affective level, why don't autistic children do it? Our early research showed that it wasn't simply that they *can't* do it. In certain circumstances children with autism are actually very competent in tracking the line of sight between another person's head direction and an object distant from it. To demonstrate this, we (Leekam *et al.*, 1997) used a task devised by Perrett and Milders in which children with autism identified what a person was looking at from photographs of the person's head or eyes directed toward one of three coloured rods. Both the spacing between these rods and the person's head–eye orientation were varied. We found that children with autism were exceptionally good at making fine discriminations and were as accurate as typically developing children in reporting what the person was looking at.

While they were competent at following another's line of sight in these circumstances, the same children were often quite incompetent at gaze-following in other circumstances. For example, we gave children two tasks. One was an 'instructed' task (Baron-Cohen 1989), which made similar demands to the study described above. The experimenter sat in a seat, opposite the child. For each trial she looked at a different target object located to the left, right, or behind the child, asking 'What am I looking at?' The other was a 'spontaneous' task (Butterworth and Cochran, 1980). In this task an experimenter first gained eye contact with the child and then immediately turned her head and eyes to look to the left, right, or behind the child towards a small target star attached to the wall at eye level, out of the child's immediate visual field. We found a dissociation of performance for these two tasks. Children with autism followed gaze and correctly reported the target in the instructed task, but were very poor at following gaze in the spontaneous task. By contrast, comparison groups followed gaze on both tasks.

These results confirmed that children with autism have a spontaneous gaze-following impairment, but the reason for this was still unclear. Given the analysis described earlier, based on evidence from non-human primates and very young infants, the impairment seemed unlikely to be due to a problem with the mentalistic aspect of gaze, or even with the affective aspect of gaze. So why should children with autism fail to follow gaze spontaneously? The hypothesis we developed focused on a problem of spontaneous orienting of attention.

2.2 Why Attentional Orienting?

The basic idea was that some rather low-level orienting capacity might be missing early in life, and if so, this might show itself in subsequent development through an impairment in joint attention development and through attention problems later in life. This idea developed from looking at research findings in infancy and research with older individuals in autism. Research studies of attentional orienting in typically developing infants suggest that there are two critical abilities that should be present as early as the first year of life: first, an ability to reflexively orient to sensory stimuli, normally present at birth; second, an ability to control attention, an ability that appears at about 3 months of age. This capacity for voluntary control shows itself in the form of two corresponding developments. These are the capacity to disengage from one stimulus and shift to another and the ability to form an expectation from a cue (Hood, 1995; Johnson, Posner, and Rothbart, 1994; Gilmore and Johnson, 1995).

Studies that trace the development of reflexive and voluntary attention have traditionally been set up to test infant responses in non-interactive settings using *non-social* stimuli. Interestingly, though, developments in orienting to social stimuli in the first year of life, by means of gaze-following, seem to correspond roughly to the same developments observed in these non-social studies. Normal infants do not engage in gaze-following at all in the early months. They are unable to follow the cue of another's gaze direction until they reach 3 months of age, and then do so only when the object linked to the gaze direction is clearly visible. Beyond that, further developments are evident. From 9 to 12 months infants become able to follow the cue of another's head turn without an object being visible. This evidence highlights the importance of a developmental trajectory in the voluntary control of attention that might reflect itself in typical developments in joint attention.

Turning to research in autism, we found that the idea of an attentional impairment was not new to literature. A number of early studies using low-level physiological measures suggested that people with autism had a low-level impairment in perception or attention. However, the original evidence for such an abnormality was mixed and appeared inconclusive. More recently, evidence has been put forward for a more specific difficulty in attentional orienting, and specifically in terms of an impairment in attention shifting. Courchesne and colleagues (1994) have made the case for a fundamental attention problem attributed to cerebellar processes. Experiments devised to test this hypothesis have used a specific experimental paradigm, and have been confined to older individuals. This paradigm tests an individual's speed and accuracy in orienting to a target (e.g. a cross) that appears at one of two locations (e.g. left or right) on a computer screen. A cue is presented before the target. This cue may be either valid (consistent with subsequent target location) or invalid (inconsistent with target location). The critical measure in these tasks is the difference in reaction time between valid and invalid trials (the validity effect). The slower response to invalid trials compared with valid trials is thought to reflect the time taken to disengage from the cued location. Abnormal validity effects have been found in several studies involving individuals with autism, leading to the conclusion that people with autism may have difficulty in disengaging and shifting attention (Townsend, Singer-Harris, and Courchesne, 1996; Casey *et al.*, 1993; Wainwright-Sharp and Bryson, 1993; Courchesne *et al.*, 1994).

Problems with disengagement and shifting attention have also been proposed as evidence for executive functioning impairments in autism (Russell, 1996; Pennington and Ozonoff, 1996). Although tests of executive dysfunction tend to rest on higher-level cognitive functions such as shifting cognitive set rather than visual orienting, this account predicts that children have problems with one particular type of attentional orienting—the disengaging and shifting of visual attention (Russell, 1996; Pennington and Ozonoff, 1996).

While problems with disengaging and shifting have been proposed as specific impairments in autism, the attentional orienting task used in these studies involves another aspect of voluntary control that covaries with disengaging and shifting— this is the ability to predict from a cue. The term 'cue' in this context refers to something that indicates something else. In the adult literature, a 'symbolic' cue such as an arrow activates a goal-directed system that is sensitive to expectation, probability, and cognitive interpretation. Several studies show that children with autism have particular problems with these 'symbolic' cues, suggesting an impairment in endogenous or voluntary control of orienting (Wainwright-Sharp and Bryson, 1993; Casey *et al.*, 1993; Swettenham *et al.*, 2000). It is therefore conceivable that this aspect—the ability to read or form an expectation from a cue—rather than the disengaging and shifting aspect might be impaired (Burack *et al.* 1997).

Not all responses to a cue activate endogenous or controlled attention, however. A peripheral cue—for example, a flash of light in the location of a potential target—has the effect of reflexively or automatically cueing attention to that location. This reflexive response is rapid and involuntary, and is impervious to higher cognitive influence. So what kind of attentional response would be elicited in an experiment that substitutes an arrow cue with a head-turn cue? Even though this kind of cue fits the description of a 'symbolic' cue at first sight, the traditional conceptual distinction between endogenous orienting (under voluntary control) and exogenous orienting (under stimulus control) has been challenged by results of such studies with normal adults. These studies, using a picture of a human head or eyes in place of an arrow, indicate that it is the exogenous rather than the endogenous attentional system that is activated in these tasks (Driver *et al.*, 1999; Friesen and Kingstone, 1998; Langton and Bruce, 1999).

The evidence from both typically developing infants, adults, and older individuals with autism gave us the background knowledge we needed to develop a working hypothesis. Possibly the development of the orienting response is delayed or arrested in autism, which then leads to the kinds of problems found in adult studies of attentional cueing.

3. AN ANALYSIS OF ATTENTIONAL ORIENTING AND GAZE-FOLLOWING

We started out with an analysis of orienting ability at two levels. At the most basic level, that of reflexive or *exogenous* orienting, the child simply needs to be able to orient spontaneously to targets and low-level cues. At the next level, that of *endogenous* orienting or voluntary control, the child needs to be able to form an expectation or interpretation of a stimulus. There is another distinction to be made within this reflexive/voluntary dichotomy, however. This is the description of a stimulus as either *social* or *non-social*. It is possible that social stimuli are special in some way, and are preferentially attended to by typically developing children, but not by children with autism. If so, the difficulty of attentional orienting may not be a general difficulty, but a problem related to social attention only.

What prediction might be made about autistic children's joint attention ability according to this conceptual scheme? Several different predictions are possible. One is that children with autism might have general difficulties with reflexive orienting. Such difficulties might affect children in a global sense, or might be specific to social stimuli. If there are difficulties at the level of exogenous orienting, this will have knock-on effects for higher-level attentional orienting. Another hypothesis is that more basic reflexive orienting ability may be intact, but there may be selective difficulties at the higher level of attentional control. Again, this might be a general impairment or might be specific to social stimuli. Given what we already know about autism, the problem is likely to take the form of a developmental delay in children who are very young and/or have very low IQ, perhaps showing impairments at both exogenous and endogenous levels, while older children at a higher level of ability show impairment at the higher, endogenous level only.

3.1 Studies of Gaze-Following and Attention

3.1.1 *Predicting from a Cue*

Our first set of studies examined children's ability to use both lower-level exogenous and higher-level endogenous orienting when predicting from a cue. The initial studies focused on the social cue of a head turn, using Corkum and Moore's (1998) gaze-following paradigm. This allowed us to assess the extent to which children are able to predict from a head-turn cue in three different conditions. Two of these conditions appeared to activate a more endogenous level of responding, one situation making slightly more rigorous demands on the ability to use the cue as a meaningful indicator, while the other involved endogenous attention at a less demanding level. The third condition appeared to activate an exogenous, or reflexive, level of responding.

In these studies, the set-up involved the child sitting opposite the experimenter. Two boxes were placed against a left and right wall, out of the child's visual field. Each box contained a concealed target, a toy train that was activated (popped out of a box with flashing lights) in the training and test phases. The task consists of three parts. For the first set of baseline trials (endogenous responding), the experimenter turned her head to the left or right (no targets visible), and the child's spontaneous gaze-following was recorded. The second set of trials (exogenous responding) was a training phase in which the experimenter's head turn was followed 2 seconds later by the activation of a remote controlled target in the location to which the experimenter turned. The third was a test phase (endogenous responding) in which activation of the target object was contingent not simply on the experimenter's head turn but also on the child's head turn. The child had to follow the experimenter's head turn when there was no target in view, and the target was activated only if the child successfully turned to the correct location. This phase was therefore similar to the baseline phase, but less demanding, as the child was reminded after each trial of the potential for a target object.

When Corkum and Moore carried out a similar task with 6–12-month-old infants, they found that infants of 6 months followed the experimenter's head turn when the target was visible in the training phase (exogenous level), but showed very little gaze-following when the target was out of sight during the baseline (endogenous level, more demanding) or test phase (endogenous, less demanding). In contrast, older infants followed head turns to targets outside the visual field. Infants of 8–9 months did this mainly during the test phase, whereas 10–12-month-olds reliably followed the experimenter's head turn both during the test phase and during the baseline phase. Moore (1999) suggested that at about 9 months, once infants discover that objects can potentially appear to the side in this procedure, they attempt to predict on which side the objects will appear using the head-turn cue to guide their response. The idea is that by this age infants are not simply learning an association between cue and target. Even if the target is not paired with the cue, the infant will still follow the head turn, as long as he or she is aware of a potential for a target. Shortly after this, the predictive meaning of cues, such as a head turn, becomes so well established that infants of 10–12 months old will follow gaze in the baseline phase without any exposure to the target. These developmental changes suggest that by the end of the first year infants come to retain the meaning of a head turn as an indicator, even when there are no target objects present.

This kind of explanation is relevant to autism. If children with autism have a problem using a head-turn cue, and if this problem amounts to a severe developmental delay, then possibly the lack of gaze-following in children with autism can be likened to the lack of gaze-following in 6–8-month-olds. If the developmental delay in children with autism follows the sequence of stages outlined by Corkum and Moore, then younger and less able children with autism should show no spontaneous gaze-following at all, whereas older and more able children with autism might show some level of spontaneous gaze-following, either partially, in the test phase only, or fully, in both the baseline and the test phase.

In studies with school-aged children (Leekam, Hunnisett, and Moore, 1998) and with pre-school children (Leekam, Lopez, and Moore, 2000), we found exactly this developmental pattern. A proportion of children with autism did follow head turns to a target out of view, just like 10–12-month-olds in Corkum and Moore's study. These children were older and had higher ability. Very few younger children, even those with higher ability, initially followed head turns to a target out of view, but a good proportion did so during the test phase, resembling infants of 8–9 months. Nearly half of the pre-school children, however, were like Corkum and Moore's 6–7-month-olds. They did not follow gaze at all, except when the target was visible in the training phase. These results contrasted with those for typically developing children and for children with learning and language disabilities, most of whom followed gaze spontaneously regardless of ability level. For children with autism, then, developmental level seems to affect gaze-following ability, whereas for the developmentally matched comparison group, gaze-following occurs spontaneously regardless of developmental level. Our interpretation of these results was that, with increased chronological age and higher mental age, the meaning of the head-turn cue becomes consolidated for children with autism, but much later than it does for non-autistic children.

In follow-up work we found further support for the possibility that it might be the endogenous nature of head-turn cues that creates difficulty. In one study we attempted to make the cue–target association more salient and explicit (Leekam *et al.*, 1998). We found that when other cues are added to a head-turn cue—for example, pointing or vocal cues (e.g. 'Look!')—children with autism performed remarkably well. In fact, in one of these studies we found that *every* autistic child followed a pointing gesture combined with a vocal cue. A similar result has been found for typically developing infants. When additional cues other than head turn, such as pointing (Butterworth and Grover, 1990) and vocal cues (Deak *et al.*, 1997) were used, these were more effective for eliciting gaze-following than head turn alone in young infants.

The results presented so far suggest that children with autism may have great difficulty in spontaneously using the information provided by a head-turn cue. Is this because such cues are social in nature? In another study, we tested children's responses to a *non-social cue* by adapting our existing experimental paradigm. Instead of another person sitting opposite the child, the experimenter's chair was replaced with a turntable upon which an object (a toy train) was placed at the child's eye level. This object was remotely controlled from behind a screen so that it rotated to face the target objects in a similar way as a person turning their head to align with a target. Recent studies with normal 12-month-old infants show that infants (and adults) follow the orientation not only of people but also of inanimate objects such as an animal shape with facial features (Johnson, Slaughter, and Carey, 1998). In our task we tested pre-school children with autism and a matched, developmentally delayed non-autism group on both the standard gaze-following task and the turning train task. For the non-human task, children had a training phase followed by a test phase with the same number of trials as for the gaze-following task. We found that children with autism did not initially perform better than the comparison group in the non-human condition than in the human condition. In fact, neither the autism nor the non-autism group were particularly good in the non-human cue condition. After some exposure to the link between non-human cue and target event, however, the performance of children with autism across trials was better than that of the comparison group. This better performance suggests that they might be more successful at applying an associative strategy in a task like this. One interpretation of these results is that children with autism tend to rely on repeated and predictable links between cue and target.

Taken together, our studies suggest that while older and more able children with autism follow gaze spontaneously, younger and less able children with autism do not. Younger children are sensitive to the association between a non-social cue and a target, however. They may also be relying on environmental 'markers' to assist them with gaze-following, as do young infants. For example, their problem with gaze-following seems to improve when either the target of the head direction is highlighted in some way, such as by activating the target object, or else the directional nature of the cue is highlighted by adding vocal cues and pointing. These results reveal a picture of gross developmental delay. Children with autism may need many more years than are required by typically developing and developmentally delayed children if they are to respond to a head-turn cue.

3.1.2 Disengaging and Shifting Attention

Given that our earlier gaze-following results revealed that nearly half of the pre-school children resembled 6–7-month-old infants in their gaze-following responses, our next task was to examine the ability of these children on a task designed to measure attention in very young infants. Our next experiment (Leekam, López, and Moore, 2000, Experiment 3) was based on the design used by Atkinson and colleagues (1992), in their experiments with 1–3-month-old typically developing infants. This task measures ability to disengage and shift attention.

In this task a central stimulus is activated before the onset of a peripheral target. However, the cue is not directional in form, and does not give information about the subsequent location of a target.

Only younger children took part. So the original twenty pre-school autistic children and the original twenty matched comparison children from our earlier experiment (Leekam et al., 2000) participated. Whereas Atkinson et al. tested infants' shifts of gaze to computer-generated patterns, we designed a task using the same equipment as we used in our gaze-following experiment. We adapted the original set-up by replacing the experimenter's chair with a box that was identical to those in the periphery containing a concealed target object (toy train). At the start of the experimental trial the remote-controlled central toy train appeared out of the box in front of the child, its side view visible to the child. For the overlap condition (half the trials), this central stimulus remained displayed while a peripheral target train appeared. For the non-overlap condition, the central stimulus disappeared into the box immediately before the peripheral target train appeared. We predicted that if children with autism have a specific problem with disengaging from a central stimulus to shift towards a peripheral target, they should be slower and less accurate than the comparison group at turning to the peripheral target on the overlapping trials only. If they have a general orienting problem, they should be slower than the comparison group in *both* the overlap and non-overlap condition.

The results were clear. Children with autism were not slower or less accurate than the non-autistic children in either condition. Both groups were slightly slower in the overlap condition than the non-overlap condition, but the children with autism were as accurate and as fast as comparison children in shifting attention to a peripheral target when a central stimulus overlapped and competed for attention. Indeed, when the low-ability children with autism and with developmental delay were compared, the autistic children were faster than the non-autistic children. Children with autism, then, at least in this task, appear to have an intact ability to orient attention to stimuli even when this requires the disengagement of attention from something they are looking at.

If children with autism are able to disengage and shift their attention, does this mean that their attentional orienting, at least to objects, is intact? Results for both conditions of this experiment showed no difference between clinical groups. This suggests that young children are fast in making overt shifts of head and eyes towards a stimulus that they were presumably motivated towards, and had no problem with disengaging head and eye movements.

Our second study explored *social* orienting ability in a face-to-face situation. Does the ability to orient reflexively to objects apply to social as well as non-social stimuli? Recent behavioural studies testing orienting to social stimuli as well as to non-social stimuli have found orienting difficulties in very young children with autism (Dawson et al., 1998; Swettenham et al., 1998). These difficulties seem to be particularly pronounced in response to social stimuli. In our study we also tested the same children's orienting responses to a person, by conducting an analysis of the face-to-face interaction between the child and experimenter as they took part in the gaze-following experiment described earlier. To investigate this, a coder who was blind to the diagnosis of the children coded the videotape during the beginning of the experimental gaze-following session. At the beginning of the session, the experimenter tried to make eye contact with the child before the experimenter turned her head. During this period, the experimenter first tried to make eye contact by looking at the child. If this attempt did not succeed, she called his or her name, and if that also failed, she called 'Look at me'. We were interested in whether the child would make an orienting response by looking at the experimenter's face in response to a vocal call for attention.

The results showed impaired responding to social stimuli. Children with autism were much less responsive than were controls to the experimenter's attempts to gain the child's attention (e.g. response to name call). They responded to significantly fewer of the bids made by looking at the adult's face. Further analysis showed that responding to attention bids was strongly related to gaze-following ability and was difficult for both high- and low-functioning children with autism. These results therefore suggest that when social stimuli are considered, there may be a problem at the level of dyadic orienting.

In summary, our findings showed that pre-school children with autism, many of whom were poor at gaze-following, were very able to orient to objects and disengage from one object stimulus to shift to another spatial location. Yet the same children seemed to have particular difficulty in orienting to the social stimulus of a name call.

3.2 Summary: Joint Attention Difficulty as an Attention Orienting Problem?

How, then, should we characterize the attentional orienting difficulty in autism and its relation to joint attention? Our results show, first, that not all children with autism have a problem with gaze-following. This problem is more likely to affect those children who are very young and/or have a low level of IQ. However, our studies show that even those children who fail to follow gaze spontaneously are good at reflexively orienting to the onset of a non-social target object. They can also disengage from a competitive stimulus, and can direct attention in space when instructed. But, relative to matched controls, they do have difficulties with cues that involve meaning or information. This applies particularly to a social cue such as a head turn, but other studies also show difficulties with cues such as an arrow. But if the cue is direct or marks out a target, then their performance seems to be much better. When presented with a non-human indicator, they seem to pick up an associative connection more effectively than other children, and one suggestion is that they may apply the same associative technique to human as well as non-human cues. In sum, they have difficulties at the level of endogenous, voluntary control of attention, but this difficulty seems to be related particularly to the predictive element of cue.

The problem for young children with autism is not confined to this higher level of endogenous orienting, however. Their most striking problem was with orienting to a person at a reflexive level. Many children had difficulty orienting towards an adult in response to a simple eye gaze or name call from an adult. This difficulty of reflexive orienting was not apparent in their responses to non-social objects. These results therefore suggest that there may be a problem with attentional orienting that particularly affects orienting to social stimuli at both exogenous and endogenous levels.

The results of our research appear to contradict the predictions made by executive function theory. The Atkinson *et al.* task that we adapted has been previously suggested by Russell (1996) to be a candidate test for executive function ability very early in life. Can we therefore conclude from this experiment that children with autism do not have an executive dysfunction, at least early on in development? This conclusion might be warranted, given that other studies of pre-school children with autism have also failed to show executive function impairments in such children (Griffith *et al.*, 1999). However, the executive functioning tests that are failed by older children tend to involve goal-directed activity and typically measure higher-level cognitive skills, suggesting that a distinction should be made between these and other tasks.

The results of our attention shifting study also seem to contradict earlier research with older children and adults with autism that suggests a fundamental impairment in attention shifting related to disengaging of attention (Courchesne *et al.*, 1994). How do our results for children with autism fit with these findings? Differences in task and subject populations make it difficult to make direct comparisons. For example, our studies measure overt rather than covert attentional processes. Nevertheless, some recent research may support our findings. As mentioned earlier, research with normal adults indicates that exogenous attention rather than endogenous attention is activated when a head or eye cue is used in a traditional Posner-type attentional cueing task. Recent research with older individuals with autism using the same paradigm shows that they are slower than controls to respond to centrally presented pictures of head direction (Swettenham *et al.*, 2000) and eye direction (Neely *et al.*, 2001). These (and our) results suggest that their difficulty may not be confined to a failure in endogenous orienting, as previously proposed, but also affects the exogenous system when *social* stimuli are involved.

Another way of looking at these findings is to think of the exogenous versus endogenous distinction as a continuum rather than a category distinction. As Posner (1980, p. 19) himself points out, no external cue is entirely reflexive, and it will only summon attention if it is important to the subject. For individuals with autism, human stimuli may simply not be important early in development, and this may have serious implications for later development.

4. RETHINKING THE NATURE OF
THE JOINT ATTENTION IMPAIRMENT

At the beginning of this chapter, I outlined four contradictions or questions that an account of joint attention needed to address. How does the investigation of joint attention described above deal with these issues?

4.1 Dyadic Interaction and Joint Attention

One of the most influential early accounts of joint attention is found in the work of Werner and Kaplan (1963). Werner and Kaplan proposed that the sharing of experiences, right from the moment of the first shared smile, is central to the development of reference and later symbolic development. The initial problem for a child with autism, therefore, may be that they fail to benefit from face-to-face interaction. They do not automatically attend to social stimuli. This then leads to a secondary problem. If autistic children are not orienting to other people, they will be less aware of what these people themselves are orienting to, and subsequently to the significance or value of these acts. This may then lead to a lack of prioritizing of social signals, which in typically developing children become automatic and reflexive. All this may mean that children with autism develop an over-dependence on non-social sensory stimuli, and may use strategies of learning based on regularities and association rather than on priorities already acquired by the use of social conventions. This may explain the reliance on repetitive behaviours, the lack of flexibility, and a host of later cognitive difficulties.

In ongoing work we are investigating the link between early dyadic gaze patterns and triadic communicative gestures and language. Our earlier experimental work already suggested that orienting to a bid for eye contact by an adult is related to gaze-following ability. More recently we have shown the same pattern in spontaneous interactions involving dyadic and triadic behaviours. Those children who fail to initiate joint attention are also the children who orient less in an observational setting, by looking less at an adult's face when she makes a vocal, visual, or tactile bid for attention (Leekam and Ramsden, in press).

Gaze-following ability is also related to higher-level declarative acts (pointing to show, holding out to show) in the same sample of children. In this study (Leekam *et al.*, 1999), we found that autistic children who spontaneously followed gaze in the experiment were more likely to initiate higher-level declarative acts (pointing to show, holding out to show) in a free play situation than those who did not follow gaze. In sum, these findings all indicate that very basic dyadic difficulties affect later triadic joint attention.

4.2 Affect, Cognition and Joint Attention

What role do affect and motivation play in the onset and development of dyadic orienting and its relationship with joint attention? The origin of the joint attention problem could be described as a lack of sensitivity to orient towards conspecific stimuli whether in the visual, auditory, or tactile domain. In the visual case this would be described as orienting eyes towards another person's face in response to another's call or response for attention. The source of this problem might be the lack of an in-built perceptual detector (Morton and Johnson, 1991), a faulty reward mechanism affecting motivation (Mundy, 1995), or a lack of affective capacity (Hobson, 1993). At the moment there is no evidence to decide between these alternatives. These accounts may not even be alternatives to each other, as motivational-affective and perceptual-cognitive abilities can be thought of as critically interrelated. Visual and auditory orienting capacities, such as the ability to detect motion or localize sound, make it possible for the infant to interact and express affect with others. On the other hand, motivation or affect itself directs this orienting ability. Although our work so far has not tackled how affect plays a role in the development of joint attention, this is clearly a factor that must be taken into account in future research.

4.3 Early Experience and Joint Attention

Experience is likely to play a crucial part in the development of gaze-following and subsequent joint attention. Two types of experience might precede the onset of gaze-following as an automated skill. The first, already mentioned, is face-to-face mutual gaze, and the second is attention to objects. With respect to attention to objects, infant research suggests that the existence of a target object in the environment is very important for triggering gaze-following at the developmental stage before the meaning of the head turn becomes consolidated. Our findings suggest that children with autism are rather like these young infants, relying for much longer on environmental markers to assist them with gaze-following. With respect to experience of mutual gaze, children with autism do not seem to lack the opportunity for social interaction. Any observation between a young child with autism and his or her parents makes clear that the social input is there, but the child for some reason cannot benefit from it. This contrasts with enculturated apes who do seem to benefit from interactions with humans as far as we can tell from their communicative gestures (Gómez, 1991) and gaze-following ability (Povinelli and Eddy, 1997). If children with autism have an in-built weakness in orienting to social stimuli, they also seem to fail to gain from the experiences of social interaction, and this lack of experience will itself have repercussions for development. A convincing transactional account along these lines has been proposed by Mundy and Neal (2001), who describe the problem at a neurological as well as a behavioural level. They suggest that an initial failure to orient will lead to lack of information input and subsequent disruptions in experience-expectant neural development and behavioural development.

4.4 Development and Joint Attention

The discussion above suggests that children with autism do not benefit from social experience. If this were true, then surely no child with autism would ever acquire joint attention? Instead, we find that a good proportion of older and more able children do in fact engage in gaze-following and in other joint attention acts. One hypothesis is that these higher-functioning, more verbal children who acquire joint attention belong to a different diagnostic group which shows milder symptoms from the start. This group might start with a greater capacity for dyadic orienting, and hence show less impaired joint attention ability. This ability would in turn facilitate their language acquisition, as it does for typically developing children. Parent reports, however, suggest that even when joint attention does develop, it appears years later than normal (at 5 or 6 years), and for some children residual problems remain in the style of joint attention—for example, showing objects by dragging people towards them (Leekam *et al.*, 1998). How then do these children acquire joint attention?

One possibility is that children with autism find different routes to language, and this in turn assists the development of joint attention. Landry and Loveland (1988), for example, reported that many children with autism had advanced language but poor joint attention. They concluded that the language development of children with autism may not be built on pre-verbal joint attention skills as it is for typically developing children. An alternative hypothesis, then, is that language acquisition itself facilitates joint attention. Evidence that children with autism might find a different route than other children is suggested by the findings of Carpenter *et al.* (2002). In an observational study, Carpenter found that children with autism appeared to show referential language without also showing gaze-following or communicative gestures. This was the opposite pattern to the one found for typically developing and learning-disabled children who engaged in joint attention before language. We found similar results in a study of parents' retrospective reports of first word onset in children with autism compared with children who had language impairments. Results showed that language was delayed for both groups. For the language-impaired groups, however, parents reported that first words appeared at about the same age or a little later than the appearance of acts of joint attention, whereas for the autism group the pattern was reversed, and first words were reported to occur first (Leekam, 2000).

Perhaps, then, children with autism may use a more direct route to learn the names for things. For example, children are believed to learn words by following the adult's direction of gaze (Baldwin, 1991, 1995). An alternative strategy for word learning might avoid engagement with another's face and gaze by using the sound directed away from the person and towards an object as the means of connecting the word with the object. A preliminary experiment with typically developing infants (Leekam and Wyver, 1999) suggests that this strategy of using sound direction for naming is used by typically developing infants. But it may be more common for children with autism and for children with visual impairments than for other children with typical development.

Bates *et al.* (1979) proposed that symbol development relies on the under-standing of the vehicle–referent relationship (Peirce, 1931). This understanding is achieved in several stages. First the child comes to understand the conventional uses of signs and gestures, 'whose form and function are agreed upon by both parent and child' (p. 36). Later, the child comes to understand the vehicle–referent relationship—that a particular sign or word can stand for its referent. The emergence of communicative intention is believed to be an important development in the transition from understanding conventions to understanding the vehicle–referent relationship (Bates *et al.*, 1979; Tomasello, 1999; Tomasello, Call, and Gluckman, 1997). Communicative intention is indicated by the child's awareness that a sign is understood by the recipient in a similar way to oneself. It appears to demonstrate awareness of the representational relationship between the sign and its referent, but this awareness is achieved through social-communicative means. The child recognizes one person's intention towards another's attentional state. Evidence of this is indicated, for example, by checking another person's gaze and alternating looking between the object and the other person. If language learning proceeds via an alternative route in children with autism, perhaps they become aware of the vehicle–referent relationship without the intentional communicative function. The possibility that children with autism can recognize the vehicle–referent relationship independently of making any social or mental inferences might be suggested by children's understanding of non-mental representations (Leekam and Perner, 1991). However, it is difficult to find research that clearly demonstrates understanding of the vehicle–referent relationship in the absence of a communicative task. More research is therefore needed in order to establish whether the inferences required for symbolic development in children with autism do in fact follow the normal pattern of development, and whether children with autism do or do not rely on communicative intention in the development of symbolic functioning.

5. WHY DO CHILDREN WITH AUTISM HAVE A JOINT ATTENTION IMPAIRMENT?

To conclude, I have proposed that the joint attention impairment arises from an orienting problem early in development. This problem, as others have suggested (Hobson, 1993; Mundy 1995; Tantam, 1992), first affects dyadic interactions before it affects triadic joint attention interactions between child, another person, and objects. This dyadic orienting problem is likely to be highly related to motivational and affective factors, and we need to know more about the way it is related, given that motivational-affective capacity may not only drive orienting but may also be driven by it.

Our findings so far indicate that children with autism differ from other children not only in triadic joint attention but also in dyadic face-to-face interaction. If their later difficulties with understanding signs and symbols stem from this dyadic impairment in engaging with others, how similar is this problem to the difficulty of non-human primates, who fail to learn communicative signals to share attention? There seem to be some distinct differences. Non-human primates seem to benefit from social experiences with humans and follow gaze direction, but do not use declarative joint attention gestures or language. Children with autism, by contrast, initially seem not to follow another's gaze direction, yet some do acquire this ability as they get older and also develop declarative gestures and language. Perhaps enculturated non-human primates have the capacity to be affected by people in a dyadic and to some extent triadic interactions, but are limited in their ability to learn communicative signals and linguistic symbols, whereas for young children with autism it is the other way around. They can learn to use communicative signals and linguistic symbols, but they are limited in their capacity for dyadic and triadic interaction. If so, this suggests two rather distinct developments. In the case of the typically developing child these developments build on each other. In the case of the child with autism, the learning of symbols may develop separately, relying on a different route to language acquisition, or, alternatively, some minimum level of capacity to engage with others is required to enable this ability to develop.

As our research may be beginning to show, if children with autism start out with a basic impairment in orienting to others, they may remain handicapped in their development of joint attention and symbolic skills, but this does not mean that they are completely unable to develop any joint attention. For older and more able children, social experience may in time equip them with the capacity for joint attention, although this development occurs much later than for typically developing children, and the quality of sharing might still be missing. They may also gain from their experience in a different way from other children. It is also possible that even if they lack the initial ability to interpret communicative intentions, they may take another route to the development of linguistic symbol use and to the acquisition of joint attention.

REFERENCES

ALLISON, T., PUCE, A., and McCARTHY, G. (2000), 'Social perception from visual cues: role of the STS region', *Trends in Cognitive Science*, 4 (7): 267–78.

ATKINSON, J., HOOD, B., WATTAM-BELL, J., and BRADDICK, O. (1992), 'Changes in infants' ability to switch visual attention in the first three months of life', *Perception*, 21: 643–53.

BALDWIN, D. A. (1991), 'Infant's contribution to the achievement of joint reference', *Child Development*, 62: 875–90.

—— (1995), 'Understanding the link between joint attention and language', in C. Moore and P. Dunham (eds.), *Joint Attention: Its Origins and Role in Development*. Hillsdale, NJ: Lawrence Erlbaum, 131–58.

BARANEK, G. T. (1999), 'Autism during infancy: a retrospective video analysis of sensory-motor and social behaviours at 9–12 months of age', *Journal of Autism and Developmental Disorders*, 29, (3): 213–24.

BARON-COHEN, S. (1989), 'Perceptual role taking and protodeclarative pointing in autism', *British Journal of Developmental Psychology*, 7: 113–27.

—— (1995), *Mindblindness: An Essay on Autism and Theory of Mind*. Cambridge, Mass.: Bradford/MIT Press.

BATES, E., BENIGNI, L., BRETHERTON, I., CAMAIONI, L., and VOLTERRA, V. (1979), *The Emergence of Symbols: Cognition and Communication in Infancy*. New York: Academic Press.

BRENTANO, F. VON (1970/1874), *Psychology from an Empirical Standpoint*, ed. O. Kraus. London: Routledge & Kegan Paul.

BURACK, J. A., ENNS, J. T., JOHANNES, E. A., STAUDER, E. A., MOTTRON, L., and RANDOLPH, B. (1997), 'Attention and autism: behavioural and electrophysiological evidence', in D. Cohen, and F. Volkmar (eds.), *Handbook of Autism and Pervasive Developmental Disorders*, 2nd edn. New York: Wilson & Sons, 226–47.

BUTTERWORTH, G., and COCHRAN, E. (1980), 'Towards a mechanism of joint visual attention in human infancy', *International Journal of Behavioral Development*, 3: 253–72.

—— and GROVER, L. (1990), 'Joint visual attention, manual pointing and preverbal communications in human infancy', in M. Jeannerod (ed.), *Attention and Performance*, xiii: *Motor Representation and Control*. Hillsdale, NJ: Laurence Erlbaum, 605–24.

CARPENTER, M. PENNINGTON, B., and ROGERS, S. J. (2002), 'Interrelations among social-cognitive skills in young children with autism', *Journal of Autism and Developmental Disorders*, 32 (2): 91–106.

CASEY, B., GORDON, C., MANNHEIM, G., and RUMSEY, J. (1993), 'Dysfunctional attention in autistic savants', *Journal of Clinical and Experimental Neuropsychology*, 15: 933–46.

CORKUM, V., and MOORE, C. (1998), 'The origin of joint visual attention in infants', *Developmental Psychology*, 34: 28–38.

COURCHESNE, E., TOWNSEND, J., AKSHOOMOFF, N., SAITOH, O., YEUNG-COURCHESNE, R., LINCOLN, A., JAMES, H., HAAS, R., SCHRIEBMAN, L. A., and LAU, L. (1994), 'Impairment in shifting attention in autistic and cerebellar patients', *Behavioral Neuroscience*, 108: 848–65.

DAWSON, G., and LEWY, A. (1989), 'Arousal, attention, and the social-emotional impairments of individuals with autism', in G. Dawson (ed.), *Autism, Nature, Diagnosis, and Treatment*. New York: Guilford, 49–74.

—— MELTZOFF, A., OSTERLING, J., RINALDI, J., and BROWN, E. (1998), 'Children with autism fail to orient to naturally occurring social stimuli', *Journal of Autism and Developmental Disorders*, 28: 479–85.

DEAK, G., FLOM, R., PICK, A., and SILBERGLITT, B. (1997), 'Perceptual and maturation factors affecting joint visual attention in infancy'. Poster presented at SRCD, Washington, April.

DRIVER, J., DAVIS, G., RICCIARDELLI, P., KIDD, P., MAXWELL, E., and BARON-COHEN, S. (1999), 'Gaze perception triggers reflexive visuospatial orienting', *Visual Cognition*, 6: 509–40.

FEIN, D., PENNINGTON, B., MARKOWITZ, P., BRAVERMAN, M., and WATERHOUSE, L. (1986), 'Toward a neuropsychological model of infantile autism: are the social deficits primary?', *Journal of the American Academy of Child Psychiatry*, 25 (2): 198–212.

FRIESEN, C. K., and KINGSTONE, A. (1998), 'The eyes have it: reflexive orienting is triggered by nonpredictive gaze', *Psychonomic Bulletin and Review*, 5: 490–3.

GILMORE, R. O., and JOHNSON, M. H. (1995), 'Working memory in six-month-old infants revealed by versions of the oculomotor delayed response task', *Journal of Experimental Child Psychology*, 59: 397–418.

GÓMEZ, J. C. (1991), 'Visual behaviour as a window for reading the mind of others in primates', in A. Whiten, (ed.), *Natural Theories of Mind: Evolution, Development and Simulation of Everyday Mindreading*. Oxford: Basil Blackwell, 195–207.

—— SARRIÁ, E., and TAMARIT, J. (1993), 'The comparative study of early communication and theories of mind: ontogeny, phylogeny and pathology', in S. Baron-Cohen, H. Tager-Flusberg and D. Cohen (eds.), *Understanding Other Minds: Perspectives from Autism*. Oxford: Oxford University Press, 397–426.

GRIFFITH, E. M., PENNINGTON, B. F., WEHNER, E. A., and ROGERS, S. J. (1999), 'Executive functions in young children with autism', *Child Development*, 70 (4): 817–32.

HARRIS, P., and MACFARLANE, A. (1974), 'The growth of the effective visual field from birth to seven weeks', *Journal of Experimental Child Psychology*, 18: 340–8.

HOBSON, P. (1993), *Autism and the Development of Mind*. Hove: Lawrence Erlbaum Associates.

—— (2002), *The Cradle of Thought*. London: Macmillan.

HOOD, B. (1995), 'Shifts of visual attention in the human infant: a neuroscientific approach', in C. Rover-Collier and L. Lipsett (eds.), *Advances in Infancy Research*. Norwood, NJ: Ablex, 163–216.

JOHNSON, M., POSNER, M., and ROTHBART, M. (1994), 'Facilitation of saccades toward a covertly attended location in early infancy', *Psychological Science*, 5: 90–3.

JOHNSON, S., SLAUGHTER, V., and CAREY, S. (1998), 'Whose gaze will infants follow? The elicitation of gaze following in 12-month-olds', *Developmental Science*, 1: 233–8.

LANDRY, S. H., and LOVELAND, K. A. (1988), 'Communication behaviours in autism and developmental language delay', *Journal of Child Psychology and Psychiatry*, 29: 621–34.

LANGTON, S. R. H., and BRUCE, V. (1999), 'Reflexive visual orienting in response to the social attention of others', *Visual Cognition*, 6 (5): 541–67.

LEEKAM, S. R. (2000), 'Joint attention and language in children with autism and children with language impairments'. Poster presented at the International Society for the Study of Behavioural Development, Beijing, July.

—— and PERNER, J. (1991), 'Does the autistic child have a metarepresentational deficit?', *Cognition*, 40: 203–18.

—— and RAMSDEN, C. A. (in press), 'Dyadic orienting and joint attention in preschool children with autism'. *Journal of Autism and Developmental Disorders*.

—— and WYVER, S. 'Joint attention without vision'. (1999), Paper presented at the European Developmental Psychology Conference, Spetses, Greece, September.

—— BARON-COHEN, S., PERRETT, D., MILDERS, M., and BROWN, S. (1997), 'Eye-direction detection: a dissociation between geometric and joint attention skills in autism', *British Journal of Developmental Psychology*, 15: 77–95.

LEEKAM, S. R. (2000) HUNNISETT, E., and MOORE, C. (1998), 'Targets and cues: gaze-following in children with autism', *Journal of Child Psychology and Psychiatry*, 39: 951–62.

—— REDDY, V., LOPEZ, B., and STAN, P. (1999), 'Gaze-following and declarative joint attention in children with autism'. Poster presented at Society for Research in Child Development, Albuquerque, April.

—— LOPEZ, B., and MOORE, C. (2000), 'Attention and joint attention in preschool children with autism', *Developmental Psychology*, 36 (2): 261–73.

LESLIE, A. (1987), 'Pretence and representation: the origins of theory of mind', *Psychological Review*, 14: 412–26.

McEVOY, R., ROGERS, S. J., and PENNINGTON, B. F. (1993), 'Executive function and social communication deficits in young autistic children', *Journal of Child Psychology and Psychiatry*, 34: 563–78.

MOORE, C. (1999), 'Gaze-following and the control of attention', in P. Rochat (ed.), *Early Social Cognition*. Hillside, NJ: Lawrence Erlbaum Associates, 241–56.

MORTON, J., and JOHNSON, M. H. (1991), 'Conspec and Conlern: a 2-process theory of infant face recognition', *Psychological Review*, 98 (2): 164–81.

MUNDY, P. (1995), 'Joint attention and social-emotional approach behaviour in children with autism', *Development and Psychopathology*, 7: 63–82.

—— and NEAL, R. (2001), 'Neural plasticity, joint attention and a transactional social-orienting model of autism', in L. Glidden (ed.), *International Review of Research in Mental Retardation*, 23: 139–68.

—— and SIGMAN, M. (1989), 'The theoretical implications of joint attention deficits in autism', *Development and Psychopathology*, 1: 173–83.

—— —— UNGERER J., and SHERMAN, T. (1986), 'Defining social deficits of autism: the contribution of non-verbal communication measures', *Journal of Child Psychology and Psychiatry*, 27: 657–9.

—— —— and KASARI, C. (1994), 'Joint attention, developmental level and symptom presentation in autism', *Development and Psychopathology*, 6: 389–401.

—— CARD, J., and FOX, N. (2000), 'EEG correlates of the development of infant joint attention skills', *Developmental Psychobiology*, 36 (4): 325–38.

MURRAY, C., and TREVARTHEN, L. (1985), 'Emotion regulation of interaction between two-month-olds and their mothers', in T. Field and N. Fox (eds.), *Social Perception in Infants*. Norwood, NJ: Ablex, 101–25.

NEELY, J., TURNER, M., and FINDLAY, J. (2001), 'Attention shifting upon social cues in high functioning individual with autism'. Poster presented at the Meeting for the Society for Research in Child Development, Minneapolis, April.

OSTERLING, J., and DAWSON, G. (1994), 'Early recognition of children with autism: a study of first birthday home videotapes', *Journal of Autism and Developmental Disorders*, 24: 247–57.

PEIRCE, C. S. (1931–5), *Collected Papers of Charles Sanders Peirce*, ed. C. Hartshorne and P. Weiss. Cambridge, Mass.: Harvard University Press.

PENNINGTON, B. F., and OZONOFF, S. (1996), 'Executive functions and developmental psychopathology', *Journal of Child Psychology and Psychiatry*, 37 (1): 51–87.

POSNER, M. I. (1980), 'Orienting of attention', *Quarterly Journal of Experimental Psychology*, 32: 3–25.

POVINELLI, D. J., and EDDY, T. J. (1997), 'Specificity of gaze-following in young chimpanzees', *British Journal of Developmental Psychology*, 15: 213–22.

RUSSELL, J. (1996), *Agency: Its Role in Mental Development*. Hove: Erlbaum Taylor & Francis Ltd.

SCHULTZ, R. T, ROMANSKI, L. M., and TSATSANIS, K. D. (2000), 'Neurofunctional models of autistic disorder and Asperger syndrome: clues from neuroimaging', in A. Klin, F. R. Volkmar and S. S. Sparrow (eds.), *Asperger Syndrome*. New York. Plenum, 179–209.

SWETTENHAM, J., BARON-COHEN, S., CHARMAN, T., COX, A., BAIRD, G., DREW, A., and REES, L. (1998), 'The frequency and distribution of spontaneous attention shifts between social and nonsocial stimuli in autistic, typically developing, and non-autistic developmentally delayed infants', *Journal of Child Psychology and Psychiatry*, 39: 747–53.

—— MILNE, E. H., PLAISTED, K. C., CAMPBELL, R., and COLEMAN, M. (2000), 'Visual orienting in response to social stimuli', *Journal of Cognitive Neuroscience*, suppl. 53D.

TANTAM, D. (1992), 'Characterising the fundamental social handicap in autism', *Acta Paedopsychiatrica*, 55: 88–91.

TOMASELLO, M. (1999), *The Cultural Origins of Human Cognition*. Cambridge, Mass.: Harvard University Press.

—— CALL, J., and GLUCKMAN, A. (1997), 'Comprehension of novel communicative signs by apes and human children', *Child Development*, 68: 1067–80.

TOWNSEND, J. SINGER-HARRIS, N., and COURCHESNE, E. (1996), 'Visual attention abnormalities in autism: delayed orienting to location', *Journal of the International Neuropsychological Society*, 2: 541–50.

TREVARTHEN, C., and HUBLEY, P. (1978), 'Secondary intersubjectivity: confidence, confiding and acts of meaning in the first year', in A. Lock (ed.), *Action, Gesture and Symbol*. London: Academic Press, 183–229.

WAINWRIGHT-SHARP, J. A., and BRYSON, S. E. (1993), 'Visual orienting deficits in high-functioning people with autism', *Journal of Autism and Developmental Disorders*, 23: 1–13.

WERNER, H., and KAPLAN, S. (1963), *Symbol Formation*. New York: Wiley and Sons.

11

Joint Attention and the Problem of Other Minds

Johannes Roessler

I

In 'The idea of perfection', Iris Murdoch writes that 'uses of words by persons grouped round a common object is a central and vital human activity'. Her account of what makes the activity central and vital consists of two connected elements. One is that joint attention is an important mechanism for acquiring knowledge and concepts. For example, 'The art critic can help us if we are in the presence of the same object and if we know something about his scheme of concepts. Both contexts [our spatio-temporal and conceptual contexts] are relevant to our ability to move towards "seeing more", towards "seeing what he sees".' The other element is that joint attention enables us to gain mutual understanding: 'Human beings are obscure to each other, in certain respects which are particularly relevant to morality, unless they are mutual objects of attention or have common objects of attention, since this affects the degree of elaboration of a common vocabulary' (1970, pp. 32–3).

This last claim needs some qualifying—it certainly seems possible to gain a detailed and deep understanding of others without the benefit of sharing attention with them. But there may still be a sense in which the capacity for joint attention plays a foundational role in understanding other minds. I take it that this suggestion has great intuitive plausibility; and, as several chapters in this volume illustrate, it receives strong support from recent work in developmental psychology. I want to begin by contrasting two general directions in which the suggestion might be pursued. It is a familiar idea that other minds are open to a distinctive kind of understanding, often characterized as an understanding 'from the inside'. This is usually taken to be a matter of (in some sense) re-creating in our own imagination some aspects of the conscious point of view of the person we are trying to understand. A proposal that would be in line with this general idea is that joint attention is important because it is a helpful setting for gaining this kind of imaginative understanding. Obviously the task of re-creating your reasoning, or imagining your experiences, or establishing what I would think if I were in your situation, becomes relatively manageable when I *am* in your situation—when we are grouped round a common object of attention. So joint attention might be seen as the natural context for developing the skills required for simulating other minds.

An alternative line to take would be to hold that the reason joint attention is important for understanding other minds is that it makes simulation dispensable.[1] On this view, when you jointly attend to an object with someone else, at least some aspects of his experience will be transparent to you. As Murdoch puts it, you may 'see what he sees'. On a natural reading, this means not just that you see the same object (and perhaps recognize the same features) as he does, but that you see the object (and its features) as something of which he is aware as well. There is simply no need for you to engage in an imaginative exercise to understand his point of view, when this is manifest to you *qua* co-attender. In a passage that is often seen as an early and radical manifesto of the simulation view, Kant writes: 'if I wish to represent to myself a thinking being, I must put myself in his place, and thus substitute, as it were, my own subject for the object I am seeking to consider' (1929, p. A 353). One thing that is wrong with Kant's view, it might be said, is that it falsifies the phenomenon of joint attention: in joint attention we experience each other as thinking beings.

An immediate question facing this proposal is what, if anything, reflection on joint attention adds to the familiar (and, many would argue, justly unpopular) idea that some mental states are directly observable. The natural response is that what is fuelling the intuition that joint attention provides me with a direct grasp of a co-attender's experience is the fact that she is *sharing* her experience with me, which in turn raises the question: how should we characterize the relevant notion of sharing, and how might sharing experiences, in that sense, provide an 'understanding from the inside' that involves no simulation? Put differently, the question is how the two elements of Murdoch's account of the importance of joint attention—its role in sharing knowledge of the world around us, and in gaining knowledge of other minds—are related to one another.

Rather than trying to tackle these questions head-on, I will approach them by considering a less purely philosophical, but closely connected, question that has been the subject of much fascinating work in developmental psychology: How should we characterize the kinds of joint attentional interactions children begin to engage in during the first half of the second year? In particular, should we think of such interactions as manifesting an understanding of other minds, and if so,

---

[1] For a suggestive discussion of this view, see Schütz, 1997, esp. pp. 165ff. Schütz draws a sharp distinction between the awareness we have of another's attention in a face-to-face situation (of which joint attention is a paradigmatic case) and what he calls 'social observation'. The latter lacks 'the many-faceted mutual mirroring characteristic of the face-to-face situation, in which the conscious content of the two partners is mutually identified'. Connectedly, 'face-to-face interaction' involves a direct 'disclosure of the motives of the other person', whereas in gleaning motives from observed behaviour, the observer is forced to adopt some 'indirect approach', such as imaginatively 'putting himself in the Other's place'. Schütz does not pretend that the participant's point of view is immune to error, or always privileged over the point of view of detached observation ('the nonparticipating listener can realize that two partners to a discussion are merely talking past one another, whereas they themselves may be totally unaware of this'). The claim is just that there are important differences, both phenomenological and epistemological, between the third-person and the second-person perspectives.

how should we characterize that understanding? I begin by spelling out what I take to be the problem; roughly: while there is a compelling case for the view that joint attention manifests some psychological understanding, standard explanations of what such understanding consists in seem to break down when applied to 1-year-olds. In sections III and IV I consider and contrast two recent developmental accounts of joint attention, Michael Tomasello's and Peter Hobson's. Drawing on Hobson's account, I will then (in section V) sketch a suggestion as to what it might mean to credit infants with psychological understanding and knowledge of other minds. In section VI I discuss a basic objection to this account. In section VII I explore its bearing on communication and knowledge of other minds in the case of subjects with fully developed psychological concepts.

II

Most infants start to point at things sometime before the end of the first year. Their pointing skills at this stage leave considerable room for further development. (For example, infants are initially oblivious to the importance of establishing mutual attention *before* pointing. See Franco, Chapter 7 above.) Even at this early stage, though, pointing seems to be part of a meaningful social interaction; it is typically accompanied by vocalizations and gaze alternation between referent and addressee. An intuitively compelling description of what is going on here is that infants are trying to show an interesting object to their caregiver: they are trying to share attention to the object with her. If this account is right, there is a powerful case for concluding that 1-year-olds have some understanding of others as subjects of attention and perhaps emotion. Data from gaze-following or social referencing generate similar and equally powerful intuitions. But there are two reasons why those arguing for 'rich' interpretations of early joint attention interactions (interpretations that credit infants with some kind of psychological understanding) tend to place particular weight on pointing. First, it seems evident that we are talking about an intentional activity here; infants point in order to achieve some goal, with gaze alternation designed to check whether the goal has been accomplished. Second, while pointing is sometimes used as a means of obtaining a desirable object (proto-imperative pointing), often it is not; and in these latter cases (proto-declarative pointing) it is simply not clear what purpose the pointing might be serving, if not that of sharing attention. So we have a basic argument for a rich interpretation: proto-declarative pointing manifests the belief that pointing is a way of drawing someone's attention to interesting objects.

While this line of reasoning has much intuitive appeal, it raises two difficult theoretical issues: (a) What does it mean to say that 1-year-olds conceive of others as subjects of attention? (b) In describing the goal of proto-declarative pointing, we naturally help ourselves to the notion of *sharing* attention. But can we spell out explicitly what sharing attention involves (specifically in the case of young children)?

The answers to (a) that can be extracted from the recent developmental literature fall, by and large, into either of two camps. Roughly, one approach (the more common one) equates psychological understanding with the possession of a (perhaps primitive) 'theory of mind', where this is normally conceived of as the ability to explain and predict a person's behaviour in terms of her psychological properties. Joint attention interactions are seen from this perspective as perhaps the earliest manifestations of children's theory of mind. By contrast, the second approach suggests we should think of such interactions as a relatively sophisticated form of intersubjective engagement—less sophisticated forms of which can be observed in infants as young as 2 months. The development of children's psychological understanding, on this view, consists, at least initially, in the development of their ability to engage with others in certain kinds of reciprocal interactions, involving mutual attention between baby and caregiver (primary intersubjectivity) and, from the age of 9 months, also shared attention to objects (secondary intersubjectivity): it is part of this development that infants learn to see and hear what other participants are doing, feeling, or attending to. Thus, while the first camp tends to think of joint attention as something of a revolution in infants' interpersonal relations, the second camp emphasizes the continuity between dyadic and triadic modes of intersubjective engagement.

Some aspects of the debate between these approaches are purely empirical (for example, some of Trevarthen's original experiments on mutual attention have been found difficult to replicate: see Rochat and Striano, 1999, for discussion); but there is also a fundamental disagreement on epistemological issues. Very crudely, on the intersubjectivity approach, the fact that others are subjects of experience is something that is perceptually given to infants, at least in so far as they engage in normal interpersonal relationships. To the extent that grasping this fact requires any activity on the part of the infant, this is a matter of joint reciprocal activities with caregivers. By contrast, proponents of the theory of mind approach tend to take it as axiomatic that, as the opening sentence of Meltzoff *et al.* (1999) puts it, 'our sensory experience of other people tells us about their movements in space but does not tell us directly about their mental states'. Infants' grip on the idea of other minds is thus seen as the result of an active interpretative effort—they have to work out that others are subjects of experience, and the task of developmental psychologists is precisely to chart the course of this intellectual achievement.

Rather than looking at this debate in general terms, I want to make some points specifically about how the two approaches bear on joint attention. My first set of comments will be largely negative: my provisional result will be that as far as a credible answer to question (a) is concerned (the question of what it means to say that 1-year-olds are aware of others as subjects of attention), neither of the two approaches looks particularly promising. So my aim in this section is to flesh out the claim that joint attention presents us with a paradox: there are strong grounds for attributing some grasp of psychological properties to 1-year-olds, but at the same time, infants this age seem to lack the kinds of psychological abilities needed to make this attribution intelligible. The methodological suggestion I will pursue in the next section is that progress with (a) depends on a better understanding of (b) (what does sharing attention come to in the case of 1-year-olds?).

As indicated, one assumption motivating the theory of mind approach is that other minds are not directly observable: to establish what others think or desire, you have to rely on inferences, specifically inferences to the best explanation. To make such inferences is precisely to make others' behaviour intelligible in terms of their psychological properties; so infants need at least a rudimentary theory of mind. A second, perhaps more important kind of consideration is this. To have thoughts about a particular psychological property, you need to understand which property is in question. Now, what individuates psychological properties, on a widely held view, is their causal-explanatory role. This suggests that to grasp a given psychological property, we need to understand something about its role in a subject's mental economy—its causal relations with the world around the subject, other mental states of the subject, and the subject's actions. Once again, this requires the ability to make someone's behaviour (and mental states) intelligible in terms of her (other) mental states and her environment.

Many assume, therefore, that to say that 1-year-olds have some understanding of others as subjects of attention just is to say that they have a theory of mind. Yet there is something prima facie baffling about the idea that 1-year-olds have the intellectual abilities required for grasping theories and giving explanations. Intuitively, this is, as Strawson put it in a different context, 'to misrepresent us as theorists before we have the means of theorizing' (1992, p. 122). A standard move to allay such worries is to remind us that 1-year-olds' theory of mind is quite primitive in certain ways. For example, 1-year-olds may not appreciate that people sometimes act on the basis of false beliefs, or that perceptual experience can be misleading. They may be limited to making observed behaviour intelligible in terms of, say, desires and opportunities for action. But there is a deeper worry—a worry about the very idea that babies possess an explanatory theory, rather than just a worry over which psychological notions the theory deploys.

On the face of it, it looks as if the theory of mind approach is committed to the idea that in so far as we have reason to ascribe to young children thoughts about others' mental states, we also have reason to ascribe to them thoughts about evidential and explanatory relations between propositions. For example, Gopnik and Meltzoff argue that data from joint attention interactions make it plausible that infants 'know that the direction of the eyes, or perhaps just the direction of the head and body, indicates something about the person's visual contact with an object' (1997, p. 104). In other words, infants know that gaze direction provides evidence about the focus of someone's attention, where this means: they understand that facts about attention often provide good explanations of facts about eye or head movements. This, in turn, implies that infants have some grasp of counterfactual conditionals: arguably, to know why something happened is, in part, to know what would have happened had things been different in relevant ways, all else being equal. Then the problem is that there are good grounds for scepticism about the suggestion that 1-year-olds grasp counterfactuals. Admittedly, there is as yet little agreement in the literature on the development of counterfactual reasoning. But the disagreement tends to be over whether or not 3- (and perhaps 2-) year-olds are able to engage in such reasoning. I think most would regard the idea that 1-year-olds grasp counterfactual conditionals as far-fetched. Note that the worry here is not about the general idea of attributing to young children some kind of grasp of causal relations. What seems problematic is the idea that they are able to give causal *explanations*. This, then, would be one way of fleshing out the charge that crediting 1-year-olds with a theory of mind is 'to misrepresent us as theorists before we have the means of theorizing'. (Related worries, which I will not pursue here, might be raised about infants' ability to deal with evidence—in particular, conflicting evidence.)

Some psychologists are careful to qualify the theory of mind they attribute to young children as 'implicit'—precisely in order to pre-empt any worries about infants' 'means of theorizing'. For example, it is sometimes argued that infants' grasp of a theory of mind should be seen as analogous to 3-year-olds' grasp of grammatical rules (Bretherton, 1991). Representations of such rules may play a causal role in both perceiving and producing sentences, regardless of the fact that 3-year-olds are unable to state the rules verbally. Similarly, possession of a theory of mind might enable infants to parse perceived movements into units that yield descriptions under which they are intended (Baldwin and Baird, 1999) or to anticipate others' behaviour. But this line of response comes at a heavy price. The price is to sever the link between infants' theory of mind and their psychological understanding. The intuition we started from, recall, was that proto-declarative pointing is an intentional action that reveals a conception of others as subjects of attention. The intuition is that infants' *reason* for pointing (roughly: the desire to share attention) entails some understanding of attention—it is integral to the intuition that pointing is to be explained at the personal level, rather than just in terms of causally relevant subpersonal mechanisms (even if devoted to processing information about others' mental states). If a theory of mind is qualified as implicit in the current sense, it provides no help in clarifying the content of that intuition. To say that 1-year-olds have some understanding of attention would be just as misleading as to claim that 3-year-olds understand grammatical categories. In reality, versions of the theory of mind approach that appeal to subpersonal information-processing tend to mix this account with personal-level explana-tions. (For example, the Shared Attention Mechanism postulated by Baron-Cohen is said to give 'the child a way of inferring a person's desires and goals from the direction of their gaze' (1995, p. 51).) The basic problem of how to characterize infants' psychological understanding remains unsolved.

The problem I am raising here is orthogonal to the dispute between advocates of the so-called theory theory, on the one hand, and the simulation theory, on the other—a point that is worth stressing, given that the term 'theory of mind' is sometimes used as a variant of 'theory theory'. The dispute between these views is usually presented as a disagreement over the nature of interpretation, where interpretation is taken to be a matter of making intelligible what someone says and does in terms of her psychological properties. However, while they offer different accounts of interpretation, advocates of the two views typically proceed on the shared assumption that the capacity for interpretation is necessary for psychological understanding. It is just this assumption that seems to be rendered problematic by reflection on the development of joint attention. The problem is that while there is a compelling intuition to the effect that 1-year-olds have some grasp of others' attention, there are also prima facie grounds for doubting that they have the conceptual abilities needed for interpretation (such as the ability to give causal explanations). In case the simulation theory might seem less vulnerable to this kind of objection, let me consider one (influential) version of it. Michael Tomasello maintains that from the age of 9 months infants conceive of others as intentional agents, and that this conception draws on two vital abilities (Tomasello, 1999). One is the disposition, present even in very young infants, to engage with others in games of mutual attention, which Tomasello describes as the 'like me stance'. (I will return to this in a moment.) The other is the ability to separate means from ends, to choose a particular method for accomplishing a given goal. In Tomasello's view, this ability emerges at around 9 months. Then the idea is that since infants are equipped with a basic sense of others as being 'like me', 9-month-olds will immediately utilize their newly acquired instrumental reasoning in simulating *others'* instrumental reasoning, thereby arriving at an understanding that others act intentionally. An interesting question raised by this proposal concerns the sense (if any) in which 1-year-olds can be described as simulating other minds. A specific worry here might be that it is hard to see how simulation might get going without the capacity for pretence (which is generally held to emerge only towards the end of the second year). But for current purposes what matters is that the assumption I am questioning is written into the explanandum of Tomasello's theory. He aims to give an account of how infants become able to explain others' behaviour in terms of their goals, where the suggestion is that the crucial mechanism lies in the development of infants' capacity for goal-directed action. What is simply assumed here is that infants have the conceptual abilities to give causal explanations.

Let us now turn to the intersubjectivity approach. Does appeal to infants' social engagement yield a more satisfactory account of their psychological understanding? There are a number of well-documented ways in which infants as young as

2 months appear to respond to the psychological properties of others. For example, they show clear patterns of responding to others' attention (in mutual attention), affect (in 'proto-conversations', where participants take turns in producing matching expressions of affect), and intentional actions (in early imitation). There is also evidence that infants actively seek to establish such face-to-face interactions, and that they sometimes show signs of distress when the adult is unresponsive (see Trevarthen, 1993; Rochat and Striano, 1999, for reviews of the literature). In interpreting these findings, it is important to distinguish two issues: (i) What is it infants are responding to? Should we think of them as responding to a caregiver's attention, or merely to certain patterns of behaviour? (ii) What kind of psychological explanation should be given of the response? In her contribution to this volume (Chapter 5), Vasu Reddy argues (convincingly, in my view) that the natural answer to (i) is that it is indeed attention, rather than mere behaviour, that infants are engaged with, and that this answer is far more plausible than any of the theoretical assumptions responsible for many psychologists' resistance to it, such as the assumption that mental states are not directly observable. It is not clear, however, whether this point provides support for Reddy's conclusion that infants have some understanding of others' attention even before the emergence of 'the third element' (before they participate in triadic joint attention formats). What matters here is (ii)—the question of what kind of psychological explanation is germane to the case of infants' dyadic intersubjective engagement.

I think many would argue that there is simply not enough structure in the way 6-month-olds pursue goals to warrant the attribution of psychological *understanding*. This is not to deny that their contribution to mutual attention interactions can be given some kind of personal-level explanations. Infants' conscious perception of others, and their emotional responsiveness, may be an essential part of the explanation. What many would question is whether such contributions are intentional actions, in the sense of being informed by practical reasons understood by the agent herself. Suppose we agree that infants are perceptually aware of someone else's attention (rather than mere 'behaviour'). This does not commit us to a picture on which such awareness provides the rational basis for infants' decisions, say, about how to keep a proto-conversation going. Rather, we might think of her disposition to respond practically and affectively to a caregiver's attention in distinctive ways as part of *what it is* for her to be aware of others' attention. A suggestive way of putting this is to say that young infants perceive others as a distinctive sort of affordance—as Peter Hobson puts it, as 'a special kind of object that affords one-to-one interaction and sharing and gives the baby a special set of feelings and tendencies to act' (2002, p. 93). More specifically, infants might be said to perceive another's attending to themas affording certain kinds of reciprocal engagement. Returning now to joint attention, part of the basic argument, recall, was the claim that proto-declarative pointing is an intentional activity—that infants use pointing as means to sharing attention. So it is not just that triadic joint attention differs from earlier (dyadic) mutual attention in virtue of the existence of a common object of attention. Rather, joint attention requires explanations in terms of infants' reasons in a way in which early mutual attention games do not, where the reasons involve an understanding of the co-attender's focus of attention. On the face of it, then, it will not do to think of joint attention merely as a continuation of earlier mutual engagement by more sophisticated means. We need an account of what the extra sophistication consists in, and in this regard the intersubjectivity approach offers little help.

III

The upshot of these considerations is that early joint attention interactions present us with a paradox. On the one hand, there is a compelling case for the claim that proto-declarative pointing is informed by an awareness of the caregiver's focus of attention. On the other hand, the kinds of abilities we want to invoke in explaining what such an awareness might consist in do not seem to be in place at the beginning of the second year. We face the unsatisfactory situation that the seemingly compelling claim may turn out to be unintelligible.[2]

I now want to turn to a set of issues that arise when we ask what is involved in sharing attention; specifically, how that notion should be understood in the case of 1-year-olds. I will suggest that our difficulties with the nature of infants' psychological understanding derive, at least in part, from an implausible answer to this question. I will argue that, by putting together some elements of an alternative picture, we simultaneously obtain materials for a way of dissolving the paradox.

The notion of sharing attention raises at least three issues: (i) What are the mechanisms by which shared attention is established? (ii) How should we understand the notion of attention here? What is it that is being shared when 1-year-olds share attention with caregivers? (iii) It is not sufficient for sharing attention, as we normally understand it, that two people happen to attend to the same object. They must attend to the object *together*, where, intuitively, this involves

---

[2] One response to the paradox might be to remind us that, quite independently of the conceptual issues, the empirical case for rich interpretations of joint attention is far from being universally accepted. For example, according to Josef Perner, an equally plausible explanation of the empirical evidence is that infants engage in proto-declarative pointing simply because they enjoy their mastery over their mothers' eyes (Perner, 1991, p. 131). Perner cautions that the intuitive appeal of a rich interpretation may reflect a bias in favour of explanations that make sense to adults: 'it appeals to our adult intuition because we feel this is the reason why we would point in that situation.' But whatever the outcome of the debate about the complex empirical issues here, it seems unlikely that it will dissolve our paradox. Even if, initially, infants lack an understanding of others as co-attenders, such understanding begins to emerge as joint attention interactions become more sophisticated over the course of the second year, as even the more cautious interpreters accept. (See Corkum and Moore, 1995, for a detailed defence of this view.) So, with a few months' delay, we find ourselves faced with the same conceptual issues.

some kind of *awareness* of attending together. But how should we characterize the content of this awareness?

I want to look at two opposing views on these issues that have recently been put forward by Michael Tomasello and Peter Hobson. The most obvious point of disagreement between Tomasello and Hobson is over what is being shared in proto-declarative joint attention. Roughly, Tomasello highlights the fact that selectively attending to something can be an intentional activity ('intentional perception', as he calls it). On his view, the 'meeting of minds' characteristic of joint attention is primarily a 'meeting of wills'. By contrast, in Hobson's view, the important point is that attending to an object involves being emotionally affected by the object. He thinks of joint attention as essentially the sharing of object-directed emotions—as a matter of being jointly affected by the world. But this point is related to a deeper disagreement about the mechanisms by which joint attention is established. Very roughly, for Tomasello, joint attention is basically a kind of rational co-operation, exploiting the participants' ability to understand each other's communicative intentions. On the other hand, Hobson appeals to something like a shared human nature: ultimately, joint attention depends on the participants' natural disposition to respond with affect to perceived affective attitudes. These views, in turn, are connected with different perspectives on the role and nature of co-attenders' awareness of each other's point of view. In this section I will look at Tomasello's account; in the next section I turn to Hobson's approach.

What is involved in comprehending a pointing gesture? Tomasello suggests that pointing is a special way of manipulating someone's attention, where the mechanism by which this is achieved is the expression of a communicative intention. Accordingly, comprehending a pointing gesture requires recognizing the communicative intention informing it. The relevant intention, of course, is not the intention for the audience to form a certain belief, familiar from Gricean accounts of assertion. Rather, the intention that infants need to recognize is: 'You intend for [me to share attention to (X)]' (1999, p. 102) On Tomasello's account, then, children recognize, and express, genuine communicative intentions at an early age, before they understand what it means to make an assertion (let alone to make an assertion that imparts new information to the audience).[3] Pointing involves a distinctive kind of co-operation: my intention to attend to a particular object arises from my realization that this is what you would like me to do. This yields at least a partial answer to the question of what is involved in being aware of attending to something together: it involves an awareness not only of the fact that you and I are

---

[3] More precisely, Tomasello suggests that infants may acquire an understanding of the communicative goal of pointing 'sometime soon after their first birthdays'. Before that, he suggests, pointing may be a case of 'ritualizing' a gesture that has been noticed to achieve desirable results. Importantly, in Tomasello's view, in so far as pointing is a mere ritualization, it is not a means for establishing genuine joint attention. (See 1999, pp. 88–9.)

attending to the same object, but also of the communicative intentions that are instrumental in bringing about our shared attention.

It is important that on this account there is a clear distinction between infants' *recognition* of a caregiver's psychological properties—specifically, their communicative intentions—on the one hand, and their *response*, on the other. The two are not unrelated (infants' recognition of communicative intentions is thought to cause and rationalize their response), but the relation is a causal relation between what Hume called distinct existences. This is connected with the fact that, for Tomasello, the development of social interaction is explained, in part, by the development of children's theory of mind: crudely, the emergence of a conception of others as intentional agents makes (certain sophisticated forms of) social interaction, such as sharing attention, possible. There is a connection, then, between Tomasello's account of what sharing attention consists in and his commitment to the idea that infants have a primitive theory of mind. Sharing attention, on his account, requires interpreting others' communicative behaviour, and thus the ability to make sense of such behaviour in terms of the intentions informing it.

But it seems to me that this account of sharing faces a serious challenge. Briefly, the problem is this. Tomasello's account of the co-operative element of joint attention shares a crucial feature with Grice's account of assertion, on which it draws. Very roughly, when you make an assertion, on Grice's account, you are trying to provide the audience with evidence regarding your beliefs. Of course you will normally be hopeful that, having correctly interpreted the evidence, the audience will eventually come to share the belief you have expressed. But they will do this only if certain further conditions are met, viz. they regard you as trustworthy, responsible, competent, and so forth (Grice, 1989, p. 294). So, as in Tomasello's account, there is a gap between the audience's recognition of the communicative intention and their intended response, a gap that is typically bridged by an inductive argument from an ascription of a communicative intention and an appraisal of the competence and character of its subject to the truth of the belief being expressed. On the face of it, Tomasello's account implies that understanding declarative pointing requires an analogous structure: the gap between recognizing that you intend for me to share attention to X and forming the intention to attend to X has to be bridged by a piece of practical reasoning, premissed on the judgement that it is desirable for me to co-operate with you.

However, on reflection, the idea that this kind of structure is in place by the end of the first year is quite implausible. One-year-olds may have acquired the beginnings of means–end reasoning, but that is not the same as the ability to weigh up potentially competing practical projects—for example, to decide, in the light of one's own desires and plans, whether to accept an invitation to share attention with someone else. Of course, children may or may not be responsive to such an invitation: if they are in a bad mood, or distracted, they may not take it up. But this does not imply that they understand the caregiver's intentions and then make a rational choice not to co-operate. Their mood may make them indisposed to even receive the invitation, as it were. The case of assertion provides an instructive parallel. Suppose it is suggested (plausibly, I presume) that 2-year-olds understand and make assertions that impart new information to the audience, and that they are able to acquire knowledge by being told things. In parallel with Tomasello's account of proto-declaratives, it might be argued that children's understanding here must take the form of their being able, first, to recognize someone's communicative intention of providing evidence of her beliefs, and, second, to reason that, given the informant's trustworthiness, the belief will very likely be true. Surely the correct response to that suggestion would be Wittgenstein's: 'A child learns there are reliable and unreliable informants much later than it learns facts which are told it' (1969, §143). A similar response to Tomasello's account would be: a child becomes able to reflect on the relative weight of her own and others' interests much later than being able to participate in joint activities.

It might be said that practical reasoning is not the only way in which recognizing communicative intentions might lead to a co-operative response. In the absence of sophisticated rational abilities, habitual causal connections may take the place of reasons—1-year-olds may simply be disposed to co-operate with others' communicative intentions. The problem with this move is that it abandons the original idea that sharing attention is a case of rational co-operation. The infant is not seen as co-operating on the basis of *her own* reasons (since the current suggestion grants that 1-year-olds lack the ability to make up their minds as to whether or not to join in a co-operative activity). But nor is it clear why recognizing the psychological fact that someone wants me to attend to X might itself amount to sharing *her* reason for attending to X. Either way, we seem to have lost the idea of a 'meeting of wills'.

It is worth considering what an analogous move in the case of 2-year-olds' use of testimony would look like. The suggestion would be that, presented with someone's testimony, 2-year-olds first establish what the informant believes, by identifying her Gricean intentions; then, being insufficiently mindful of the existence of untrustworthy or careless informants, they habitually jump to the conclusion that what their informant believes is the case. Quite apart from problems with the implication that 2-year-olds can be credited with the concept of belief, the picture is unattractive in that it depicts young children's testimony-based beliefs as systematically irrational (rather than as rational in a less demanding sense than the sense relevant to thinkers with more fully developed conceptual abilities). Certainly on this picture it is hard to see how the resulting beliefs might constitute knowledge: they are not based on the infants' own reasons (in the sense that an ascription to the informant of a certain belief serves as a premiss in an argument that establishes the truth of that belief); nor is it clear how recognizing someone's belief might simply amount to sharing a reason for accepting the proposition which forms its content. An alternative proposal here would be that 2-year-olds have some (perhaps in some ways primitive) notion of knowledge, and come to share the beliefs expressed by their informants because they—rigidly, but surely not unreasonably—think of testimony as a matter of sharing knowledge. I will return to this idea, and its bearing on joint attention.

IV

In the light of these difficulties, the following seems to be an attractive thought. To interpret proto-declarative joint attention as a matter of expressing, recognizing, and acting on communicative intentions is to over-mentalize the phenomenon. In reality, infants follow a caregiver's attention, as expressed in her pointing, not because they understand that this is what the other would like them to do, but because it is natural for them to do so. I take it that this 'naturalist' approach would be in line with Peter Hobson's account of joint attention. In Hobson's view, when a 1-year-old 'takes the role of other people by imitating them and assuming their attitudes', 'she does this automatically, in the sense that she is drawn into doing it.' He also writes that 'the infant is moved by others, and this happens because infants are innately equipped to be moved in this way' (2002, pp. 74–5).

Is this naturalist account guilty of *under*-mentalizing 1-year-olds' social inter- actions? One reason for thinking it is not is that Hobson's account of early social interaction gives a central position to infants' own activity. True, there is a crucial element of passivity, in so far as the whole engagement hinges on the capacity to be 'moved' by perceived affective attitudes. But sharing experiences in this way is something that infants actively try to bring about. In fact, this is true even at the stage of primary intersubjectivity, before the emergence of triadic joint attention. Even at this stage the infant finds 'that sharing experiences is something that hap- pens and then stops, but is also something that can start again and stop again. It can be sought and achieved' (Hobson, 2002, p. 252). There are two important implications here, which in turn give rise to a problem. One implication is that infants must have some kind of awareness of sharing experiences, even at the level of primary intersubjectivity. It is clear, though, that this awareness cannot be a matter of explicitly representing the fact that you and I have the same kind of experience. For one thing, it is implausible to assume that 6-month-olds grasp first-person thoughts. Just as importantly, as indicated earlier, while primary intersubjectivity manifests impressive practical social abilities on the part of the infant, there is no reason to think that these abilities involve the possession of psychological concepts. Hobson, for one, certainly does not think they do. Accordingly, the second implication is that young infants' sense of sharing experi- ences should be characterized in pre-reflective terms, as it were. They may have an experience of sharing before they understand what it is to share experiences, just as they have an experience of others' attention, as a certain kind of affordance for social interaction, before they begin to understand the concept of attention. (Another parallel might be young infants' sense of causal efficacy, which arguably pre-dates their ability to think of themselves as an object and to reflect on their own causal powers. See, for example, Lewis, 2003.)

Suppose this idea of a pre-reflective sense of shared experience can be made good. Then the problem this raises for Hobson's account of joint attention is: How does triadic joint attention differ from earlier mutual attention games in respect of infants' awareness of sharing experiences? As we saw earlier, Tomasello's response to this is that proto-declarative joint attention involves a fully-fledged, explicit awareness of the fact that both participants are attending to the same object. On this view, there are only two models to choose from: on the one hand, young infants' pre-reflective sense of shared experience, and on the other hand, the kind of common knowledge involved in intentional communication. By contrast, Hobson thinks of proto-declarative joint attention as a kind of half-way house between pre-reflective and fully reflective sharing. He suggests that 12-month-olds perceptually 'register' the object-directed attitudes they come to share. For example, in the case of social referencing, where the infant looks to the adult for guidance on how to deal with an unfamiliar object and is naturally 'moved' to adopt the adult's stance towards the object, Hobson thinks that the infant registers or recognizes the caregiver's attitude. This goes beyond pre-reflective sharing, in that infants have the beginnings of an understanding of the shared property, but it falls short of an explicit awareness of the fact that the property is being shared. (On Hobson's account, explicit self-awareness, which would be required to grasp this fact, emerges only towards the end of the second year.)

Hobson's half-way house, it seems to me, is a very attractive position. However, it brings us back to the question of how to characterize 12-month-olds' psychological understanding. And here the problem of doing justice to the qualitative differences between primary intersubjectivity and triadic joint attention resurfaces. A crucial element of Hobson's own account of infants' psychological understanding is his rejection of the idea that awareness of other minds provides a rational basis for infants' response to perceived attitudes.[4] In a social referencing situation, he insists, infants are aware of the caregiver's attitude, but this awareness is not the infant's *reason* for her affective response, or part of her reason. The infant does not infer that the object is kosher from the fact that the caregiver looks unconcerned. The response is generated by a more primitive mechanism—infants are naturally responsive to perceived attitudes. This makes room for Hobson's positive suggestion that coming to share the attitude is part of *what it is* for infants to recognize it in others, which he illustrates thus: 'to perceive a smile as a smile (to take the simplest example) is to respond with feeling, in such a way that

---

[4] In fact, Hobson makes a distinction between 12-month-olds' ability to 'register' others' attitudes and older children's ability to understand attitudes. But I take it that this is best interpreted as a distinction between more or less developed forms of understanding.

through the smile one apprehends the emotional state of the other' (Chapter 9 above, p. 190).

How does appeal to infants' affective response help to clarify the nature of their psychological understanding? In elaborating his proposal, Hobson emphasizes the importance of a (pre-reflective) sense of interpersonal causal relations: 'the child's movement in psychological stance is accompanied by awareness (which may be intermittent) that this is occurring through the child's responsiveness to another person' (Chapter 9, p. 189). But a sceptic might argue that this is not enough to distinguish joint attention from earlier dyadic interactions, and hence not enough to give substance to the intuition that joint attention manifests psychological understanding. To use Hobson's example, responding to a perceived smile 'with feeling' is surely quite a basic phenomenon that need not (and, in the case of 6-month-olds, arguably does not) involve any grasp of psychological concepts or any understanding of the other's emotional state. So what reason, if any, is there for thinking that being responsive, specifically, to other's *object-directed* attitudes involves recognizing, and in some sense understanding, the attitude?

V

I want to suggest that the issue here turns on the following noteworthy feature of proto-declaratives (which Hobson emphasizes, though not in these terms): the project in proto-declarative joint attention is not simply that of reciprocally responding to expressions of emotions, but that of sharing an appreciation of *what the object is like*. Franco and Butterworth (1996) highlight just this feature when they argue that, from its inception, proto-declarative pointing is usually accompanied by some sort of 'comment' on the object. The general idea—that joint attention involves both reference and some kind of predication—goes back to Werner and Kaplan's classic discussion of the 'primordial sharing situation'. One of their claims is that the emergence of triadic joint attention marks a shift from perceiving objects purely as 'things-of-action' to perceiving them as 'objects-of-contemplation' (1963, p. 44). A natural gloss on their use of the term 'contemplation' is the following: to contemplate an object is to attend to it in a particular mode—roughly, with a view to becoming aware of what the object is like, rather than with a view to, say, obtaining or manipulating the object. Werner and Kaplan argue, further, that it is in the context of joint attention that infants acquire the ability to 'contemplate' objects: 'the act of reference emerges not as an individual act, but as a social one: by exchanging things with the Other, by touching things and looking at them with the Other' (1963, p. 43).

How does this proposal bear on the issue of infants' psychological understanding? The most immediate point here is that 'contemplation', whether practised individually or jointly, is an essentially reflective project. This is not to deny that we often engage in the project spontaneously, nor that it is one in which one can lose oneself, with one's attention being wholly absorbed by the perceived scene. To say that the project is essentially reflective is just to make explicit that the project has certain conceptual prerequisites. I take it that the idea of a 'contemplative' stance, as opposed to a purely practical, or immersed, mode of engagement with the world, is not the idea of an absence of activity, but of activities aimed at the acquisition of knowledge, specifically knowledge of the objective world around us. It follows immediately that a subject engaging in the project needs certain conceptual abilities. Most obviously, she needs concepts that may be used in noticing what kinds of features a perceived object has. But arguably, she will also need certain normative and psychological notions. The project of looking to see what an object is like is not just that of getting the answer to some question about the world around one, or even that of getting the *right* answer. It is the project of getting an answer that is manifestly right, where this means something like: you can satisfy yourself that the answer is correct (e.g. by looking). So getting things right is an essential part of the project, and this requires some grasp of the distinction between truth and falsity. It also requires some idea of the kind of state that is being pursued—being aware of what an object is like. This will include some understanding of the conditions that have to be met for someone to enjoy such awareness, where these conditions will in part be specific to particular sensory modalities: to see an object, you need to be placed at a suitable distance from it, with your eyes open, with no object blocking the line of sight, etc. It is important to stress that the involvement of psychological notions here derives from their role in the pursuit of truth and knowledge, not from the role normally emphasized by the theory of mind approach, viz. explanation and prediction of behaviour. Put differently, the concepts are required for knowledge in a completely general sense: not for knowledge of a particular phenomenon, such as the causes of others' behaviour, but for knowledge in general.[5]

At this point two questions arise. First, if we understand the notion of a contemplative stance in this way, is it not too sophisticated to be helpful in interpreting proto-declaratives? Second, supposing it is not, how does the notion cast light on infants' conception of others as subjects of attention (specifically, on the connection between recognizing an attitude and being 'moved' by it)?

A natural worry behind the first question is that the notion of truth is available only as part of a package that includes notions such as those of belief, knowledge, assertion, entailment, and so forth, and that these latter notions are not available to 1-year-olds. But I think we can find a promising response to this worry, or part

---

[5] The distinction I am drawing here has a parallel in the case of the concept of belief. The theory of mind approach emphasizes its role in belief–desire explanations of actions. But there is also what might be called the deliberative role of the concept of belief: the capacity to engage in theoretical deliberation requires a grasp of notions such as belief, truth, and evidence, notions which help to define the goal of deliberation.

of such a response, by looking at the kinds of examples of early shared 'comments' we find in the developmental literature. They tend to concern evaluative features of objects, such as being scary, disgusting, interesting, funny, nice, etc.—features that are closely associated with particular kinds of affective attitudes. One reason why this matters is that it is relatively easy, in these cases, to make sense of the idea of a non-linguistic mode of expressing a comment about an object, through facial and other expressions. But another reason is this. In the case of evaluative features like being scary or funny, it seems impossible to divorce someone's understanding of the feature from her understanding of the corresponding attitude. More precisely, borrowing a formulation from David Wiggins, to understand that an object is scary is to understand that the object is such as to make it appropriate to be afraid of it (Wiggins, 1987). So to grasp what it is for an object to be scary is to have some understanding of the normative relation between the feature and the attitude. But this does not mean that grasping particular evaluative features requires an explicit understanding of general normative concepts such as truth, justification, or appropriateness. The more specific notions may be developmentally more basic. Importantly, they may not require the general idea of a true or false belief.

There are two problems with this response, though. First, if proto-declarative pointing involves not just reference but something like a comment upon the object, then in so far as infants understand the point of the project in which they are engaged—getting right what the object is like—it looks as if they do have some grip on the general distinction between truth and falsity (even if it may initially be put to use primarily in relation to affectively significant features). (See MacNamara, 1986, for a similar argument to the effect that infants' early assertions manifest a grip on the concept of truth.) Then, supposing there are independent reasons to be sceptical about the idea that infants possess the concept of truth, this should perhaps lead us to reconsider the claim that proto-declaratives serve to establish joint contemplation. Second, even if particular pairs of evaluative features and attitudes may in some ways be easier to grasp than the concept of belief, it is far from clear that infants can be credited with an understanding of an inappropriate attitude (say, someone's being afraid of a perfectly harmless object), any more than with an understanding of false beliefs. However, the difficulties here may be more apparent than real. Suppose we accept that proto-declaratives, like assertions, aim at truth. It seems conceivable that infants' understanding of truth is essentially tied to the context of pursuing it. They may be able to engage in truth-directed projects like proto-declarative pointing, and to distinguish a correct answer from an incorrect one, without appreciating the *explanatory* role of false beliefs or inappropriate attitudes—without being able to appeal to such states in making someone's behaviour intelligible (which is what standard false belief tasks test for).

This point bears immediately on the question of how to understand the *point* of early joint attention interactions. Consider Bernard Williams's account of the point of making statements that are 'plainly true' (whose truth is evident both to the speaker and the audience). One function of such statements, Williams writes, is that they 'remind us that we share the same world and find the same things salient, and help us to discover where we do and do not agree' (2002, p. 72). This kind of project may well be too sophisticated for 1-year-olds. To be interested in the extent to which we agree, you need to appreciate that some of my attitudes towards an object may be incorrect (by your lights). So you need to be able to reflect on your own attitude, independently of considering mine, and to become aware of my attitude without thereby coming to share it. Neither of these abilities may be in place at the beginning of the second year. It seems to be consistent with the evidence to suppose that at this early stage infants assume a pre-established harmony between an object's significance and the caregiver's attitude to the object: in cases where they are unable to share the other's attitude, they will also find it difficult to become aware of it. So the point of proto-declaratives may be a more basic one, to be characterized in terms of knowledge rather than belief: infants may be concerned to share their awareness of what things are like (where this will typically involve affective attitudes).

It is sometimes said that young children fail to appreciate the separateness of subjects of experience, that their awareness of mental states involves an undifferentiated 'we', not decomposable into 'I' and 'you'.[6] If this is intended to mean that infants' conception of others' psychological properties is such as to leave no room for any divergence between their own and others' points of view, early joint attention interactions provide straightforward counter-evidence: the whole point of proto-declaratives is to bring someone else's focus of attention in line with one's own. However, on a weaker reading, the undifferentiated 'we' claim may simply be taken to mean that young children initially lack the conceptual prerequisites for understanding disagreements. They may not yet be able to reflect on their own attitudes, as opposed (or at least potentially opposed) to someone else's. Agreement may be the product of infants' natural tendency to share perceived attitudes, rather than of some form of joint deliberation. Note, though, that this weaker reading is consistent with the view that infants do become aware of a co-attender as a subject of experience (individuated in the same way as other physical objects).

Turning now to our second question, how, if at all, might the notion of contemplation help to explain infants' ability to recognize a co-attender's attitudes? Recall the paradox rehearsed in section II: proto-declarative pointing seems to manifest a grasp of a co-attender's focus of attention; yet, given that infants lack the conceptual abilities required for a 'theory of mind', it is not clear what this grasp consists in. The suggestion I extracted from Werner and Kaplan's account of joint attention was that a crucial context in which we exercise psychological concepts is the pursuit of truth and knowledge, where this requires reflective abilities,

---

[6] See e.g. Barresi and Moore, 1996; Merleau-Ponty, 1964.

such as reflecting on whether or not you are aware of something, or which attitude is the correct one to adopt to a particular object. In response to the paradox, then, it might be said that infants' psychological understanding consists in their developing ability to engage in reflective projects such as contemplating perceived objects. But how does that response bear on an explanation of infants' conception of *other minds*? Ordinarily we associate the notion of reflective awareness with the first-person (singular) perspective. How might the development of reflective abilities yield an awareness of a co-attender's mental states?

At this point we need to return to Hobson's proposal that infants' understanding of others' attitudes is grounded on their natural affective responsiveness. If Franco and Butterworth, amongst others, are right about the role of shared comments in proto-declarative joint attention, such responsiveness undergoes a profound change towards the end of the first year. Infants are 'moved' by a caregiver's display of emotions no longer just to feel happy or amused, they are moved to find a particular object interesting or scary or funny: the response has some (perhaps primitive) conceptual content. This is not to say that the response is no longer an exercise of infants' natural capacity to be moved, as Hobson puts it. But it means that the interaction is informed by an interest in the significance of objects in the common environment, with caregivers providing infants with the correct answer to a question. (The answer may resolve uncertainty on the part of the infant, as in a social referencing situation; or it may reinforce her own impression of the object, as when a caregiver echoes a comment expressed by the infant in proto-declarative joint attention.) Now, infants may not be able to challenge others to offer reasons for their claims, but nor is it clear that they come to share others' attitudes merely as a blind reaction, devoid of any understanding of what makes it the right attitude to have. An alternative picture here would be that infants relate to caregivers as to something like an authority: a source, and a potential sharer, of knowledge of what objects are like.[7] Suppose for a moment that this intuition can be made good. Then it is plausible to suppose that infants are no longer aware of the source of their affective response to an object (the caregiver's affective engagement with it) just as an affordance for further mutual engagement; they are aware of it as the right attitude to the object, as an attitude that is appropriate, given the nature of the object. So there are two mutually dependent kinds of interest that inform such interactions: an interest in the significance of the perceived object and an interest in the caregiver's response to the object. Correlatively, there are two kinds of concepts infants begin to grasp when they participate in joint attention: they learn to perceive objects as having certain evaluative features and people as having propositional attitudes directed at objects.

---

[7] Compare the following observation by Philip Rochat: 'it appears that from 9 months of age, infants become explicitly aware of others as potential teachers and informants to solve problems.... In particular, infants construe others as having authority with the power to judge because they know better' (2001, p. 356).

The suggestion might be put by saying that infants' developing understanding of the normative relation between the world and the mind is closely connected with their developing understanding of interpersonal normative relations. Even quite young infants are good at perceiving contingencies between their own and others' contributions in games of mutual attention. What is new about triadic joint attention is that interpersonal causal relations assume a normative significance. A central issue facing this proposal, therefore, concerns the sense in which we may speak of normative relations, or authority, here. A sceptic might take the view that so long as infants are unable to give and ask for reasons, a caregiver's influence over the infant's attitudes will be an exercise of sheer causal power, not of any kind of authority recognized by the infant. Indeed, what might such recognition consist in, in the absence of a fully developed normative vocabulary? Without pretending to be able to do justice here to the complex issues raised by this question, I want to make one brief comment. If I understand the developmental work correctly, the early stages of triadic joint attention show an interesting kind of role reversal: infants begin by being moved to adopt a caregiver's attitude to an object, but after a few weeks they will also be able to take a more active role, actively pointing and expressing comments about objects, and thereby moving the caregiver to share *their* attitude. Infants seem increasingly able to single out interesting objects, and to expect the caregiver to share the relevant attitude to them. So, from an early stage, the relationship is a *reciprocal* one, and this implies that infants conceive of others' attitudes not only as a standard to follow, but also as answerable to the standard set by the nature of objects. It is not as if, for the infant, the correct response just is whatever response the caregiver displays. (If this were the case, one might well question whether infants have a genuine grasp of the distinction between correctness and incorrectness at all.) Rather, what the capacity for role reversal suggests is that infants begin to appreciate that the caregiver to whom they are responsive is herself responsive to the world, as seen by the infant.

It might be said that since proto-declarative communication tends to be about plain truths in Williams's sense, truths that are plain for both participants to see, the issue of trust and authority does not in fact arise. The case of social referencing may be sufficient to refute this claim: in such situations infants look to a caregiver for an appraisal of a perceived object precisely because it is not obvious to them what the object is like (e.g. whether it is safe to explore). But the claim also overlooks the possibility that some truths may *become* plain ones for the infant in virtue of her coming to share the caregiver's attitude. (Recall Iris Murdoch's remark that joint attention may enable us to 'see more'.) This is not only so in the sense that joint attention may prompt an infant to notice or realize something about an object that she failed to notice (but could have noticed) on her own. Joint attention may also be a mechanism for the transmission of new concepts; it may enable infants to notice new aspects, or new kinds of evaluative features, of an object. And of course it provides the context in which infants acquire much of their early vocabulary. Some recognition of a caregiver's authority, then, is involved even in the case of proto-declarative joint attention.

VI

The suggestion I have been pursuing is that an early form of psychological understanding may consist in the ability to recognize pairs of evaluative features and affective attitudes in the context of sharing an appreciation of such features, rather than in the ability to explain someone's behaviour in terms of their mental states. The suggestion raises a number of specific developmental issues which would require a more detailed treatment than I can offer (most importantly, issues concerning infants' sense of interpersonal causal relations and their understanding of authority). But there is also a more general problem. It is easy to feel that, however it is spelled out in detail, the very idea that infants' psychological understanding is constitutively related to their interaction with others must be misguided. The idea seems to give rise to a dilemma. Either one's participation in the joint project is a rational action, or it is not. If it is rational, then it must be informed by a *prior* understanding that the other participant is a subject of conscious mental states, and that she is aware of, and shares, my desire for us to engage in the joint project. This suggests that rational social interaction presupposes, and hence cannot constitute, psychological understanding. On the other hand, if infants' participation in the interaction is merely an automatic, natural response to a perceived affordance, rather than being informed by practical reasons, then it is hard to see how it can contribute to an explanation of infants' grasp of other minds.

The problem with this line of objection is that the blanket notion of rational action is liable to muddy some important issues. Suppose that for an action to be rational, at least in the basic sense relevant here, is for it to be intentional, i.e. to be informed by a belief as to how to achieve a particular objective. It is a familiar point in the philosophy of action that a particular action may be intentional under one description but not under another. You may intentionally make a witty remark and thereby unintentionally drop a clanger. So the idea that infants' participation in joint attention is intentional prompts the question: under which description?—which in turn should lead us to ask: which beliefs make it rational? Now, one suggestion might be that infants' participation in joint attention is intentional in the sense that they wish to share attention with another subject of mental states, and believe that the caregiver is such a subject. As adults, we are seldom confronted with the question of whether or not a particular human being is a subject of mental states, but some psychologists take the task facing new-borns to be precisely that of working out that others are subjects, that 'those entities are like me' (Meltzoff *et al.*, 1999; see also Tomasello, 1999). On this view, it would be natural to suggest that once infants have acquired the belief that certain entities have mental states, their very participation in social interaction with others becomes intentional in a sense in which it was not when they were lacking that belief.

It is not obvious, however, that infants'—or indeed anybody's—participation in social interaction is intentional in this sense. For one thing, it is not clear that anyone, apart from professional psychologists and philosophers, holds the general belief that others are subjects of mental states. And it is arguable, anyhow, that this belief is no one's reason for engaging in interpersonal activities. The question of whether or not to participate in social interaction at all is not a genuine issue for adults, let alone infants. One suggestion here might be that we would do well to think of our participation in social interaction as analogous to our belief in the existence of mind-independent objects, of which Hume observed, 'nature has not left this to his [the sceptic's] choice, and has doubtless esteemed it an affair of too great importance to be trusted to our uncertain reasonings and speculations' (1978, p. 187).[8]

In any case, there is an alternative account of what makes infants' social interaction intentional. On this account, their engagement with others is intentional in so far as it involves specific intentional actions—for example, looking to a caregiver to see what she makes of an unfamiliar toy, or pointing at something to direct the caregiver's attention to it. What make the actions intentional, under these descriptions, are specific beliefs about other people—say, the belief that the caregiver knows whether the object poses any danger, or the belief that pointing is a way of attracting her attention to an object. (The claim that proto-declarative pointing is intentional in this way is of course the upshot of the basic argument for a rich interpretation of proto-declaratives: see section II above.) Then the question is: How do infants acquire such beliefs? And how, if at all, might appeal to social interaction help to answer this question?

One thing that is clear is that if infants' conception of others as subjects of mental states is based on some kind of analogical reasoning, then the role of intersubjective engagement is bound to be strictly limited. Compare Meltzoff and Moore's suggestion that realizing that one's actions are being imitated by someone else provides 'grounds for an important realization by the infant: "I intend to produce these acts, the adult performs these same acts, they are not chance events; therefore, the adult intends his acts" ' (1995, p. 89). On this view, understanding how infants come to think of others as subjects of intentions requires giving an account of the evidence on the basis of which infants ascribe intentions to others. Social interaction (specifically, on Meltzoff's account, caregivers' imitation of infants' behaviour) matters in so far as it provides such evidence, but it does not play any constitutive role in relation to infants' grasp of psychological concepts.

---

[8] See Strawson, 1985, for a detailed discussion of the naturalist approach, as applied to both knowledge of the external world and knowledge of other minds.

What is assumed here is that infants know what intentional action is from their own case; the task facing an infant is to extend the concept to the case of entities whose intentions and experiences are not manifest to her from the first-person perspective. Given this description of the situation, the general belief that others are 'like me' in being subjects of intentions or attention has some real work to do. Infants need to get their heads round this general point before they can form specific beliefs about other people's perspectives.

But suppose we are sceptical both about the idea that analogical reasoning can provide a rational basis for the belief in the existence of other minds and about the possibility of acquiring knowledge of what it is to have a given psychological property 'from one's own case'. Then we may find the following picture an attractive alternative: infants begin to think of others as subjects of experience by acquiring specific perceptual beliefs about their attitudes—they learn to see and hear, for example, what others are attending to or what they feel about perceived objects. So the task facing developmental psychologists is not that of mapping the kinds of evidence on the basis of which infants attribute mental states to others, but that of giving an account of the way in which infants' perceptual experience becomes imbued with psychological concepts. It is here that social interaction may have a constitutive role to play. Thus the suggestion of the previous section was that the ability to perceive what someone else feels about an object emerges as part of the ability to engage in a simple kind of conversation about objects. Of course, in so far as we are talking about an intentional activity here, it is intentional in virtue of infants' beliefs about others' attitudes. (We may also be appealing to various pre-intentional aspects of the interaction, aspects that may be purely affordance-driven; but for current purposes it is the intentional aspects that matter.) So it might be said that there is a risk of circularity: infants' beliefs about others' attitudes are supposed to be constitutively linked to social interaction, yet the intentions informing the social interaction depend on those very beliefs. However, it is not clear that the circle here must be a vicious one. Instead, we may adopt the view that intentional social interaction and psychological understanding are mutually dependent. Proto-declarative pointing may be intentional in virtue of infants' beliefs about caregiver's focus of attention and their attitudes; at the same time, infants' grasp of these properties constitutively involves the capacity for (and an interest in) shared contemplation.

We can clarify the point by distinguishing between two aspects of the causal role of a psychological property. (See Campbell, 2002, pp. 175–6.) On the one hand, there is the intra-personal causal role of the property, the patterns of causal relations between it and other properties of the same individual, including her actions. On the other hand, there is its interpersonal causal role, the way it affects other individuals. On one view, grasping a psychological property is primarily a matter of understanding its intra-personal causal role. This is the view that underpins the theory of mind approach. In contrast, on Hobson's view, what is foundational for psychological understanding is infants' sense of interpersonal causal relations, of the way in which participants in joint attention affect each other's attention and attitudes. More precisely, the idea is that infants' sense of interpersonal causal relations, and hence their psychological understanding, is inseparable from their own engagement in social interaction—psychological understanding is simply not available from the point of view of detached observation and explanation. It is this idea that provides a clear rationale for the mutual dependence view: it suggests that the transformation of purely affordance-driven social interaction into joint activities that are intentional under certain descriptions, on the one hand, and the development of psychological understanding, on the other, are two sides of the same coin.

VII

How does this whole discussion bear on the case of mature psychological concepts and knowledge? I have argued that the ability to explain someone else's behaviour in terms of their psychological properties is not a (developmentally) fundamental element of our conception of other minds. What is fundamental is the ability to share attention and attitudes. But it might be said that while this may be so, it tells us little about knowledge of other minds in the case of adults. The difference between the two cases may be precisely that, with the emergence of mature psychological concepts, social interaction ceases to play any constitutive role; mature knowledge of other minds rests on inference to the best explanation. The opposite view would be that it is illuminating to think of mature psychological understanding as a descendant of the more basic form. I want to end with some (sketchy and programmatic) remarks on this latter view.

We can distinguish two aspects of the development of increasingly sophisticated psychological concepts over the first few years. On the one hand, there is a growing sophistication in children's capacity for sharing attitudes. Thus, in their joint attention interactions children become increasingly sensitive to differences in the spatial perspectives of the two participants. For example, they become progressively better at taking into account what can and cannot be seen from the caregiver's point of view, and they learn to show objects in a non-egocentric way (in a way that makes it impossible to see the object from one's own point of view). Again, with the emergence of linguistic communication the repertoire of attitudes that can be shared expands rapidly, as regards both the content and the type of shared attitudes. Eventually, sharing attitudes can take the form of offering reasons in trying to convince someone of one's own beliefs or the merits of one's projects. On the other hand, we can describe the developmental trajectory in terms of the increasing range of psychological properties that children begin to understand, and the increasingly subtle nature of their understanding. One suggestion, in line with the argument of the previous section, would be that the two developments are inseparable, in the sense that, in explaining children's grasp of more complex psychological properties, we need to advert to advances in their capacity for sharing attitudes. So it is not that increasing sophistication in psychological understanding causally explains progress in social interaction. At least in some central respects, the latter is partly constitutive of the former.

There is no room here to explore in detail how this approach might deal with particular psychological concepts. (See Chapter 12 below for an illuminating discussion of the case of episodic memory.) Instead, I will consider some general epistemological issues raised by the inseparability claim.

Suppose we accept that infants' natural responsiveness to perceived attitudes, together with their emerging capacity for (joint) contemplation, enables them to perceive a co-attender's attitude to an object, or, in Murdoch's phrase, to see what she is seeing. The question is whether this ability can survive the numerous and major alterations in their conceptual abilities that take place over the following years. On the face of it, it is hard to see how it can, given that, certainly by the end of this development, the close connection between becoming aware of others' attitudes and coming to share them seems to be broken: we have no difficulty understanding utterances as expressive of beliefs, even if we regard the beliefs as false or the utterances as insincere. So it looks as if the capacity to be 'moved' by perceived expressions of attitudes can no longer play any significant role in our explanation of knowledge of other minds.

A striking statement of this version of the problem of other minds is to be found in Jean Starobinski's analysis of an incident in Rousseau's childhood, related near the beginning of the *Confessions*. Rousseau was accused of breaking a comb, and his (as he tells us) sincere and true denial was not believed. Commenting on the intense and enduring anguish this event caused Rousseau, Starobinski writes: 'From that moment, paradise was lost, since paradise was the reciprocal transparency of consciousnesses, a total and confident communication between them.'[9] The significance of this incident for Rousseau, or at least the significance he later read into it, may be compared with that of the argument from illusion in the case of knowledge of the external world. In both cases, the most immediate effect is to make direct, non-inferential knowledge seem impossible, which in turn gives rise to doubts as to the possibility even of inferential knowledge of the facts in question. (Starobinski speaks of a 'moment of crisis in which the "veil" of separation is lowered...in which minds become opaque to one another and mistrust makes friendship impossible' (1988, p. 11).)

One line to take here would be to accept that, post-paradise, mutual transparency is no longer available, but to insist that there are sound inferences that provide a basis for knowledge of other minds. Communication may be viewed as

---

[9] Quoted (in Williams' own translation) in Williams, 2002, p. 174.

a matter of producing stimuli that allow the hearer to make such inferences (Sperber and Wilson, 1995). But it might be said that this is mistaken in the same way that the rejection of direct realism is a mistaken response to the argument from illusion. Communication may continue to render consciousnesses mutually transparent, even when it is understood that informants can be unreliable or insincere. The important point here is that we should not let cases of illusion or mistrust dictate the terms in which we describe the basic case. Rather, it may turn out that these cases are in some sense parasitic on the basic case of mutual transparency—the abilities involved in dysfunctional communication may rely on the more fundamental capacity for sharing attitudes.

In 'Meaning, communication, and knowledge', McDowell defends a conception of communication that seems to answer to this general description. Interestingly, central to McDowell's account of the basic case is a story about the way in which mature linguistic communication has developed from a more primitive form of communicative behaviour. Briefly, the idea is that at the primitive level, communicative behaviour serves simply to transmit information, without expressing any propositional attitudes. Examples include instinctive communicative behaviour in non-human animals (e.g. 'a bird might instinctively emit a characteristic sort of squawk on seeing a predator'), but also the communicative repertoire of children in the early stages of language learning, described as 'a matter of something like a conditioned reflex'. Although communication in this sense does not impart knowledge (or any other propositional attitudes), it does amount to 'a further mode of sensitivity to the presence of [for example] predators, over and above more direct kinds of perception' (1998, pp. 40, 47). McDowell's central claim is that '(i)t is plausible that the assertoric core of linguistic behaviour is a descendant, now under intentional control, of the sort of instinctive communicative repertoire we have been considering' (p. 45). One thing this means is that, in the right circumstances, assertions, just like the primitive communicative behaviours from which they descend, constitute 'cognitive stand-ins for the state of affairs that they represent' (p. 46). In this way, McDowell aims to show how communication can be an immediate *sharing of knowledge*, rather than a matter of providing evidence of one's beliefs. Of course, the audience may decide not to accept an assertion; they may treat it as merely expressive of belief. But McDowell's claim is that this ability is parasitic on the more basic role of assertions: 'their antecedent capacity to represent reality is what makes them capable of expressing beliefs' (p. 48).

As is clear from many chapters in this volume, McDowell's description of communication in the early stages of language learning as a conditioned response will be contested by many psychologists. But this in itself need not undermine the explanatory value of McDowell's developmental story. A fictional genealogy may potentially yield real illumination. (See Williams, 2002.) A more serious worry is that, given the vast distance between the primitive and the mature case, it is not entirely clear how the latter may have retained some of the essential features of the former. But I want to focus on a more specific point. It seems to me that McDowell's account of how communication transmits knowledge is unsatisfactory in a crucial respect. The genealogy is intended to flesh out the idea that hearing someone assert that *p* may be a source of knowledge that *p*, and that this cannot always be explained in terms of the hearer's ability to draw an inference from the speaker's supposed reliability and sincerity to the truth of her assertion. I take it that the idea has much appeal, both intuitive and theoretical. And it seems indeed to be inconsistent with the Gricean picture that McDowell rejects, on which assertoric communication yields, most immediately, beliefs about the speaker's beliefs, rather than about the subject-matter of her beliefs. However, McDowell's explanation of knowledge by testimony appears to divorce such knowledge from knowledge of the informant's mind altogether. What is supposed to make such knowledge possible is a feature that assertions have inherited from primitive communicative behaviour, viz. that they serve as 'cognitive stand-ins for the state of affairs that they represent'. But surely what is distinctive of knowledge by testimony is that it involves coming to know that *p* by becoming aware *of the informant's knowledge* that *p*. Appeal to the primitive case, as conceived by McDowell, provides no help in understanding this essential link between testimony and knowledge of other minds.

It is at this point that I think a genealogy that takes proto-declarative joint attention as its starting-point may be more illuminating. In one respect, of course, this resembles the starting-point of McDowell's account: just like his primitive communicative behaviour, proto-declaratives precede an understanding of the fact that informants may not be trustworthy. One significant difference is that while McDowell's primitive communication involves the transmission of information that is not perceptually available to the receiver, the subject-matter of proto-declarative communication tends to be truths that are plain to both participants (though, as I suggested earlier, joint attention may be an important factor in making the relevant truths plain to infants). But the most profound difference is that there is a sense in which infants *comprehend* what is being communicated (as McDowell's birds do not). On the kind of picture discussed earlier, their comprehension is initially quite limited. It consists of two things: (a) infants come to share the caregiver's affective attitude to a common object, where this shows some rudimentary grasp of the evaluative features that are being jointly contemplated; (b) they are aware of the caregiver's attitude, as the attitude that matches, or is made appropriate by, the relevant feature.

To get the genealogy going, I want to enrich this picture, though, to begin with, only very slightly. Consider a stage in development at which infants have sufficient linguistic abilities to comprehend assertions not only of plain truths, but of (currently) unobservable truths as well. We may also suppose that they understand communicative intentions—for example, the intention to let someone know something—and that they show signs of being able to think of themselves as an object with the use the first person. I suggest that these developments do not compel us to make any fundamental change in our explanation of infants' comprehension. Rather, their comprehension of assertions may be seen as a development of their natural capacity to be moved by perceived attitudes: what they have acquired is the ability to be moved by an assertion in a certain way—namely, to come to share the belief expressed by it. Correlatively, they perceive the assertion as an expression of knowledge on the part of their informant—just as before, the interaction is informed by a basic form of trust in the authority of caregivers. (While their conception of knowledge may be primitive in certain ways, it will include the idea that knowledge is the norm that governs assertions.) Again, in being aware of being moved by someone else's assertion, infants may become aware of the informant's intention to share her knowledge, and go on to form similar intentions themselves. The important point is that these forms of comprehension are based on, rather than providing a basis for, the hearer's coming to share the attitude that is being communicated. There is a basic link between comprehension and trust here. The hearer's understanding of assertions is correlative with her acceptance of the authority of her informants. That trust does not have any rational basis, though it may be sustained by various forms of reciprocal interaction between caregiver and infant.

Let us now fast-forward to the stage where children have taken on board the fact that beliefs can be false and utterances insincere. One thing they will now be able to do is comprehend an assertion without adopting the belief expressed by it. So, it might be said, the 'veil of separation' has fallen—the passage of attitudes from one mind to another is no longer a matter of the natural capacity to be moved by perceived expressions of attitudes, but has to be explained in terms of the hearer's reasons for accepting the speaker's testimony. Connectedly, this natural capacity can no longer play any part in explaining knowledge of other minds, which will now have to be based on inference to the best explanation. But I want to suggest that these conclusions do not follow at all. An alternative account would be this. What children learn when they acquire the capacity for comprehension without sharing is a new way of using their ability to be moved by assertions. A perceived assertion that p will still engender the thought that p (supposing of course that the right language is used and the relevant concepts are in place); only children are now able to resist being saddled with the belief that p, by prefixing this thought with the concept 'she believes that...', or 'she is telling me that...'. In this way, they may exploit their earlier capacity for receiving knowledge by testimony in a new way, enabling them to become aware of (potentially false) beliefs or (potentially mendacious) communicative intentions.

This account will not, and is not intended to, convert a determined sceptic who thinks we never have reason to trust others' reliability and sincerity. The most immediate point is simply that it is a mistake to assume that once children understand these things, the basic case to focus on in giving an account of comprehending assertions is the case of comprehension without sharing. On the contrary, our account of that case may have to appeal to the more basic ability to comprehend assertions by coming to share the beliefs expressed by them. But it is natural to combine this point with the view that assertions may transmit knowledge directly, in a way that does not rely on the hearer's being in a position to infer the truth of what she is being told from her informant's trustworthiness. Such inferences are required only if the hearer has a good reason not to take an assertion at face value; in that case (but only in that case) the hearer has no choice but to prefix the attitude communicated to her in the ways suggested earlier.[10] Correlatively, unless there is reason for doubt, assertoric communication remains a source of direct knowledge of what the speaker knows.[11]

REFERENCES

BALDWIN, D., and BAIRD, J. (1999), 'Action analysis: a gateway to intentional inference', in P. Rochat (ed.), *Early Social Cognition*. Mahwah, NJ: Erlbaum, 215–40.

BARON-COHEN, S. (1995), 'The eye direction detector (EDD) and the shared attention mechanism (SAM): two cases for evolutionary psychology', in C. Moore and P. J. Dunham (eds.), *Joint Attention: Origins and Role in Development*. Hillsdale, NJ: Erlbaum, 41–59.

BARRESI, J., and MOORE, C. (1996), 'Intentional relations and social understanding', *Behavioral and Brain Sciences*, 19: 107–54.

BRETHERTON, I. (1991), 'Intentional communication and the development of an understanding of mind', in D. Frye and C. Moore (eds.), *Children's Theories of Mind*. Hillsdale, NJ: Erlbaum, 49–75.

BURGE, T. (1993), 'Content preservation', *Philosophical Review*, 102: 457–88.

CAMPBELL, J. (2002), *Reference and Consciousness*. Oxford: Clarendon Press.

CORKUM, V., and MOORE, C. (1995), 'Development of joint visual attention in infants', in C. Moore and P. J. Dunham (eds.), *Joint Attention: Origins and Role in Development*. Hillsdale, NJ: Erlbaum, 61–83.

FRANCO, F., and BUTTERWORTH, G. (1996), 'Pointing and social awareness: declaring and requesting in the second year', *Journal of Child Language*, 23: 307–36.

GOPNIK, A., and MELTZOFF, A. (1997), *Words, Thoughts, and Theories*. Cambridge, Mass.: MIT Press.

GRICE, P. (1989), 'Meaning revisited', in his *Studies in the Way of Words*. Cambridge, Mass.: Harvard University Press, 283–303.

HOBSON, P. (2002), *The Cradle of Thought*. London: Macmillan.

HUME, D. (1978), *A Treatise of Human Nature*, ed. L. A. Selby-Bigge. Oxford: Clarendon Press.

[10] This is a way of putting Tyler Burge's 'Acceptance Principle': 'A person is entitled to accept as true something that is presented as true and that is intelligible to him, unless there are stronger reasons not to do so' (1993, p. 467).

[11] Many thanks to Naomi Eilan, Christoph Hoerl and Teresa McCormack for their extremely helpful comments on a previous version of this chapter.

KANT, I. (1929), *Critique of Pure Reason*, Trans. Norman Kemp Smith. London: Macmillan.

LEWIS, M. (2003), 'The development of self-consciousness', in J. Roessler and N. Eilan (eds.), *Agency and Self-Awareness*. Oxford: Oxford University Press, 275–95.

MACNAMARA, J. (1986), *A Border Dispute: The Place of Logic in Psychology*. Cambridge, Mass.: MIT Press.

McDOWELL, J. (1998), 'Meaning, communication, and knowledge', in his *Meaning, Knowledge, and Reality*. Cambridge, Mass.: Harvard University Press, 29–50.

MELTZOFF, A. and MOORE, K. (1995), 'A theory of the role of imitation in the emergence of self', in P. Rochat (ed.), *The Self in Early Infancy*. New York: Elsevier, 73–93.

—— GOPNIK, A., and REPACHOLI, B. (1999), 'Toddlers' understanding of intentions, desires, and emotions: explorations of the dark ages', in P. Rochat (ed.), *Early Social Cognition*. Mahwah, NJ: Erlbaum, 17–41.

MERLEAU-PONTY, M. (1964), 'The child's relations with others', in his *The Primacy of Perception*, ed. J. Edie. Evanston, Ill.: Northwestern University Press, 96–155.

MURDOCH, I. (1970), 'The idea of perfection', in her *The Sovereignty of Good*. London and New York: Routledge, 1–45.

PERNER, J. (1991), *Understanding the Representational Mind*. Cambridge, Mass.: MIT Press.

ROCHAT, P. (2001), 'Social contingency detection and infant development', *Bulletin of the Menninger Clinic*, 65: 347–60.

—— and STRIANO, T. (1999), 'Social-cognitive development in the first year', in P. Rochat (ed.), *Early Social Cognition*. Mahwah, NJ: Erlbaum, 3–34.

SCHÜTZ, A. (1997), *The Phenomenology of the Social World*. Evanston, Ill.: Northwestern University Press (orig. pub. in 1932).

SPERBER, D., and WILSON, D. (1995), *Relevance: Communication and Cognition*, 2nd edn. Oxford: Blackwell.

STAROBINSKI, J. (1988), *Jean-Jacques Rouseau: Transparency and Obstruction*. Chicago and London: University of Chicago Press.

STRAWSON, P. (1985), *Scepticism and Naturalism: Some Varieties*. London: Methuen.

—— (1992), *Analysis and Metaphysics*. Oxford: Oxford University Press.

TOMASELLO, M. (1999), *The Cultural Origins of Human Cognition*. Cambridge, Mass.: Harvard University Press.

TREVARTHEN, C. (1993), 'The self born in intersubjectivity: the psychology of an infant communicating', in U. Neisser (ed.), *The Self Perceived*. Cambridge: Cambridge University Press, 121–73.

WERNER, H., and KAPLAN, B. (1963), *Symbol Formation*. New York: Wiley.

WIGGINS, D. (1987), 'A sensible subjectivism?', in his *Needs, Values, Truth*. Oxford: Blackwell, 185–214.

WILLIAMS, B. (2002), *Truth and Truthfulness*. Princeton: Princeton University Press.

WITTGENSTEIN, L. (1969), *On Certainty*, ed. G. E. M. Anscombe and G. H. von Wright. Oxford: Blackwell.

12

Joint Reminiscing as Joint Attention to the Past

Christoph Hoerl and *Teresa McCormack*

The other chapters in this volume are concerned primarily with the phenomenon of children and adults jointly attending to physical objects in the visual field, and address important issues regarding the developmental significance of joint attention, understood in this sense. In this chapter, we are concerned with a phenomenon that has traditionally been considered quite independently of this body of research—joint reminiscing, or memory sharing. Our aim is to show how the general notion of joint attention can also be applied to the case of joint reminiscing, and that characterizing joint reminiscing as joint attention to the past, and spelling out the implications of such a characterization, provides us with a way of shedding light on its developmental significance.

There is clearly some intuitive appeal in the idea that, when two people are engaged in sharing memories of an incident they have experienced together, that past incident becomes the focus of their joint attention, much in the same way as an object in the current environment could become the focus of their joint attention through their looking at that object together. This way of putting things, however, may be thought to mask a crucial difference. On the face of it, the terms 'memory sharing' or 'joint reminiscing' stand for an activity that necessarily involves the use of a shared language. More specifically, it seems that it is only the existence of certain linguistic devices, such as the past tense, that makes it possible for two people to jointly focus attention, not just on aspects of their current environment, but also on past events and circumstances.

A central theme in the literature on joint attention is the idea that certain kinds of joint attentional abilities can be seen as precursors to linguistic abilities. The idea that language, and the existence of certain linguistic devices, can, in turn, make available other, more sophisticated, forms of joint attention has received less discussion. Indeed, the latter idea might be seen to raise a puzzle for developmentalists. For how is it that children come to grasp the meaning of these linguistic devices? How, for instance, do children come to understand the specific nature of the contribution the past tense makes to the meaning of a sentence? Consider the following passage from Elizabeth Anscombe:

> It seems possible to show someone what to mean when one wants him to say 'red' with meaning, but impossible to show him what to mean by 'was red'; for how does one get his attention directed to what he is to speak of? When one has to teach 'red' one can at least

ensure that the learner's eyes are looking in the right direction; and one would not expect to be able to teach him except on this condition. But if one is to teach the use of the past tense, then there is...nothing in him to direct in the hope of directing the attention, as in the other case it was possible to direct the eyes. Yet it seems that a necessary condition of his being able to grasp the meaning of 'there was red' *is* his attending to the right thing. (Anscombe, 1981, p. 105)

We might get a better grip on the point Anscombe is getting at in this passage by considering a particular approach to language development championed, for instance, by Michael Tomasello (1999). The background idea informing this approach is that linguistic exchange, in general, is a matter of securing and sustaining joint attention (cf. also Campbell, 1998; Heal, Chapter 2 above). Thus, basically, what children learn when they come to grasp the meaning of a new piece of language is how this piece of language can be used as a means of achieving joint attention to a certain aspect of the world. The key proposal is that children are initiated into this use in the context of adult–child interactions in which joint attention to the relevant aspects of the world can already be achieved through other means. As Tomasello (1999, p. 109) puts it, 'the child acquires the conventional use of a linguistic symbol by learning to participate in an interactive format...that she understands first nonlinguistically, so that the adult's language can be grounded in shared experiences whose social significance she already appreciates.'

One way of understanding Anscombe's point is in terms of the claim that this picture of language acquisition cannot be used to explain how children come to grasp the meaning of the past tense. Put crudely, one sense in which it seems 'impossible to show [a child] what to mean by "was red"' is that there is no way of establishing a shared attentional focus on particular past events that can ground the child's understanding other than by using past-tensed expressions in the first place. In other words, in learning the meaning of the past tense, children are not simply learning a new means of securing and sustaining a kind of joint attention that they already have an independent purchase on. Rather, how children learn to participate in interactions involving a joint attentional focus on past events and how they come to grasp the meaning of the past tense are two aspects of the same developmental question.

There is, however, also a further, more radical claim that is perhaps hinted at in the passage we have quoted from Anscombe. There is a more fundamental sense in which it might be 'impossible to show [a child] what to mean by "was red"', if, prior to the emergence of a grasp of the meaning of the past tense and the capacity to talk about the past with others, children are simply unable to turn their attention away from the present, so to speak, and focus it on particular past events and circumstances instead. In other words, the more radical claim that Anscombe might have in mind is that the very ability to make the past a possible focus of one's attention—to have one's mind 'looking in the right direction' (Anscombe, 1981, p. 105) in the first place—only emerges in the context of learning how to participate in linguistic interactions that involve the sharing of such attention to the past with others.

The bulk of this chapter will be taken up with an attempt to articulate one way in which this claim might be fleshed out. If it can be made good, as we believe that it can, it indicates a deep connection between a particular aspect of memory development, on the one hand, and a particular aspect of socio-communicative development, on the other.

As we will put it, our suggestion is that participation in joint reminiscing has a key role to play in the development of what Endel Tulving (1972, 1983) has called *episodic memory*. In the first half of this chapter, we will argue that what is needed to explain the difference between episodic memory and other forms of memory is precisely the idea that episodic recall, uniquely, involves turning one's attention to the past. In order to give substance to this idea, we will draw on work on perceptual attention to arrive at a general characterization of the role of attention that can also be put to work in giving an account of episodic recall. A key claim here will be that perceptual attention is the mechanism by which certain kinds of cognitive capacities can have an influence on the way in which information is processed in perception. We will argue that, for episodic recall to occur, information retained from past events must similarly be processed in a specific way, informed by certain kinds of cognitive capacities. This, we will suggest, can explain a sense in which episodic recall, uniquely, involves making particular past events the focus of one's attention.

It is by considering in detail the way in which certain kinds of interactions with others can turn on the sharing of such attention to the past that we will then, in the second half of the chapter, try to clarify the idea that joint reminiscing plays a crucial role in the development of episodic memory. Our strategy will be to focus on one specific kind of cognitive capacity underpinning the ability to turn one's attention to the past in episodic recall, possession of which is, roughly speaking, a matter of grasping the way in which causality unfolds over time. Put briefly, we will argue that, in order to give substance to the distinction between the past and the present, children need to grasp the idea that how things are in the present depends not just on what happened at one point in the past, but also on what happened subsequently. We will also suggest, however, that children first grasp this idea in the context of conversations in which an adult is trying to exert some rational influence on the child by reminding her of specific past events. In other words, our key developmental claim will be that the ability to attend to the past in episodic recall recruits a certain type of causal understanding, and that children acquire this type of causal understanding in the context of learning how to participate in a particular kind of rational engagement with others that turns on the sharing of episodic memories.

To illustrate the nature of the argument we will put forward, it might help to consider one particular way of drawing an analogy between joint reminiscing and joint visual attention. Much existing work on the latter is concerned with articulating what is being seen as an important difference between genuine joint attention and other, more primitive types of behaviour, such as following the other's gaze merely because it might serve as a clue to the location of a desirable object, or as a means to predict the other's behaviour in a competitive situation (see e.g. Call and Tomasello, Chapter 3 above). Two claims, in particular, can be found in the literature that aim to bring out why such behaviour falls short of joint attention. The first is the claim that joint attention turns on what Werner and Kaplan (1963, p. 43) call the shared *contemplation* of objects (see also Franco, Chapter 7 above). The second is the claim that, in joint attention, such shared contemplation is the vehicle for a type of interaction that is essentially *mutual* or *social* in nature (see e.g. the passage we have quoted from Tomasello, above; or Hobson, Chapter 9 above). Adopting a phrase used by Bates, Camaioni, and Volterra (1976, p. 59), we might summarize these two claims by saying that participating in joint attention is a matter of '[using] objects as a means to the [other]', where the key contrast is with ways of engaging with objects, and with other people, that are governed by purely individual, and purely practical, concerns.

Part of what we want to show is how similar considerations can be applied in giving an account of the nature and development of joint reminiscing. The type of remembering that is shared in joint reminiscing—i.e. episodic remembering—might also be said to involve an element of contemplation, in that it is concerned with what happened in the past in its own right. As we will show, this can be contrasted with a more primitive kind of remembering in which the significance of information retrieved from memory is exhausted by its capacity to yield expectations about the current environment. At the same time, however, we will also try to show how the sharing of episodic memories in joint reminiscing can serve as the vehicle for a specific type of social-communicative interaction that would not be possible in the absence of episodic memories. Adopting Bates *et al.*'s terminology, the general idea is that, as children learn to participate in joint reminiscing, they learn how to use not just particular objects in the current environment, but also particular past events as a distinctive kind of 'means to the other'. Thus, just as in the case of joint attention, giving an accurate account of joint reminiscing requires spelling out the distinctive form of engagement, both with the world (here the past) and with others, it involves. Our suggestion will be that, by doing so, we might also get a better grip on the suggestion that joint reminiscing in fact provides the first context in which children exercise the capacity to attend to the past in episodic recall.

1. EPISODIC RECALL AS AN ATTENTIONAL PHENOMENON

Whilst the term 'episodic memory', first introduced by Tulving (1972), is widely used in current psychological literature, there is a great deal of disagreement over the precise nature of the difference between episodic memory and other forms of memory—so much so, in fact, that the usefulness of the distinction is sometimes called into question (see e.g. Tulving, 2002, for a review). In this section, we want to make a proposal that, in our view, has the potential to dissolve some of the existing disagreement by framing the question as to what makes episodic memory distinctive in a new way. We want to argue that it is useful to think of the difference between episodic memory and other forms of memory in terms of a distinct way in which attention is deployed in episodic recall. In other words, episodic recall uniquely involves the exercise of a particular form of attention, which might be described as attention to particular past events.

Consider the following example, adapted from Alfred Ayer (1956) and Gareth Evans (1982; see also Campbell, 2001). Suppose that a friend tries to remind you of an incident in your past of which she was a witness. As Ayer points out, you need not be in any doubt that the incident occurred; in fact, you might even form an accurate mental image of it. Even so, it is still possible that you cannot get yourself to remember the incident. Suppose also, however, that after a while, the incident does come back to you. This may happen quite suddenly, 'in a flash of recollection', as Evans (1982, p. 308) puts it. The question now is: How should we describe what has happened to you—i.e. what this change in your state amounts to?

Evans thinks that the change at issue can be described as a change in the causal history of your state. As he puts it, the relevant state of recollection only sets in once 'the *right* information is retrieved' (ibid.)—i.e. information that traces back to your own experience of the incident. On closer inspection, however, it is not obvious that your failure to recollect must imply the absence of a causal connection between your present mental state and your past experience, as this suggests. As the literature on priming brings out, there are a number of ways in which particular past experiences can have a causal influence on a person's subsequent mental state in the absence of conscious recollection (cf. e.g. Mayes, 2001, for examples). Thus, it is not clear why we should rule out the possibility that your friend's attempts to jog your memory succeeded in activating information retained from your experience of the incident, even before the flash of recollection occurred. Indeed, such information might play a part in explaining your ability to form an accurate mental image, say, of the location and people involved.

By way of developing a possible alternative to, or modification of, Evans's account of recollection, it might be worth considering an example of a different situation, discussed by Naomi Eilan (1998), which, we believe, shares some similarities with the example just discussed. Suppose you are trying to find your keys, and you are looking for them on your kitchen table, which is cluttered with a variety of objects. The keys are in fact right there in front of you, but it still takes you some time to notice them, and you might later describe the situation by saying, '[They] were staring me in the face all the while I was looking for them, until something clicked' (Eilan, 1998, p. 189).

As in the case of the flash of recollection, we might ask how this change in your state is to be characterized. What exactly is missing before you come to notice the keys? The idea that what is missing is information of a certain sort, or with a certain causal ancestry, is, if anything, even less appealing here. At least, it is difficult to see how the notion of information might be sharpened up in the required way, as, intuitively, there is also a sense in which the right information has been available to you all along.

We believe that a more promising way of approaching the question as to what it takes for you to notice the keys is in terms of Ulric Neisser's (1976, p. 20) idea that 'we can see only what we know how to look for'. Both Eilan (1998) and Johannes Roessler (1999) take this general idea as their starting-point and emphasize an active ingredient in the relevant notion of 'looking'. Put briefly, their suggestion is that the content of perceptual experiences depends, in part, on the particular kind of perceptual project the subject is engaged in, such that 'having a particular experience can be an achievement on the part of the subject' (Roessler, 1999, p. 57). In terms of our example, Eilan's and Roessler's point might be put as follows. Whether or not you notice the keys does not just depend on their presence (and visibility) on the table, but also on your capacity to formulate the question as to whether or not the keys are on the table in front of you and bring that question to bear in the process of looking.

We can think of two crucial factors that must be in place in order for you to engage in this project of answering the question as to where the keys are by looking. Arguably, your project must be informed by your possession of the specific concepts needed for framing the question, such as the concept 'keys'. On a more fundamental level, however, your project must also be informed by an understanding as to how, in general, perception can make the presence of physical objects, such as your keys, manifest to you. Put briefly, the thought here is this. The question you are trying to answer, broadly speaking, is a question as to how the world is, independently of you. And, in order to appreciate how perception can yield an answer to such a question, you must be able to make sense of how the circumstances you are aware of in perception might have obtained without your being aware of them. What makes intelligible the mind-independent existence of the perceived world, in this sense, according to Eilan and Roessler, is a grasp of the fact that further conditions have to be fulfilled, over and above things' being a certain way in the world, if you are to perceive that they are that way. They both connect this idea with Evans's notion of a 'simple theory of perception' (see also Campbell, 1994). According to Evans (1982, p. 222), a subject can be said to possess such a simple theory in so far as he is able 'to think of his perception of the world as being simultaneously due to his position in the world, and to the condition of the world at that position'. In short, it is your having a grip on the idea that what you can perceive is determined, in part, by facts about your own spatial location, which makes it possible for you to use perception to answer questions about the mind-independent world.

Thus, the basic idea here is that your having a perceptual experience in the content of which your keys can figure as such is the outcome of an active perceptual project you are engaged in, in so far as it involves the bringing to bear of certain cognitive capacities. The key notion that, according to Eilan and Roessler, is needed to explain this sense in which perception involves an active ingredient, is that of attention. Attention, as Eilan (1998, p. 194) puts it, is 'the means by which we answer... questions about the environment'. In other words, the appeal to attention can capture a sense in which a perceiver is not just a passive receiver of information, but is actively and rationally involved in the picking-up of information. What happens when you stare at the table without noticing your keys, for instance, is that information is not picked up in a way that engages with your project of answering the question as to where your keys are. It is only when the selection of information is successfully guided by that question that you come to notice the keys—i.e. when you attend to them in the required way.

We have introduced the example of coming to notice the keys as an example of a cognitive change that seems difficult to account for in terms of the idea of a change in the information available to the subject. Our other example of such a change was that of being reminded of an incident that happened in one's past, and the incident coming back to one in a flash of recollection. Assuming that Eilan's and Roessler's analysis of the change that occurs when you come to notice the keys is along the right lines, is there an analogous way of explaining what is involved in the flash of recollection?

One way of developing the analogy here is in terms of the idea that episodic recall, too, involves a particular form of attention. Put briefly, the suggestion might run as follows. Just as we can ask what it takes for a subject to use perception to answer questions about her current environment, so we can ask what it takes for a subject to use her memory to answer questions about her past environment. The answer, in each case, turns on the general notion of attention as a mechanism mediating a particular kind of active involvement on the part of the subject in the processing of information. Putting this notion of attention to work in an analysis of episodic recall requires acknowledging that successful recollection of a past event depends on two factors: (a) the subject's having experienced the event and having retained information from that experience, and (b) the subject's being able to draw on such information in a specific way. There are ways in which a subject can be said to draw on such information that do not amount to the subject's recollecting the particular event in question—one such way, for instance, is in forming a mental image of what an event of that type might look like. By contrast, genuine recollection occurs only when such information is drawn on in a way that engages with the subject's project of answering the question as to what actually happened.

John Campbell (2002, p. 27) has argued that the notion of attention is the key linking notion 'connecting our psychology, at the level described by common sense, with the information-processing described by psychologists'. It is this idea that, ultimately, also stands behind our suggestion that episodic recall should be seen as involving a particular form of attention. Episodic recall involves attending to the past, as we might put it, in so far as episodic recall is not just dependent on the availability of information retained from the past, but also on the subject herself having a particular kind of active influence on the processing of that information. Thus, the connection between common sense and information-processing psychology that Campbell speaks of might be spelled out as follows. Episodic recall is a matter of a subject's using her memory to pursue certain kinds of questions about the past; for an answer to come forward, however, the subject's pursuing the relevant question must have a causal influence on the way information retained from past experience is being processed. It is only then that the 'flash of recollection' occurs.

So much for the general suggestion that episodic recall can be seen as involving a particular form of attention. In what follows, we will try to flesh out this suggestion by arguing that it can provide for a useful way of thinking about certain aspects of the development of episodic memory.

2. EPISODIC RECALL AND CAUSAL UNDERSTANDING

We have suggested that recollecting a past event can be understood as involving attending to the past, in the sense of bringing certain kinds of cognitive capacities to bear in the process of remembering. To make this suggestion more concrete, we need to ask what those cognitive capacities might be. One way of framing this question is in developmental terms. What are the kinds of reasoning or understanding that must be in place if children are to be said to be able to use their memory to answer questions about what happened in the past?

One possible starting-point here would be the idea that using one's memory to answer questions about what happened in the past requires grasp of a simple theory akin to the simple theory of perception that, according to Eilan and Roessler, must be in place if a subject is to be capable of using perception to answer questions about her current environment. To repeat, the appeal to such a simple theory, in the case of perception, was meant to explain how the subject can give substance to the idea of the mind-independent existence of the perceived world. Roughly speaking, what makes it intelligible, for the subject, that circumstances she is consciously aware of in perception are not dependent for their existence on being perceived is the idea that what she can perceive is the joint upshot of two factors: what is the case in the world and where the subject herself is located within that world (cf. also Campbell, 1994). Similarly, it could be argued that, if a subject is to be capable of using her memory to answer questions about what happened in the past, she must grasp that her being able to remember a certain event depends not just on that event's having happened, but also on certain other conditions being fulfilled, such as her having been in the right place when that event happened. Again, the idea here would be that this is (part of) the way in which the subject gives substance to the idea that events she can remember could have happened without her being able to remember them (cf. Hoerl, 2001, for further discussion).

In what follows, however, we wish to concentrate on a specific aspect of the ability to use one's memory to answer questions about what happened in the past that is already taken for granted in the above description. In doing so, we will follow Michael Martin, who describes as a crucial achievement in the development of episodic memory the child's being able to 'make sense of how there can be specific, and hence actual, events of which it has . . . conscious awareness, but which are nevertheless not part of the present scene' (2001, p. 280). In other words, the issue that Martin raises is what it takes for a child to be able to give substance to the distinction between the past and the present in recollecting particular past events. Central to resolving this issue, he suggests, is the idea that the child acquires 'a grasp of the concept of time as a causal structure' (ibid.).

We might get a better grip on the issue raised by Martin, and develop one way of reading the suggestion he makes, by considering the following example. Imagine a child carrying a toy, who visits a sequence of three locations in turn (not revisiting any locations in the sequence) and discovers afterwards that she no longer has the toy. Memory may yield to her a mental image of the toy at a specific location—say, location 2—that she visited earlier (or some other type of information that links the toy and that location), and thus she may return to location 2 to look for the toy. Although the child may be successful in retrieving the toy, and the information yielded by memory undoubtedly stems from a specific past event, we can still question whether the child is able to give any substance to the distinction between how things were in the past and how they are now.

To bring out the force of this question, consider a case in which the child returns to location 2, as above, but is unable to find the toy there. We can think of a primitive use of memory that is exclusively guided by an interest in how the world is, or might be, right now, which would allow the child to retrieve the toy from location 2, if it is there, but leave her at a loss if it is not there. The function of memory, in this sense, would be exhausted by its capacity to yield expectations about the present environment. If those expectations are frustrated, however, there is no function left for this type of memory to serve. The child might well continue searching, but these further searches would be directed merely randomly at the other two locations.

We can contrast this primitive use of memory with a more sophisticated ability to make use of the memory of the toy as being at location 2, even in a situation where the toy can no longer be found at that location. Given that the toy was seen at location 2, but is no longer to be found there, the place where the child should search next is the place she visited subsequently, i.e. location 3. We can point to two factors that must be in place if the child is to be able to make use of her memory in the way called for here. On the one hand, she must have a grip on how her memory of the toy as being at location 2 might be correct, even though the toy is no longer to be found there. This much is required if it is to be so much as possible for her to continue making rational use of her memory, even after her search at location 2 was unsuccessful. On the other hand, to put her memory to actual use, in the required way, she must be able to integrate it with further knowledge. Specifically, she must be able to draw on knowledge of the temporal order in which the three locations were visited, and use that knowledge in conjunction with her memory of the toy as being at location 2, in order to constrain her search.

What connects these two factors, we want to argue, is a particular kind of causal understanding they both require, relating to a fundamental aspect of the way in which causality works in time. First, what makes available the thought that the toy may indeed once have been at location 2, even though it is no longer there, is the idea that what is the case now depends not just on what was the case at a certain time in the past, but also on what happened subsequent to that time. In other words, it is the idea of a further event, which happened after her being at location 2, and which made it the case that the toy is no longer there, that allows the child to hold on to her memory of the toy as being at location 2, and make use of that memory in further reasoning. Second, it is the same general idea of a sequence of events, later stages of which can obliterate or change the effects of earlier ones, that is also needed for the child to be able to make use of knowledge of the order in which the three locations were visited in constraining the search. We might describe the kind of reasoning that is required here as follows. There is no point in the child revisiting location 1 if she remembers the toy being at location 2, because, given the order in which she visited the locations, the toy must have been removed from location 1 to show up in location 2. Instead, since it is no longer in location 2 either, it must have been lost subsequent to her visit to location 2, i.e. during or after her move to location 3.

Note that, in the preceding paragraph, we have described the child's reasoning in a way that, arguably, entails that the child can grasp the notion of the past, and of particular past events. This is deliberate, in so far as the point we want to make is that it is precisely the ability to engage in reasoning of this general type—i.e. reasoning which turns on the causal significance of the order in which sequences of events unfold—that can explain a sense in which the child can give substance to the difference between the past and the present. Specifically, it is only when the ability to engage in such reasoning is in place that the child can be said to use her memory in a way that involves a grasp of the fact that things might no longer be the way they once were. As we might put it, recollecting past events in their own right—i.e. *as* past events—requires the ability to conceive of them as belonging to a sequence of events leading up to the present, and to give causal significance to the temporal order of that sequence in terms of the idea that later events in the sequence can obliterate or change the effect of earlier ones.

If these considerations are along the right lines, they might provide us with a way of cashing out both the claim that episodic recall involves a particular form of attention and the claim that 'a grasp of the notion of time as a causal structure', as Martin (2001, p. 280) puts it, plays a crucial role in episodic recall. As we have argued in the previous section, episodic recall can be seen to involve a particular form of attention in so far as it involves using one's memory to answer questions as to what happened in the past. The argument of this section has been that giving substance to the difference between the past and the present requires the ability to engage in the particular kind of causal reasoning we have described. In other words, it is only if the ability to engage in such reasoning is in place that a subject can be said to attend to past events in their own right in episodic memory.

If what we have said so far is correct, one important empirical question regarding the development of episodic memory is this: At what point in development do children start to grasp the causal significance of the temporal order in which events take place? This is the question we wish to focus on in the next section. So far, we have given only one example of a task that might be used to measure such a grasp (i.e. serial search), and we will discuss two studies that have found that young children do have difficulties with this type of task. However, we will also discuss other developmental studies, involving quite different experimental paradigms, which support the idea that there is a specific aspect of causality, relating to how causality works in time, that children have difficulties with well into the third year of their lives.

3. YOUNG CHILDREN'S CAUSAL UNDERSTANDING

The causal reasoning abilities of young children have become a particular focus of attention in recent developmental research, some of which points to important continuities between causal reasoning in such children and the mature causal reasoning of adults (Corrigan and Denton, 1996; Gopnik and Sobel, 2000, Gopnik *et al.*, 2001; Schlottman *et al.*, 2002). Much of the recent research on children's causal reasoning has been carried out within the general framework of the 'theory-theory' (Gopnik and Meltzoff, 1997), which claims that children's understanding of the world develops in a way that bears close resemblance to the process of theory formation and change in science (Gopnik *et al.*, 2004). Gopnik *et al.* argue that young children have simple theories about various domains (e.g. biology or psychology) that are underpinned by a body of causal knowledge, and that they learn causal relationships systematically and efficiently through their observations of events. In fact, they suggest that infants' perceptual sensitivity to the causal relationships in Michottean displays of colliding objects (Leslie, 1982;

Oakes, 1994; Oakes and Cohen, 1990) may be evidence of causal understanding in the physical domain from very early in life.

Although some researchers may object to this rich interpretation of infants' abilities (e.g. White, 1995), there is ample evidence from an older body of research that children as young as 3 years can not only make explicit judgements about the causal powers of familiar objects (e.g. Bullock, Gelman, and Baillargeon, 1982; Gelman, Bullock, and Meck, 1980; Shultz, 1982), but can also make rapid and accurate inferences about the causal powers of completely novel objects in ways that are systematic and can be described in terms of certain principles (Shultz, 1982; Shultz and Kestenbaum, 1985). Nevertheless, we want to suggest that the causal understanding underpinning these abilities might still fall short of a mature grasp of causality in one crucial respect, in that it may not encompass an understanding of how causality unfolds over time. Appreciating the causal powers of objects is a matter of being able to judge which events usually take place when those objects feature in certain ways in certain situations. However, this is, at least in principle, separable from being able to grasp how causal influence is propagated through a succession of such events.

One way of making this clear is by contrasting two versions of a picture task that has been used with 3- and 4-year-olds. Gelman, Bullock, and Meck (1980) examined children's ability to complete a sequence of three line-drawings depicting a simple causal transformation. They found that 3-year-olds correctly chose, e.g., a picture of a knife to put in between a picture of an apple and a picture of a cut apple, or a picture of a cut apple to put next to a picture of an apple and a picture of a knife. However, Das Gupta and Bryant (1989) argued that children could solve the Gelman *et al.* task purely on the basis of associating an instrument (e.g. a knife) with a certain type of outcome (e.g. a cut object) without using the idea of a causal transformation leading from an earlier state of affairs to a later state of affairs. In their own studies, Das Gupta and Bryant used picture sequences beginning with, for example, a cut apple and ending with a wet and cut apple. To complete this type of sequence, they argued, children were required to reason from the initial state of the object to the end state, rather than simply choosing an object with associated causal powers (e.g. in this example, they would have to choose a picture of a jug of water rather than a picture of a knife). They found that 3-year-olds had difficulties under such circumstances, suggesting that although they were familiar with the causal powers of the relevant objects, they were unable to take account of the temporal order in which events must happen to yield the sequence indicated by the pictures.

One of the few studies aimed explicitly at investigating connections between children's general understanding of time and their causal reasoning abilities is that of Povinelli *et al.* (1999). The question they were interested in was whether young children have an 'explicit understanding of time as a successive series of causally interdependent states of the world' (pp. 1426–7). They addressed this question by examining whether 3- and 5-year-olds can recruit information about the temporal order in which two past events took place in working out a current state of the world. In one of Povinelli *et al.*'s experiments, children took part in two games with an experimenter, one after the other. Unbeknownst to the child, while he or she was playing the first game, a second experimenter hid a toy in one box behind him or her. While the child was playing the second game, this experimenter then moved the toy to a different box. Immediately after the children finished playing the second game, they were shown videotape clips of themselves playing each of the games, with each of the two hiding events that they had previously been unaware of now clearly in view. They were then asked to find the toy. The crucial manipulation in the study was that children were not always shown the videotape clips in the order in which the games had actually occurred. To pass the task, children thus had to draw a connection between what they could see on the videotape clips and what they knew about the order in which they had actually played the two games. They had little difficulty in working out, based on what they had been shown, that there was now a toy in one of the boxes. Yet, the 3-year-olds were unable to work out which of the videotape clips depicted the toy's current location, even if they were explicitly reminded, while watching the videotape clips, which game they had played first and which they had played last.

We have recently carried out a study involving a different experimental paradigm, which also examined whether children can take account of the order in which two events occurred in making judgements about a present state of affairs (McCormack and Hoerl, forthcoming). In our task, children were familiarized with a box that had two different buttons. Pressing one button resulted in a marble appearing in a window, whereas pressing the other button resulted in a toy car appearing in the window. There was only ever one object in the window at any one time. The apparatus was then covered, and the buttons were pressed one at a time. Children were required to infer the current contents of the window when given retrospective cues about the temporal order in which the buttons had been pressed. We found that children younger than 5 were unable to infer the current contents of the window, even if explicitly encouraged to take order information into account.

Finally, there is also evidence that children have difficulty in using knowledge of the temporal order in which a series of events took place in situations that are closely analogous to the example of searching for a toy we used in the previous section. Wellman, Somerville, and Haake (1979) conducted a task in which 3-, 4- and 5-year-old children visited a series of eight well-defined locations. At location 3, the experimenter took a picture of the child with a camera, but at location 7, the experimenter told the child that he or she could no longer find the camera. Although many of even the youngest children initially searched in location 3, their second searches were often at locations 1 and 2, even if children were able to recall where they had seen the camera. Wellman *et al.* suggested that the younger children in their study may have been employing a simple associative strategy (which led to searches at the location most strongly associated with the missing object), rather than trying to infer where it was possible that the object might be. Haake and Somerville (1985) used a simpler task, in which the child observed the experimenter visiting four hiding locations while holding an object that was at some point left under one of the locations. Like Wellman *et al.*, they found that the second searches of young children were often not logically constrained by the temporal order in which the locations had been visited.

Although the studies that we have described have used quite disparate tasks, and each of them assesses a number of abilities in addition to causal and temporal reasoning, together their findings point to a specific difficulty that 3–4-year-olds seem to have with what we might call *temporal-causal reasoning*, i.e. reasoning that turns on the causal significance of the temporal order in which sequences of events unfold. In the preceding section, we argued that it is just this type of reasoning which a subject must be capable of, if she is to be able to attend to the past in episodic memory. Thus, if what we have said is correct, one useful way of approaching questions about the development of episodic memory is by asking how children acquire the ability to engage in such temporal-causal reasoning.

4. JOINT REMINISCING AND CAUSAL UNDERSTANDING

In the opening paragraph of his 1983 monograph, Tulving characterizes episodic memory as the only form of memory which involves 'travel[ling] back into the past in [one's] own mind' (Tulving, 1983, p. 1). One of the key aims of what we have said so far has been to show how Tulving's claim might be fleshed out in terms of the idea that episodic recall, uniquely, involves a particular form of attention, which might be called 'attention to the past'. In the remainder of this chapter, we wish to investigate a developmental claim which Nelson, drawing on Tulving's characterization of episodic memory, puts as follows: '[E]stablishing a past that can be travelled through [in one's mind] depends on socially shared remembering' (1988, p. 266). In light of our own discussion, another way of capturing the claim is this: it is through participating in communicative exchanges that centre on the sharing of memories of particular past events, i.e. joint reminiscing, that children acquire the capacity to attend to the past.

Our discussion so far has focused in particular on the role that a specific form of causal reasoning, which we have called 'temporal-causal reasoning', can be seen to play in making possible such attention to the past. This might provide us with one way of understanding the significance of joint reminiscing for the development of episodic memory. The idea, in short, would be that children first learn to engage in temporal-causal reasoning in the context of joint reminiscing. But how exactly should we think of the developmental mechanism whereby participation in this particular kind of communicative activity makes available a new type of reasoning ability?

A key claim in what follows will be that there is a particular kind of normative dimension to temporal-causal reasoning. So far, we have characterized this type of reasoning primarily in terms of the kinds of causal relationships it picks up on. Here our concern is also with a specific form of rationality it can be seen to involve. To illustrate, consider once again, for instance, the serial search task we described in section 2, above. In the version of the task that was critical to our argument, the child had a memory of the toy as being at location 2 (out of three that had been visited), but the toy was no longer to be found there. We have said that, in order to constrain her subsequent search, the child must integrate her memory of the toy as being at location 2 with her knowledge of the order in which the three locations were visited. A natural way of describing what this involves is by saying that the child must treat the content of her memory as evidence or support for the toy's being in one location rather than another, given the content of her knowledge about the order in which the three locations were visited. Christopher Peacocke has described the general kind of reasoning at issue here as 'second-tier thought, since it involves thought about relations of support, evidence or consequence between contents, as opposed to first-tier thought, which is thought about the world where the thought does not involve any consideration of such relations between contents' (1996, p. 130). What we want to suggest in this section is that there is a close connection between the capacity to engage in temporal-causal reasoning, conceived of as a species of such second-tier thought, and the capacity to engage in a particular kind of communicative exchange in which the sharing of memories is the means by which one person exerts rational influence on another. Furthermore, we also want to suggest that it is in this sense that 'socially shared remembering', as Nelson puts it, might be seen to provide the first context in which children exercise the type of reasoning abilities required to attend to particular past events in episodic memory.

To begin with, it might help to consider a case in which communication falls short of its goal. The following extract is from a conversation in which an adult experimenter (E) wants to find out what a child (C) did during a recent camping holiday.

E: You slept outside in a tent? Wow, that sounds like a lot of fun.
C: And then we waked up and had dinner. First we eat dinner, then go to bed, and then wake up and eat breakfast.
E: What else did you do when you went camping? What did you do when you got up, after you ate breakfast?
C: Umm, in the night, and went to sleep.

(Fivush and Hamond, 1990, p. 231)

Intuitively, what seems to go wrong in this conversation is that the child does not really understand the import of the adult's use of the past tense. The child responds to the adult's questions by producing what is typically called a 'script', i.e. a schematic story of how things usually go (Nelson, 1986; Schank and Abelson, 1977). In recounting such a script, the child of course makes use of knowledge that was in fact acquired in the past. However, what is missing from the child's response is any indication that she herself can give significance to the difference between the way things went on a particular occasion in the past (i.e. her camping holiday) and the way they continue to go on a typical day.

Recent developmental research has focused in particular on the significance of adult–child conversations that differ from the example just quoted in two important respects. First, they are conversations concerning past events that the child has experienced together with the adult (usually a caregiver). Secondly, they are conversations that involve so-called scaffolding by the adult; that is to say, the adult draws on her own memory of those events in guiding the conversation—by providing some of the relevant information herself, by explicitly confirming the child's recollections, or by asking leading questions. In particular, such scaffolding seems to be aimed at eliciting, or rather jointly generating, a temporally structured account of a sequence of events, in contrast to simply asking 'What else happened?' Consider the following conversation between a mother (M) and her child (C), which seems rather more successful than the one we quoted before:

M: What happened to your finger?
C: I pinched it.
M: You pinched it. Oh boy, I bet that made you feel really sad.
C: Yeah . . . it hurts.
M: Yeah, it did hurt. A pinched finger is no fun . . . But who came and made you feel better?
C: Daddy!

(Fivush, 1994, p. 149)

In what follows, we want to focus on two kinds of contribution the mother makes to this conversation: First, she explicitly confirms the child's memory of her pinching her finger ('You pinched it', 'It did hurt'). Secondly, she introduces a further topic: another event that happened after the child pinched her finger ('who came and made you feel better?'). What we want to suggest is that these contributions can be seen to serve the aim of helping the conversation come to a success in two different, but closely connected, senses. On the one hand, they aim at aiding the child's thinking about the two events in question, and specifically their relationship to each other. On the other hand, they also aim to effect a change in the child's current emotional attitude. We believe that it is by looking at how these two aims are connected with each other, and how what the mother says might help in achieving them, that we might also better understand the general idea that parent–child conversations about the shared past, and the particular types of parental scaffolding they involve, might have a crucial role to play in children's own developing understanding of the past.

Let us look, first, at the content of the mother's contributions. What seemed to be lacking in the previous example involving the child who had been on a camping holiday was any indication that the child was able to give substance to the difference between the past and the present. Part of what the mother does in this second example is to give the child the means to do just this. What she flags, in her contributions to the conversation, is that the event mentioned by the child did take place—the child did pinch her finger, and it did hurt—but also that there was another event—Daddy making the child feel better. It seems clear that, at least in the mother's view, this later event had the power to obliterate the effects of the earlier event—acting as an 'intervening cause' between the first event and the present, as we might put it. And it is precisely the general idea of such an intervening cause which makes intelligible why things might no longer be the way they once were.

However, there is another aspect to this conversation that is not just a matter of what is being said, and if we think that the child can see the relevant connection between the two events, it also has something to do with that aspect. Perhaps the most natural way of understanding what the mother is trying to communicate to the child in this example is that there is no longer any reason for the child to be distressed about her finger. Here we are assuming, as Fivush (1994, p. 149) does, that the rekindled memory of what happened to her finger initially causes some distress to the child, which the mother wants to alleviate. If this is true, the question we should ask is how the mother attempts to do this. For instance, one option for her would have been simply to try and exert some causal influence on the child's emotional state, by introducing another topic of conversation purely as a means of distracting the child. But, intuitively, she does something quite different. Note that the mother is actually quite careful not to distract the child from the truth that, indeed, she did pinch her finger, and also the general truth that 'A pinched finger is no fun'. Rather, as we might say, her strategy is to show the child that these truths have no direct bearing on how the child should feel, because of what happened after the child had pinched her finger.

Ultimately, our interest here is not in whether the child in this example does in fact understand that this is what the mother is getting at. Rather, what we want to highlight is that, if she does so, her understanding the content of the mother's words is closely tied up with her appreciating the point they have in the conversation. We might get clearer on this issue by considering again a distinction between two aspects or dimensions of what we have called temporal-causal reasoning, which we discussed at the beginning of this section. On the face of it, it is precisely a particular instance of temporal-causal reasoning that the mother in the current example is prompting the child to engage in. The reasoning in question turns on a grasp of a particular kind of causal relationship obtaining between two events in virtue of the fact that the later event changed or obliterated the effects of the earlier event. As we have suggested, however, there is also a further, normative dimension to such reasoning, in virtue of it being a species of what Peacocke has called 'second-tier thought'. In connection with the current example, the basic idea here might be spelled out as follows. The child's being able to grasp the relevant relationship between the two events at issue is, in part, a matter of her being able to appreciate relations of support (or lack thereof) between the content of her memories of these events and the contents of certain attitudes towards the present. That is to say, unless the child can, for instance, rationally revise her feelings in light of those memories, it is difficult to see how she can be said to have picked up on the way the two events are related to each other.

We have considered this example in some detail because we believe that it can illustrate at least one way in which the sharing of memories of past events can serve as a means of a particular form of rational interaction between two individuals. As such, it might also help us to understand better Nelson's claim that participation in 'socially shared remembering' is a crucial factor in the emergence of the very ability to attend to the past in episodic memory. Broadly speaking, the general idea here is that a specific type of reasoning ability that must be in place for episodic memory to be possible is in fact first exercised in a socio-communicative context. At the start of this section, we suggested that one key to unpacking Nelson's claim lay in the idea (developed in more detail in previous sections) that the ability to engage in temporal-causal reasoning plays a crucial role in making possible the kind of attention to the past involved in episodic recall, by allowing the child to give substance to the distinction between the past and the present. However, we have also sought to bring out a particular kind of normative dimension to temporal-causal reasoning. It involves the ability to assess relations of support, evidence, or consequence between the content of one's memories and the content of certain attitudes towards the present, in light of one's knowledge about the order in which different past events unfolded. Thus, one way of understanding Nelson's claim is in terms of the idea that children first come to use their memory in this way in a dialogical situation in which the relevant memories are shared with an adult, and in which the adult is using the sharing of those memories as a means of exerting rational influence on the child. In other words, it is through coming to appreciate the point that the adult's appeals to certain past events have in conversation that the child develops the ability to assess the relevant relations between the content of her memories and the content of her attitudes towards the present. In more concrete terms, this also involves the child's coming to understand that things might no longer be the way they once were. And it is in this sense that the development of episodic memory, which involves such an understanding, might be seen to be tied to children's participation in joint reminiscing with others. In what follows, we will try to flesh out this suggestion in the context of a discussion of recent work in developmental psychology that centres on the notion of a narrative.

5. THE ROLE OF NARRATIVES IN MEMORY DEVELOPMENT

According to Nelson (1996), a central aspect of the developmental significance of joint reminiscing can be captured as follows. Initially in development, she claims, 'memory as such has no value in and of itself, but takes on value only as it contributes to the individual's ability to behave adaptively' (Nelson, 1996, p. 265). It is only when children learn how to engage in joint reminiscing with others that memories emerge which, as she puts it, 'appear to be valued for themselves' (p. 266). Key to explaining this developmental shift, according to Nelson, is the notion of a *narrative*. Her idea is that learning to engage in joint reminiscing involves acquiring a specific set of linguistic skills—narrative abilities—and the possession of these skills forms the background to a distinct kind of engagement with the past, which she describes as valuing memories for themselves.

We wish to conclude our chapter by taking a closer look at the notion of a narrative, which has become a central notion in much recent writing on memory development (see also Fivush, 1991, Miller, 1994, Pillemer and White, 1989, among others). Specifically, we want to argue that there are at least two different, though interconnected, ideas that might be seen to inform the claim that narrative abilities play a crucial role in memory development. The first is the idea that narratives provide a crucial framework for recollecting particular past events in their own right, independently of any direct relevance they may have for current behaviour and expectations. The second is the idea that narrative abilities also serve to make such memories of particular past events socially accessible, and thus make it possible for memory to assume a new function, over and above its function in guiding behaviour and expectations. In discussing these two ideas, we also wish to compare our own account of memory development to other accounts that can be found in the existing literature.

Against the background of the argument we have outlined, one way of reading Nelson's claim that memory development is, at least in part, a matter of the child's coming to value memories for themselves, might be as follows. We have argued that there is a sense in which memory is initially used only to answer questions about how things are (or may be) in the child's current environment. It is only with development that children begin to use their memory in a way that involves a grasp of the fact that things might no longer be the way they once were, and thus that genuine episodic memories emerge.

A similar line of thought can be seen to be at work in developmental accounts which give narrative abilities a central role in making possible stable, enduring memories of particular past events. Nelson (1993, 1996), for instance, argues for the existence of a developmentally primitive memory system that is geared, primarily, at the retention of generic information. That is to say, information gleaned from particular events is typically quickly forgotten, unless reinforced by the experience of further events of the same type and retained in the form of a general schema or script for the type of event in question. The development of language, Nelson claims, makes possible a new mechanism for establishing persistent memories by a process of reinstatement. Such reinstatement takes the form of generating memory narratives, either internally or with a social partner. And it is through such reinstatement, according to Nelson, that memories for particular past events can acquire longevity.

Similarly, Fivush and Hamond (1990) have observed that young children's recall, when asked about a certain event, appears to be quite fragmented and context-dependent. They suggest that such children are 'relying on the adult's questions to provide retrieval cues' (p. 243), and consequently recall different aspects on different occasions. With the acquisition of narrative abilities, by contrast, children acquire a consistent framework for recounting events, including the 'who, what, when and where' (Neisser, 1982), which they can use to guide their own retrieval (see also Hudson, 1990; Hudson and Shapiro, 1991).

On our account, we can retain the notion that the development of narrative skills plays a crucial role in memory development. However, our emphasis here is on a fundamental type of reasoning ability involved in narrative construction— i.e. the ability to engage in what we have called temporal-causal reasoning— whose significance is often not fully recognized or made explicit. Nelson, for instance, assumes that narrative construction can exploit a developmentally more primitive 'capacity for holding in mind a sequence of events, involving self and others, temporally and causally arranged' (1993, p. 17). There is considerable evidence to support such a claim, if it is to mean that even quite young children can reproduce a sequence of events behaviourally, or describe it verbally, and do so in a way that tends to be faithful to the temporal and/or causal relations between individual events in the original sequence (see e.g. Bauer and Mandler, 1989, 1992; Nelson, 1986). Yet, as we have tried to argue, there is also evidence suggesting that young children still lack an important kind of causal understanding, which might be described as an explicit grasp of the causal significance of the temporal order in which events happen (see also Pillemer, 1998; Povinelli *et al.*, 1999; Welch-Ross, 2001). And, arguably, it is this kind of causal understanding which is required for full-blown narrative construction.

In fact, one way of understanding the notion of a narrative is to see narratives as the very vehicle of this more sophisticated form of causal understanding. That is to say, construction of a narrative is the form that a subject's grasp of the causal significance of the temporal order of events takes. Narratives, on this view, embody an understanding of how the overall outcome of a sequence of events depends on the temporal order in which they happened: i.e. how events that came later in the sequence might have changed or obliterated the effects of earlier events. A detailed defence of this view of what narratives are is beyond the scope of this chapter. But, if it is along the right lines, narratives might be thought to play an even more fundamental role in memory development than Nelson, Fivush and Hamond, and others suppose. Part of our argument has been that attending to the past in its own right, in episodic memory, depends on being able to give substance to the idea that things might no longer be the way they once were. This, we have argued, is the reason why episodic recall requires the ability to conceive of remembered events as belonging to a sequence of events, later stages of which can obliterate or change the effects of earlier ones. Thus, if narratives can indeed be seen as the vehicles for the particular kind of causal understanding involved here, narrative abilities, in fact, have an essential role to play in making genuine episodic memory possible in the first place.

6. NARRATIVES AND THE SOCIAL FUNCTION OF MEMORY SHARING

In the previous section, we interpreted Nelson's claim that a crucial stage in memory development consists in the child's coming to value memories for themselves as a claim about the *content* of a sophisticated form of memory, i.e. episodic memory. That is to say, we have argued that recollecting particular past events in episodic memory involves attending to the past in its own right, independently of any direct bearing it may have on the present. Further, we have suggested that narrative construction, involving a certain form of temporal-causal understanding, might have a crucial role in making such attention to the past possible.

In talking about children coming to value memories for themselves, however, Nelson herself seems to have a stronger claim in mind, which also encompasses the idea of a fundamental change in the *function* of memory. To say that episodic memories are valued in themselves—say, in the sense that they involve a grasp of the fact that things might no longer be the way they once were—does of course not preclude that they can, on occasion, be put to a practical purpose. In an earlier section, we discussed the example of a child searching for a lost toy, and tried to show how rationally constraining her search, even if the toy is no longer at the location where she remembers it as being, involves attending to the past in episodic memory. For Nelson, however, the paradigm case of memories' being valued in themselves is one in which the very activity of recollecting and constructing a narrative of the past is, in some sense, valued in and of itself.

One way of understanding Nelson's point is in terms of a further distinction sometimes drawn in the developmental literature between episodic memories and autobiographical memories (see e.g. Fivush, 2001; Nelson, 1996; Reese, 2002). In particular, autobiographical memories, on this view, are held to embody a particular form of understanding of the self, and this might go some way towards explaining Nelson's idea that constructing a memory narrative can sometimes be valued in and of itself.

For Fivush, for instance, '[e]pisodic memories are representations of what happened; autobiographical memories are memories of what happened *to me*'

(2001, p. 36, original emphasis). According to her, the crucial difference between these two types of memory lies in the fact that the latter requires what she calls a particular form of 'representational awareness' (p. 37). That is to say, autobiographical memory can only emerge once children come to understand that memories are representations of the past, which, on Fivush's view, involves understanding that one's own representation of a particular past event can differ from those of others. It is in this context that Fivush also talks about the role of joint reminiscing in memory development. Joint reminiscing, she argues, plays a crucial role in the development of autobiographical memory, because sharing memories with others provides experience of contrasting perspectives on past events. This, as she puts it, 'is how children come to understand memories *as* representations, a critical step in the development of a subjective perspective' (Fivush, 2001, pp. 42–3, original emphasis; see also Fivush, Haden, and Adam, 1995; Haden, Haine, and Fivush, 1997; Nelson, 2001; Welch-Ross, 1997).

The idea of a difference between episodic and autobiographical memory, drawn along these lines, has not been a feature of the account we have put forward. Fivush's account can be seen as part of a larger group of theories which frame developmental questions (e.g. also questions about the significance of joint visual attention) in terms of questions about the acquisition of a 'theory of mind', which is held to centre on an understanding of the representational nature of mental states (see e.g. Baron-Cohen, 1995; Perner, 1991). As Jane Heal (Chapter 2 above) points out, however, this approach makes it difficult to see why carrying out certain activities jointly with others should have any particular importance in development. Applying Heal's argument to Fivush's account, it is at least unclear why something like the representational understanding of memory described by Fivush could not develop in the absence of genuine joint reminiscing. To be sure, joint reminiscing might be seen as a context in which differences in the way two people remember a particular event become particularly salient. However, such differences might also, at least in principle, become apparent to a child who simply observes that other people's reactions after a certain event are different from her own.

Heal's general aim is to argue against the usual conception of a 'theory of mind' as the end-point of development, instead replacing it with a view according to which development is a matter of the child's 'learn[ing] with growing sophistication to play his or her part in [a shared] life' (above, p. 41). Interestingly, Welch-Ross (2001) has criticized Fivush's (2001) account on related grounds. Picking up on Fivush's notion of a 'subjective perspective', she argues that the development of such a perspective is not, as Fivush portrays it, a matter of noticing differences between one's own perspective on past events and that of others. Rather, she suggests that such a perspective first emerges 'because children begin to organize events according to personal and emotional evaluations that are shared with others' (Welch-Ross, 2001, p. 116).

Like Welch-Ross, we believe that the primary significance of joint reminiscing lies not in making evident differences in perspective, but rather in establishing a shared outlook on the past in the first place. An example here might be the conversation involving the child who had pinched her finger, as discussed above. According to our reading of this example, the rekindled memory of what happened to her finger initially causes some distress to the child, which the mother tries to alleviate by reminding the child that Daddy subsequently came and made her feel better. Thus, jointly constructing a structured account of what happened in the past, in this example, might actually be seen to serve as a means of resolving differences between two people's perspectives.

However, implicit in this interpretation is a further idea that is unrecognized, or at least not made explicit, by Welch-Ross. It seems that it is precisely *by way of* organizing events according to such a jointly constructed structured account that, at least in this case, mother and child arrive at the kind of shared personal and emotional evaluation of the past of which Welch-Ross speaks. Picking up on our earlier suggestion regarding the notion of a narrative, one way of developing this point might be in terms of the idea that narratives of the past are not just the vehicle of a certain form of causal understanding, but also the vehicle of a certain form of normative understanding. What we have suggested, in fact, is that there is a close connection between these two features, in that giving significance to the causal order in which events happened is, at least in part, a matter of being able rationally to revise one's current attitudes in light of memories of particular past events. It is in this sense that joint narrative construction might be understood as a way of arriving at a shared appreciation of how certain attitudes are, or are no longer, rationally appropriate.

Again, we do not have the space to discuss this way of construing the notion of a narrative in more detail. Rather, we want to end our discussion by coming back, once more, to Nelson's claim that children come to value memories for themselves as they learn how to participate in joint reminiscing with others. One reading of this claim that we have as yet left under-explored is in terms of the idea that it is the activity of sharing memories with others that children come to value in and of itself. Bernard Williams has argued that any plausible account of language in general needs to recognize 'the immense importance that human beings find in exchanging assertions which offer no news to any of them' (2002, p. 47). Many of our conversations about the past, in particular, clearly take the form of such exchanges of 'plain truths' (p. 45). What we want to suggest, in short, is that the notion of a narrative, as just outlined, might help us shed light on the importance that we nevertheless attach to them.

To develop the point, it might be helpful to note a parallel with issues regarding joint attention discussed in some of the other chapters in this volume. Several of them can be seen as trying to articulate a sense in which engaging in joint attention is a fundamental feature of what Jane Heal describes as living a 'shared life'.

This issue comes to the fore specifically in connection with two, closely interrelated claims about the significance and nature of joint attention, different variants of which are discussed by a number of the authors. The first is the claim that joint attention has a fundamental role to play in grounding (further) collaborative activities, such as communication and joint action. The second is the claim that what makes these activities genuinely collaborative is the particular kind of mutual awareness that they involve and that joint attention provides for. What connects these two claims, on Heal's own view, is the idea that it is by way of engaging in joint attention that we recognize, and make manifest that we recognize, 'what reasons [others] already acknowledge and what kinds of discussion and project it might be fruitful to engage with them' (p. 42 above).

To adopt Heal's words, one way of understanding the view that we have outlined is in terms of the idea that there is a specific way in which conversation can also turn on such a mutual acknowledgement of reasons, that has to do with the possibility of jointly constructing a narrative of the past. Thus, part of the importance we attach to joint reminiscing, even when it amounts to no more than the exchange of plain truths, lies in the fact that joint reminiscing is an activity through which others can become available to us as subjects with whom certain forms of rational engagement can be entered into. We value memories of particular past events for themselves, on this view, because the sharing of such memories is a way of establishing, maintaining, or negotiating a distinctively social relationship with others.

REFERENCES

Anscombe, G. E. M. (1981), 'The reality of the past', in *Collected Philosophical Papers*, ii: *Metaphysics and the Philosophy of Mind*. Oxford: Oxford University Press, 103–19.

Ayer, A. J. (1956), *The Problem of Knowledge*. London: Pelican Books.

Baron-Cohen, S. (1995), 'The eye direction detector (EDD) and the shared attention mechanism (SAM): two cases for evolutionary psychology', in C. Moore and P. J. Dunham (eds.), *Joint Attention: Its Origins and Role in Development*. Hove: Erlbaum, 41–59.

Bates, E., Camaioni, L., and Volterra, V. (1976), 'Sensorimotor performatives', in E. Bates, *Language and Context: The Acquisition of Pragmatics*. New York.: Academic Press, 49–71.

Bauer, P. J., and Mandler, J. M. (1989), 'One thing follows another: effects of temporal structure on 1- to 2-year-olds' recall of events', *Developmental Psychology*, 25: 197–206.

——— ——— (1992), 'Putting the horse before the cart: the use of temporal order in recall of events by one-year-old children', *Developmental Psychology*, 28: 441–52.

Bullock, M., Gelman, R., and Baillargeon, R. (1982), 'The development of causal reasoning', in W. Friedman (ed.), *The Developmental Psychology of Time*. New York.: Academic Press, 209–54.

Campbell, J. (1994), *Past, Space and Self*. Cambridge, Mass.: MIT Press.

CAMPBELL, J. (1998), 'Joint attention and the first person', in A. O'Hear (ed.), *Current Issues in the Philosophy of Mind*. Cambridge: Cambridge University Press, 123–36.

—— (2001), 'Memory demonstratives', in C. Hoerl and T. McCormack (eds.), *Time and Memory: Issues in Philosophy and Psychology*. Oxford: Oxford University Press, 169–86.

—— (2002), *Reference and Consciousness*. Oxford: Oxford University Press.

CORRIGAN, R., and DENTON, P. (1996), 'Causal understanding as a developmental primitive', *Developmental Review*, 16: 162–202.

DAS GUPTA, P., and BRYANT, P. E. (1989), 'Young children's causal inferences', *Child Development*, 60: 1138–46.

EILAN, N. (1998), 'Perceptual intentionality, attention and consciousness', in A. O'Hear (ed.), *Current Issues in the Philosophy of Mind*. Cambridge: Cambridge University Press, 181–202.

EVANS, G. (1982), *The Varieties of Reference*. Oxford: Oxford University Press.

FIVUSH, R. (1991), 'The social construction of personal narratives', *Merrill-Palmer Quarterly*, 37: 59–82.

—— (1994), 'Constructing narrative, emotion, and self in parent–child conversations about the past', in U. Neisser and R. Fivush (eds.), *The Remembering Self: Construction and Accuracy in the Self-Narrative*. Cambridge: Cambridge University Press, 136–57.

—— (2001), 'Owning experience: developing subjective perspective in autobiographical narratives', in C. Moore and K. Lemmon (eds.), *The Self in Time: Developmental Perspectives*. Mahwah, NJ: Lawrence Erlbaum, 33–52.

—— and HAMOND, N. R. (1990), 'Autobiographical memory across the preschool years: toward reconceptualizing childhood amnesia', in R. Fivush and J. A. Hudson (eds.), *Knowing and Remembering in Young Children*. Cambridge: Cambridge University Press, 223–48.

—— HADEN, C., and ADAM, S. (1995), 'Structure and coherence of preschoolers' personal narratives over time: implications for childhood amnesia', *Journal of Experimental Child Psychology*, 60: 32–56.

GELMAN, R., BULLOCK M., and MECK, E. (1980), 'Preschoolers' understanding of simple object transformations', *Child Development*, 51: 691–9.

GOPNIK, A., and MELTZOFF, A. (1997), *Words, Thoughts and Theories*. Cambridge, Mass.: MIT Press.

—— and SOBEL, D. M. (2000), 'Detecting blickets: how young children use information about causal properties in categorization and induction', *Child Development*, 71: 1205–22.

—— GLYMOUR, C., SOBEL, D., SCHULZ, L., KUSHNIR, T., and DANKS, D. (2004), 'A theory of causal learning in children: causal maps and Bayes nets', *Psychological Review*, 111: 1–31.

—— SOBEL, D. M., SCHULTZ, L. E., and GLYMOUR, C. (2001), 'Causal learning mechanisms in very young children: two- , three- , and four-year-olds infer causal relations from patterns of variation and covariation', *Developmental Psychology*, 37: 620–9.

HAAKE, R. J., and SOMERVILLE, S. S. (1985), 'Development of logical search skills in infancy', *Developmental Psychology*, 21: 176–86.

HADEN, C., HAINE, R., and FIVUSH, R. (1997), 'Developing narrative structure in parent–child conversations about the past', *Developmental Psychology*, 33: 295–307.

HOERL, C. (2001), 'The phenomenology of episodic recall', in C. Hoerl and T. McCormack (eds.), *Time and Memory: Issues in Philosophy and Psychology*. Oxford: Oxford University Press, 315–35.

Hudson, J. A. (1990), 'The emergence of autobiographical memory in mother–child conversation', in R. Fuvish and J. A. Hudson (eds.), *Knowing and Remembering in Young Children*. Cambridge: Cambridge University Press, 166–96.

—— and Shapiro, L. R. (1991), 'From knowing to telling: the development of children's scripts, stories, and personal narratives', in A. McCabe and C. Peterson (eds.), *Developing Narrative Structure*. Hillsdale, NJ: Lawrence Erlbaum, 89–136.

Leslie, A. M. (1982), 'The perception of causality in infants', *Perception*, 11: 173–86.

Martin, M. G. F. (2001), 'Out of the past: episodic recall as retained acquaintance', in C. Hoerl and T. McCormack (eds.), *Time and Memory: Issues in Philosophy and Psychology*. Oxford: Oxford University Press, 257–84.

Mayes, A. R. (2001), 'Aware and unaware memory: does unaware memory underlie aware memory?', in C. Hoerl and T. McCormack (eds.), *Time and Memory: Issues in Philosophy and Psychology*. Oxford: Oxford University Press, 187–211.

McCormack, T., and Hoerl, C. (forthcoming), 'Children's reasoning about the causal significance of the temporal order of events', *Developmental Psychology*.

Miller, P. J. (1994), 'Narrative practices: their role in socialization and self-construction', in U. Neisser and R. Fivush (eds.), *The Remembering Self: Construction and Accuracy in the Self-Narrative*. Cambridge: Cambridge University Press, 158–79.

Neisser, U. (1976), *Cognition and Reality*. New York: W. H. Freeman and Co.

—— (1982), 'Snapshots or benchmarks?', in U. Neisser (ed.), *Memory Observed*. San Francisco: Freeman, 43–8.

Nelson, K. (1986), *Event Knowledge: Structure and Function in Development*. Hillsdale, NJ: Lawrence Erlbaum.

—— (1988), 'The ontogeny of memory for real world events', in U. Neisser and E. Winograd (eds.), *Remembering Reconsidered: Ecological and Traditional Approaches to Memory*. Cambridge: Cambridge University Press, 224–76.

—— (1993), 'The psychological and social origins of autobiographical memory', *Psychological Science*, 4: 7–19.

—— (1996), *Language in Cognitive Development: Emergence of the Mediated Mind*. Cambridge: Cambridge University Press.

—— (2001), 'Language and the self: from the "experiencing I" to the "continuing me"', in C. Moore and K. Lemmon (eds.), *The Self in Time*. Mahwah, NJ: Lawrence Erlbaum, 15–33.

Oakes, L. M. (1994), 'Development of infants' use of continuity cues in their perception of causality', *Developmental Psychology*, 30: 869–79.

—— and Cohen, L. B. (1990), 'Infant perception of a causal event', *Cognitive Development*, 5: 193–207.

Peacocke, C. (1996), 'Entitlement, self-knowledge and conceptual redeployment', *Proceedings of the Aristotelian Society*, 96: 117–58.

Perner, J. (1991), *Understanding the Representational Mind*. Cambridge, Mass.: MIT Press.

Pillemer, D. B. (1998), *Momentous Events, Vivid Memories*. Cambridge, Mass.: Harvard University Press.

—— and White, S. H. (1989), 'Childhood events recalled by children and adults', in H. W. Reese (ed.), *Advances in Child Development and Behavior*, xxi. New York: Academic Press, 297–340.

Povinelli, D. J., Landry, A. M., Theall, L. A., Clark, B. R., and Castille, C. M. (1999), 'Development of young children's understanding that the recent past is causally bound to the present', *Developmental Psychology*, 35: 1426–39.

Reese, E. (2002), 'Social factors in the development of autobiographical memory: the state of the art', *Social Development*, 11: 124–42.

Roessler, J. (1999), 'Perception, introspection and attention', *European Journal of Philosophy*, 7: 47–64.

Schank, R. C., and Abelson, R. P. (1977), *Scripts, Plans, Goals and Understanding*. Hillsdale, NJ: Erlbaum.

Schlottmann, A., Allen, D., Linderoth, C., and Hesketh, S. (2002), 'Perceptual causality in children', *Child Development*, 73: 1656–77.

Shultz, T. (1982), 'Rules of causal attribution', *Monographs of the Society for Research in Child Development*, 47: 1–51.

—— and Kestenbaum, M. (1985), 'Causal reasoning in children', *Annals of Child Development*, 2: 195–249.

Tomasello, M. (1999), *The Cultural Origins of Human Cognition*. Cambridge, Mass.: Harvard University Press.

Tulving, E. (1972), 'Episodic and semantic memory', in E. Tulving and W. Donaldson (eds.), *Organization of Memory*. New York.: Academic Press, 381–403.

—— (1983), *Elements of Episodic Memory*. Oxford: Oxford University Press.

—— (2002), 'Episodic memory: from mind to brain', *Annual Review of Psychology*, 53: 1–25.

Welch-Ross, M. K. (1997), 'Mother–child participation in conversation about the past: relationships to preschoolers' theory of mind', *Developmental Psychology*, 33: 618–29.

—— (2001), 'Personalizing the temporally extended self: evaluative self-awareness and the development of autobiographical memory', in C. Moore and K. Lemmon (eds.), *The Self in Time*. Mahwah, NJ: Lawrence Erlbaum, 97–120.

Wellman, H. M., Somerville, S. C., and Haake, R. J. (1979), 'Development of search procedures in real-life spatial environments', *Developmental Psychology*, 15: 530–42.

Werner, H., and Kaplan, B. (1963), *Symbol Formation*. Hillsdale, NJ: Erlbaum.

White, P. A. (1995), *The Understanding of Causation and the Production of Action: From Infancy to Adulthood*. Hove: Erlbaum.

Williams, B. A. O. (2002), *Truth and Truthfulness*. Princeton: Princeton University Press.

13

Joint Attention and Common Knowledge

John Campbell

1. A RELATIONAL VIEW OF JOINT ATTENTION

Joint attention requires an object to which to attend and two or more people to attend to it. In principle there seems to be no limit to the number of people who could be jointly attending to the same object, but for present purposes I will assume that we are dealing only with the two-person case. So one canonical form for a report of joint attention is:

x and y are jointly attending to z.

We cannot, though, suppose that this will be the fully analysed form of a report of joint attention. For when a report of the form 'x and y are jointly attending to z' is true, it will be true in virtue, in part, of the individual psychological states of the two participants x and y. So we ought to be able to say just which psychological states of x and y matter here. And no doubt the analysis should impose the same conditions on x as on y; the two participants have to meet the same conditions for them to be jointly attending.

One basic issue we have to address here can be stated as follows. Suppose that you are sitting on a park bench watching a swan, and someone comes to sit beside you. Perhaps there is some rudimentary conversation. So you shift from solitary attention to the swan, through a condition in which both you and your neighbour are coincidentally watching the swan, to full joint attention. Should this transition be thought of as affecting the intrinsic nature of your perceptual experience of the swan? On what I will call a 'non-experientialist' view, your perceptual experience is just the same whether you are engaged in solitary attention to the swan or in joint attention to it. What is distinctive of the case in which you and another are jointly attending is that (a) you are monitoring the direction of the other person's attention, and (b) one of the factors controlling the direction of your own attention is the direction of the other person's attention. Any account will have to find some place for these 'monitoring and control'

Thanks to Michael Bacharach, Christopher Peacocke, and the participants in the Joint Attention meeting at Warwick in 1999 for stimulating discussion of these issues. This is a lightly edited excerpt from the discussion of these topics in my *Reference and Consciousness* (Oxford: Oxford University Press, 2002).

elements in joint attention. The non-experientialist view holds that these elements are external to the perceptual experience of attention itself. On what I will call an 'experientialist' account, by contrast, there is a shift in the nature of your perceptual experience itself when you shift from solitary attention to joint attention.

Within experientialist accounts, we can distinguish between relational and reductive analyses. I will say that an analysis is 'reductive' if it is possible to say which individualistic states of x matter here, without this already implying that there is joint attention involving x and another. By contrast, an analysis is 'relational' if ascribing the relevant psychological states to x already implies that there is someone with whom x is jointly attending. On a relational view, joint attention is a primitive phenomenon of consciousness. Just as the object you see can be a constituent of your experience, so too it can be a constituent of your experience that the other person is, with you, jointly attending to the object. This is not to say that in a case of joint attention, the other person will be an object of your attention. On the contrary, it is only the object that you are attending to. It is rather that, when there is another person with whom you are jointly attending to the thing, the existence of that other person enters into the individuation of your experience. The other person is there, as co-attender, in the periphery of your experience. The object attended to, and the other person with whom you are jointly attending to that object, will enter into your experience in quite different ways. In this essay I want to state the case for this relational view of joint attention.

2. CAUSAL CONDITIONS ON JOINT ATTENTION

An experientialist account can accept that there are 'monitoring and control' dimensions to joint attention. To fill out the experientialist account, then, we could say that for it to be true that x and y are jointly attending to z, x and y must be co-ordinating their attention to z, in that one of the factors sustaining x's attention to z is that y is attending to z, and one of the factors sustaining y's attention to z is that x is attending to z. This co-ordination of attention may involve the use of subpersonal mechanisms, rather than explicit, personal-level thoughts about the direction of the other person's attention, or explicit intentions to attend to whatever the other person is attending to, as on a non-experientialist model. On an experientialist account, what is distinctive of joint attention, at the subjective level, is that the other person enters into your experience. There surely are causal conditions on this happening; we could say:

> *Causal Conditions on Joint Attention:* If x and y are jointly attending to z, then x's experience of perceptual attention will have a certain functional role, and that functional role may be realized by a brain state. For x's experience

to be an experience of jointly attending, with y, to z, both of the following conditions must be met:

(a) z must have played a causal role in bringing it about that x is in that brain state, and

(b) the fact of y's continued attention to z must be one of the factors causally sustaining x's continuing to attend to z.

On a non-experientialist account, by contrast, the monitoring of the direction of the other person's attention involves personal-level perception and judgement about the other person, and bringing your own attention into line with the other person's involves explicit intention and planning. On a non-experientialist view, though, the experience of attending to the object is intrinsically the same whether it is solitary or joint attention.

On the relational version of the experientialist view, the individual experiential state you are in, when you and another are jointly attending to something, is an experiential state that you could not be in were it not for the other person attending to the object. The other person enters into your experience as a constituent of it, as co-attender, and the other person could not play that role in your experience except by being co-attender. So when it is true that 'x and y are jointly attending to z', it will on the relational experiential view be true that x has the experience of jointly attending, with y, to z. And from this ascription of a psychological state to x, it follows that x and y are jointly attending to z.

Of course, it can happen that you think you are involved in joint attention when you are not. You and I might start out jointly attending to one of the fish in a pond, but at a certain point, having for a long period taken myself to be jointly attending with you to that fish, I might find that you have silently slipped away, perhaps long ago. In that case, on a relational view, I did not have the kind of experience I took myself to be having. I took it that you were a constituent of my experience, as co-attender to the fish, when in fact you were not.

It would also be possible to have a non-relational or, as I called it earlier, a reductive version of the experiential view. On this account, when we are describing the psychological states in which x and y must be, individually, when x and y are jointly attending to z, we can describe x's states without presupposing that y exists, and we can describe y's states without presupposing that x exists. Of course, in giving a full analysis of what it is for it to be true that 'x and y are jointly attending to z', the reductionist may have to appeal to causal relations between the direction of x's attention and the direction of y's attention. At that point, the analysis will indeed presuppose the existence of both x and y. It remains true that on the reductionist account, the relevant psychological states ascribed to x in the analysis will not themselves presuppose the existence of y, and similarly the psychological states ascribed to y will not of themselves presuppose the existence of x. So those psychological states can be described individually without presupposing that the subject is engaging in joint attention with another. By contrast, as we saw, on a relational account the other person is a constituent of your experience when you are jointly attending to something, and present in the capacity of co-attender; so on this account a characterization of the individual subject's psychological state does after all presuppose that this individual is engaged in joint attention with another person.

Which, if any, of these pictures of joint attention is correct? I think we have to be quite explicit here about why we need the notion of joint attention at all. It is, after all, not needed for knowledge of what someone else is talking or thinking about. Knowledge of the reference of someone else's demonstrative term does not demand joint attention by the two of you. Suppose that I am hiding in the bushes as you come out into the moonlight, and as you look around, you soliloquize. You use demonstratives in your soliloquy, referring to, for example, 'that star'. There seems to be no reason why I can't understand what you are saying and know what you are thinking; I can see the star myself, and I know that it is what you are talking and thinking about. Of course, there is a sense in which your perspective on the star will be a bit different from mine, since you are seeing it from a different position; but I can compensate for that, either by imagining how it would look from your perspective or by explicit reasoning about what you can see. All this, without you even knowing that I am there. So to determine which picture of joint attention we want, we still have to explain why any such picture is required, since there is a basic understanding of other people's demonstratives that can be achieved without the benefit of joint attention.

3. CO-ORDINATED ATTACK

If I am to know which demonstrative thought you are having, there has to be some way in which it is indicated to me which thing you are thinking about. If you are expressing your thought to me, using a demonstrative term, there has to be what Kaplan (1989) called the demonstration accompanying the demonstrative— a pointing gesture, some descriptions indicating where to look, maybe a sortal term, and so on. Suppose we consider a case in which the demonstration is a little bit unusual. Suppose that you and I are both sitting in front of the same big screen, but in separate compartments, so that we cannot see or hear each other directly, though we can type messages on to the screen. And the screen contains a number of differently coloured circles. You type on to the screen, 'That circle is the target'. How do I know which circle you are referring to? To let me know which circle you are attending to, you have a set of buttons which will light up lamps in my compartment. To signal that you are attending to the green circle, you push the green button, and the green lamp lights up in my compartment. Then I know that you are attending to the green circle. This is not to be thought of as a descriptive identification of the object, though, but an attention-orienting demonstration (if you prefer, we might consider an apparatus of electronic arrows which point to the object). The only problem is that the electronic apparatus functions only about 50 per cent of the time; the signal gets through only about 50 per cent of the time. So although I know that you are attending to the green circle, you do not know that I know that, since you do not know whether your message got through.

What I need, to let you know that your message got through, is an acknowledgement button, so that I can light a lamp in your compartment confirming receipt of your message. Once you get that, you know that I know that you are attending to the green circle. But again, the electronic apparatus works only about 50 per cent of the time, so I do not know whether you got my acknowledgement. You have to be able to confirm receipt of my acknowledgement; then I will know that you know that I know that you are attending to the green circle. And again, the apparatus works only about 50 per cent of the time. And so on. Just to be fully explicit about this, the electronic apparatus never sends an incorrect message; it either works or sends no message at all. And you and I have to interest in sending wrong messages. So any message we get is accurate.

Suppose you and I are playing a war game, and we have to co-ordinate our attack on a single target. If we do manage to agree on the target, then victory is certain, but it will be a disaster if only one of us attacks; anything is better than that scenario. You type up on the screen, 'Let's attack that one at noon', pushing the green button to demonstrate to me which one you mean. The green lamp goes on in my compartment, so I know which one you have in mind. Does this make it rational for me to attack at noon? The problem is that you do not know whether your message has got through. So you do not know whether I will attack, so it is not rational for you to take the chance of attacking alone. So I do not know that you will attack, which makes it irrational for me to attack. I can try to improve the situation by pushing my acknowledgement button, but I will not know whether the message has got through, and you will know that I don't know that, so we will still be sitting tight. And so on; no finite iteration will allow us to manage the co-ordinated attack that is available to us and will secure victory (Rubinstein, 1989).

The trouble is that we can in practice achieve success in co-ordinated attacks. If you and I are sitting side by side, not in booths, but in an ordinary situation, it could be fully apparent to us that we will succeed. But how can we have achieved this? Michael Bacharach sums up the standard response, given by Lewis (1969) and Schiffer (1972), as follows (he is discussing the case in which two people are sitting at a table with a carafe in full view between them):

A normal human will not only see the carafe, but will also see the *normality* of the other co-present normals; lastly, normality has the reflexive property that it is part of being normal to know the perceptual and epistemic capacities of normal people. ... These characteristics of normality imply that in the carafe situation an inferential process is set in motion which leads asymptotically, if the agents are logically omniscient, to common knowledge. (Bacharach, 1998, p. 309)

But we have to acknowledge that agents are not usually logically omniscient. Since a rational attack by either or both of us seems to require that we have the infinitary knowledge, it seems to follow that we could never be in a position to attack. You might say that what all this shows is that it would not, in an ordinary situation, without the booths, ever be rational for you and I to launch a co-ordinated attack on the basis of one of us saying, 'Let's attack that one!' Perhaps at best there is a thought, 'Well, we'll have to do something sooner or later', that might drive you to take the risk. But this really would be irrational, since we are considering a case in which there are known to be no time-limits on effective action, and the pay-off structure is that mismanaged attack means disaster, while a successful attack yields only a significant but limited reward. The trouble is that it seems perfectly evident that even with that pay-off structure in place, in the ordinary case, without the booths, a co-ordinated attack on the basis of the demonstrative utterance, 'Let's attack that one!', could be quite rational. Intuitively, in an ordinary case, with you and I looking at the screen and no booths, everything is out in the open to such an extent that we can rationally attack. How can that be? This is the puzzle raised by co-ordinated attack.

Suppose we go back to considering the ways in which we might analyse the report, 'x and y are jointly attending to z'. Suppose we consider the non-experiential view, on which what this requires of x is that x should be (a) attending to z and (b) monitoring the direction of y's attention and having the direction of y's attention function as one of the factors causally determining the direction of x's own attention. It seems evident that on this view the puzzle is insoluble. The mere fact that x is attending to z does not of itself mean that anything is out in the open. And when we add the monitoring and control conditions to that, it seems evident that x would need, from monitoring y, to achieve infinitary knowledge of what they both know about the direction of their attention to z, by the argument above.

Similarly, if we consider the reductive version of an experientialist view, it seems evident that again, on this view, the puzzle of co-ordinated attack will be insoluble. The subject x will still have to achieve infinitary knowledge of their joint attention in order to make the attack rational.

It does seem to be different on what I called the relational version of the experiential view. On this view, what the subject in an ordinary context begins with is experience of the object to which she is attending, with the co-attender present as a constituent of the experience. This kind of relational experience is simply not available to the players in the booths. No matter how many iterations they go through, the end state will never be such a relational state, with the other person figuring as co-attender in one's experience. But on this view, the availability of the relational experience in the ordinary case is what makes it possible for us, in the ordinary case, to be rational in executing a co-ordinated attack.

4. TWO CHALLENGES

There are two challenges that this view faces. The first is to check whether being in the relational experiential state it describes could provide anything more than n-level knowledge of the situation, for some particular finite n. The further challenge is this: suppose we can establish that being in the relational experiential state transcends n-level knowledge, for any particular n. We need to determine whether that is because the relational experiential state merely provides the basis for n-level knowledge, for any finite value of n. That is, if the situation is merely that the logically omniscient subject could derive infinitary knowledge from the relational experiential state, then we have not progressed beyond the idea of an appeal to normality set out in the quotation from Bacharach above.

I begin with the first challenge, which we can address inductively. Suppose someone claims that being in the relational experiential state can provide only knowledge of what the other person is attending to—that it can provide only level-1 knowledge. We can see that the significance of the relational experiential state goes beyond that, by reflecting that if x is in such a state, with y present, as co-attender, as a constituent of the state, then it follows that y too must be in such a relational experiential state. So y has the experience of attending to z, jointly with x, and on that basis y can know that x is attending to z. And x knows that y has such an experience. So x is in a position to have the level-2 knowledge that y knows that x is attending to z. Hence, x's relational experiential state is not exhausted by its implications for level-1 knowledge. Suppose now that, for some finite n, we agree that x has n-level knowledge of the situation. Then on the basis of y's relational experience, y too has n-level knowledge of the situation. And x can know this. So x can achieve $n + 1$-level knowledge of y's knowledge of the direction of x's attention. The derivational possibilities of the relational experiential state do not have a finite bound.

Now the second challenge comes. Does this show anything more than that the relational experiential state can serve as the basis on which a logically omniscient subject—perhaps given auxiliary knowledge of the context (that y's experiences do yield y knowledge)—could derive infinitary knowledge? If not, then we have made no progress beyond the appeal to 'normality'. I think that this challenge has not yet been met; to meet it, we have to consider just what it means to say that in x's experience, y is 'present as co-attender', that y too is a constituent of the experience. I think that as long as we think of the role that y is playing in the experience as something that we have to understand in broadly representational terms, then this challenge really is lethal. For when you think of the experience in representational terms, all that is happening is that y has been introduced as a constituent of x's experience, but we have as yet been told nothing about how the relationship between x and y is being represented within x's experience. And when we ask what relation is being represented, it seems entirely obscure how that relation, whatever it is, could be anything more than the provision of a basis on which *n*-level finitary knowledge could be derived, for arbitrary *n*.

I think that the problem here is the representational view of experience, and it is, indeed, just to counter the representational view that the relational account takes the co-attender to be a constituent of the experience. Suppose we consider for a moment the case of ordinary, solitary attention to an object you can see. Suppose that your eye is resting on a scene—say a garden—and your attention is now on one plant, now on another. What change does it make to your experience when you shift from highlighting one plant to highlighting another? On a representationalist account, the difference must be a difference in the representational content of your experience. But it seems quite evident that there need be no such difference in representational content. The tree seems no greener than it did before you attended specifically to it, for example. And although in some cases the shift in attention will result in your obtaining more information about just that tree, as we saw, that is not definitive of the attentional shift; a covert shift in attention will not typically lead to any enrichment of your representation of the object. The change, when you shift attention from one plant to another, has to do rather with the functional role of your experience of the object. When you attend specifically to it, you are in a position to harvest knowledge from it, and to act specifically on it.

Suppose now we consider the case in which another person enters the content of your experience, not as the object of your attention, but as your co-attender: not as the thing to which you are attending, but as the person with whom you are attending to a specific object. There is again no reason to think that this shift, from solitary attention to having the other person enter your experience as co-attender, should be thought of as a shift in the representational content of your experience. Rather, there is a shift in functional role. If the other person enters your experience as co-attender, then you and the other person are now in a position to engage rationally in joint projects with regard to the object, whether co-ordinated attack, joint investigation of the object, or some other project, such as fighting over it or jointly moving it. This is not in itself a representational change; there is no representation of your relation to the other person, and the way in which the other person seems to you to be may be exactly the same as before you became involved in the exercise of joint attention.

I am here only saying that attention and joint attention have functional roles; I am not saying that they are exhausted by those functional roles. Rather, attention and joint attention should be regarded as the categorical bases for the kinds of project we can carry out, whether those projects are solitary or joint verification and action. In either case, being in the state confronts one with the rational basis for one's actions. As we saw, this picture does not seem to be available on either the non-experiential or the reductive views of joint attention; only the relational experiential account can sustain this non-representational analysis.

There is an analogy here between the puzzle of co-ordinated attack and Lewis Carroll's (1895) famous puzzle of Achilles and the tortoise. Having crossed the line first, Achilles claims to have beaten the tortoise, a claim the tortoise disputes. But, says Achilles, 'If I crossed the line first, then I won; and I did cross the line first.' The tortoise agrees to that, but resists the conclusion that Achilles won. 'All right', says Achilles, 'but you must agree that if it's the case that if I crossed the line first, then I won, and if it's the case that I crossed the line first, then I did win. Moreover, it is the case that if I crossed the line first, then I won. And it is the case that I crossed the line first.' The tortoise agrees to all that. 'So I won!,' says Achilles. But here the tortoise disagrees. Setting up the problem in this way can make it seem that what the tortoise really needs to appreciate the validity of Achilles' inference is some infinitary knowledge; and the puzzle then is how we can rationally engage in inference without having such infinitary knowledge. But this generates the puzzle only by supposing that our appreciation of logical validity must be a matter exhaustively of the representation of logical rules. Similarly, the puzzle of co-ordinated attack is generated by supposing that the relations between the two joint attenders x and y must be a matter of how, in experience or thought, they represent their relations to one another. What I am proposing is that, on the contrary, in both cases we have to go beyond these appeals to representational states, and consider the categorical basis of what it is that the subjects can do. Rational transitions do not always have to be underpinned by explicit representations of their rationality.

5. WHY JOINT ATTENTION?

I am, then, proposing that we should think of joint attention as a more primitive phenomenon than common knowledge; but that joint attention can none the less have something of the force, in rendering an action rational, of infinitary common knowledge. The suggestion I want to make is that we can view joint attention as a primitive phenomenon of consciousness; just as the object can be a constituent of your experience, so too it can be a constituent of your experience that the other person is, with you, attending to the object. What I am suggesting is that joint attention, so conceived, could of itself have the force usually envisaged for infinitary common knowledge in rationalizing action, and that this explains how we can in practice succeed in tasks such as co-ordinated attack, for which no finite level of mutual knowledge is sufficient.

You might point out that Co-ordinated Attack scenarios can arise in many different cases, not just those involving perceptual demonstratives. The classical cases, indeed, would involve commanders on a battlefield, out of earshot of one another, exchanging messages by means of faulty equipment. And the kind of appeal to joint attention that I am proposing would be out of place in such cases.

But the puzzle of co-ordinated attack does not arise in such cases either. The puzzle arises only because it seems evident that in the cases involving a perceptual demonstrative, things are in fact sufficiently out in the open that Co-ordinated Attack could be rational. Then the puzzle is to understand how this could be, in the absence of infinitary knowledge. In the non-perceptual cases, however, it does not seem at all obvious that Co-ordinated Attack would be rational in the absence of infinitary knowledge. So there is no need to explain how co-ordinated attack might after all be rational in such a case.

I have been talking about the bearing of joint attention on our understanding of each other's perceptual demonstratives. It is easy to feel that the causal co-ordination of attention, which I have emphasized as an element in joint attention, though plainly of practical importance, does not play any role in an account of communication involving demonstratives, because of the following kind of case. Suppose that you and I look out of our windows at a dog barking in the moonlight. We are attending to the same thing, but this does not count as joint attention, because we may not even be aware of each other's existence. But suppose, as we lean out of our windows, that you and I catch sight of each other. Perhaps you and I have quarrelled, so that the mere fact that you are looking at the dog has not the slightest tendency to dispose me to continue looking at it. The fact that you are looking at the dog may actually dispose me somewhat to look away, but in fact I remain fascinated by the commotion. So it is not that you are causing me to attend to the dog, or that I am causing you to. There is no 'co-ordination' between us. I would be attending to the thing whether or not you existed. If, as we look out of our windows, you say to me, 'That dog is barking', I will on the face of it have no trouble in interpreting your remark, which thing you are talking about or what aspect of it you are commenting on, even though there is no co-ordination of the control of attention. But this case is only one step away from the case in which I hear you soliloquizing while hiding in the bushes. It is not a case in which we have full openness of communication; we are not yet in a position to launch a co-ordinated attack on the dog.

The case of the dog in the moonlight is a much more unusual case than might at first appear, because it really has to be a case in which there is zero causal co-ordination of attention. And that is not at all what would usually happen, even in the case of the quarrelling neighbours. Once you have any interest, however slight, in interpreting the other person's remark, there would ordinarily be some moves towards causal co-ordination by you; and likewise if the other person has any interest in being understood. The case in which the auditor has no interest whatever in whether he is attending to the same thing as his neighbour, and meanwhile the neighbour is speaking without any interest in whether her audience is able to interpret her correctly, is far removed from ordinary communication, and cannot be used to establish that causal co-ordination is not necessary in ordinary communication.

REFERENCES

BACHARACH, MICHAEL (1998), 'Common knowledge', in *New Palgrave Dictionary of Law and Economics*. London: Macmillan, 308–13.

CARROLL, LEWIS (1895), 'What the tortoise said to Achilles', *Mind*, 4: 278–80.

KAPLAN, DAVID (1989), 'Demonstratives', in Joseph Almog, John Perry, and Howard Wettstein (eds.), *Themes from Kaplan*. Oxford: Oxford University Press, 481–563.

LEWIS, DAVID (1969), *Convention*. Cambridge, Mass.: Harvard University Press.

RUBINSTEIN, A. (1989), 'The electronic mail game: strategic behaviour under "almost common knowledge"', *American Economic Review*, 79: 385–91.

SCHIFFER, STEPHEN (1972), *Meaning*. Oxford: Oxford University Press.

14

Joint Attention: Its Nature, Reflexivity, and Relation to Common Knowledge

Christopher Peacocke

Two parents are watching their son take his first upright steps in learning to walk. Here we have a paradigm of joint attention. The two parents are attending to their son; they are aware of each other's attention to their son; and all this attention is wholly overt. Everything is in the open, nothing is hidden. In what does this openness consist? Can we characterize it explicitly, without using metaphors?

The parents are likely to switch their attention to each other and smile during this episode. This would be a case of what is sometimes called 'contact attention'; and here too everything is in the open. Again, we can ask: what is a literal, explicit characterization of this openness?

As a stipulation, and following some but not all writers in the field, I will restrict the terms 'joint attention' and 'contact attention' to episodes which fully possess this openness. So our first task is to say what, constitutively, joint attention and contact attention are. We cannot hope to be clear about the relations of joint attention and contact attention to other phenomena and capacities until we have an answer to this foundational question. The question is not one of giving an analysis of the meaning of some word in English which has a determinate sense which is hard to make explicit. We use such metaphorical terms as 'openness' precisely because there is no such English word. So our task here is not conceptual analysis: it is rather that of characterizing properly a complex psychological phenomenon, of saying what it is.

After offering such a characterization, I will go on to consider the relation of joint attention to common or mutual knowledge. I will argue that the openness of joint attention is more fundamental than mutual knowledge; that in many cases it makes mutual knowledge possible; and that a range of phenomena that have

I thank Naomi Eilan for encouraging me to write up in more systematic form the remarks I made about the relations between joint attention and common knowledge in the general discussion session at the 1999 Warwick Conference on Joint Attention. (This is also known as calling my bluff.) I have been greatly helped by the challenge of responding to Stephen Schiffer's incisive critical comments on an earlier draft; by Gilbert Harman's guidance on the massive existing literature on some of the topics discussed here; by the editorial comments of Christoph Hoerl, Naomi Eilan, and Johannes Roessler; and by the discussion at a presentation of this material at the NEH Summer Institute on Consciousness and Intentionality at UCSC in 2002, run by David Chalmers and David Hoy, where I learned from the comments of George Downing, Michelle Montague, Scott Sturgeon, and Deborah Tollefsen.

been characterized in terms of mutual knowledge should rather be elucidated in terms of joint attention. If I am right, joint attention and its properties should receive a much more prominent position in the philosophy of mind and language than it has been accorded hitherto.

1. CHARACTERIZING THE OPENNESS OF JOINT ATTENTION

Joint attention involves much more than two subjects attending to the same object. Two subjects could each be attending to the same object without either being aware that the other is attending to the same object. More strikingly, two subjects could each be aware, and it could also be part of the content of their experience, that the other is attending to the same object, without the episode having the openness of joint attention and contact attention. Consider two people who are standing facing each other, separated by a thick pane of glass. Suppose each person falsely believes that this glass is a one-way mirror, allowing him to see the other, but preventing the other from seeing him. So each really sees the other, while believing the other cannot see him. This is far from having the openness of contact attention. Similarly, we can suppose that in this situation, both are attending to something—an animal, say—in their common field of view, off to one side of the glass between them. Each may have a genuine perception of the other attending to exactly the same thing as he is attending to, viz. the animal. But because each believes that the other cannot see him, this too is far from having the openness present in our paradigm cases of joint attention.

It might be suggested that these are not cases of joint attention, because each person does not perceive that the other is jointly attending with him in our strong, favoured sense of joint attention. That is a true statement about these cases. It is indeed true that in joint attention, subjects do perceive, or can be aware, that they are jointly attending. But this point cannot answer our original question, for it embeds the notion of joint attention within the content of psychological states such as attention, perception, and awareness. If our task is to say what joint attention and contact attention are, we do not fully answer that question by giving a condition which embeds that very notion within certain mental states.

The point bears upon the suggestion that what is distinctive of joint attention is that the co-attender figures, as someone who is co-attending to the same object, as a constituent of the subject's perceptual experience.[1] What does 'co-attender' mean in such a condition? If 'co-attender' means just 'attends to the same object', that condition will be met in our example of the glass barrier that is falsely believed to be a one-way mirror, in the case in which both subjects attend to the

---

[1] This proposal is made by John Campbell in Chapter 13 above, and in Campbell, 2002, ch. 8.

animal off to one side. In that example, each perceives that the other is co-attending in that sense. If 'co-attender' means something stronger, and implies full joint attention to the object to which both are attending, the notion of a co-attender simply embeds the property which is to be explained, the openness of joint attention.[2] This is not to say that such embeddings do not provide an important constraint upon what joint attention is. It is just to say that they cannot be the full account. Compare: to be fashionable, something must be believed to be fashionable. But this cannot be a complete account of what it is to be fashionable. We cannot fully or completely individuate the property of being fashionable by saying that it is that property P such that to have P, something must be believed to be P. Too many other properties besides that of being fashionable meet this condition; and correspondingly, it intuitively leaves out too much of what is involved in being fashionable.

How, then, are we to say, in a more informative way, what it is that is missing from the glass-barrier example, and is present in paradigm cases of genuine joint attention?

At this point, it is almost a reflex of a contemporary philosopher of mind to suggest that what is missing from the glass-barrier example is arbitrarily high iteration of some mental state. This would be an instance of the general style of approach that has proved so fruitful in the case of the special kind of overtness found in the much-discussed phenomenon of mutual or common knowledge, so carefully identified and discussed by David Lewis (1969, ch. 2, sect. 1) and Stephen Schiffer (1988, ch. 2, sect. 2). Let us follow Schiffer and take this as our definition of x and y's having mutual knowledge* that p (the asterisk is simply to indicate that we have a defined term here):

x knows that p

y knows that p

x knows that y knows that p

y knows that x knows that p

x knows that y knows that x knows that p

y knows that x knows that y knows that p

etc.

If we have only a finite initial segment of this series of conditions holding of x and y, we do not have fully overt knowledge between x and y that p. It has seemed plausible to suppose that in at least some cases, the overtness of x and y's knowledge consists in the holding of every proposition in this iteration. Could we not simply apply the same kind of idea to the case of the overtness of full joint attention?

---

[2] This means that if co-attention is construed in the weaker, first way, there will be a gap in Campbell's argument that perception of co-attention provides a basis for mutual knowledge.

There is a problem in trying to do so, and the problem stems from one of the differences between knowledge and perception. It is part of any plausible defence of the view that Schiffer's definition actually applies to a particular pair of individuals that for a person to have a belief captured in one of the longer iterations of belief, it is required only that the believed content is something the person could infer from what he indisputably currently believes. The thought of the believed content in a complex embedding does not have to enter his consciousness for the attribution of the belief to be correct. Many beliefs are indeed like this, as Schiffer notes: 'I trust that it is true of each philosophy don in Oxford that he knows that his maternal grandmother was never married to Benito Mussolini' (1988, p. 36). Now suppose we offered this hierarchy as distinctive of what is involved in joint attention of x and y to o:

x perceives that x and y are attending to o

y perceives that x and y are attending to o

x perceives that y perceives that x and y are attending to o

y perceives that x perceives that x and y are attending to o

x perceives that y perceives that x perceives that x and y are attending to o

etc.

The problem is that the observation which defends the applicability to real people of the definition of mutual knowledge* does not carry over to the perceptual case, nor to any other state of occurrent awareness. The sense in which each philosophy don in Oxford has the belief about his maternal grandmother is a counterfactual sense. It is something he would infer from currently stored beliefs by principles he already accepts. But perception and other states of occurrent awareness are not merely counterfactual at all. Someone perceives something to be the case only if in the actual world he is in a conscious state with the representational content of what he perceives to be the case. And it is quite implausible that in all cases that display the openness of joint attention, subjects are in the perceptual states mentioned above, with arbitrarily complex embeddings of the 'perceives that' operation, or any other operator expressing occurrent awareness.

The situation is yet more demanding on the philosophical theorist who wants to give a constitutive account of this openness. Even though arbitrarily high iterations of 'perceive that' or 'is occurrently aware that' do not obtain, nevertheless the openness of genuine joint attention is not something dispositional or counterfactual either. In fact, intuitively, what we are still characterizing metaphorically as the openness of the situation of joint attention and of contact attention is not merely something which exists: it also seems to be present to the consciousness of the participants. How are we to account for this combination of characteristics, the presence of such openness in consciousness, combined with the absence of arbitrarily complex embeddings within 'perceives that...'?

We can make a start on this task by characterizing what it is for a state of affairs to have what I will label 'mutual open-ended perceptual availability' to two subjects. To be thus available, a state of affairs must meet the following condition:

> If the obtaining of the state of affairs, and the operation of perceptual and attentional mechanisms in the two subjects, bring it about that one of them perceives that the state of affairs obtains, or bring it about that one of them perceives that the other perceives that it does, or brings it about ... etc., then the state of affairs (thus brought about) of his so perceiving is available for the other to perceive.

The other does not actually have to perceive the state of affairs so brought about for mutual open-ended availability to obtain. The availability to the other of the state of affairs brought about suffices. For the perceptual state of one person to be available to a second is for there to be information in the public environment of the second person which permits a sound computation to the content that the original person is in the perceptual state, using computational principles of the same kind (possibly differing only in complexity of the contents involved) as those already employed by the second person. Information can be available to a subject, but not in fact be accessed by that subject. This is not the same as its being hidden. In the case of joint attention, the state of affairs of the two subjects each attending to a given object is one which has mutual open-ended perceptual availability to them.

This description of open-ended availability is a little too stringent. You may see the other as seeing that you see that *p*. Now suppose the other then becomes occurrently aware of this third-order seeing of yours. Do we really want a characterization of open-endedness that excludes iterations that, at the higher levels, involve occurrent awareness that is not actually perceptual? That seems too strong. The distinctive openness can be present provided occurrent awarenesses at higher levels are available, even if they are not actually perceptual (they remain different from the results of conscious inference). We should indeed still require genuine perception that the other perceives that *p*. It is distinctive of the phenomenon we seek to characterize that any iterations are based on conscious awareness, rather than reached by personal-level inference. We can relax the definition of mutual open-ended perceptual availability to accommodate these points. Henceforth I take the mutual open-ended availability of a state of affairs *s* to two people to mean this:

> Each perceives that the other perceives that *s* obtains; and if either is occurrently aware that the other is aware that he is aware ... that *s* obtains, then the state of affairs of his being so occurrently aware is available to the other's occurrent awareness.

Here I take it that perceiving that something is so is one, but not the only, form of occurrent awareness that it is so.

No finite mind can accommodate arbitrarily long embeddings of contents beginning *perceives that* or *is occurrently aware that* in its representational contents. What is available for a subject to perceive will eventually not be capable of entering the content of the perceiver's states, because of cognitive and computational limitations in the perceiver's psychological economy. These limitations should not be taken as limitations on the openness of the situation of full joint attention, but as limitations on the ability of the subject to take advantage of what is made available by such openness. If we were to have a definition of openness which can be satisfied only by infinite minds, it could not capture the openness which is enjoyed in joint attention by actual finite human beings such as ourselves.

The mutual open-ended perceptual availability of x's and y's attending to a particular object seems to be a necessary condition for the openness of their joint attention to the object. It is not sufficient. Consider someone who is surprised and delighted when he discovers that when he is attending to an object, the other person notices that fact. This can be the situation of someone who is just coming to appreciate the possibility of joint attention, but is not yet fully engaging in it. This is a case of *incipient* joint attention. Yet this person and his partner's attention to an object may have the property of mutual open-ended perceptual availability. Having this property is consistent with merely incipient joint attention. It is one thing for a state of affairs to have that property; another for the participants to have some awareness that it does. I think this awareness that the case is one of open-ended availability is essential to the full openness of joint attention.

More generally, when there is full joint awareness between two subjects, there is awareness of full joint awareness. That is, full joint awareness has what logicians would call a fixed-point character. The phenomenon of full joint awareness shows that this logical property corresponds to something psychologically real. Now, if mutual open-ended perceptual availability can be present without awareness of its presence, and if full joint attention cannot be present without awareness of *its* presence, then it follows that full joint awareness does not consist merely in mutual open-ended perceptual availability. Mutual open-ended perceptual availability can be at most part of what is involved in full joint attention.

Mutual open-ended perceptual availability is a notion that it takes some intellectual reflection to formulate. It might be doubted for this reason whether it can really enter the content of perceptual experience. I would contest the objection. There are other clear cases in which a person experiences something as being a certain way, does not necessarily have a word or recognitional concept for that way, and in which his experiencing it as being that way consists in his experiencing it as having other features, which he may find it quite hard to articulate. To take a familiar example, someone may experience something as diamond-shaped. Someone can have this experience without having formed a recognitional concept *diamond-shaped*. To experience something as diamond-shaped is to experience it as a shape which is symmetrical about the bisectors of its angles (see Peacocke,

1992, ch. 3). Even quite sophisticated thinkers find it hard to say what it is about something that is diamond-shaped that makes them experience it as so. All the same, the experience of symmetry about the bisectors of the angles is real and effective in producing the distinctive way the whole shape is experienced as being. At a much greater level of complexity, there is no difficulty of principle in two people experiencing their joint attention to an object as having a certain feature, a feature which consists in their experiencing certain properties and relations as instantiated, properties and relations they may find it hard to articulate despite the familiarity of the experience.

We might try another hypothesis, and appeal not just to mutual open-ended perceptual availability, but to awareness thereof. Is awareness by two people, attending to the same object, of the mutual open-ended perceptual availability of their situation sufficient for the intuitive openness which is characteristic of joint attention? Such awareness can be occurrent; and since it does not involve an arbitrarily high iteration of occurrent attitudes, it is immune to the objections against the earlier naïve extension from the case of mutual knowledge. None the less, even considering the possibilities in the abstract, we would have to say that this awareness is still not sufficient for full openness. For someone could be aware that his situation has the property of mutual open-ended perceptual availability, without being aware that the other had the same awareness. One could think of cases in which someone is told that the other, unlike oneself, does not have such awareness, and in which one has come to internalize this, so that it affects one's perceptions of the other.

In actual cases of joint attention, each is aware of the mutual open-ended perceptual availability because he sees the other, he sees the object to which both are attending, and sees the spatial relations between these three things, and the other's perceptual organs. So does it suffice to add a requirement to that effect? We might try to add to the conditions that

> *x* and *y* are fully jointly attending to *o* iff
>
> (a) *x* and *y* are attending to *o*;
>
> (b) *x* and *y* are each aware that their attention in (a) has mutual open-ended perceptual availability;

this further requirement:

> the awareness in (b) results from *x*'s and *y*'s perception of their spatial relations to o, and to one another, and to the sense-organs involved in their attention in (a)?

That would not suffice. If a person who informs each of *x* and *y* that their attention in (a) has mutual open-ended perceptual availability does so only when he has checked on the spatial relations of *x*, *y*, and *o*, and the properties of their sense-organs, the 'results from' relation in the proposed third requirement could hold. But this would not be a case of full joint attention. Besides being wrong in detail, such a style of modification is taking a wrong turn for several reasons. The most fundamental is that we are aiming to characterize the experience of openness itself, not what makes it available.

I suggest that one distinctive feature of full joint attention is as follows. Suppose you are a participant in a situation of full joint awareness. Concerning the total awareness which is involved in your joint attention, you are aware of the following: that both you and the other person are aware that this total awareness exists.

On this view, the total awareness has an indexical intentional content which makes reference to the total awareness itself. Is this coherent and intelligible, and if so, what does it involve?

There are many examples of mental states and events whose intentional contents contain indexical components that make reference to those very same mental states and events. Suppose I am being lazy, and my friend encourages me on urgent practical grounds to start thinking. I may then think:

This thinking is coming too late.

My thought is about the very event of thinking itself; and the thought may very well be true. If I am interrupted in my thinking, that may be my only thought on this occasion. The episode of thinking 'This thinking is coming too late' may be the only thinking to which the demonstrative component 'This thinking' refers. Mental events and states, like linguistic items, can sometimes refer to themselves indexically.

The phenomenon is to be distinguished from cases falling under two other descriptions, cases whose coherence is doubtful. It is prima facie plausible that awareness of something is always distinct from what it is awareness of. (A closely related claim would be that awareness that something is the case is always distinct from the holding of the proposition of which it is awareness.) If that is so, no state can be, or consist in part in, an awareness of itself. But the indexical mental self-reference of which I have been speaking does not involve such incoherence. To say that a mental state of awareness has an intentional content which refers to that awareness is not to say that it is an awareness that consists in part in an awareness of itself. The indexical component *this awareness* can refer to an awareness without the awareness referred to having itself as an individuating component. Such reference no more involves a regress of individuation than does the intentional component *this thinking* in 'This thinking is coming too late'. Such a self-referential thought does not require that some event of thinking be a constituent of itself. For something to have an intentional content which refers to itself is not for it to be individuated by its relations to itself. There is no kind of objectionable ungroundedness here.

Indexical mental self-reference is also distinct from the use of such vacuous contents as 'This intentional content is thus-and-so'. Here the indexical component purports to refer to an intentional content; and arguably it cannot succeed in doing so. The indexical intentional contents with which I am concerned refer, by contrast, not to other intentional contents or their constituents, but to mental events or states. So they do not have this second kind of ungroundedness either.

Indexical self-reference can generate iterations. The extent to which this possibility is realized depends upon what notions feature in the content in which the indexical self-reference is made, and on what principles hold for those notions. To illustrate how indexical self-reference can generate iterations, I will first consider a linguistic case, since it shows the phenomenon in relatively pure form, free of extraneous complications. The basic structures illustrated in this simple case are present also in much more complex examples.

Suppose we have a rather powerful encyclopaedia E. It contains not only first-order information about the world, but also contains information about encyclopaedias, including itself. In particular,

(i)   The encyclopaedia E says:

(C)   Rome is Italy's capital and this encyclopaedia E contains this conjunction.

We can raise the question of which propositions this encyclopaedia is committed to. There is a notion of commitment, and an entailment-like notion of implication, for which we have the following principle of closure of commitment under implication:

(Closure Principle) If E is committed to A, and A implies B, then E is committed to B.

From E's containing the self-referential information (C) together with the Closure Principle, we can obtain arbitrarily complex iterations of 'E is committed to E is committed to E is committed to . . . C', as follows.

From the statement of the example, proposition (i), we have

(ii)   E is committed to C.

Now C itself implies that E contains C, and hence that E is committed to C . That is, we have

(iii)   C implies E is committed to C.

We can now apply the Closure Principle, taking the proposition C as the value of 'A' and the proposition 'E is committed to C' as the value of 'B' in our formulation of the Closure Principle. From that Principle, (ii), and (iii), it follows that

(iv)   E is committed to: E is committed to C.

That gives our first iteration. We have also just shown:

(v)   (ii) implies (iv).

We can now apply the Closure Principle again, taking the proposition (ii) as the value of 'A', and the proposition (iv) as the value of 'B'. By the Closure Principle, (iv), and (v), we can conclude:

(vi)   E is committed to: E is committed to: E is committed to C.

It is clear that this pattern of argument can be repeated to obtain arbitrarily long iterations of 'E is committed to' preceding C.

Self-reference within (C) is wholly essential to obtaining these iterations. Suppose we had only the following information, which does not involve self-reference, about a variant encyclopaedia F:

> (i′) The encyclopaedia F says:

> (D) Rome is Italy's capital, and the encyclopaedia F contains the information that Rome is Italy's capital.

Arbitrarily high iterations do not follow from this. F says that it says that Rome is Italy's capital; but it leaves it open (on the basis of the information given) as to whether it is committed to saying that it says it. In our little derivation above (iii) was crucial in arguing for the iterations. The analogue of (iii) does not hold in the case in which we have only (i′). (D) itself does not imply that F contains (D). (D) implies only that F contains the information that Rome is Italy's capital, and not that it contains the information (D) itself.

Now we can return to mental states and events with indexical self-referential contents. Do they generate arbitrarily high iterations? To apply and extend a remark of Barwise (1988) to our example of the encyclopaedia: commitment travels at the speed of logic, but awareness and knowledge travel at the speed of the mind. We can add that sometimes that speed is zero. Consider someone who has a genuinely reflexive awareness of his own pain. He is not merely aware that he is in pain. He rather meets the condition (vii):

> (vii) he is aware that he is in pain, and he is aware this whole awareness exists.

Do arbitrarily high iterations of 'he is aware that' applied to 'he is in pain' follow from (vii)? They would if we had the following unrestricted principle:

> If our subject is aware that an awareness exists, and this latter awareness involves his being ϕ (for a suitably tight notion of involvement), then he is aware that he is ϕ.

This unrestricted principle does not hold, if humans are not capable of arbitrarily complex states of awareness—as, to say it again, they cannot be if their minds are finite. But there is a clear sense in which the materials are available for a subject to rise to any particular level of iteration once he meets the reflexive condition (vii). For (vii) is stronger than any finite iterations of 'he is aware that' applied to contents that do not refer to the mental state of awareness in question.

So it is with full joint attention. The account of full joint attention by x and y to o that I am now suggesting is this:

> (a) x and y are attending to o;

> (b) x and y are each aware that their attention in (a) has mutual open-ended perceptual availability; and

(c) x and y are each aware that this whole complex state of awareness (a)–(c) exists.

For any particular level of iteration of 'x is aware that y is aware that . . .', it could in principle be reached by x and y, if each co-operates and each extracts everything from the state of awareness that is required to reach that level. No finite mind can reach every level given that we are concerned with a non-dispositional form of awareness. But (a)–(c) remain very different from a non-self-referential state of awareness with finitely many iterations and a cut-off point.[3]

The elements of the finitely many iterations which do hold in a particular case of full joint attention also have a single common explanation: awareness with an indexically self-referential content. More generally, just as (vii) is a case of individual genuinely reflexive consciousness, this account (a)–(c) of full joint attention can be regarded as treating it as a simple two-person case of genuinely reflexive social consciousness.

Full joint attention, even if its participants cannot fully articulate its nature, is a relatively sophisticated state. Its reflexivity is possible only for beings who have some way of representing attention, mental states, and employing some form of indexical reference to mental states. Between the most primitive forms of mutual awareness required for simple co-ordinated joint actions and the mature phenomenon of full joint attention, there will be a series of increasingly rich types of mental representation, content, and operations upon them. The conceptual, as well as the empirical, investigation of this series is one of the many tasks for future work suggested by the present approach. It is, for example, well known that infants are perceptually sensitive to the distinction between those events which appear to be actions and those which do not. But looking at something, and attending to something, are actions. The ability to identify actions will be the first step into the territory in which the mature phenomenon of full joint attention is located.

Important questions also arise at this point about the relation of awareness with self-referential intentional contents to the possibility of self-involving situations, and to other self-referential mental states. It can be very tempting to use self-involving situations in describing the reflexivity of full joint attention. Such an approach raises many metaphysical issues: I pursue some of them in the Appendix to this paper, in order not to lose the main thread of the argument in the philosophy of mind proper. That thread now leads us to consider the relation

---

[3] States with indexical contents have been used by Gilbert Harman in the characterization of mutual knowledge. He observes: 'A group of people have mutual knowledge of p if each knows p AND WE KNOW THIS, where "THIS" refers to the whole fact known' (Harman, 1977, p. 422). Harman also makes use of self-referential intentions to analogous iterative effect in his review of Schiffer, 1988, (Harman, 1974). For more general remarks on self-referential attitudes, see Harman, 1986, esp. ch. 8. The views I defend in the text above do not imply that all intentions, theoretical conclusions, or perceptual experiences have self-referential contents.

between full joint attention as characterized here and the kind of openness involved in mutual knowledge.

2. JOINT ATTENTION AND MUTUAL KNOWLEDGE

I start this section by arguing that the classical account of common or mutual knowledge developed by Lewis and Schiffer does not capture the openness of some of the situations to which it has been applied in the literature.

Lewis's and Schiffer's accounts, which are in their essentials identical, are justly famous and beautiful accounts of a phenomenon with which previous writers had grappled and failed. I do not question that the Lewis–Schiffer account gives a good philosophical explanation of some cases of mutual knowledge as Schiffer defines it. I think it gives the correct explanation of mutual or common knowledge of such truths as that George W. Bush is currently President of the USA, and that people here in New York drive on the right, speak English, and use dollars and cents as money. But I think there is a class of cases to which the Lewis–Schiffer account does not apply, even though these cases nevertheless display a distinctive kind of mutual openness. This class includes even some examples by reference to which the notion of mutual knowledge was introduced in this literature. The class of cases in question is that in which there is a distinctive kind of knowledge made available by full joint attention.

To substantiate these claims, we need to look in more detail at the classical account. I will use Schiffer's formulation (points corresponding to those I will make could be set out *pari passu* for the Lewis formulation). First, here is Schiffer's development of an example, a case in which we 'Suppose that you and I are dining together and that we are seated across from one another and that on the table between us is a rather conspicuous candle' (1988, p. 31). He continues (I will change his notation for uniformity with the preceding, but otherwise this is verbatim):

Clearly I know that there is a candle on the table. So

Kxp.

I also know that you know that there is a candle on the table. How do I know this? First, I know that if a 'normal' person (i.e. a person with normal sense faculties, intelligence, and experience) has his eyes open and his head facing an object of a certain size (etc.), then that person will see that an object of a certain sort is before him. Secondly, I know that you are a 'normal' person and I see that your open-eyed head is facing the candle... So

$KyKxp$.

Further, I do not presume to be the only person aware of the above-mentioned law about normal people in certain circumstances; I also know that you know that normal people see things that are in their line of vision when their eyes are open, etc. And I have seen that you see that my open-eyed head is facing the candle. So I know that you know that I know that there is a candle on the table; i.e.

KxKyKx*p*.

Schiffer's account relies on what we can call *generating properties* (my termi-nology) and iterated inferences from these generating properties and their char-acteristics. In the example of mutual knowledge* about the candle, the person *x* has the following generating property: that of being a visibly 'normal', open-eyed, conscious person who is identical with *x* and who, at a close distance, is directly facing the candle, and *y*, who has the same properties *vis-à-vis x* (cf. p. 35). The idea is that in a case of mutual knowledge between *x* and *y* that *p*, if *F* is the gen-erating property for *x* (with respect to *p*), and *G* is the generating property for *y* (with respect to *p*), *F* will have two crucial characteristics:

> First, being *F* is sufficient for knowing that *p*, for knowing that *x* is *F*, and for knowing that *y* is *G*. The same holds for *G* correspondingly.

> Second, for any proposition *q*, if being *F* and being *G* are each sufficient for knowing that *q*, then both being *F* and being *G* are sufficient for knowing that sufficiency condition.

Schiffer provides a finite basis for cases of mutual knowledge* in terms of such generating properties. His theory is then that *x* and *y* mutually know that *p* iff there are generating properties of *x* and *y* with respect to the proposition *p*.[4]

The hierarchy of iterations of knowledge on the part of each mutual knower is attained by the knower by inference from his knowledge that he and the other have the relevant generating properties. These iterations really do follow from this simple theory. The elegance of the approach is undeniable.

I will be arguing for three points. The first point, a negative claim, is a Thesis of Non-Necessity, to the effect that the Schifferian conditions are not required for the openness distinctive of many of the examples discussed. The second point, more positive, is that an Alternative Account can be given of a kind of openness and the knowledge it generates, an account which does not require mutual knowledge*. The third claim is that this openness and knowledge of the sort characterized in the Alternative Account are in fact what characterize a significant range of the phenomena for which mutual knowledge was invoked by earlier writers.

The Thesis of Non-Necessity implies, then, that in some basic cases of full joint attention, there is no Schifferian generating property and there are no Schifferian iterated inferences. That is, the openness of the situation is not an inferential mat-ter. It is rather a matter of perceptual awareness. The openness of the situation is not captured by any finite basis for inference, because it is not a (personal-level) inferential matter at all.

---

[4] This summarizes in my terminology his formulation on pp. 34–5.

As a further elaboration of this Thesis of Non-Necessity, I also suggest that the cases in which there is no such inference are in a certain sense basic. The existence of these cases makes possible examples of mutual knowledge* as characterized by Schiffer's theory.

Two people, one or both of whom may be 6 years old, can jointly attend to a candle without so much as having the conception of a normal person, let alone beliefs or knowledge about the psychological capacities of normal people. Each person may simply see that the other sees the candle.[5] They can also have the more complex forms of mutual awareness involved in our characterization of joint attention without engaging in inference at all, and *a fortiori* without employing a finite basis for inference.

Could it be replied that the finite basis, the relevant generating properties, are actually merely tacitly known, and that there is tacit inference from this tacitly known finite basis? Maybe so: but tacit knowledge and tacit inference, or computation, therefrom is entirely compatible with the finally attained state being a perceptual state, rather than being a personal-level inferential state. This is precisely our conception of tacit knowledge of the rules of a grammar for English. Unconscious operations which draw on the information stated in grammatical principles result in perceptual states, of perceiving a sentence as grammatical or otherwise, or of hearing it as having a certain semantic and syntactic structure. But this is not personal-level inference, under rational control. Far from being an alternative to a perceptual account of the openness involved in joint attention, merely tacit knowledge is rather one particular kind of account of how a perceptual phenomenon might arise.

How, as things actually are, do people ever come to know that in general, normal people see things that are in front of them, that normal people know this, and so forth? It seems to me that this knowledge is attained by generalization from experience with particular situations in which one sees that someone is seeing something, and in which this is wholly open in the way in which I have tried to characterize joint attention. Experience with, and knowledge of, particular situations is rationally prior to knowledge of generalizations about normal persons. It is not clear that there is a plausible alternative way, as things actually are, in which knowledge about normal people could be acquired otherwise. Further, for the relevant properties of normal people to have the distinctive characteristics of Schiffer's generating properties, one needs experience not merely of others seeing things, but of the openness of such situations. Otherwise one would not be in a position to know that normal people can attain knowledge about what normal people are like (as opposed to merely having that knowledge oneself). Common knowledge of such matters of driving conventions, and geographic and political

---

[5] Schiffer himself slips into the very natural, and in my view true, description of one person as seeing that the other sees something to be the case (1988, p. 31).

facts, all rely on common knowledge of facts about perception; which in turn relies on the phenomenon of full joint attention.

In fairness to Schiffer, I should add that his intention may simply have been to show that a finite basis for mutual knowledge* is a genuine possibility. His concern may not have been the correct treatment of the particular example of the candle, but simply to show how mutual knowledge is so much as possible for finite minds. He did make clear one way in which mutual knowledge* can be attained, and in that sense he gave an existence proof. All the same, we still need a correct treatment of the example of the candle, and of the openness present in various basic joint interactions with the world.

We cannot simply leave the matter with this Non-Necessity Thesis, resting content to note that not all cases of joint attention meet the conditions for mutual knowledge as characterized in Schiffer's theory. For it is highly intuitive to say that there is some kind of openness to the knowledge that there is a candle on the table when there is joint attention to the candle. That is, there is a kind of openness to that knowledge that there is a candle on the table, an openness which is captured neither by the classical theory nor by the definition of mutual knowledge*.

At this point, in attempting to characterize this openness, we have at least two options. One option is to seek to modify the classical theory of mutual knowledge. We might try to change some of the parameters of the classical theory, in a way that respects the perceptual character of this openness. It is not easy to see how to do this. We cannot simply replace 'knows' by 'perceives' throughout Schiffer's theory. Recall that in a case of mutual knowledge that p, the generating property F for a person x had to be such that if it is sufficient for knowing an arbitrary proposition, it is also sufficient for knowing that it is so sufficient. We cannot simply replace 'know' by 'perceive' here, and obtain something true. When we consider the sort of generating properties with which Schiffer was concerned—being a 'normal' perceiver, awake, where there is light, etc.—it is implausible that when those conditions are sufficient for the subject knowing some given proposition, it is also literally perceived, rather than known, that they are so sufficient. If one says merely that this sufficiency is known, nothing follows about the availability of higher-order perceptions. Perceptual content is, as I have commented before, not closed under a priori operations on its contents. Actually this point would apply even if it were maintained that in some cases the sufficiency of the generating property for perceiving certain propositions to hold could itself be perceived. From the facts that a given thinker perceives A to be the case, and perceives B to be the case, and the fact that A and B together trivially entail C, it does not follow that our subject perceives C to be the case. I will not pursue the option of modifying the Schifferian account in any more detail, because I think that account is suited only to the inferential case. The essentially inferential character of Schiffer's account is not well-suited to phenomena of perceptual awareness.

Instead of trying to modify the classical account, I will pursue the other theoretical option. That is the option which holds that there is an openness of knowledge in cases of joint attention that is not captured by the classical theory of mutual knowledge and its inferential mechanisms. At this point I aim to develop an Alternative Account. Let us speak of *open knowledge* in its own right. In particular, consider open perceptual knowledge. We can say that

x and *y* have open perceptual knowledge that *p* iff

(a′) *x* and *y* both perceive that *p*;

(b′) *x* and *y* are both aware that their perceptions that *p* are mutually open-ended; and

(c′) *x* and *y* are aware that they are both aware of this very awareness (a′)–(c′).

Two people jointly attending to a candle between them may have open knowledge that the candle is flickering, even if they do not meet Schiffer's finite basis for mutual knowledge that the candle is flickering.

The more general case of open knowledge, be it perceptual or non-perceptual, could be characterized in terms of open perceptual knowledge and what is mutually known about each other's memory and inferential procedures. This more general case would be a mixture of the perceptual character of joint attention and the inferential character of Schifferian mutual knowledge.

What are the properties of open perceptual knowledge? Open perceptual knowledge that *p* does not imply arbitrarily high iterations of knowledge, since, as we saw, arbitrarily high iterations of awareness are not implied by our description of joint awareness. Failure to imply arbitrarily high iterations of knowledge is not, however, the most fundamental difference between open knowledge and common knowledge. Indeed, Lewis notes that his particular formulation of common knowledge does not imply arbitrary iterations of actual knowledge or expectation, since the rationality assumptions required on his account for such a derivation become more demanding and implausible as we rise through higher levels (1969, pp. 55–6). What is distinctive of cases of open knowledge is not the absence of arbitrary iterations of knowledge, but rather the means by which such finite iterations as do hold are reached. Suppose that in the case of joint attention to the candle, *x* does reach this state:

x sees that *y* sees that the candle is flickering.

Seeing that *p* is a form of knowledge that *p*: 'seeing that' is a factive mental state operator with the properties noted by Williamson (2000, pp. 34–41). It follows that

x knows that *y* sees that the candle is flickering.

This is something that follows from the nature of *x*'s state: it is not a matter of *x* making any transition in thought. By contrast, the next and final step is a matter of x himself making some transition in thought. Suppose that x has some appreciation that seeing is a form of knowledge. Then from that fact, some minimal inferential competence, and the last displayed sentence, we have that

x knows that y knows that the candle is flickering.

There are two notable features of this derivation of second-level iterated knowledge. One feature is that the iteration has not been derived from a Schifferian finite basis. It has not been reached by any inferences about 'normal' people. It has instead been extracted from a complex state of awareness present in a case of joint attention. The openness of a situation of joint attention consists in the facts, perceptual facts, given in our characterization of joint attention. Open knowledge is a by-product of that perceptual openness.

The other notable feature of the derivation is that it requires x to appreciate that seeing something provides a way of gaining knowledge about that object. Autistic children, even able ones, do not in general have this appreciation. A study by Josef Perner, Uta Frith, Alan Leslie, and Susan Leekam (1989) suggests that only one third of able autistic children realize that seeing something provides a means of coming to gain knowledge about that thing.[6] If their figure is roughly right, it follows from their work and the present account that most autistic children will not be capable of attaining open knowledge. Even if an autistic child sees that someone else is looking at something, he does not thereby gain knowledge of what the other knows. This state of affairs may greatly reduce the interest, for the autistic child, of situations in which he sees that he and another are seeing the same thing. Actually, we can distinguish two points at which there may be failure to make a transition to the attribution of knowledge to the other person. Perner *et al.*'s questions to autistic children were framed in terms of what the other person was looking at (1989, p. 693). To reach open knowledge by the route I have been describing, one must first be able to make the move from information about which objects the other is seeing or looking at to information about what the other sees to be the case; and then one must be able to move from this information to an attribution of knowledge. Failure could occur at either of these two points.

3. WIDER APPLICATIONS

My third claim was that there is a range of phenomena for which the Alternative Account, in terms of open knowledge and its source in joint attention, does better than mutual knowledge. Before generalizing, I take first the openness of linguistic communication. Suppose I say to you 'It's time for lunch'. My utterance is

[6] See esp. Perner *et al.*'s (1989) discussion of knowledge-formation tasks.

successful if we are jointly aware that I am saying that it is time for lunch. More generally, the paradigm of a successful indicative utterance in which one says that *p* is an utterance of which utterer and audience are jointly aware that it is a saying that *p*. A similar point applies *pari passu* for moods other than the indicative. The utterer aims to bring about a state of joint awareness whose content involves the meaning or, better, the intentional content of the utterance itself.

It is essential for this account that the intentional content of the utterance be part of the representational content of the perceptual experiences (in this case auditory experiences) of utterer and listener. If the assignment of meaning to the utterance were merely a matter of personal-level inference on the part of the hearer, then joint awareness that I've said that it's time for lunch would not be perceptual. But it seems that in the paradigm cases of successful communication, it is so.

The openness of communication does not require the inferential structures in Schiffer's account of mutual knowledge. The openness of my communication consists rather in the fact that you and I have full joint awareness that I am saying that it's time for lunch. We equally have open knowledge that I said it's time for lunch.

I don't need to have any beliefs about what normal people in our linguistic community do, or how they interpret utterances, to perceive you as saying that it's time for lunch. Nor do I need such beliefs for us to be jointly aware of this fact about what you are saying. In fact, in the cases in which I do have such knowledge, it seems to me once again to be based on experience of communications with relatives and acquaintances which already involve the kind of joint awareness I am identifying, in advance of any knowledge about the community. Even if some of my beliefs about what the wider community would mean by utterances of certain expressions are false, that need not prevent me from hearing your utterance correctly, and from our having full joint awareness of my saying that it's time for lunch. Just as false beliefs about the mechanisms of perception do not prevent one from having ordinary perceptual knowledge about the world—since that knowledge does not rest on beliefs about the nature of perceptual mechanisms—so also having false beliefs about language in the community does not prevent one from being aware of what someone has said on a particular occasion.

Sometimes, when an expression or a surface syntactic structure has to be disambiguated, beliefs about one's circumstances, and the likely topic of conversation, will affect how one hears one's interlocutor's utterance. But this does not mean that knowledge of meaning is purely inferential. The point is analogous to perceptual cases outside those of linguistic communication. Your knowledge of your peaceful circumstances means that you will discount an apparent perception as of a machine-gun firing as incorrect. You may realize that, say, some ball-bearings have tumbled in rapid succession on a metal surface; and you may (but need not) come to hear the continuing event as such a tumbling. Perception remains distinct from judgement and belief; but it is false to say that it cannot be influenced by them, or by hypotheses entertained by the thinker. Sometimes also, disambiguation itself is not a matter of conscious inference. The continuing context disambiguates without any entertaining or thought of alternative readings. The end state of the understander is still something perceptual, rather than merely judgement reached by inference.

I have concentrated on particular single instances of full joint attention; but in fact full joint attention is rarely a matter of one-off single events. Joint attention and contact attention between two people are commonly extended over time. Examples are ubiquitous, and so important, that one is inclined to say that their possibility is part of what it is to be distinctively human. Cases range from temporally extended games and interaction with a child, to adult interactions, both conventional and non-conventional.

In an extended encounter between two people involving joint attention and contact attention, we can speak of the mutual world which is created between the participants. This mutual world involves the events which are jointly attended to, the participants' relations to them, the development of both of these over time, and what is known at each stage about what has happened earlier in the mutual world of joint attention. Nagel's well-known paper 'Sexual perversion' (1969) was right to emphasize the role of iterated psychological states in mutually open sexual interactions between two people. Here too I believe the phenomena are best characterized in terms of full joint attention and full contact attention, rather than in terms of common knowledge. In such interactions too, a joint-attentional world is created between the participants.

Extended discourse between two people also creates such a mutual joint-attentional world. Some of the matters that David Lewis calls score-keeping in a language-game concern the created world of joint attention constructed and developed in the discourse to which the participants are jointly attending. Language has multiple special features; but I suggest that the openness of linguistic communication should be seen as a special case of the philosophically prior and more general phenomenon of the openness of joint attention.[7]

---

[7] In discussing the openness of linguistic communication, Simon Blackburn writes: 'The ideal of full openness is more simply captured if we just add the want that nothing about my wants be concealed' (1994, p. 115, in a section entitled 'Openness and communication'). Blackburn's discussion is in several respects consonant with the claims of the present paper; but I would add that the best way for such a want as he cites to be fulfilled is to create a situation of full joint attention. When an intention to produce such a situation is fulfilled, a certain openness will be present as intended, even if the agent does not have self-referential wants of the kind Blackburn discusses. Blackburn also writes, congenially, 'But in the restaurant is it really plausible to say that when our eyes meet in full mutual awareness, I (and she) have an endless stock of wants?' He says that his condition that the subject wants no concealment of his wants describes the situation better. I would say that this still does not pick out a distinctive state of awareness, whatever the beliefs and desires of the participants. What distinguishes our two people in the restaurant is that they have open perceptual awareness that they are attracted to each other.

APPENDIX: REFLEXIVITY, SELF-INVOLVING SITUATIONS AND SELF-REFERENTIAL STATES

This Appendix discusses the relation between the above treatment of full attention and two other approaches found in the extensive but scattered literature on other issues about mutual psychological properties. The first of these other approaches makes use of self-involving situations; and it plunges us into metaphysical issues.

Self-Involving Situations

It can be tempting to elucidate the openness of full joint attention in terms of self-involving situations thus: when x and y are engaged in full joint attention to o, there is a situation S such that:

(si) S is a situation in which x and y are attending to o;

(sii) S is a situation in which x's and y's awareness that they are both attending to o is open-ended; and

(siii) S is a situation in which x and y are perceptually aware of S.

Such a situation S is not merely self-involving. It is more specifically what we can call *psychologically self-involving*, in the sense that it involves a psychological relation to itself. Self-involving situations have been invoked by several writers, in a range of disciplines including psychology, philosophy, and linguistics, to account either for mutual knowledge, or for weaker versions of mutual mental states.[8] One of the most vigorous, and formally creative, proponents of this style of approach, Jon Barwise, went so far as to write that 'Shared understanding in all its various guises (mutual belief, common knowledge, public information) rests on circular, or at least non-wellfounded situations. In as much as there are assumptions of such shared understanding throughout game theory, law, communication theory, and the like, we are constantly caught in non-wellfounded situations' (1989, p. 198).

Psychologically self-involving situations also have the power to give rise to iterations of attitudes. Once again, for the sake of illustration, we start with a state other than awareness, to make the formal structures clear. Suppose we have a person—John—and a situation S, which consists in the holding of (sa) and (sb):

(sa) p

(sb)   John knows that S exists.

Let us write $S \vDash A$ for 'A holds in situation S' (as in 'A is a fact of situation S' in the way this is used in the situation theory of Barwise and Perry (1983; see also Barwise, 1989)). Suppose also that we have the following Principle K holding of John's knowledge:

(Principle K) If John knows that S exists and $S \vDash A$, then John knows that A.

From (Principle K), (sa), and (sb), it follows that

(1)   John knows that p.

Hence

(2) $S \vDash$ John knows that p.

---

[8] There is significant and illuminating use of self-involving situations in Clark and Marshall, 1981; Barwise, 1988; Sperber and Wilson, 1995, p. 42.

So from (Principle K), (sb), and (2), we have

(3) John knows that John knows that *p*.

Hence

(4) $S \models$ John knows that John knows that *p*.

And so forth, for arbitrarily many iterations of 'John knows that' applied to *p*. All of these follow from Principle K and the individuation of the psychologically self-involving situation *S*. The individuation of *S* together with Principle K are jointly clearly stronger than any finite list of iterations of 'John knows that' applied to *p*. No finite set of such iterations, however long, has the same implications as the self-involving situation *S* when combined with Principle K. So arbitrary iterations can be obtained from a psychologically self-involving situation, in the presence of a suitable principle governing the psychological relation in question.

Now we can return to full joint attention and its situation-theoretic characterization in conditions (si)–(siii). Actual perceivers are not like ideal knowers. Consider the principle

If *x* perceives situation *S*, and $S \models A$, then *x* perceives that A.

We cannot expect such a principle to hold without restriction. When *S* is psychologically self-involving, as in our characterization of full joint attention, this principle would imply the existence of arbitrarily high iterations of 'perceives that' in *x*'s perceptual states. Since these states—unlike beliefs conceived as inexplicit in Schiffer's account—are not dispositional, this principle would imply the existence of actual occurrent perceptual states that full joint attenders do not in fact enjoy. Ordinary perceivers go only so far in extracting what it is in principle possible to extract from a perceptually self-involving situation. So the clauses (si)–(siii) do not commit us to saying that *x* and *y* actually have arbitrarily complex perceptual states with contents like 'He perceives that I perceive that he perceives . . .'. When *x* is perceptually aware of the state *S* described in clauses (si)–(siii), *x*'s perceptual system has the information to compute correctly from states it is already in to new contents, such as '*y* is aware of a state in which I'm aware of a state in which he's attending to o'. But it does not follow from the fact that *x* has the information to compute, subpersonally, this content, that he actually carries out the computation. On all of these most recent points, the advocate of self-involving situations for characterizing full joint attention can say much the same as I said in the main text, in defending the treatment in terms of mental states and events that are self-referential. So why not describe all the phenomena with which this paper is concerned by using the apparatus of self-involving situations?

The main reason must be concern that self-involving situations are not metaphysically legitimate. They seem to involve an unacceptable regress of individuation. Anyone who has been brought up on the iterative hierarchy as the intended model of ZF set theory will have been trained to find self-involving situations suspect. No doubt training can induce acceptance of almost anything—but if we want a rational articulation of the concern, it can be formulated as the principle that the world itself must be well-founded. I call this position 'insistence on objective well-foundedness'. Opponents of objective well foundedness have developed illuminating formal theories of what self-involving situations would have to be like, and of what is involved in commitment to them. Peter Aczel's (1988) theory of non-well-founded sets is a particularly elegant exposition of the foundations of such a treatment, and of its commitments. Aczel shows that the existence of non-well-founded sets is implied by nothing more than the axiom that every graph has a unique decoration. Valuable as this formal development is, I do not think that by itself it can answer the doubts of someone who insists on objective well-foundedness. The simplest case of a one-element graph which generates a set which is a member of itself seems to involve something which is individuated in terms of itself (Aczel, 1988; Barwise and Moss, 1996, ch. 10). This will concentrate, rather than answer, the doubts of those who insist on objective well-foundedness.

I will be offering some arguments and theses in favour of the conjecture that reality is well-founded. One of the major tasks facing anyone who holds this position is to explain how, consistently with that position, there can exist all the examples which Barwise cites and which he says require the existence of self-involving situations (1989, pp. 194–8; Barwise and Moss, 1996, pt. II, esp. ch. 4).

The first step in elaborating this position is to draw a distinction between *eliminable* and *ineliminable* self-involving situations. An eliminable self-involving situation is one whose existence can be fully explained in terms of situations or other entities that are not self-involving. The person who insists that reality must be objectively well-founded should not have any quarrel with the existence of eliminable self-involving situations. How could a self-involving situation be eliminable? Here is one way, which draws upon the materials of the preceding discussion. Some self-involving situations consist in the occurrence of self-referential mental states or events. In such cases, the self-involving situations can be obtained from self-referential mental states by what I call 'an inside-out transformation'. Suppose a person x has the following properties:

x is aware that p; and

x is aware that this whole awareness exists.

I suggest that we can, quite generally, transform such a state of affairs into the following true statement about a self-involving situation:

There is a situation S which is constituted by the facts that

x is aware that p, and

x is aware that S exists.

A self-involving situation which is attainable by such a transformation is in the nature of the case eliminable in the above sense. Its existence is wholly consistent with reality being objectively well-founded. Provided a self-involving situation is attainable by an inside-out transformation, we can legitimately use it in characterizing full joint attention and other phenomena of mutuality, whilst continuing to insist that reality is well-founded. The main text of the present paper can then be regarded as doing the following. If the self-involving states usable in characterizing full joint attention are obtainable by an inside-out transformation, it ought to be possible to specify the well-founded states from which they are so obtainable. The main text of the paper then aims to answer the question: which are those well-founded states? Certain mental states with indexically self-referential contents provided the answer.

If this is correct, then the permissibility of using self-involving situations in the description of these psychological phenomena does not by itself legitimize self-involving situations that are not reachable by use of inside-out transformations. These psychological phenomena cannot be used in support of the claim that the world is not well-founded. It would take some real phenomenon describable only by self-involving situations that are ineliminable to refute objective well-foundedness.

These considerations can be generalized to provide a case in support of objective well-foundedness. The case can be presented in a series of four theses, of which these are the first three:

> Thesis 1: There is a range of types of well-founded states of affairs that generate legitimate, eliminable self-involving states of affairs.

> Thesis 2: Indexically self-referential mental states form just one of these types.

> Thesis 3: What all these types have in common is that from well-founded states of affairs, they generate the infinitary characteristics distinctive of self-involving situations.

One example of a well-founded state of affairs which generates eliminable self-involving states of affairs is Schiffer's classical inferential account of mutual knowledge. He gave a finitary, inferential explanation which applies to the case of mutual knowledge between you and me that people in the USA drive on the right, in terms of the generating properties we noted in Section 2 above. The conditions cited in Schiffer's inferential explanation are wholly well-founded. They are also the conditions in virtue of which there exists a self-involving situation S with the following properties:

> $S \vDash$ People in the USA drive on the right.

> $S \vDash$ I know S.

> $S \vDash$ You know S.

(Here I follow the style of characterizing mutual knowledge found in Barwise, 1989, and in Barwise and Moss, 1996, p. 49.) The relevant infinitary consequences of this self-involving situation are also consequences of Schiffer's finitary characterization. There is, then, a legitimate self-involving situation that can be mentioned in the explanation of some cases of mutual knowledge; but it is generated by conditions—those formulated by Schiffer—which are wholly well-founded.

A non-psychological case cited by Barwise as non-well-founded is an example due to John Perry. I quote:

Imagine two parallel mirrors of the same size, facing each other, one A with an 'X' painted on it, the other B with an 'O'. This is a simple finite physical situation which is, in some sense circular. We can think of it as three situations, a situation s with two sub-situations s_A and s_B the scenes reflected in A and B, respectively. In s_A we have the facts that B has an 'X' and that B reflects s_B, while in s_B we have the symmetric facts about A. The facts of s are those of $s_A \cup s_B$ plus the facts that A and B are parallel and facing one another. (Barwise, 1989, p. 194)

This description is highly intuitive: but the self-involving situations used in the description are also eliminable. They exist in virtue of the wholly well-founded spatial relations between A and B, the markings on them, and the laws of reflection. These well-founded conditions have infinitary consequences about reflection (if we prescind from the minimum size of particle which can reflect light, and other minima). Nothing here involves ineliminably self-involving states of affairs.

More generally, I suggest that what holds of the mirror example holds also of the other examples cited in support of the claim that the world is not well-founded. I suggest:

> Thesis 4: Each of the examples of 'circular' situations cited by Barwise (1989) and by Barwise and Moss (1996) is either

> (a) not really self-involving, or

(b) it is a self-involving situation generated by one of the types of well-founded situation mentioned in Thesis 1, and so is a case of merely eliminable self-involvement.

I won't enumerate every single example developed in the works by Barwise and by Barwise and Moss. I will rather take a few as exemplars, and aim to give responses available to one who holds that reality is well-founded, responses which can be transferred to other cases.

Some of the cases which are described as cases of circularity do indeed meet that description, but do not amount to the postulation of self-involving situations. Barwise and Moss describe, for instance, one way of solving a particular probability problem, that of finding the probability that the first time we get heads in a series of tosses of a fair coin, it will be on an even-numbered flip. An elegant solution to this problem involves characterizing the unknown, x, as identical to a number picked out by a condition involving x. (Barwise and Moss, 1996, p. 53).[9] This gives an equation with x on both sides, which can be solved.

There are no self-involving situations in this case at all. For there to be a complex condition on x that involves x itself, and which is uniquely satisfied, is not for any entity or state of affairs to be individuated in terms of itself. It is an important point that a specification of an object x may involve x itself, and may uniquely fix x. This is something that is relied upon in functional specifications of states in the philosophy of mind, and in the individuation of concepts in some theories of concepts (Lewis, 1970, 1972; Peacocke, 1992, esp. ch. 1). But it does not require self-involving situations or non-well-founded states of affairs.

The same seems to me to be true of self-reference, and of reference by tokens or events to larger tokens or events of which they are a part. Some words in a sentence may refer to the whole sentence of which they are a part, as in Barwise's example of an airline announcement which concludes, 'This announcement will not be repeated'. Barwise and Moss say that 'Such examples show that the relation "refers to" is circular, that is, that things sometimes refer to themselves, or to other things that refer back to them' (1996, p. 56). This falls short of showing that the world is not well-founded. The token utterance-events in the airline announcement—the utterance of 'this announcement' and the utterance of the whole announcement—are neither of them individuated in terms of themselves, nor circularly in terms of each other. No utterance-token, or inscription, or even an event of reference in thought, is individuated in terms of itself, in the way that the non-well-founded sets of Aczel's theory are individuated in terms of themselves.

But perhaps we are looking in the wrong place for the non-well-founded. Barwise and Moss's remark is explicitly about the relation of reference: so is that relation itself not well-founded? For a relation not to be well-founded is for it to be individuated in terms of itself. To establish that a relation has that property, one has to show something about what it is in general for the relation to hold, and in particular to show that the conditions for its holding can be given only in terms of that very same relation itself. Barwise and Moss do not do that: it is entirely consistent for a well-founded relation to hold between an entity and itself, or an entity and some other entity of which it is a part. Further, to be an objection to the well-foundedness of the world, it would have to be shown that any self-involving

---

[9] The example is from Donald Newman.

characterization of the reference relation is ineliminable. The arguments in these works of Barwise and of Barwise and Moss have not done that either.

Several of Barwise's (1989) examples concern mental events and states. He discusses Descartes's thought 'I think therefore I am', and writes of it that 'it is a mental act that comprehends itself as a constituent' (p. 194). Barwise's point is that it is Descartes's thinking of this very thought that convinces Descartes, in the face of the doubt, that he exists. But this is then a case of the sort we discussed in the first section: it is a mental event with an intentional content one of whose components refers to the mental event itself. In fully explicit form, the content is 'I think in this very thinking, therefore I am' (indeed, this is very close to the later exposition in Barwise and Moss, 1996, p. 51). But, once again, for a mental event to have an intentional content one component of which refers to that mental event is not for anything in the world to be individuated in terms of itself. In my judgement, the same applies to Barwise's other psychological examples.[10]

Finally, a case which is more challenging and demands a more detailed response is Barwise's (1989) example of the situations involved in the game of poker. Barwise notes that certain parts of a play of a game of poker are public information, and that what is public—such as the information that 3♣ is an 'up' card—are circular (p. 197). What is public is a situation in which not merely is it seen by all players that 3♣ is an 'up' card, but they all see that it is, they all see that they all see that it is, and so forth. An advocate of self-involving characterizations would say that there is a self-involving situation S which consists in

(i)   each player seeing 3♣ face up on the table, and

(ii) each player seeing this very situation S.

This self-involving situation will then have the familiar iterative consequences which we require if we are to describe the public part of this play of the game fully and accurately.

As before, I do not object to this description of the situation, but I do hold that this self-involving situation is eliminable. The well-founded state of affairs in virtue of which it holds is this. Each player x of the game is in the following state:

x sees that 3♣ is face up on the table, and

x sees that this whole seeing is seen by the other players.

This well-founded state has the relevant iterative consequences. To give the barest outlines of how the consequences follow, suppose we have as a premiss that this seeing by x is a seeing that p. We know that this seeing is seen by the other players; so (under the circumstances of the present case), the other players see that in this seeing x sees that p. We can apply this form of reasoning to conclude that the other players see that in this seeing x sees that 3♣ is face up on the table. But if the player x is computationally competent, he sees that these premisses hold and can compute soundly from them, and will thereby come to see, in this seeing, that the other players see that he sees that 3♣ is face up on the table; and so forth. As before, the indexically self-referential seeing has more iterative consequences than any finite series of iterations without self-reference. Barwise was right to emphasize this feature of the situation; but we can have that feature, and explain its presence, without postulating ineliminably self-involving situations.

---

[10] Barwise cites what he calls a Gricean intention that that very intention be recognized. This too is a case of a mental state with an intentional content one of whose components refers to the mental state.

Fixed-Point Characterizations

As we noted, a principle which characterizes a notion informatively in terms of itself is what logicians call a fixed-point principle. One approach developed by some theorists of mutual notions is to try to use fixed-point principles to individuate those very notions themselves. In the case of mutual knowledge, for instance, we can say that *x* and *y* mutually know that *p* iff

> *x* and *y* know that *p*, and
>
> *x* and *y* know that it is mutual knowledge that *p*.

In his paper 'Three Views', Barwise noted that this fixed-point characterization will not be equivalent to the characterization in terms of repeated finite iterations of knowledge when *x* and *y* have limited logical abilities (1988, p. 378). Joint attention under the approach I have been suggesting also supports a fixed-point principle. *x* and *y* are jointly attending to o iff:

> *x* and *y* are attending to o;
>
> *x* and *y* are aware that this attention is open-ended; and
>
> *x* and *y* are each aware that they are jointly attending to o.

The above discussion shows that we do not require ineliminable self-involving situations to explain how it can be that a particular fixed-point principle holds. Fixed-point characterizations, taken in themselves, are of course not well-founded; but in all the cases discussed here, the fixed-point characterizations of mutual psychological states that are true hold in virtue of psychological states and events that are well-founded.

REFERENCES

ACZEL, PETER (1988), *Non-Well-Founded Sets*, CSLI Lecture Notes 14. Stanford, Calif.: CSLI.

BARWISE, J. (1988), 'Three views of common knowledge', in M. Vardi (ed.), *Proceedings of the Second Conference on Theoretical Aspects of Reasoning about Knowledge*. Los Altos, Calif.: Morgan Kaufmann, 365–79.

—— (1989), *The Situation in Logic*, CSLI Lecture Notes 17. Stanford, Calif.: CSLI.

—— and Moss, L. (1996), *Vicious Circles: On the Mathematics of Non-Wellfounded Phenomena*, CSLI Lecture Notes 60. Stanford, Calif.: CSLI.

—— and PERRY, J. (1983), *Situations and Attitudes*. Cambridge, Mass.: MIT Press.

BLACKBURN, SIMON (1994), *Spreading the Word: Groundings in the Philosophy of Language*. Oxford: Oxford University Press.

CAMPBELL, JOHN (2002), *Reference and Consciousness*. Oxford: Oxford University Press.

CLARK, H., and MARSHALL, C. (1981), 'Definite reference and mutual knowledge', in A. Joshi, B. Webber, and I. Sag (eds.), *Elements of Discourse Understanding*. Cambridge: Cambridge University Press, 10–63.

HARMAN, GILBERT (1974), review of original edition of Schiffer, 1988, *Journal of Philosophy*, 71: 224–9.

—— (1977), review of Jonathan Bennett, *Linguistic Behaviour, Language*, 53: 417–24.

—— (1986), *Change in View*. Cambridge, Mass.: MIT Press.

LEWIS, DAVID (1969), *Convention: A Philosophical Study*. Cambridge, Mass.: Harvard University Press.

LEWIS, DAVID (1970), 'How to define theoretical terms', *Journal of Philosophy*, 67: 427–45.

—— (1972), 'Psychophysical and theoretical identifications', *Australasian Journal of Philosophy*, 50: 249–58.

NAGEL, THOMAS (1969), 'Sexual perversion', *Journal of Philosophy* 66: 5–17.

PEACOCKE, CHRISTOPHER (1992), *A Study of Concepts*. Cambridge, Mass.: MIT Press.

PERNER, JOSEF, FRITH, UTA, LESLIE, ALAN, and LEEKAM, SUSAN (1989), 'Exploration of the autistic child's theory of mind: knowledge, belief and communication', *Child Development*, 60: 689–700.

SCHIFFER, STEPHEN (1988), *Meaning*. Oxford: Oxford University Press.

SPERBER, D., and WILSON, D. (1995), *Relevance*, 2nd edn. Oxford: Blackwell.

WILLIAMSON, TIMOTHY (2000), *Knowledge and its Limits*. Oxford: Oxford University Press.

Author Index

Abelson, R. P. 275
Aczel, P. 318–19, 321
Adam, S. 281
Adamson, L. 86, 87, 89, 95, 99, 104, 105, 106, 165
Agnetta, B. 47, 50
Akhtar, N. 171, 176–7
Alexander, S. 94
Allen, J. 196
Allison, T. 208
Angelopoulos, M. 178
Anscombe, G. E. M. 260–1
Ashburn, L. 180
Assanelli, A. 142, 159
Astington, J. 92
Atkinson, J. 217, 218, 220
Ayer, A. J. 264

Bacharach, M. 291, 293
Baillargeon, R. 271
Baird, J. A. 172, 179, 180, 235
Bakeman, R. 86, 87, 89, 104, 105, 165
Baldwin, D. A. 85, 154, 158, 223, 235
Baranek, G. T. 196, 207
Bard, K. A. 68,131
Baron-Cohen, S. 36, 67, 78, 79, 89, 117, 131, 155, 180, 196, 198, 206, 208, 211, 235, 281
Barr, D. J. 168
Barresi, J. 247 n.
Bartlett, E. 167
Barton, M. 167, 175, 176
Barwise, J. 307, 317, 319, 320–2, 323
Bates, E. 15, 16, 18–19, 50, 67, 86, 88, 90, 95, 102, 105, 117, 121, 135, 137 n.,140, 145, 154, 158, 209, 224, 263
Bauer, P. J. 279
Bennett, P. 178
Bergman, T. 114
Bertenthal, B. I. 190
Bierschwale, D. T. 48
Bill, B. 173, 174
Blackburn, S. 43, 316 n.
Blake, J. 129
Block, N. 36
Bloom, L. 154, 166, 169, 173, 176
Bloom, P. 170
Bonvillian, J. 167

Borzellino, G. 129
Brand, R. 180
Brazelton, T. B. 96, 97
Brentano, F. 206
Bretherton, I. 235
Brown, R. 160, 202
Bruce, V. 214
Bruner, J. 1, 7, 67, 71, 86, 88, 104, 105, 111, 114, 135, 166, 167
Bryant, P. E. 271
Bryson, S. E. 213
Buber, M. 94
Bullock, M. 271
Burack, J. A. 213
Burge, T. 258 n.
Butterworth, G. 16, 51, 67, 110, 114, 117, 119, 135, 136, 137, 138, 139, 140, 142, 145, 152, 153, 155, 158, 211, 216, 244, 248
Byrne, R. W. 59, 60, 68

Call, J. 27, 72, 76, 224, 263
Camaioni, L. 15, 90, 95, 102, 105, 135, 137 n.,140, 145, 263
Campbell, J. 22, 24, 29, 252, 261, 264, 265, 266, 267, 299 n., 300 n.
Card, J. 208
Carey, S. 167, 217
Caron, A. J. 114
Carpenter, M. 57, 90, 117, 123, 131, 139, 171, 176, 180, 223
Carroll, L. 295
Carruthers, P. 42
Casey, B. 213
Cech, C. G. 48
Charman, T. 78, 79, 157, 196, 198
Clark, H. 165, 168, 317 n.
Cochran, E. 110, 211
Cohen, L. B. 271
Cohn, J. F. 98
Collingwood, R. G. 43
Collis, G. M. 167
Conti-Ramsden, G. 159
Corboz-Warnery, A. 88
Corkum, V. 118, 215, 216, 238 n.
Corrigan, R. 270
Costall, A. 94
Courchesne, E. 212, 213, 220

Crompton, R. 77
Cross, D. 170
Csibra, G. 117
Cutting, J. E. 190

D'Entremont, B. 90, 93, 114
D'Odorico, L. 141
Dahlgren, S. O. 196
Das Gupta, P. 271
Davidson, D. 7–14, 20, 22, 23, 25, 30,
    31, 32
Davies, M. 36, 42
Dawson, G. 196, 207, 218
Deak, G. 216
Denton, P. 270
Descartes, R. 322
Desrochers, S. 119, 121
Diesendruck, G. 178
Doherty, M. 171
Dore, J. 130 n.
Driver, J. 114, 174, 214
Dunham, P. J. 36, 38, 91
Dunham, X. 91

Eddy, T. J. 46–7, 48, 50, 55, 68, 69, 158, 174,
    211, 222
Eilan, N. 264, 265, 266, 267
Elman, J. 154, 158
Emery, N. 50
Evans, G. 264, 265

Fantz, R. L. 96
Farrar, J. 158, 166, 167
Farroni, T. 74
Fein, D. 207
Fish, D. 160
Fivaz-Depeursinge, E. 88
Fivush, R. 274, 275, 276, 278, 279, 280–1
Flavell, J. H. 59, 124, 170, 171
Fodor, J. 42, 170
Fogel, A. 121, 133, 134
Fox, N. 208
Franco, F. 16, 21, 22, 27, 232, 244, 248, 263
Friesen, C. K. 214
Frith, U. 314
Fujita, K. 75

Gagliano, A. 133, 142, 145, 147, 152
Gelman, R. 271
Gergely, G. 171
Gibbs, R. 168
Gibson, E. J. 60, 104

Gillberg, C. 196
Gilmore, R. O. 212
Gluckman, A. 47, 224
Goldin-Meadow, S. 161
Golinkoff, R. 129, 138, 141, 178
Gomez, J. C. 27, 57, 131, 209, 222
Goodman, J. 154, 158
Gopnik, A. 37, 92, 118, 198, 234, 270
Grant, J. 167
Greenfield, P. M. 103
Grice, P. 168, 239, 240, 241, 256
Griffith, E. M. 220
Grover, L. 110, 119, 216
Guajardo, J. J. 117, 119–20, 122
Gunnar, M. R. 99

Haden, C. 281
Haine, R. 281
Hains, S. M. J. 114
Haith, M. M. 114
Halliday, M. A. K. 132, 154, 159
Hamond, N. R. 274, 279, 280
Hannan, T. E. 121, 133, 134
Happe, F. 67, 171
Hare, B. 47, 48, 49, 50, 51, 52, 53,
    56, 72, 76, 174
Harman, G. 308 n.
Harris, M. 166, 167
Hauser, M. D. 56
Heal, J. 30, 31, 189, 261, 281, 282, 283
Heibeck, T. H. 167
Heyes, C. 59
Hirsh-Pasek, K. 178
Hobson, P. 24, 26, 73, 74, 80, 95, 206,
    207, 222, 224, 232, 237, 239, 242,
    243–4, 248, 252, 263
Hollich, G. J. 178, 179
Hood, B. M. 114, 174, 212
Hopkins, W. 68, 131
Hornik, R. 99
Horton, W. S. 169
Huber, E. 75
Hubley, P. 89, 207
Hudson, J. A. 279
Hume, D. 240, 251
Hunnisett, E. 209, 216

Itakura, S. 48, 50, 56, 57
Iverson, J. M. 161

Jarrett, N. 51, 110, 114, 117, 119
Johansson, G. 190

Johnson, M. H. 96, 97, 114, 212, 222
Johnson, S. 217
Jones, D. 167
Jones, O. 36

Kant, I. 231
Kaplan, B. 7, 15, 17–19, 21, 27, 30, 32, 87, 90, 95, 102, 105, 106, 121, 130, 135, 136, 221, 244, 247, 263
Kaplan, D. 290
Karin-D'Arcy, M. R. 72
Karmiloff-Smith, A. 66, 73
Kasari, C. 99, 131, 207
Kedesdy, J. 166
Kessler-Shaw, L. 158
Kestenbaum, M. 271
Keysar, B. 168, 169
Kingstone, A. 214
Klinnert, M. D. 98
Kohler, W. 66

Laa, V. 69, 79
Landry, S. 196, 223
Langton, S. R. H. 69, 214
Leavens, D. 68, 99, 131
Lee, A. 95, 190, 191, 194, 198, 202
Leekam, S. 24, 78, 79, 188, 189, 196, 314
Lempers, J. D. 119, 121
Leonard, L. B. 159
Lepore, E. 42
Leslie, A. M. 67, 206, 270, 314
Leung, E. 119, 136
Levorato, M. C. 141
Lewis, D. 42, 291, 300, 309, 313, 316, 321
Lewis, M. 243
Lipsitt, L. P. 92
Lock, A. 133
Locke, J. 166, 167, 173
Lopez, B. 78, 209, 216, 217
Lord, C. 195
Loveland, K. A. 196, 223
Lycan, W. 75

MacArthur, D. 99
McCarthy, G. 208
McDowell, J. 255–6
McEvoy, R. 207
McGinn, M. 43
MacNamara, J. 246
McNeill, D. 133, 161
Malle, B. F. 180
Mandler, J. M. 279

Markman, E. M. 167, 172
Marshall, C. 317 n.
Martin, M. G. F. 268, 270
Maurer, D. 114
Mayes, A. R. 264
Meck, E. 271
Meltzoff, A. 118, 171, 198, 233, 234, 250, 251, 270
Menzel, E. W. 68
Merleau-Ponty, M. 247 n.
Messer, D. J. 119, 121
Miklosi, A. 48
Miller, P. H. 124
Miller, P. J. 278
Moore, D. G. 190
Moore, M. J. 114
Moore, C. 36, 38, 79, 90, 91, 93, 118, 178, 209, 211, 215, 216, 217, 238 n., 247 n, 251
Morgan, S. B. 198
Morrissette, P. 119
Morton, J. 96, 222
Moses, L. J. 85, 125, 170, 172, 179, 180
Moss, L. 319, 320–2
Muir, D. W. 114
Mundy, P. 77, 78, 102, 131, 196, 207, 208, 209, 222, 224
Murdoch, I. 230, 231, 249, 254
Murphy, C. M. 119, 121
Murray, C. 209
Murray, L. 98
Myowa-Yamakoshi, M. 74

Nadel, J. 98
Nagel, T. 316
Nagell, K. 90, 117, 139, 180
Namy, L. L. 179
Neal, R. 208, 222
Neely, J. 220
Neisser, U. 265, 279
Nelson, K. 167, 273, 274, 275, 277, 278–9, 280, 281, 282
Newman, D. 321
Ninio, A. 166

O'Neill, D. K. 103
O'Reilly, A. 93
O'Rourke, P. 129
Oakes, L. M. 271
Ontai, L. L. 173, 174
Osterling, J. 196, 207
Ouston, J. 191
Ozonoff, S. 213

Papafragou, A. 170
Peacocke, C. 25, 29, 274, 277
Peirce, C. S. 224
Pennington, B. F. 198, 207, 213
Perner, J. 88, 90, 92–3, 99, 101, 170, 171, 224,
    238 n., 281, 314
Perrett, D. I. 174
Perry, J. 317, 320
Perucchini, P. 139, 142, 155
Phillips, A. T. 120, 125
Phillips, W. 78, 79, 80
Piaget, J. 66, 73
Pillemer, D. B. 278, 279
Plunkett, K. 166
Posner, M. 212, 220
Povinelli, D. J. 46–7, 48, 50, 54, 55, 56, 68,
    69, 70 n., 72, 74, 158, 174, 211, 222,
    271–2, 279
Premack, A. J. 180
Premack, D. 117, 180
Proffitt, D. R. 190
Prutting, C. A. 196
Puce, A. 208

Quine, W. V. O. 172

Rader, N. 60, 104
Ramsden, C. A. 221
Rattray, J. 88
Reaux, J. E. 47
Reddy, V. 32, 237
Reese, E. 280
Repacholi, B. M. 125
Rheingold, H. L. 119, 136
Ricard, M. 119
Rochat, P. 233, 237, 248 n.
Roessler, J. 27–8, 265, 266, 267
Rogers, S. J. 198, 207
Romanski, L. M. 208
Rothbart, M. 212
Rubinstein, A. 291
Rumbaugh, D. M. 57
Russell, C. 106
Russell, J. 213, 220

Salapatek, P. 114
Salerni, N. 142, 159
Samuelson, L. K. 166, 169, 173, 176, 177, 178
Sarria, E. 209
Savage-Rumbaugh, E. S. 57
Saylor, M. M. 169
Scaife, M. 114

Schafer, G. 166
Schaffer, H. R. 117, 121
Schank, R. C. 275
Scheiffelin, B. B. 167
Schiffer, S. 1, 291, 300, 301, 308 n., 309–14,
    315, 318, 320
Schlottman, A. 270
Schultz, R. T. 208
Schütz, A. 231 n.
Segal, G. 37
Shapiro, L. R. 279
Shatz, M. 21, 93
Sherwood, V. 86, 88
Sherzer, J. 133
Shinn, M. 133 n.
Shultz, T. 271
Sigman, M. 102, 131, 196, 207, 208
Sigueland, E. R. 92
Simone, L. 103
Singer-Harris, N. 213
Slaughter, V. 217
Smith, L. B. 166, 169, 173, 176, 177, 178
Smith, N. V. 66
Smith, P. 36, 42
Sobel, D. M. 270
Somerville, S. C. 273
Sommerville, J. A. 117
Spelke, E. S. 125
Sperber, D. 1, 65, 80, 255, 317 n.
Starobinski, J. 254
Stone, W. L. 155
Stone, T. 42
Strawson, P. 234, 251 n.
Striano, T. 233, 237
Swettenham, J. 213, 218, 220
Symons, L. A. 114

Tamarit, J. 209
Tanaka, M. 48, 56, 57
Tantam, D. 224
Teixidor, P. 69, 79
Theall, L. A. 47, 70 n.
Tinker, E. 154
Todd, B. 99
Tomasello, M. 15, 16–17, 19, 20, 21, 23, 24,
    27, 28, 29, 30, 31, 32, 38, 71, 72, 76, 87,
    90, 91, 95, 106, 117, 129, 130, 131, 132,
    139, 141, 158, 166, 167, 171, 174, 175,
    176, 180, 209, 224, 232, 236, 239, 240,
    241, 243, 250, 261, 263
Tomonaga, M. 74
Townsend, J. 213

Tremblay-Leveau, H. 98
Trevarthen, C. 67, 73, 89, 98, 133, 134, 165,
    207, 209, 233, 237
Tronick, E. Z. 98
Tsatsanis, K. D. 208
Tulving, E. 262, 263, 264, 273

Vaughan, A. 102
Vecera, S. P. 97, 114
Volterra, V. 15, 90, 95, 102, 105, 135, 137 n.,
    140, 145, 263
Vygotsky, L. S. 66, 130, 135, 136, 201

Waal, F. De 71
Wainwright-Sharp, J. A. 213
Watson, J. K. 170
Waxman, S. R. 179
Welch-Ross, M. K. 279, 281, 282
Wellman H. M. 37, 92, 120, 125, 170, 171,
    272, 273
Werner, H. 7, 15, 17–19, 21, 27, 30, 32, 87,
    90, 95, 102, 105, 106, 121, 130, 135, 221,
    244, 247, 263

Wetherby, A. M. 196
White, P. A. 271
White, S. H. 278
White, T. G. 166
Whitehurst, G. J. 166
Whiten, A. 60, 68, 118, 174
Wiggins, D. 246
Willen, D. 114, 174
Williams, B. 246–7, 249, 254
    n., 255, 282
Williamson, T. 313
Wilson, D. 1, 65, 80, 255, 317 n.
Wimmer, H. 170
Wimpory, D. C. 195
Wishart, J. 142, 157
Wittgenstein, L. 43, 180,
    190, 241
Wolff, P. H. 97
Woodward, A. L. 171, 179
Wrangham, R. W. 56
Wyver, S. 223

Yaniv, I. 21

Subject Index

aboutness 74–5
Achilles and the tortoise 295
autism 94–5, 102, 155, 157, 189–202, 205–29
attention:
    attention contact 65–6, 68–71, 74, 78–80
    attention following 65–6, 71, 79–80
    attentional orienting 173–5, 212–14, 217–20
    attention-seeking behaviour 70–1, 98, 100–3
    nature of attention 92–3, 104, 185–7, 239,
      266–7
    to the past 103, 262–70, 273–7
    to self 98, 100–3, 106
    understanding of 3, 59–61, 69, 74, 87–91,
      94–106, 144–50, 187–9, 191–3, 202, 239–44

causal conditions on joint attention 4–7, 288–9
causal understanding 244, 262, 269–73
checking, visual 50, 140–5, 160
chimpanzees 45–62, 68–73
co-attender as constituent of experience 29,
    288–90, 292–4, 299–300
common knowledge 22–30, 39, 66, 291–5,
    300–1, 309–14
communicative intentions 55–6, 72, 239–41
competition vs. co-operation, understanding of
    gaze behaviour in 52–4, 56, 72
contact gestures 67, 76, 78
contemplative stance 7, 17–19, 26–8, 90, 130,
    244–5, 263
co-ordinated attack 290–2, 295–6

demonstratives 290, 295–6
dogs 48, 57
Down's syndrome 102, 157

episodic memory 262–70, 277–80
    see also attention, to the past

flash of recollection 264–7

gaze-following 15–16, 39, 91, 96
gaze-following paradigm 49–51
generating properties 310–11
gesture choice paradigm 46–7, 55–6, 68–9
grasping and reaching 111–14

imitation 198–200, 251
interaction:

dyadic 38, 85–106, 195, 237–8
    triadic 39, 85–106, 195, 243
intersubjectivity 73, 88, 190–202, 236–8
iteration 2, 25–6, 291–2, 300–8, 313–14

joint attention:
    communicative-intention vs. intersubjective
      theory 16–17, 19–22, 24–33, 206,
      221–2, 239–44
    experientialist vs. non-experientialist view
      287–92
    relational vs. reductive view 288–93
joint reminiscing 260–3, 273–83

language development 39, 132, 151–4, 158–60,
    165–83, 261–2

memory development 262–3, 268, 273–83
metarepresentation 66, 73–4, 206
    see also theory of mind
mutual knowledge, see common knowledge
mutual open-ended perceptual availability
    302–4
mutuality 22–30, 94, 102, 106, 263, 283

naming 151–4
    communicative intentions account
      of 167–9
    covariation-detection account of 166–7
    simple heuristics account of 172–80
narrative 278–83

object choice paradigm 47–9, 51, 55–7, 72
objective thought 7–10, 19–22, 27–8, 265, 267
occluder test 52–4
open knowledge 313–16
openness 28–30, 292, 298–316
    of linguistic communication 314–16
other minds, grasp of 10–11, 40, 90–9, 104–6,
    187–9, 230–1, 250–8
    see also co-attender as constituent of
      experience

past tense, understanding of 260–3, 268–9,
    275–7
perspective taking 59, 171–2
pointing 39, 79–81, 129–61, 119–25
    gesture 133–9

proto-declarative 67, 76, 78, 91, 101–3, 131,
    136–9, 145, 232–50
proto-imperative 67, 78–9, 131, 136–9,
    145, 232
psychological concepts 34–8, 40–3,
    234, 244–50
psychological understanding:
    simulation theory of 42–3, 230, 236
    theory theory of 42, 236
    see also seeing, understanding of; attention,
        understanding of; theory of mind

rationality 41–2
    see also second-tier thought
reflexivity, *see* self-reference, indexical
representational vs. relational view of experience
    293–5

scripts 275, 279
second person representations 30–2, 40–3, 66,
    80, 94, 231
second-tier thought 274, 277

seeing, understanding of 19–22, 45–62, 68–9,
    76, 144
self-involving situations 317–22
self-reference, indexical 305–8, 317–22
sensorimotor notion of subject 66–7, 73–4, 80
serial search 268–70, 272, 274, 280
sharing of affective attitudes 188–202, 242–3,
    245–8
simple theory of perception 19–22, 26–8, 245,
    265, 267–8
simulation, mental 42, 61, 230, 236
social cognition, in apes vs. humans 59–61, 201
social referencing 91, 98–9, 189, 243
spatial cognition 21–2, 265, 267, 304–5

temporal-causal reasoning 273–7, 279–82
theory of mind 36–8, 58–9, 73–4, 132, 160,
    170–2, 233–6, 281
    see also metarepresentation
triangulation 7, 15, 88, 90, 100

visual barriers 50–4, 58–60, 72, 145–50